HISTORY

OF

TENNESSEE

From the Earliest Time to the Present; Together with an Historical and a Biographical Sketch of the County of Shelby and the City of Memphis, Besides a Valuable Fund of Notes, Original Observations, Reminiscences, Etc., Etc.

ILLUSTRATED.

NASHVILLE:
THE GOODSPEED PUBLISHING CO.,
1887.

This volume was reproduced from
An 1887 edition located in the
Knoxville Public Library,
Knoxville, Tennessee

All rights reserved. No part of this publication may be reproduced, stored in a retrieval system, transmitted in any form, posted on to the web in any form or by any means without the prior written permission of the publisher.

Please direct all correspondence and orders to:

www.southernhistoricalpress.com
or
SOUTHERN HISTORICAL PRESS, Inc.
PO BOX 1267
375 West Broad Street
Greenville, SC   29601
southernhistoricalpress@gmail.com

Originally published: Nashville, 1887
Reprinted with New Material by:
Southern Historical Press, Inc.
Greenville, SC 2018
New Material Copyright 2018 by
Southern Historical Press, Inc.
Greenville, SC
ISBN #0-89308-231-7
All rights Reserved.
Printed in the United States of America

SHELBY COUNTY

SHELBY COUNTY is situated in the southwest corner of the State of Tennessee. It is bounded on the north by Tipton County, on the east by Fayette County, on the south by the State of Mississippi and on the west by the Mississippi River. In area it contains about 700 square miles. Generally speaking the surface is either level or gently undulating, and the soil is extremely fertile. Outside of the bottoms, at the lowest points the La Grange sands outcrop. This is a stratified mass of sand mostly argillaceous and quite variable in color. Their thickness is not known, and in them occur veins of lignite, as at Raleigh. The Orange sandstone also appears at the slopes at the bluff, and at the surface in the eastern part of the county. Above all lies what is known as the Bluff deposit or loess loam. This is a stratum of fine siliceous loam, and is usually of a light ashen, yellow or buff color. In thickness it varies from a few feet to about 100 feet. Memphis is built on this deposit. The loess deposits are famous the world over for their excellence as a subsoil, on account of their porosity and fertility, by which crops growing above them are enabled to survive long periods of drought better than those growing above most other kinds of subsoil. Above all is a rich alluvial deposit or vegetable mold, furnishing abundant material for the sustenance of crops, and is as rich as is anywhere to be found. The surface of the county is interspersed with a few creeks and small rivers, and the upland back from these creeks and rivers frequently rests upon a bed of reddish fire brick clay. The water courses are as follows: Wolf River, Loosahatchie River, Big Creek, Nonconnah Creek and Bayou Gayoso. There are two sets of mineral springs, one of Raleigh, the other at Nashoba, both containing sulphur and iron; but neither has as yet become famous as a health or summer resort. For convenience of reference the bluffs may be here enumerated: The first Chickasaw bluff is at Fulton in Lauderdale County, the second at Randolph in Tipton County, the third at Old River, and the fourth or lowest at Memphis. It is generally believed and it is probably true that it was from this bluff that De Soto crossed the Mississippi River, instead of at Randolph, as is suggested by Killebrew. The remains of extinct animals found in the county are thought by geologists to be representatives of the *genera* mastodon, megalonyx, castor and castoroides. Some think these remains belong to diluvium of the Mississippi Valley, but Prof. Safford thinks they are more probably from the Bluff loam.

The general trend of testimony seems to be that De Soto first saw the Mississippi at the lowest or fourth Chickasaw bluff, and that Chisca was located thereon, at the point where Fort Pickering was afterward built, where are the remains of two Indian mounds, since called the Jackson mounds. Authorities differ somewhat as to the date of De Soto's approach to the Mississippi River. Bancroft fixes the date at April 25, 1541, while others with perhaps too little investigation prefer the 8th of the same month. From this time forward for a period of 132 years the foot of white man is not known to have trod the sacred soil of West Tennessee. In June, 1673, two of the most celebrated personages known to the early religious history of this country, Father Marquette and M. Joliet, entering the Mississippi from the Wisconsin, passed down the Father of Waters to the mouth of the Arkansas, stopping on their way at the fourth Chickasaw bluff, where they were kindly received by the native Indians. After their return to the North a map, prepared by Marquette, was published in 1681, on which dense settlements are marked along the "Mitchisipi Highlands," corresponding to the first, second and fourth Chickasaw bluffs. After Father Hennepin returned from his trip down the Mississippi, made shortly after 1680, the Chevalier de La Salle in 1682 passed down the Mississippi to the Gulf of Mexico, and on his way down stopped at the fourth Chickasaw bluff, built a cabin thereon and erected a fort which he named *Prud 'homme*.* In 1686 Chevalier de Tonti stopped at this same bluff on his way down the Mississippi, and in 1699 M. D'Iberville, ascending the Mississippi, landed at this bluff and found here a letter written by De Tonti thirteen years before addressed to La Salle. In 1735 Bienville also visited the country, as did also D'Artaguette.

In 1739 Bienville again entered the Chickasaw country, this time passing up through Arkansas, crossing the Mississippi River at the fourth Chickasaw bluff and remaining there all winter. In March, 1740, a portion of his troops having sunk under the climate and all having become discouraged, he made a treaty of peace with the Chickasaws; returned to New Orleans, leaving Fort Assumption (now Memphis) in their possession, But little is known about the history of this portion of the country from this time until the arrival at this point in 1783 of Benjamin Foy, sent by Gen. Don Gayoso, and who in that year erected at the mouth of Margot (Wolf) River fortifications, to which he gave the name of Fort San Fernando. The Spaniards remained in possession

---

*See page 111 in the General History.

of this fort until the ratification of the treaty by which Louisiana was ceded to the United States, and the thirty-third degree of North latitude made the boundary line between the two countries.

Soon after this treaty Lieut. Pike was sent by the United States Government to take possession of the fort and the Spanish troops, evacuating it, crossed the river and established Camp L'Esperance, afterward called Camp Good Hope, near the terminus of the Military Road. Gen. Wilkinson came on soon after the arrival of Lieut. Pike, dismantled Fort San Fernando and established Fort Pickering about one mile below on the Mississippi River. The Chickasaws remained in possession of this country, then, more as a hunting-ground, however, than as a residence country until the treaty of 1818, by which they ceded West Tennessee to the United States. This treaty was ratified in 1819, and proclaimed by the President January 7, that year. By its terms the Chickasaws removed to the Indian Territory and received $20,000 annually for fifteen years.

But long previous to this treaty North Carolina, while Tennessee was yet under territorial government, made numerous large grants to individuals, mostly at the rate of £10 for every 100 acres so granted. The first grant recorded in the register's books of Shelby County is North Carolina Grant, No. 17, to Samuel Harris for 5,000 acres, lying on the North Fork of Looshatchie River, near the mouth of that fork and adjoining Grant No. 1010 to John McKnitt Alexander, and Grant No. 572 to Robert Goodloe; Grant No. 561, for 2,000 acres in favor of William Alston, lay on the north side of Looshatchie River adjoining No. 465 of 2,000 acres to James Robertson. John Gray Blount and Thomas Blount had granted to them eight separate tracts of land each containing 1,000 acres and numbered 117, 178, 190, 195, 219, 224, 225 and 239. Grant No. 86 for 5,000 was in favor of Richard Cross, and lay on the North Fork of Looshatchie. No. 306 lay on Big Hatchie and was for 5,000 acres in favor of Robinson Mumford. Alexander McCullock had two grants, No. 41 for 3,000 acres and No. 42 for 2,000 acres. But perhaps the most interesting grants made within the limits of Shelby County were those to John Rice and John Ramsey, because of their connection with the great city of Memphis. The John Rice grant was No. 283 and was described as follows:

> Know ye that we, in consideration of £10 for every 100 acres hereby granted, paid into our treasury by John Rice, have given, granted and by these presents do give and grant unto the said John Rice, a tract of land containing 5,000 acres lying and being in the western district on the Chickasaw bluff, beginning about one mile below the mouth of Wolf River at a white oak tree marked J. R.; running thence north 20° east 226 poles; thence north 27° west, 310 poles to a cotton-wood tree; thence due east 1,377.9 poles to a mulberry tree; thence south 625 poles to a stake; thence west 1,304.9 poles to the beginning, as by the

plat hereunto annexed doth appear, together with all woods, mines, minerals, hereditaments and appurtenances, to the said land belonging or appertaining, to hold to the said John Rice, his heirs and assigns forever; this grant to be registered in the register's office in our western district within twelve months from the date hereof, otherwise the same shall be void and of no effect.

In testimony whereof we have caused these our letters to be made patent, and our great seal to be hereunto affixed.

Witness: Samuel Johnson, Esquire, our Governor, Captain-general and Commander-in-chief, at Halifax, the 25th day of April, in the XIII year of our independence and of our Lord 1789.

By his Excellency's command.   SAM. JOHNSON.
    J. GLASGOW, *Secretary*.

The John Ramsey grant was No. 19,060, and was recorded May 10, 1823, the record in this case being as follows:

Know ye, that in consideration of Warrant No. 383, dated the 24th day of June, 1784, issued by John Armstrong, entry officer of claims for the North Carolina western lands, to John Ramsey for five thousand acres, and entered on the 25th day of October, 1783, by No. 383 there is granted by the said State of Tennessee unto the said John Ramsey and John Overton, assignee, &c., a certain tract or parcel of land, containing five thousand acres by survey bearing date March 1, 1822, lying in Shelby County, Eleventh District, Ranges Eight and Nine, Sections One and Two, on the Mississippi River, of which to said Ramsey four thousand two hundred eighty-five and five-sevenths acres, and to said Overton seven hundred and fourteen and two-sevenths acres, and bounded as follows, to wit: Beginning at a stake on the bank of said river—the southwest corner of John Rice's five thousand acre grant, as processioned by William Lawrence in the year 1820— running thence south 85° east with said Rice's south boundary line, as processioned aforesaid, one hundred and seventy-five chains to a poplar marked R.; thence south two hundred chains to an elm marked F. R.; thence west, at sixty-two chains crossing a branch bearing south, at seventy chains crossing a branch bearing southeast, at one hundred and nineteen chains crossing a branch bearing south, and at one hundred and sixty chains a branch bearing south, in all two hundred and seventy-three chains, to a cottonwood tree marked F. R., on the bank of the Mississippi River; thence up the margin of said river with its meanders (here follows a minute description of the course of the river) to the beginning, with the hereditaments and appurtenances, to the said John Ramsey and John Overton and their heirs forever.

In witness whereof William Carroll, governor of the State of Tennessee, hath hereunto set his hand and caused the great seal of the State to be affixed, at Murfreesborough, on the 30th day of April, in the year of our Lord, 1823, and of the independence of the United States the forty-seventh.

By the governor,
    DANIEL GRAHAM, *Secretary*.   WILLIAM CARROLL.

At the time the county was organized, May 1, 1820, there were probably less than twenty actual settlers within its limits, and no other settlement within seventy-five miles. The office of the Eleventh Surveyor's District was opened about the 6th of December, 1820, at the house of Thomas D. Carr on the fourth Chickasaw bluff. Those in attendance at that time, as near as can now be ascertained, were Jacob Tipton, William Lawrence, John Ralston, W. L. Byler and the clerk of the office, Alfred Taylor. The land locators were Gideon Pillow, O. B. Hays of Nashville, in behalf of R. Hightower & Sons; James Vaulx in behalf of McLemore, Vaulx & Caruthers; M. H. Howard, on behalf of Samuel Dickens & Co.; James Walker and Col. James Brown, on behalf of Polk, Porter & Co. John Overton, one of the proprietors of the new town of Memphis, then recently laid out, was present with his plans of the upper part of the place and made attempts to sell some of his lots, but did not meet with much success, selling only a few at from $40 to $100 per lot. Mr. Overton was well satisfied in his own mind, notwithstanding, that Memphis was destined to be one of the great cities of the United States, if indeed it did not at some future day rival in splendor the ancient city of Memphis on the Nile. Mr. Overton's liberality toward various people and interests deserves to be perpetuated in this work. He gave two lots to T. D. Carr upon which to build a tavern; to A. B. Carr he gave a lot for the location of a mill, and he also donated one on Bayou Gayoso for a tannery yard.

In order that it may be understood what is meant above by the Eleventh Surveyor's District, it is proper to explain that during the session of the Legislature which convened in October, 1819, the western district of Tennessee was laid off into five land districts, numbered from 9 to 13 inclusive. District No. 9 embraced the southeast part of West Tennessee, beginning on the Tennessee River, where the line previously run between Tennessee and Alabama crossed it, the presumption then being that this line was on the $35°$ of north latitude, running thence due west thirty-five miles; thence north fifty-five miles; thence east to the Tennessee River, and thence up the Tennessee River to the beginning. The Tenth Surveyor's District adjoined the Ninth on the west, extending west thirty miles; thence north fifty-five miles, and thence east to the Ninth District. The Eleventh District lay between the Tenth and the Mississippi River, including Shelby County. Jacob Tipton was appointed surveyor of this district. The Twelfth District embraced the northeastern part of West Tennessee, commencing at the intersection of parallel of latitude $36° 30'$, north with the Tennessee River, and extending with this parallel westward to a point midway between the Tennessee and Mississippi Rivers; thence south to the north line of the Tenth District, and thence east to the Tennessee River; and the Thirteenth District lay west of the Twelfth, extending to the Mississippi River.

The names of the early settlers in Shelby County, so far as can be consistently given in this work, are introduced in connection with the sketches of the towns in the vicinity of which they settled. It is deemed appropriate here to present a brief outline of the famous institution of Frances Wright, about which much has been written and much misapprehended, the name of which was Nashoba.

Nashoba (the name in the Chickasaw language meaning wolf) was an institution established by Miss Frances Wright in the year 1826 upon lands purchased in 1825, for the purposes of benevolence and the emancipation of the slave. The lands of Nashoba, amounting in the aggregate to 1,940 acres, lay on both sides of Wolf River, in Shelby County, in the vicinity of Germantown and Ridgway, and are described as follows:

    1st. A tract of 640 acres, granted by the State of Tennessee to William Lawrence and William A. Davis by Grant No. 21,815, and conveyed by them to Miss Wright.
    2d. A tract of 240 acres, granted to her as assignee of William Fewkes.
    3d. A tract of 240 acres, granted to her as assignee of James Richardson.
    4th. A tract of 200 acres, granted to her as assignee of Andrew Jones.
    5th. A tract of 200 acres, granted to her as assignee of John Gilliam.
    6th. A tract of 200 acres, granted to her as assignee of Powel Busby.
    7th. A tract of 200 acres, conveyed to her by the grantee, Richard Hensband.
    8th. A tract of 20 acres, entered in the name of T. H. Persons, by entry No. 907 under date of August 5, 1824, and conveyed by Mr. Persons to Miss Wright.

In order to accomplish the purpose she had in view, Miss Wright appointed certain trustees to manage the institution, giving the lands described above in trust to them. Their names were the following: Gen. Lafayette, William McClure, Robert Owen, Cadwallader D. Colden, Richardson Whitby, Robert Jennings, Robert Dale Owen, George Flowery, Camilla Wright and James Richardson.* The lands, according to the deed of trust, were to be held by them, their associates and successors in perpetual trust for the benefit of the negro race. The object of the trust was confided to the discretion of the trustees, with the limitation that a school for colored children should always be a principal part of the plan, and with the further limitation that all negroes emancipated by the trustees should on quitting the limits of Nashoba be sent outside of the limits of the United States. The trustees were not at any time to permit their own number to be reduced below five, and the trustees on the lands of Nashoba, provided their number should not be less than three, should be a quorum for the transaction of business. Besides the trustees, coadjutors were provided for, and the trustees were permitted to admit other coadjutors, with the unanimous consent of the trustees, and provided the proposed coadjutors had lived six months on the lands of Nashoba; but the coadjutors were not to have anything to do with the management of the affairs of the institution. In order to secure the independence of every one connected with the institution it was provided that no one admitted as either trustee or coadjutor should be liable to expulsion for any reason, but from the moment of admission each person was to have an indefeasible right to the enjoyment of the

---

*The supposition that Andrew Jackson was one of the trustees is not sustained by the deed of trust.

comforts afforded by the institution, i. e., to food, to clothing, to lodging, to attention during sickness and protection in old age. No member, whether trustee or coadjutor, who might quit the institution was to be entitled to any compensation for past services in addition to the participation he might have had in the comforts of the institution while residing therein. Every admission to the institution was to be strictly individual, except in cases of children under fourteen years of age, who were to be admitted with one or both parents, and reared and educated by the institution until they should be twenty years of age, when they should either be admitted into the institution or assisted in forming themselves into a community elsewhere. Among other provisions was the following: That on the Fourth of July, 1876, the trust should devolve on the then existing trustees and coadjutors jointly, and thenceforward every member was to be a trustee; and Miss Wright said: "Notwithstanding the legal inconsistency such a reservation may seem to involve, I reserve to myself all the privileges of a trustee."

Miss Wright proposed a system of education for the young black people which should fit them for self-support, and a system for the young white people having the same end in view, and her institution at Nashoba was founded on the principle of community of property and labor. Following is a bit of philosophy by Miss Wright: "Were a system of prevention adopted instead of punishment, laws would be unnecessary. In all the transactions of life the only effective precautions seem to be those which provide against the occurrence of evil, not those which attempt to remedy the evil after it has occurred." She made an appeal "to all the friends of men and of their country, to those who respect the institutions of the Republic and to all endowed with favorable principles, to all who believe in the possibility of the improvement of man, to all who sympathize in the sentiments expressed in this paper," to aid in the prospective work of the institution of Nashoba. This paper was dated December 17, 1826.

On January 6, 1827, Miss Wright gave to the trustees of the lands of Nashoba above mentioned, and to their associates and successors in office, the following named slaves: Willis, Jacob, Grandison, Frederick, Henry, Nellie, Peggy and Kitty and the male infant of Kitty, on the condition that when their labor—together with the labor of another family consisting of female slaves entrusted to her by Robert Wilson of South Carolina—should have paid to the institution of Nashoba a clear capital of $6,000, with six per cent interest on that capital from the 1st of January, 1827. and in addition a sum sufficient to defray the expenses of colonizing them, they should all be emancipated and colonized by the trustees.

The institution of Nashoba did not, however, by far come up to the expectation of its founder, and in about four years it failed. During three years she was from ill health compelled to be in Europe, and the institution's failure she attributed, not to any defect in the scheme or plan nor to the intractability of the negro, but wholly to the base conduct of those she left in charge. But to the negroes named above, whom she had placed in the institution, she was true, at her own expense sending them to Hayti and establishing them there in independence. Then, on the 1st of November, 1831, "on account of its being impracticable for them to conduct the school or to be of service as trustees of the lands of Nashoba, Gen. Lafayette, William McClure, Robert Owen, C. Colden, Richardson Whitby, Robert Jennings, Robert Dale Owen, George Flowery and James Richardson resigned their trusteeship," and also for the further reason "that Miss Wright had emancipated the slaves and colonized them on the island of Hayti." After this failure of her cherished schemes Miss Wright continued for a number of years to manage her estate in her own way, and at length it became involved in litigation, which is sufficiently traced in the history of the courts of Shelby County.

Commencing with 1840 the political history of Shelby County is succinctly as follows: In that year William Henry Harrison received 950 votes for President of the United States while Martin Van Buren received 681. In 1843 James C. Jones received 1,352 votes for governor; James K. Polk received 1,026, and in the next year Henry Clay received 1,625 votes for President while James K. Polk received 1,352. In 1845 E. H. Foster received for governor 1,307 votes and Aaron V. Brown 1,316; in 1847 Neill S. Brown received 1,409 votes, and Aaron V. Brown 1,207. In 1848 Zachary Taylor received 1,828 votes for President, to 1,607 for Lewis Cass. In 1849 there were cast for Gen. William Trousdale for governor 1,405 votes to 1,453 for Neill S. Brown. For congressman, F. P. Stanton received 1,426, and Harris 1,425; for the State Senate George W. Fisher 1,351, and Farrington 1,464. In 1851, for governor, Gen. William Trousdale received 1,490 votes, and William B. Campbell 1,563; for the State Senate William C. Dunlap 1,543, and Mr. Wickersham 1,480; for representative, M. B. Winchester 1,490, and Pope 1,474. In 1852 Winfield Scott received for President 1,824, and Franklin Pierce 1,628. In 1855 Meredith P. Gentry received 1,831 votes for governor, and Andrew Johnson 1,467. At the presidential election of 1856 James Buchanan received 2,016 votes, and Millard Fillmore 2,083. By a review of the votes given above it will be seen that at every presidential election during those twenty years the Whig candidate, considering Millard Fillmore a Whig, received a majority of the popular vote in this county, as was the case in nearly every gubernatorial election. In 1859 Isham G. Harris received 2,231 votes, to John Netherland 2,026. In 1860, the most important presidential year thus far in the history of the country, the vote in Memphis was as follows: for John Bell 2,319, Stephen A. Douglas 2,250 and John C. Breckenridge 572; and in the rest of the county, for Bell 3,048, Douglas 2,959 and Breckenridge 744.

On the 7th of February, 1861, a meeting was held to discuss the questions of the day at which Luke W. Finlay and James Brett delivered enthusiastic speeches in favor of secession, the latter gentleman especially dwelling eloquently upon the "Government as it was and as it is." This meeting was held preparatory to the election which was to take place on the 9th, at which the following votes were cast. Marcus J. Wright received 2,089 votes for State senator from Shelby and Fayette Counties; Solon Borland 1,574 and David M. Curry 2,088 for representative from Shelby County, and Humphrey 2,087 votes for floater from Shelby, Fayette and Tipton Counties. On the question of convention or no convention the vote stood: For the convention 4,720 votes, against it 209. The Union ticket and votes for each candidate were as follows: Dunlap, 2,711; Harris, 2,722; Topp, 2,808; Carroll, 2,715. These votes were cast in Memphis, and indicate the state of feeling then existing; but when the vote was taken in June following on the question of separation or no separation the result showed that meanwhile a great change had taken place in public sentiment. The vote on the 8th of June, 1861, for separation and representation was in the entire county 7,132, against both, five, the five being cast in Memphis; and the vote in Memphis for separation was 5,608, for representation 5,604.

In 1867 the vote for congressmen was as follows: For David A Nunn 4,414, and for John T. Leftwick 2,745; and for governor, W. G. Brownlow 4,419; for Emerson Etheridge 3,009. In 1868 Gen. U. S. Grant received 5,004 votes as candidate and Horatio Seymour 3,009. This was one of the most remarkable elections ever held in Shelby County, and was watched, particularly in Memphis, with the keenest interest, as it was the first presidential election at which the newly enfranchised colored man cast his ballot. In order to know with certainty how he did vote, separate ballot boxes were prepared for the white and black electors, and the result found to be as follows: In Memphis Gen. Grant received 535 from white men and from colored men 4,283, a total vote of 4,818; Horatio Seymour received from white men 2,436 votes, and from colored men 86; in all 2,522. The total white vote was 2,971, and the total colored vote 4,369. On congressman the vote stood for W. J.

Smith white vote 291, colored vote 4,212; for John T. Leftwick, white vote 2,431, colored vote 85; David A. Nunn, white vote 232, colored vote 71. In the entire county, however, Mr. Leftwick was elected over W. J. Smith by a majority of 633 votes.

In 1870 the vote for governor was, W. H. Wisener 2,968, John C. Brown 6,713; for congressman, Smith 2,804; Shaw (colored) 170; DuBose 6,506. The total city vote at that election was 6,726, and the total county vote, including Memphis, was 9,687. In 1872 occurred another remarkable election for President, the two candidates being President Ulysses S. Grant and Horace Greeley. In Shelby County Mr. Greeley received 6,356 votes, and President Grant 8,445. For governor, John C. Brown (Liberal Republican) received 6,598, and A. A. Freeman (Grant Republican) received 8,275 votes. At the county election held that year the vote for sheriff was W. J. P. D.——7,797; A. P. Curry 6,081; for trustee A. Woodward 7,747; T. Foley 5,042; privilege tax collector, J. H. Mathes 12,614, no opposition; chancellor, S. P. Walker 8,210, J. B. Bigelow 4,574; supreme judge, R. McFarland 9,735, J. B. Cook 2,416. The vote in 1874 for governor was James D. Porter (Democrat) 8,828, Horace Maynard (Republican) 5,877; for congressman, H. Casey Young 8,841, —— Lewis 5,849. The presidential vote in 1876 was more nearly equal, Samuel Tilden (Democrat) receiving 8,539 votes, R. B. Hayes 8,127; for congressman, H. Casey Young received 8,503 votes, and —— Randolph 8,092. In 1878 E. M. Wright (Republican) received 1,817 votes for governor, A. S. Marks (Democrat) 2,099, and R. M. Edwards (National) 1,729; for congressman the vote stood, H. Casey Young 5,522, ——Randolph, 3,199. In 1880 James A. Garfield (Republican) received 7,788 votes, W. S. Hancock (Democrat) 6,927, and J. B. Weaver (Greenback) 264; for governor Alvin Hawkins (Republican) received 7,758, and John V. Wright 5,265. In 1882 Alvin Hawkins as candidate for governor received 5,421 votes, William B. Bate 5,524, and Joseph H. Fussell (low credit Democrat) 257.

In 1884 James G. Blaine for President received 9,165 votes and Grover Cleveland 7,627. For governor that year Frank T. Reid received 9,290 votes and William B. Bate 7,296. The vote for congressman stood, Zach Taylor 8,732, James M. Harris 7,671. For State Senate Smith received 8,565 votes, Ramsay 7,638, and Jacob S. Galloway 7,583, and J. D. Montedonico 7,715. For representatives the following were the candidates and their respective votes: James F. Hunter 7,812, M. R. Patterson 7,838, Alfred Frohman 6,868, Morgan Kelly 7,795, and J. S. McKinley 7,465, Haynes 8,800, Fields 8,591, Vernon 8,618, Evans 8,446, and Brogan 8,987.

The most remarkable election of recent years, both for methods and results, was that of August 5, 1886. Following are the names of the various candidates and their respective votes: Sheriff—W. D. Cannon (Democrat), in the city 11,537, country 6,122, total 17,659; Silvers (Republican) 1,449; total vote for sheriff 19,108. County trustee—Andrew J. Harris (Democrat), city 8,689, country 2,877, total 11,566; Rumsey (Republican) 7,546; total vote for trustee, 19,112. Register—N. F. Harrison (Democrat), city 9,294, country 2,971; total 12,265. Fields (Republican), 7,017; total for register, 19,282. Attorney-general—George B. Peters (Democrat), city 8,599, country 2,985, total 11,584; Haynes (Republican), 6,536; G. P. M. Turner (Independent Democrat), 1,280; total vote for attorney-general, 19,400. Chancellor—Henry T. Ellett (Democrat), city 8,820, country 3,934, total, 12,754; Smith (Republican), 7,270; total vote for chancellor, 20,024. Criminal court judge—J. J. Dubose (Democrat), city 10,127, country 2,647, total, 12,774; Moss (Republican), 6,437; total vote, 19,211. Probate judge—J. S. Galloway (Democrat), city 8,750, country 2,794, total, 11,544; Eldridge (Republican), 7,653; total vote, 19,197. Circuit court judge—L. H. Estes (Democrat), city 8,132, country 3,856, total 11,988; Vernon (Republican), 7,323; total vote 19,311.

In November, 1886, the votes for the respective candidates for governor were, Robert L. Taylor (Democrat), city 4,871, country 2,144, total 7,015; Alfred A. Taylor (Republican), city 1,403, country 2,102, total, 3,505; total vote in the county for governor, 10,520, against 20,024, the total vote for chancellor in August previous.

The following are the general statistics: The population of Shelby County in 1860 was whites 30,861, blacks 17,229, total 48,090; in 1870 it was whites 39,737, blacks 36,640, total 76,377, and in 1880 it was whites 34,508, blacks 43,903, total 78,411. In 1880 the assessed valuation of real estate was $17,794,085; of personal property, $1,074,370. The amount of taxes was for the State, school purposes, $35,879; other purposes $18,868. County purposes—schools, $36,309; other purposes, $86,842. The number of manufacturing establishments in the county was 186; capital invested, $2,452,425; value of materials, $2,646,910; value of product, $4,759,691; the number of males employed above sixteen years of age, 2,278, and the number of females above fifteen, 69. The total amount of wages paid was $876,566.

Shelby County was named in honor of Gen. Isaac Shelby of Kentucky. It was erected by an act of the General Assembly, passed at Murfreesboro, November 24, 1819. The act creating the county, directed Jacob Tipton, surveyor of the Eleventh Surveyor's District, to run the boundary line of the county. This was done by William Lawrence, deputy surveyor, for which the county court allowed him the sum of $142.75. The work was completed July 30, 1823. The whole contained 625 square miles. A correct location of the thirty-fifth parallel added a fractional row of sections from the State of Mississippi.

On the third day of court $175 was set apart to Thomas D. Carr, with which to employ laborers and erect a temporary log courthouse, jury-room and jail on the public square. This house was ready for occupancy in August, 1821. In November, 1822, Lewis Williams received $72.50 for repairs on said courthouse. This house seems to have been wanting in capacity or comfort or both, as the courts frequently met at private houses. While sitting at Memphis, "Chickasaw Bluffs" was designated as the place of holding the first courts. In December, 1824, the commissioners, James Fentress, Benjamin Reynolds, William Martin and Robert Jetton, who had been selected by the General Assembly to choose sites for the various county seats for the counties of West Tennessee, selected Sanderlin's bluff, on the north side of Wolf River as the most suitable site for the county seat of Shelby County. The land embraced a little over fifty acres, twenty-nine of which was owned by Wilson Sanderlin and twenty-two by James Freeman. The town was laid out and the lots sold, the profits from which were to be used in the erection of public buildings. This new site was named Raleigh, in honor of Raleigh, N. C., in deference to Joseph Graham, who was a native of that State. Raleigh was laid off by Frederick Christian, John B. Holmes, John R. Kent and Benj. Robins. In January, 1827, the commissioners of Raleigh were allowed to draw on the county for $180 to complete the public buildings; if found necessary they were allowed $370 more out of funds not otherwise appropriated. This house was a small frame building built by Joseph Coe. This was replaced by a good brick building in 1834-35 about 40x50 feet and two stories high. In 1836 the old house was sold for $231 and the money spent in building a fence around the new brick courthouse. This house served the county until the courts were brought back to Memphis. In July, 1860, a committee consisting of J. W. A. Pettit, A. H. Montgomery, J. S. Dickerson, J. H. Goodlet and W. H. Walker with the county judge and the justices of the peace, was appointed to consult with the municipal authorities of Memphis, on the question of erecting a new courthouse at that city for the common law and chancery court, and the criminal court. The committee was to report on the propriety or necessity of building a new house, the cost of grounds and building, the amount Memphis was willing to pay and the amount of rents that would have to be paid for buildings until new ones could be built. A lot was purchased of W. B. Richardson, and in April, 1861, a loan of $150,000 at 6 per cent, payable in two, three, four and five years, in bonds of Shelby County, was offered to raise money for the new courthouse. The war coming up about this time, the matter was delayed until after the reorganization after the war.

In 1874 the large building known as the Overton Hotel was purchased at a total cost of building and repairs of nearly $150,000, and in September, 1874, all the courts were moved into that building. The federal courts, with their officers and effects, were moved into the same building in 1875.

At the August term, 1820, the court appointed Wm. A. Davis and Marcus B. Winchester commissioners to build a jail, and appropriated $125 for that purpose. They reported the completion of their work on November 6, 1821, and were paid $125 for the same. On the following day the court fixed prison bounds as follows: "Beginning and running so as to include the public square on which the courthouse now stands, and the two lots on which Sam'l R. Brown now keeps entertainment, and the street intervening between the two." On the removal of the county seat to Raleigh, a new jail had to be built. A permanent jail was built about the time of building the brick courthouse. This building stood east of the court square on the Somerville road. For the erection of these buildings a tax of $18\frac{3}{4}$ cents on each 100 acres of land, $37\frac{1}{2}$ cents on each town lot, $18\frac{3}{4}$ cents on each white poll and $37\frac{1}{2}$ cents on each black poll was levied. On July 4, 1842, prison bounds one mile square in extent were established, the court square being in the center. In 1866 the present large, expensive jail was begun. J. B. Cook was the architect, and J. J. Powers the builder. The contract price was $144,000, but the total cost was largely in excess of that amount.

The first county court levied a tax of $6\frac{1}{4}$ cents on each 100 acres of land, also $6\frac{1}{4}$ cents on each white and each black poll for a jury and poor tax. The first official expenditure for the poor was the appropriation of $13 on February 7, 1821, for the support of Phillip H. Friend, a pauper of the county. The first commissioners of the poor were T. D. Carr, William Irvine and Jacob Tipton. The poor were kept by allowances made by the county court through the commissioners of the poor till 1836 when steps were taken to have them all kept at one place instead of farming them out individually to different ones throughout the county. No permanent asylum, however, was built till 1873–74 when the present asylum was erected. The county now owns forty acres of land on which stand the asylum buildings. These are mainly brick and are well kept. The farm lies about seven miles from Memphis on the old Raleigh road.

The asylum contains about 200 inmates, including all classes. The superintendent is Dr. G. K. Duncan, under whose management the institution has been remarkably successful. A comparison of the number of inmates and the expense of keeping the same will illustrate this point. In 1875 with eighty-five inmates, the expense of the institution was over $29,000; with 200 inmates in 1886, the expense of the institution was but little over $9,000. This amount includes salary of superintendent and all other expenses.

Public roads being a public necessity, early attention was given to them. On May 3, 1820, the county court ordered Thomas H. Persons, Charles Holman, Joshua Fletcher, M. B. Winchester, J. C. McLemore and William Irvine to mark out a road from Memphis to the county line in the direction of Taylor's Mill settlement on Forked Deer River. This was the first public road in the county. The second road in the county was established in May, 1821, by Jessee Benton, John Ralston, Nat. Kimbrough, John Kimbrough, E. Deason, Edward Bradley, D. C. Tradewell, Robert Mickleberry and John Reeves. This road led from Memphis to the settlement on Big Creek and Loosahatchie, thence to Forked Deer River. Joseph Graham was appointed overseer to cut out a road from Memphis to the east line of the county in the direction of the old Cherokee trace and Colbert's wagon road. In 1829 post-roads were established leading from Memphis by way of Raleigh, Somerville, Bolivar and Jackson; also one from Memphis by way of Randolph, Covington, Brownsville and Jackson. The Memphis & La Grange Railroad was chartered in December, 1835. The road was to be about fifty miles in length, connecting Memphis and La Grange. The capital stock amounted to $250,000 individual subscriptions and $125,000 furnished by the State. The work was not begun till 1838 and it was not till 1842 that six miles of the road was completed. The road came into the city on Washington Street, and where said street crosses Main Street the cut was so deep as to require a bridge. The track or rails were of bar iron laid on streamers which rested on cross-ties. A few passenger coaches were run over the road and some cord-wood hauled from Col. Eppy White's plantation, the terminus of the road. The funds of the company having become exhausted the road was soon abandoned.

In 1850 the charter of this road was purchased by the Memphis & Charleston Railroad Company. In this the State gave 2,202 bonds of $1,000 each or $2,202,000, and in the same year the city of Memphis subscribed $500,000 stock in the same road. This road was completed and opened for traffic in May, 1857. The road was originally chartered by the State of Tennessee, February 2, 1846. The capital stock of the company, of which Samuel Tate was president, was $800,000. This company now owns 272 miles of road and operates 310 more under lease. The freight handled within the last year amounted to 68,000,000 tons moved one mile, and 18,000,000 passengers carried one mile. The earnings of ten months, ending November 30, 1886, was $1,228,851. The Memphis & Tennessee Railroad was chartered February 2, 1846. In April, 1852, the city of Memphis voted $250,000 stock to aid this road, and the State of Tennessee made it a loan of $97,500. This road connects Memphis with Grenada, Miss., a distance of 100 miles. At Grenada it intersects with the Illinois Central. The earnings of this road for the year 1886 were $425,718.

The charter to the Memphis & Ohio Railroad was granted February 4, 1842, and rechartered January 29, 1858. It was intended to run to the Kentucky State line in the direction of Cairo; work was not begun on this road till 1869, but was soon suspended. In 1871 it was consolidated with the Paducah & Gulf Railroad, and took the name of Memphis & Paducah Road. It was afterward sold under mortgage, and was reorganized as the Memphis, Paducah & Northern. It is now known as the Chesapeake, Ohio & Southwestern. It extends a distance of 345 miles. The last report shows the net earnings to be $301,806. The original cost of this road was estimated at $30,000 per mile. Shelby County voted $250,000 stock to aid this road at its first organization. The Memphis & Little Rock Railroad was incorporated January 11, 1853. Besides the individual stock, and the stock owned by the city of Little Rock, also the contractor's stock, the city of Memphis took $350,000 stock, and the Government donated 487,000 acres of public land. This road, however, was not completed until a few years since. The first president of this road was J. M. Williamson; the present president is R. S. Hays, of St. Louis. The general offices of this road are in St. Louis and Little Rock. The road extends a distance of 135 miles, and is a great cotton route. The Louisville, New Orleans & Texas Railway Company was organized in 1882 with Maj. R. T. Wilson, of New York, as president. This company purchased the interests of the Tennessee Southern, the Memphis & Vicksburg, the New Orleans & Baton Rouge, the Vicksburg & Memphis, and the New Orleans & Mississippi Valley Railway, and they were consolidated in 1884 under the name of Louisville, New Orleans & Texas Railway. This forms a connecting link between the Chesapeake & Ohio and the Southern Pacific, these making a continuous line of 4,070 miles, said to be the longest line in the world—the main line with its branches, an aggregate of 6,354 miles of line. This company also owns 4,255 miles of steamship line. The company owns 750,000 acres of Yazoo delta lands, which have been reclaimed. The yearly tonnage of this line is 380,000 tons, and the number of passengers carried is 500,000 persons. The Kansas City, Springfield & Memphis, one of the new roads centering into Memphis, is one of the great systems of road belting the country. G. H. Nettleton is president of the road. The general offices of the company are in Kansas City. The gross earnings of this road, for the ten months ending November 30, 1886, were $1,338,831. This company purchased, in November, 1886, $50,000 worth of additional ground in Memphis. The Louisville & Nashville Railroad, which has a branch into Memphis, shows, by its report for the ten months ending November 30, 1886, gross earnings to the amount of $12,718,144 for the whole system of its roads, which amounts to 3,281 miles. There are two other important roads to the city, the Memphis, Birmingham & Atlantic Road, of which George H. Nettleton is president, and the Newport News & Mississippi Valley (C. and O. route), of which C. P. Huntington is president. The Iron Mountain Railroad Company also has purchased, in the city of Memphis, $80,000 worth of grounds for depot and other purposes. A charter has just been filed for the Baltimore, Memphis & Nashville Railroad. The incorporators are E. W. Cole, Jas. M. Head, Wm. Morrow, B. F. Wilson, A. S. Colyar and J. C. Neely. It is intended to build the road across the State, from Memphis to Bristol.

The first telegraph line into Memphis was chartered October 18, 1847, and built soon after. The capital stock of the company was $28,000. The president of the company was Thomas Allen; secretary, James Coleman; treasurer, J. W. Smith.

The telegraphic interests have grown wonderfully. There are now located the offices of the American District Telegraph Company, the Gold & Stock Telegraph Company, and the Western Union Telegraph Company, in the Cotton Exchange Building. The system of which this is a part has connection with nearly all the great cities. It sends over 1,000,000 messages yearly, and uses 3,600 cells of battery, and has invested $80,000,000 capital, and owns 75,000 miles of line. At this point are employed twenty-two skilled operators and thirty-three other persons.

The principal express company operating in Tennessee is the Southern Express Company, of which H. B. Plant, Augusta, Ga., and New York, is president; M. J. O'Brien, general superintendent; Geo. H. Tilley, secretary; Hon. W. S. Chisholm, general counsel, and C. L. Loop, general auditor. The accounting department is divided into two divisions, the eastern and the western. The western division is located at Memphis. Of this division Mr. F. J. Virgin is auditor, and Mr. A. J. Signaigo is cashier. The operating department is divided into five divisions, of which the southwestern division is located at Memphis, under the superintendence of H. C. Fisher. The general accounting department at Memphis employs about forty clerks. There are purchased and distributed from the same headquarters supplies to the value of $25,000 annually.

From about 1845 to 1860 great attention was paid to the building of turnpikes and plank roads through Shelby County. The first road chartered was the Memphis & Somerville Road. This road was chartered on January 28, 1846, and rechartered February 17, 1854. The Pigeon Roost & Chulahoma Road was incorporated on October 31, 1853, with a capital stock of $41,000. It was chartered by Thomas Holman, F. A. Owen and thirty-five others for a period of ninety-nine years. The Memphis & Horn Lake Road was chartered by W. L. Lundy, John Arnold, W. Mathews, H. D. Small and S. Bailey on January 28, 1854, with a capital stock of $50,000. Owing to the peculiarity of this soil, rendering it difficult to keep up these roads, and the disorganization caused by the war, these roads were allowed to fall into decay, and in 1866 the charters of most of them were dissolved. The Memphis & Wolf River Pike Road was chartered in December, 1866, by D. Pearson, W. M. James and others. Several roads were subsequently chartered, but all have been allowed to fall into decay. Under a general law of 1875, counties are allowed to build turnpikes and employ workhouse convicts in their construction. This law has worked very successfully in Hamilton and Shelby Counties and possibly a few others. Under the act of March 23, 1883, Shelby County began work on her roads. The levy of 10 cents on each $100 yielded about $20,000; to this may be added one-half the privilege tax, and a subscription of about one-half is usually obtained without difficulty along the line of the road from the property holders. This money is expended under the direction of the turnpike commissioners. These commissioners consist of the chairman of the county court, who is *ex officio* chairman of the commission, and two other commissioners, who are appointed by the county court. In this county the convicts are hired at 10 cents per day. Under this law from two to three miles of good pike have been built on each of the various public roads leading into the city. The average number of convict laborers is about fifty-five. The salary of the chairman of the committee is fixed by law at $1,000 per annum; that of the others at $250 per annum. Squire Thomas is the present superintendent. The county owns forty acres of ground in connection with the present workhouse building. It also owns twenty head of mules, wagons, farming implements and other supplies. The buildings are of brick, and are comfortable and substantially built. They are kept scrupulously clean and the inmates are furnished three good meals per day during the work season, and two while not at work. The convicts are worked on the county roads and on the farm, the product of which goes toward the support of the institution. The female inmates are employed mainly in the laundry and in cooking. The average cost of the institution is between $7,000 and $8.000. The labor of the convicts amounts to about $2 per day as estimated by railroad work. It will be seen that the profits of the institution almost equal the expenses. The following is a list of the county officers:

Sheriffs: Thomas Taylor, *pro tem.*; Samuel R. Brown, 1833; J. K. Balch, 1835; John W. Fowler, 1842; L. P. Hardaway, 1846; J. B. Moseley, 1852; W. D. Gilmore, 1856; J. E. Felts, 1862; P. M. Winters, 1864-66; A. P. Curry, 1870; M. J. Wright, 1871; W. J. P. Doyle, 1872; C. L. Anderson, 1875: W. L. Anderson, 1878; P. R. Athey, 1881; W. D. Cannon, incumbent.

County court clerks: John Read, *pro tem.*; Wm. Lawrence, 1823; Robert Lawrence, 1831; John W. Fuller, 1848; W. L. Dewoody, 1852; J. P. Trezevant, 1862; John Teague, 1872; James Reiley, 1878; Owen Dwyer, 1882; H. B. Cullen, 1886; P. J. Quigley, incumbent.

Circuit clerks: Joseph Graham, 1832; S. R. Brown, 1848; M. D. L. Stewart, 1870; Frank Taft, 1876; B. F. Coleman, 1878; Joseph Uhl, 1886; D. Schloss, incumbent.

Registers: Thomas Taylor, 1820; M. B. Winchester, 1831; Joseph Graham, 1836; A. B. Taylor, 1842; W. P. Reaves, 1852; Henry Lake, 1862; J. W. King, 1862; C. W. Johnston, 1868; G. M. Greeley, 1870; John Brown, 1877; H. W. Grible, 1879; F. R. Hunt, 1883; John McCallum, 1886; N. F. Harrison.

Rangers: Alexander Ferguson, 1823; Tilman Bettes, 1825; L. Bostick, 1826; James Weaver, 1831; J. C. Cody, 1842; Hugh McAdam, 1848; J. A. Rudisill, 1854; A. S. Thomas, 1860; J. R. King, 1862.

Chairmen: William Irvine, 1823; M. B. Winchester, 1825; Isaac Rawlings, 1832; John Pope, 1838; J. S. Edwards, 1848; J. B. Hodges, 1854; Sylvester Bailey, 1858; J. W. A. Pettit, 1862; J. W. Smith, 1866; Thomas Leonard, 1870; T. C. Blackley, 1874; Thomas Holeman, 1880; C. E. Smith, 1885; D. C. Slaughter, incumbent.

Attorney-generals: James P. Perkins, 1822; Alex. B. Bradford, 1824; V. D. Barry, 1832; T. J. Turley, 1836; E. W. King, 1843; J. P. Caruthers, 1848; D. M. Leatherman, 1852; J. L. T. Sneed, 1855; G. M. Hardin, 1856; B. J. McFadden, 1858; J. L. Harris, 1860; W. F. Talley, 1862; George W. Reeves, 1868; Walker Woods, 1870; Luke E. Wright, 1878; G. P. M. Turner, 1886; Geo. B. Peters, incumbent.

SHELBY COUNTY. 815

Circuit judges: Joshua Haskell, 1826; Parry W. Humphreys, 1832; William B. Turley, 1834; L. M. Bramblett, 1840; W. C. Dunlap, 1850; William R. Harris, 1858; William Reeves, 1866-68; George W. Reeves, 1870; C. W. Heiskell, 1878; James O. Pierce, 1886; L. H. Estes, incumbent.

Commercial and circuit judges: E. W. M. King, 1846-50; J. C. Humpheys, 1862.

Criminal judges: J. R. Flippen, 1872; J. D. Adams, Thomas H. Logwood, P. T. Scruggs, J. E. R. Ray, J. M. Greer, L. B. Horrigan, A. H. Douglass, J. J. Du Bose, incumbent.

Chancellors: Andrew McCampbell, 1840-47; Calvin Jones, 1850; W. R. Harris, 1854; J. P. Caruthers, 1862; William M. Smith, 1865-68; E. M. Yerger, 1870; W. L. Scott; S. P. Walker, 1872; Charles Kortrecht, 1878; W. W. McDowell, 1886; H. T. Ellett, present judge.

Clerks and masters: Joseph H. Talbot, 1847; James M. Williamson, 1854; John C. Lanier, 1860; M. D. L. Stewart, 1862; Augustus Alston, 1865-70; E. A. Cole and Robert J. Black, 1876; E. L. McGowan, 1882; S. I. McDowell, incumbent.

Probate judges: J. E. R. Ray, 1870-78; Thomas D. Eldridge, 1886; J. S. Galloway, incumbent.

Pursuant to an act of the General Assembly, passed November 24, 1819, the court of pleas and quarter sessions was organized on May 1, 1820, at Chickasaw Bluffs for the new county of Shelby. Jacob Tipton having been qualified before and having made proclamation, proceeded to open court. He did so by taking his seat and administering the oath to Anderson B. Carr, Marcus B. Winchester, William Irvine, T. D. Carr and Benj. Willis, all of whom took the oath to support the Constitution of the United States, the constitution of Tennessee, the oath against dueling and the oath as justice of the peace. The organization of the court was made known by notice posted on the courthouse door and signed by the chairman. For temporary organization John Read was chosen clerk, and Thomas Taylor, sheriff. On the next day William Irwine was made permanent chairman; William Lancaster, clerk; Samuel R. Brown, sheriff; Thomas Taylor, register, and Alexander Ferguson, ranger. Paul Bayless and William A. Davis each received the same vote for trustee, but the following day Davis was elected. Gideon Carr was chosen coroner. William Bettes and William Dean received a tie vote for constable but the matter was settled the next day by electing both to that office. J. P. Perkins was chosen solicitor. The bonds for the clerk and constables were fixed at $2,000 and the other officers $5,000 each, and but one man outside the officers was on a bond. Deeds from Andrew Jackson *et al.* to Benjamin Foy for Lot 55; Peggy Grace to T. D. Carr for Lot 43 were ordered recorded. The court made the rule that the county business should be attended to on the first Wednesday of each term. Ordinary licenses were granted to Joseph James and to Patrick Meagher, at Memphis. On May 3 the court granted a ferry license to William Irvine across the Mississippi at the public wharf called Irvine's Landing. The rates allowed would seem rather high now, as $1 was allowed for a man and horse, 50 cents for loose horse, 50 cents for each head of cattle or hogs, $3 for a two-horse carriage loaded, and $5 for a four-horse carriage loaded. The ordinary rates fixed for the above were, board and lodging per week, $3.50; board alone, $2.50 per week; board and lodging per day, $1; lodging per night, $12\frac{1}{2}$ cents; horse feed, 25 cents; French brandy or gin, 25 cents per half pint; whisky, $12\frac{1}{2}$ cents per half pint; apple or peach brandy, $18\frac{3}{4}$ cents; Jamaica spirits, 25 cents per half pint. The first jury "to inquire into the body of the county" consisted of J. W. Padam, John Bettes, Patrick Meagher, T. F. Person, Charles Holiman, Joshua Fletcher, Russell Bean, Gideon Carr, Joseph James, John M. Riddle, Robt. McAllister, Humphrey Williams, William Thompson, Jacob Bean, John Grace, L. Bettes, George Allen, B. Ashford and Thomas Swarford. Benj. Willis resigned his office as justice of the peace and Thomas Carr was appointed tax-lister for the county. The first bill of sale was made by Jacob Bean to William Irvine for a negro boy. Two offenses against the State were tried at the May term of court; one against Henry Gibson and the other Patrick Magee for assault and battery. On May 4, 1820, the court appropriated $175 to Thomas D. Carr with which to build a courthouse, jury-room and jail. On the same day an indictment was found against Thomas Patterson, but the case was not sustained; however the court insisted on charging the defendant with the costs of his prosecution. Marcus B. Winchester filed notice of contest against Thomas D. Taylor for the office of register to which Taylor had been elected. The ground for contest was that at the time of his election Taylor was sheriff of White County, and as Winchester had the next highest vote he claimed the office. On November 1, 1820, the court declared Taylor was not constitutionally elected and ordered a new election the next day at the house of William Lawrence. At this time Winchester was elected "during good behavior in office." In February, 1821, the court met at the house of William Lawrence. The sheriff, solicitor and clerk were each allowed $37.50 for *ex officio* services to January 1, 1821. D. W. Maury was admitted to the bar as an attorney on August 2, 1821. At the August term F. W. Master was fined for assault and battery but took an appeal to the circuit court. At November term, 1821, M. B. Winchester and Wm. A. Davis were allowed $125 for the completion of the new jail.

The following attorneys were admitted in May, 1822; Robt. Hughes, Alex. B. Bradford, R. C. Allen, Thomas Taylor, John Brown and William Stoddert. Bradford was solicitor and was for many years a resident of Jackson. Stoddert was also a member of the Jackson bar. In November, 1822, an indictment was filed for assault and battery upon the body of Robt. M. C. Stewart by Jesse Benton. Jesse Benton was a brother of the distinguished Thomas H. Benton. He was justice of the peace of Shelby County from 1822 to 1824 and was the owner of a considerable tract of land on Big Creek. The February term of court of 1823 met at the house of Thomas D. Carr. The rate of taxation for 1823 was $18\frac{3}{4}$ cents on each town lot, $18\frac{3}{4}$ cents on each 100 acres of land without regard to value, $6\frac{1}{4}$ cents on 100 acres land for the poor and $6\frac{1}{4}$ cents on each $100 of the destruction of wolves. The elections of 1823 were held at the houses of Jacob Tipton, Robt. G. Thornton and Thomas C. Person. The first commissioners for the poor were T. D. Carr, William Irvine and Jacob Tipton. In 1824 the court met at the house of T. D. Carr again and ferry rates for Wolf River and the Loosahatchie were fixed. Deeds of conveyance for Lots 1 and 2 in the town of Memphis were made by N. B. Winchester attorney in fact for Andrew Jackson, John Overton and the heirs of James Winchester. Sam. Gibson was fined $1 for beating Thomas Johnson and was refused a new trial. The plea entered was that the time was not proven in the evidence. The court held that such proof was not necessary. Polly Spira and others were fined $5 and costs, and the sheriff returned a *nulla bona* when the State was compelled to pay the costs. On January 18, 1830, Abram Bayless was allowed $5 for holding an inquest on the body of John Barrow. Seth Wheatley was admitted as attorney on April 29, 1829, and W. C. Dunlap, July 19, 1830, H. W. Moseley in April, 1830, W. H. Humphries, July, 1831, and John D. Martin in April, 1832. The record of sale of Charlotte, a negro girl ten or eleven years old, to Au-fat-char or Brown Sam, a Chickasaw Indian, by Jesse Benton was confirmed July 28, 1825. Lewis Shank and Neil McConnell, free negroes, were given permission to live in the county on giving bond for good behavior. Ferry license was granted William Irvine to keep a ferry across the Mississippi at the public warehouse, otherwise called Irvine's Landing. Jacob T. Swarford and Patrick Meagher each gave bond in the sum of $1,250 to keep an ordinary; rates for ferries and ordinaries are given above. The first grand jury consisted of Thomas H. Persons, foreman; William Roberts, John Grace, John W. Oldham, Drury Bettes, Patrick Meagher, Thomas Palmer,

Humphrey Williams, J. M. Riddle, J. Fetcher, Joseph James and Robert Quimby. August 4, 1820, Patrich Meagher was fined $1 for retailing spirits.

Isaac Rawlings, John Ralston and Thomas Persons were the first commissioners to settle with the trustee and collector of taxes. The sheriff, county court clerk and solicitor were each allowed $42.50 for *ex officio* services for 1821. R. Reynolds was allowed $12 for four full grown wolf scalps. The coroner was allowed $16 for burying a man named McCrere who had committed suicide. Russell Bean, William Dean, J. M. Riddle, Joab Bean, J. W. Oldham and John Mazles were appointed patrollers of Shelby County. Benj. E. Person was licensed to practice law May 5, 1823. The following marriage licenses were issued from May to July, 1820; O. W. Carr to Mary Hill, Russell Bean to Mary C. Harklerood, John Chandler to Sarah Cockraham, William Irvine to Mary Carr, Thomas W. Floyd to Polly Campbell, Jacob Beard to Peggy Grace, and Lindsey Shoemaker to Jane Moore. The marriage ceremonies were performed by Jacob Tipton, John Ralston, A. B. Carr and M. B. Winchester, justices of the peace respectively. The commissioners before mentioned selected Sanderlin's bluff on Wolf River as a site for the seat of justice for Shelby County, and on July 17, 1826, Frederick Christian, John B. Holmes, John R. Kent and Benjaman Robbins were appointed commissioners to lay off the county town. Elijah Bunch was fined $50 for trading with slaves. The county court met for the first time at Raleigh, Jan. 19, 1829. In Jan., 1827, the court levied a tax of 25 cents on each 100 acres of land for the improvement of the navigation of Wolf River and appointed Daniel Dunn, Robert Fearn and Charles Boulton as commissioners of navigation. The idea of fixing a specific tax on land having no regard to its value seems now absurd ; also an attempt to improve the navigation of Wolf River seems equally ridiculous. The Raleigh Academy was established in 1829 with William Battle, David Dunn, Jas. S. Lamaster and James Rembert as trustees. Abram Bayless, coroner, was allowed $5 for holding an inquest on the body of J. Barnes, on January 18, 1830. H. W. Moseley was admitted as an attorney in April, 1830, H. W. Humphreys in July, 1831, and J. D. Martin in April, 1832. The jury for the first circuit court was drawn on August 7, 1823, to meet the fourth Monday in October following. The following composed this jury; Tilman Bettes, Geo. Allen, Henry James, W. B. Dare, Daniel Burns, Wm. Hunter, John Davis, Jacob Hunter, John Bledsoe, Samuel Smith, James McKinzie and William Harris. It is probable Joshua Haskell was the first judge, but Minutebook A of the circuit court is missing and the fact can not be ascertained. The circuit court met for the first time at Raleigh in 1828 with P. W. Humphreys on the bench, Joseph Graham as clerk, and V. D. Barry as solicitor, a position to which he had been elected in 1824. Numerous civil cases were tried. Isaac Rawlings obtained judgment against B. B. J. Robins for $26,777 on an appeal from the county court. A forfeiture of recognizance for $250 was entered against William Savage and J. M. Gillam as sureties for J. P. Porter charged with house-breaking. A. W. G. Davis was fined 1 cent for an affray with costs. On June 17, 1829, a jury of J. Messick, A. Smith, J. H. Markham, J. D. Graham, J. Young, Benj. Robins, I. B. Nickerson, J. C. Doty, J. B. Edwards, Thomas Perkins and James G. Shepherd found J. W. Allen guilty of murder in the first degree. A motion for new trial, also for arrest of judgment, was overruled by Judge Haskell and he was ordered to be hung at Raleigh on September 25, 1829. Jacob B. Painter was indicted for horse stealing but died before trial. Indictments were found, and fines of $5 each were assessed against Milton Coleman, Eppy White, John Wilson, William Powell, William Berryman, John Gregory, William Davis, Joe Porter, William Harris and John Wilford for riot, June 21, 1832. James Chandler brought suit against his wife Rachel for divorce about the same time. Wm. B. Turley appeared as judge of this court from 1832 to 1834. The opening of the State penitentiary in 1832 furnished a new field of punishment.

In that year Oliver Griffith, A. A. Norris and Joe Blackwell were sent to that institution for grand larceny, the former for four years; the second for two and the latter for three years; R. Valentine got ten years for murder in the second degree and B. Bunch three years for passing counterfeit money. Judge L. M. Bramblett appeared on the bench in December, 1834. James Walker was convicted of murder in the second degree and sentenced to the penitentiary for ten years from December 23, 1834. Sam, a slave, was convicted of manslaughter on June 8, 1835, and was ordered to be branded in the hand with the letter "M" and lie in jail till the next morning. On September 8, 1836, a jury consisting of William T. Turner, Isaiah Day, J. W. Guthridge, Thomas Loyd, J. M. Hunt, J. Pennington, J. McNeal, David Bently, John Groom, William Menton and Samuel Acock found Nimrod Hooper guilty of negro stealing and he was ordered hung in the vicinity of Raleigh on December 1, 1836. The bill of cost on this amounted to $360.99, a large sum for the time. George W. Payne and B. Huskey, were sentenced to the penitentiary, the former for five years and the latter for eight years for arson in January, 1837. E. Fraser got three years for horse stealing at the same time. Suits of foreclosure were brought by the Bank of Tennessee and Planters Bank against individuals amounting to more than half a hundred in 1837–38. These were doubtless hastened by the financial embarrassment of the times. On October 4, 1842, Abram Spiers was indicted for the murder of Simon Carmon by cutting him with a knife on September 26, 1842; Thomas S. Wynn for stealing two slaves from John B. Person, and Patrick Hay for biting off the ear of G. S. Oldham, all of whom were eventually acquitted. More naturalization papers were issued in 1844 than for all previous time. The very curious will of Andrew Rembert was made October 12, 1844. It is divided into three parts, one of which is in verse.

W. C. Dunlap became circuit judge in 1840. W. H. Looney was appointed special judge in October, 1844, for the trial of W. M. Mill for the murder of William C. Claiborn. On June 6, 1846, a meeting of the bar was called to take suitable action on the death of Andrew Jackson. W. C. Dunlap was called to the chair and E. J. Shields was made secretary. A similar meeting was called on May 13, 1846, in honor of E. J. Shields who had just died in Texas. J. R. Christian was indicted for shooting F. P. Stanton with a pistol on July 30, 1845, and escaped punishment on a $1,500 forfeiture. W. G. Parr received a sentence of four years for stealing a horse from E. D. Wade. James Hunter and William McBride got a three years' sentence on December 4, 1845, for stealing an ox from Charles D. McLean. The commercial and criminal court was established February 16, 1846, with Ephraim W. M. King as judge. The first important case before this court was W. C. Covington for stealing a slave, Maria, the property of James Dollar. A sentence of five years was imposed on him February 24, 1846, and also the case of William Brown for horse-stealing who also got five years. Samuel H. Forbes killed Martin S. Goldsby with a knife on September 6, 1846, and was sent to the penitentiary for a term of fifteen years. In 1848 there were forty-eight suits brought by the Planters Bank against individuals and forty by the Union Bank. The cases of Stephen Ross for putting out the eye of Jacob Sawyer, Peter D. Wynn for shooting Marcus D. Bolton, Thomas Osborne et al. for an attempt to murder A. Greenlaw were all nollied. Sterling, a slave of Bailey Anderson, was indicted for killing his master at the navy yard February 18, 1850, and was hung at Raleigh June 22, 1851.

The first legal hangings took place in Memphis on May 31, 1861. It was the hanging of Moses, a slave, for killing an Italian organ-grinder and Isaac, a slave, for killing his overseer near Horn Lake in Nonconnah bottom. The crimes were committed in 1858 and the cases were taken before the supreme court at Jackson and the decision of the lower court confirmed. A man named Stover or Stephens was hung on June 20, 1861, for the murder of a man on Presidents Island in 1857. This case had also been to the supreme court. Two criminal executions occurred in 1866, James Galvin and Samuel Moody, each for the murder of a policeman. The chancery court was established for the city of Memphis by an act of the General Assembly December 15, 1840. Joe H. Talbot was appointed clerk and master. On March 8, 1847, Calvin Jones became chancellor and in that year Joe H. Talbot by "visitation of Divine Providence was deprived of his reason" and James M. Williams was appointed clerk and master in his stead. The business of this court has grown wonderfully within the last twenty years entirely out of proportion to the circuit and criminal courts. One of the most interesting suits ever before the chancery court was a suit growing out of the rights of title to the Nashoba lands which were purchased by Frances Wright in 1824. In 1827 these lands were deeded to Gen. Lafayette and others in trust. In 1832 these lands were redeeded to Frances by the trustees. Frances married Count Phiquepal d'Arusmont but separated from him afterward. In 1852 she deeded her possession to her beloved but "estranged daughter, Frances Sylva." In 1853 Frances Wright died. On January 1, Sylva conveyed the remaining part, 1,422 acres of the Nashoba lands to Eugene d'Lagerty for the sum of $30,000 to be paid in installments annually of $5,000 each. d'Lagerty soon after leased the lands to Charles Patton for twenty per cent of profit from the lands. d'Lagerty was to furnish supplies for cutting lumber, brickyards, etc. Miss d'Arusmont and d'Lagerty moved to New Jersey and in 1867 they went to Scotland for an estate belonging to her. On December 23, 1873, he died while they were in Italy. In 1865 Charles Patton brought suit against the estate to enforce a claim amounting to $25,000. The land was sold under decree of court on October 5, 1866, and purchased by Charles Speer of Cincinnati for $21,335 and all claims settled by him in February, 1867. In 1874 Nelson Speer conveyed his interest to Charles Patton by deed. In 1871 the heirs of d'Lagerty brought a bill to set aside the decree to Speer as procured through fraud. This suit finally resulted in a compromise between the heirs and Charles Patton and a division of the property. In a short time Miss d'Arusmont appeared in Memphis where she had not been seen since 1860 and filed a bill against Patton and d'Lagerty heirs, seeking to enforce her claim against d'Lagerty. The claim which she endeavored to enforce amounted to $50,000. The case finally resulted in a decree providing that she could recover lands on payment of certain debts, amounting to about $10,000, against the estate. Some minor points are still unsettled.

The case for the defendants was managed by T. W. Brown, H. M. Hill and Geo. Gillham. A partnership was formed in business in 1850. Parties connected with this firm were Wade H. Bolton, Isaac Bolton, Washington Bolton and Thomas Dickens. The firm continued till 1857. Washington Bolton died and Sarah W. Bolton filed a bill in the chancery court in 1868 for her share in the property of the firm. Thomas Dickens filed a cross bill for the same purpose. On August 10, 1868, Wade H. Bolton made the following extraordinary will. A part only of this is given. It contains eighteen different clauses as follows: "I, Wade H. Bolton, at my home and place in Shelby County, Tenn., being in good health * * * First, it is my will and desire after all my just debts are paid that my ashes repose in Pleasant Ridge Church burying-ground * * * Second, I give and bequeath to my beloved wife, Lavinia Ann Bolton, * * * a life time dowry in my Hoboken plantation. Second, I give and bequeath to her * * * * $10,000 in fee simple. Third, I give * * * to her $10,000, my life policy. Fourth, I give and bequeath to Seth W. Bolton $5,000, provided he lends an assisting hand and helps to defeat the gigantic swindle of old Tom Dickens and his tool, Sarah W. Bolton, has instituted against her father's estate and mine. In event Seth W. Bolton be married or does marry a white woman of his own choice, the $5,000 shall be invested in a piece of land for them. But if Seth W. Bolton remain in a state of celibacy which he is likely to do, my executor is instructed to loan the $5,000 and pay him the interest annually. Fifth, I give and bequeath to Mary L. Bolton, wife of E. C. Patterson, $5,000 provided * * * Sixth, I give &c., to Lucassa Bolton $5,000, provided she help to defeat that gigantic swindle of old Tom Dicken and his tool, Sarah W. Bolton * * * Seventh, I give * * * to my niece, A. Wade Bolton, $5,000, provided * * * * I also give her my gold watch. Eighth, I give and bequeath to my niece, Josephine Bolton, now wife of the notorious Dr. Samuel Dickens (the Judas of the family) $5, one sixth of what Judas Iscariot got for betraying the Lord. Poor Jo, her cup of iniquity will be full after while if she ever gets time to stop in her mad career, trying to help swindle her sister out of her money, and will let her mind reflect back upon her childhood days when she sat under the shade trees and roof of her father and saw the streaming tears and heard the bitter sobs of her father and her mother portraying in the ear of her father that some distant day that old Tom Dickens would swindle them out of all they had and bring them to want. The prophecy is fulfilled in 1868 and her daughter is lending a helping hand. Eleventh, I give and bequeath to the widow of Gen. T. J. Jackson, who fell at the battle of Chancellorsville, $10,000. Twelfth, I bequeath * * * to my loyal servants now called freedmen * * * Fourteenth, I give and bequeath my Hoboken farm for the public schools of Shelby County and $10,000 to build a college to be called Bolton College. Fifteenth, I give and bequeath the rest of my estate to the chairman of the county court to be a perpetuity for the education of the poor white children of the First District. Eighteenth, I appoint E. M. Apperson my executor without security, and Beecher & Belcher my attornies."

The greatest feud was connected with the suit resulting in the death of seven persons. In 1857 a man named McMillan was killed, and in 1868 one Wilson and a servant girl, Nancy, working for Wade H. Bolton; were also killed. Soon after, two men, Inman and Morgan, were tracked into a cave in North Alabama and killed. On July 14, 1869, Wade H. Bolton was shot by Tom Dickens at the gate of the court square and mortally wounded. On July 30, 1870, Dickens was waylaid and killed in the Hatchie bottom, a short distant from Memphis. For the killing of Bolton, Dickens was arrested and put under bond of $5,000. After a trial of twenty-seven days, in which the ablest attorneys were engaged, Dickens was declared "not guilty." The trial ended February 12, 1870. In all the litigation but one conviction was secured. The estate involved in the various suits amounted to over $226,000. These were tried before Chancellor McDowell and appealed to the supreme court. The style of the suits before the supreme court were Cannon *vs.* E. M. Apperson and Maddox *vs.* E. M. Apperson. The executor of the will refused payment to some of the legatees on the ground that they had not fulfilled their part in the "infamous lawsuit." The supreme court confirmed most of the clauses of the will. The provision of the will providing for Bolton College in the First District are being carried out. The sale of lands and the other funds amount to about $65,000. Of this $10,000 is to be spent in erecting buildings on the Hoboken plantation about twenty-five miles northeast of Memphis.

In 1879 the city of Memphis had become so involved in debt from the visitation of the yellow fever, and the public improvement rendered necessary from it, also from extravagant and corrupt city government that it was bankrupt. The taxables of the city amounted to about $21,000,000, and the debts were about $5,800,000. Mandamus after mandamus was heaped upon the city officials demanding increased levies of taxes to meet the indebtedness. To put a stop to further increase of indebtedness and liquidate the old on an equitable basis there was passed "An act to establish taxing districts in this State and to provide the means of the government for the same." This was a part of "An act to repeal the charter of certain municipal corporations and to remand the territory and inhabitants thereof to the government of the State." This act passed the General Assembly January 29, 1879, and received the signature of the governor January 31, 1879, and the sanction as to its constitutionality by the supreme court of the State May 31, 1879. A receiver was appointed who proceeded to wind up the affair of the old corporations. The assets of the city amounted to something near $2,000,000. Severe tests as to the constitutionality of the taxing districts were made by them holding claims against the city, and the matter was carried to the supreme court of the United States, but the new corporation stood the test and the larger claims have been compromised at 50 cents on the dollar. The debt has been refunded in bonds against the taxing district, drawing five per cent interest. These bonds are now about par. The first receiver was Minor Merriwether, who was succeeded by Lawrence Lamb.

The criminal court docket for the last two decades has been quite full. Among the most noted cases may be mentioned the cases of J. W. Davis, J. C. Creighton, Ed Titus, John Cosgrove, Graves & Poston, J. Schoefield, E. J. Eason, Angello Morrow, J. W. Brown and Charles Clinton. In 1882 the execution of Shin Forrest for the murder of David Cruise and Jane Forrest was ordered, also Bill Rivers, for the murder of Amanda Jenkins, and Sandy Matthews was also executed in 1882. Robert Wilson was hung in the jail July 20, 1883, for the murder of Frank Russell. The last person hung was John McKeever, for the murder of Wm. T. Trainor on December 17, 1884. The crime was committed about four miles south of Memphis while the two were hunting. The case was worked up on circumstantial evidence but resulted in conviction. The judgment of the lower court was affirmed by the supreme court. Before his execution on June 26, 1885, McKeever made a full confession. It appears from the docket that for the last eight years the criminal court has convicted 350 persons per annum. Cases in which vast sums of money were involved, were the State *vs.* Proudfit; State *vs.* Anderson, public administrator, and the Extein-Norton bond cases *vs.* Shelby County. In the Anderson case about $200,000 were involved; the latter nearly as much, which was gained for the county by Gen. G. P. M. Turner, for which he has since been allowed $1,000 in fees.

A few of the distinguished dead among the judges and lawyers may be mentioned: W. T. Brown, W. C. Dunlap, V. T. Berry, Ed Yerger, Henry Barry, Henry Small, L. H. Coe, R. Topp, W. B. Turley, E. W. M. King, E. J. Shields, D. M. Leatherman, J. C. Humphreys, J. P. Caruthers, W. R. Harris, Seth Wheatley, B. N. Hart, J. D. Adams, T. H.

Logwood, P. T. Scruggs, J. E. R. Ray, L. B. Horrigan, J. L. Wheatley, G. D. Searcy, F. D. Kortrecht and Archibald Wright. Many others deserve mention. It would be impossible to do justice to the distintinguished living members of the bar. Judges A. H. Douglass and J. L. T. Sneed are among the oldest and most distinguished.

On the declaration of the existence of war between the United States and Mexico in 1846, the President at once called for 50,000 volunteers and Congress appropriated $10,000,000 to defray the expenses of the war. The number of volunteers called for from Tennessee was 2,000; however, 2,400 were accepted under the first call for one year's service. These men were divided into the infantry and the cavalry service, there being 1,600 of the former and 800 of the latter. Gov. A. V. Brown set himself earnestly to work to furnish that number. The feeling against Mexico had so wrought on the minds of the people that through patriotism or a spirit of adventure, many more were led to offer their services as volunteers than could be accepted. The first steps toward raising troops for the war was a meeting held at the Gayoso Hotel on May 8. Four companies almost immediately tendered their services—the Memphis Rifle Guards, Gaines Guards, Eagle Guards and the Jackson Guards. Only three of these companies were accepted. The two first above mentioned were infantry companies and the third was a cavalry company. The two infantry companies were ordered into camp on June 15, at Camp Carroll, near Memphis. They were mustered into the service by Gen. Hays. The officers of the Memphis Rifle Guards were E. F. Ruth, captain; J. B. Nelson, first lieutenant; E. M. Anderson, second lieutenant; G. J. Slaughter, ensign; S. H. Whitsett, orderly sergeant; W. S. Echols, Benj. O'Haver, W. A. Porter, sergeants; R. J. Dye, S. T. Woodson, John Glenn, Robt. Torrey, corporals; J. S. Foster, sergeant-major. The officers of the Gaines Guards were M. B. Cook, captain; W. B. Davis, first lieutenant; E. J. Wyatt, second lieutenant; C. Gill, ensign; R. C. Sneed, orderly sergeant; J. D. Beatty, H. L. Bynum, J. L. Wilbar, sergeants; J. C. Anderson, O. Teslard, R. P. Ford, W. H. Linn, corporals. The Eagle Guards organized by electing W. N. Porter, captain; J. L. Penn, first lieutenant; R. M. Anderson, second lieutenant; C. R. Wheat, ensign; Orville Yerger, orderly sergeant; Cyrus Marshall, Chas. Irvine, sergeants; G. Mattoon, R. Dresser, T. B. Hyler, G. L. Rolon, corporals. The two infantry companies were attached to the Second Regiment, of which Wm. Trousdale was elected colonel. The Second Regiment embarked on board the "Brownsville" on the 10th, for New Orleans and reached New Orleans the last of June; thence was sent to the Brazos in July and was afterward stationed at Camargo till in August, and in September aided in the capture of Monterey. The place fell on September 21. The troops suffered severe losses at this place; hot weather and climatic changes had proved equally as fatal as the arms of the enemy. The Shelby County troops in the invasion thus far, were attached to the brigade commanded by Gen. Gideon J. Pillow. After the capture of Monterey the main body of Taylor's troops were withdrawn from him and sent to assist Gen. Scott in an attack upon Vera Cruz. Both regiments of Tennessee troops had now been placed in the command of Gen. Pillow. The troops started for Tampico on December 14, to embark for Vera Cruz where they arrived on March 9, 1847. After some heavy fighting, Vera Cruz and all its defenses fell into the hands of the Americans on March 29. The army began its advance toward the City of Mexico on April 9, but the progress of the army was disputed by the Mexicans at Cerro Gordo Pass on April 10. It was determined to carry the place by assault. The Second Regiment was on the left of the line. They became entangled in the chapparal in front of the works and suffered terrible losses amounting to seventy-one men. Among the wounded was Gen. Pillow. After the capture of Cerro Gordo the army moved forward to Jalapa. The time of the Second Regiment had expired at this time and the regiment returned to Vera Cruz and embarked for New Orleans where they were discharged and sent home. The Eagle Guards also encamped at Camp Carroll at the Bigspring, two miles east of Memphis. The company consisted of ninety-seven men. Their uniform was of blue cloth faced with yellow. They awaited the arrival of the other troops from Middle and East Tennessee, the last of whom did not arrive until July 2, 1846. The whole force at that time in camp consisted of ten companies of cavalry and four of infantry. By a vote in Camp Carroll J. E. Thomas was elected colonel; Robt. D. Allison, lieutenant-colonel, and Richard Waterhouse, major. The regiment crossed the river at Memphis on July 27, and marched to Little Rock, a distance of 150 miles; thence to Fulton, Ark., 139 miles; thence to Robbins' Ferry, 287 miles; thence to San Antonio, Tex., 246 miles, whence it joined Gen. Taylor's forces at Matamoras. The cavalry was principally engaged in guard duty and had little of the heavy fighting to do. Among those who died of disease was Capt. W. N. Porter. The regiment returned after its year's service and before the volunteers of the second call reached the front, the City of Mexico had surrendered and negotiations for peace were under way.

On April 25, 1861, Gov. Harris directed Gen. S. R. Anderson to proceed to Memphis to organize the various bodies of troops into regiments. He remained till May 3, when Gen. J. T. L. Sneed was appointed to fill the place till the arrival of Maj.-Gen. Gideon J. Pillow on May 9. Active steps were taken to place the city and country in a position of defense. Gen. Pillow issued an order that no company should be received with less than sixty-four men, nor should any one be allowed over one hundred. On May 23 Gen. Pillow ordered all companies that were full into camp at Camp Jackson. Much difficulty was experienced in providing arms and equipments for the men. There were few arms and fewer manufactories for them. The new government set itself earnestly at work to provide means for carrying on the war, which all foresaw was inevitable. The foundry of Quinby & Robinson began casting cannon in May. As fast as men could be armed and equipped they were sent to the front. The whole county became a military camp, or at least an organization. Speakers were sent to every district in the county. All who were not regularly enlisted in the army became members of the committee of safety, of which F. Titus was president. The city of Memphis issued $50,000 in script to furnish supplies to soldiers, and in a short time $25,000 additional was issued. In May the county court issued $25,000 in script to aid in arming and equipping the men of the county. The court allowed $12 a month for the wife, and $6 per month for each child of a volunteer soldier. The men in the various civil districts were organized into companies over which were chosen captains and lieutenants. J. S. Dickason was chosen general commander for the county on May 20, 1861; $30 were allowed for three months' guard service. All surplus arms were turned over to the commanding general, for which warrants on the county were issued. Special taxes were levied for military purposes. On June 3 the county judge appointed Gen. Henry G. Smith a committee to purchase arms, guns, etc. On the 20th of May Gen. Pillow ordered reprisals to be taken of all Northern property passing through the city by river or rail, and a close scrutiny of all goods in transit. On June 1 he ordered all shipments of cotton north to be stopped. The city was organized for military purposes by wards. The ladies, under the leadership of such women as Mrs. S. C. Law, Mrs. Lockhart, Mrs. Pope and others were organized for the purpose of furnishing comforts and delicacies to the soldiers in the field and in the hospitals. On August 22 Gov. Harris issued a proclamation to the women of the State urging them to organize themselves into societies for the purpose above mentioned. In July the troops that had been enlisted in the State service were transferred or mustered into the Confederate States' service. The concentration of the Federals at Cairo led the Confederates to suspect a descent along the river from that point. To forestall such a movement strong works were established near Memphis, at Randolph, Fort Pillow, New Madrid, Island No. 10, and elsewhere along the Mississippi. On July 26 Gen. Pillow went to the front to supervise the works of defense. Soon after Gen. Albert Sidney Johnston, who was commander of the Department of Tennessee, established his headquarters at Memphis. Owing to the threatening attitude of the Federals large bodies were concentrated at points along the Mississippi River, also along the Tennessee and the Cumberland Rivers. On the transfer of the Tennessee troops to the Confederate Government, Gov. Harris issued a call for 30,000 volunteers for a reserve corps. On the fall of Forts Henry and Donelson the entire available force of the State was called out. This call was made on February 19, and the Legislature was convened at Memphis, the public archives having been removed to that place. The threatening attitude of the Federals soon led to another change. The fall of Fort Henry on February 6, and the fall of Fort Donelson on the 16th led to the fall of Columbus. New Madrid fell; Island No. 10 with its garrison surrendered on April 7-8; Fort Pillow was abandoned on June 4, and Randolph was evacuated soon after. The Federals advanced and captured Memphis in June 6.

One Hundred and Fifty-fourth Senior Tennessee Regiment was incorporated on March 22, 1860, as a militia regiment and took the above number in that line of service. It was incorporated with Wm. H. Carroll as colonel, Preston Smith as lieutenant-colonel, A. H. Douglass as major, and M. J. Wright, second major; Dr. N. Thumel, surgeon, and G. H. Monsarat, adjutant. It had also a full line of company officers. On the outbreak of the war the regiment reorganized and tendered its services to the State for twelve months. Preston Smith was then elected colonel, M. J. Wright, lieutenant-colonel; Ed. Fitzgerald, major; W. H. Stovall, adjutant. Seven of the ten companies were from Memphis and Shelby County. These consisted of Company A, Light Guards, captain, J. Genet; B, Bluff City Grays, captain, J. H. Edmonson; C, Hickory Rifles, captain, J. D. Martin; D, Southern Guards, captain, James Hamilton; E, Memphis Zouaves, captain, Sterling Fowlkes; F, Jackson Guards, captain, Michael McGaveney; G, Crockett Rangers, captain, M. Patrick.

In May Col. Wright was ordered by Gov. Harris to Randolph. At this place the Southern guards withdrew from the regiment and formed an artillery company. The Beauregards of Memphis, captian, Moreland and the Maynard Rifles, captain, E. A. Cole, were soon attached to this regiment. The One Hundred and Fifty-fourth took part in the skirmishing around Belmont and the various movements in Kentucky, till after the fall of Forts Henry and Donelson. The regiment then moved south and took an active and conspicuous part in the battle of Shiloh, where it lost several men. At the end of the year's service the regiment reorganized at Corinth, Cols. Smith and Wright both having been promoted to brigadier-generalship. Maj. Fitzgerald was elected colonel, Capt. McGaveney, lieutenant-colonel, and Capt. John W. Dawson, major. After the end of the siege of Corinth the army retreated to Tupelo, thence by way of Chattanooga began its advance into Kentucky. In the engagement at Richmond, Ky., Col. Fitzgerald was killed. The regiment was hotly engaged at Perryville, October 8, 1862. After the death of Col. Fitzgerald, Lieut-Col. McGaveney became colonel, Maj. Dawson lieutenant-colonel and Capt. Marsh Patrick, major. The army retreated back to Tennessee, and this regiment was again heavily engaged at Murfreesboro, on December 31, and January 1-2, 1863. After this battle the Bluff City Grays were attached to Forrest's cavalry, and their place was filled by DeGraffenried's company, from Fayette County. The army fell back to Shelbyville, Tullahoma and Chattanooga, and September 19, 20 was fought the furious battles of Chickamauga and Missionary Ridge on November 25. The regiment wintered near Dalton, Ga., and was engaged in the battles from May 7, 1864, to July 22. At Murfreesboro the regiment lost a third of the men engaged, also heavily at Chickamauga, Missionary Ridge; and from Dalton to Altanta one company lost twenty-seven men out of twenty-nine, nine of whom were killed, two disabled permanently and the remainder returned to duty. After the fall of Atlanta the regiment followed the fortunes of Hood through Tennessee to Franklin, Nashville and back again. It was then transferred to the east and was engaged at Bentonville, near which place the remnant of the regiment surrendered. Out of 1,100 men belonging to the One Hundred and Fifty-fourth, less than one hundred were left at the surrender. This regiment furnished its share of general officers, i. e., Gens. W. H. Carroll, Preston Smith, M. J. Wright and J. D. Martin.

The Fifth Regiment was made from a consolidation of the Second and Twenty-First Regiments. The Second Regiment was known as J. Knox Walker's regiment. The regimental officers were J. K. Walker, colonel; J. A. Ashford, lieutenant-colonel and W. B. Ross, major. The regiment was organized about the 1st of May and was at once ordered to duty at Randolph under Gen. J. L. T. Sneed. It was first engaged at Belmont, on November 7, where with inferior arms it gained a victory. Capt. Armstrong and Lieut. James Walker were killed in the engagement. The regiment was then engaged in duty at Columbus till the retreat to Corinth. The Twenty-first Regiment was raised about the last of April, at Memphis. The regimental officers were Ed Pickett, colonel; H. Tillman, lieutenant-colonel and J. C. Cole, major. The regiment reported for duty to Gen. Cheatham, at Union City, but was soon sent to Columbus, Ky., and was also engaged at Belmont, on November 7. The regiment returned by way of Union City, thence south to Corinth. This regiment and also the Second Regiment were engaged in the bloody battle of Shiloh, on April 6 and 7, 1862. After the evacuation of Corinth, the army fell back to Tupelo. Owing to the great depletion of the two regiments the Second and Twenty-first Regiments were consolidated and formed into the Fifth Regiment. On the reorganization on May 28, 1862, J. A. Smith was elected colonel, J. C. Cole, lieutenant-colonel, and R. J. Parson, major. The companies from Shelby were A, captain, Thomas Stokes; B, captain, C. W. Frayser; C, captain, W. H. Brown; D, captain, L. D. Greenlaw; E, captain, J. H. Beard; F, John Fitzgerald; G, captain, W. H. Carroll; H, captain, A. A. Cox. In August the Fifth Regiment was transferred to Mobile, thence to Tyner Station near Chattanooga, preparatory to the advance into Kentucky. It was with the main body of Bragg's army and passed by way of Sparta, Glasgow, to Bardstown, thence to Munfordsville, and assisted in its capture. It was engaged at Perryville, October 8, and retreated from Kentucky by way of Knoxville, thence moved by way of Tullahoma to the vicinity of Murfreesboro, where it was engaged in that sanguinary battle. It wintered in 1863 at Tullahoma, and fell back with the army across the Tennessee, through Chattanooga, and was in the battle of Chickamauga, on September 19, 20, and again at Missionary Ridge, on November 25. The winter of 1863-64, was spent near Dalton. From Dalton to the fall of Atlanta the Fifth Regiment was engaged almost daily. At Peach Tree Creek, on July 22, private Robt. Coleman shot the distinguished Federal, Gen. McPherson. Coleman was captured and afterward died from wounds. The Fifth Regiment followed Hood into Tennessee, and was almost annihilated at Franklin on November 30. From Nashville the regiment retreated to Corinth, where it was consolidated with the fragments of other regiments. It was then transferred to North Carolina, and was at Bentonville and surrendered at Greensboro on April 26, with less than one hundred men. The regiment was composed almost entirely of Irish, few of whom had families, in consequence of which there were few desertions and very few ever asked for a furlough.

The Fourth Tennessee Regiment was organized May 18, 1861, with R. P. Neely, colonel; O. F. Strahl, lieutenant-colonel; J. F. Henry, major; Henry Hampton, adjutant; J. A. Williams, sergeant; L. P. Yandell, assistant sergeant, and W. C. Gray, chaplain. The regiment contained 962 men. The companies from Shelby County were the Shelby Grays, captain, Somerville; Pillow Guards, captain, James Fentress; Raleigh Volunteers, captain, A. J. Kellar; Harris Guards, captain, J. H. Dean. The other companies were from Lauderdale, Dyer, Hardeman, Obion, Gibson and Tipton Counties. The regiment rendezvoused at Germantown May 15, under Gen. W. H. Carroll. It left Memphis May 20, on board the "Ingomar" for Randolph, where it was placed in the brigade of Gen. J. L. T. Sneed. On July 18 it was sent to Fort Pillow, where it was engaged in drilling. It was mustered into the Confederate service by Gen. J. A. Smith on August 17. It was soon sent to New Madrid; thence to Camp Benton, Mo.; thence back to New Madrid, and on September 3, to Columbus, Ky. On November 7 it was engaged at Belmont, on February 4 at Island No. 10; thence it went to New Madrid. On March 17 it was sent to Tiptonville and there embarked for Memphis, where it arrived on March 20. It was sent by the Memphis & Charleston Railroad to Corinth. It was in the advance, on April 4 and 5, and in the engagements of the 6th and 7th. It captured a Federal battery but lost 31 killed and 161 wounded. The regiment was now reduced to 512 men. It was reorganized at Corinth, on April 25, by electing O. F. Strahl, colonel; A. J. Kellar, lieutenant-colonel, and L. W. Finlay, major. From Corinth it went to Tupelo, Mobile, Montgomery, Chattanooga; thence (August 17) to Kentucky by way of Walden's Ridge, the Sequatchie Valley, Pikeville, Sparta, Gainesboro, Mumfordsville, Elizabethtown, Bardstown, Perryville, Danville, Big Springs, near Harrodsburg; thence back to Perryville October 7; was engaged on October 8. It moved to Camp Dick Robinson; thence by Cumberland Gap, Rodgersville, Knoxville, Bridgeport and Murfreesboro and wintered at Shelbyville. On June 23 it fell back toward Chattanooga. In July O. F. Strahl was made a brigadier-general. Other changes followed in the regiment. The regiment fought at Chickamauga, September 19 and 20, and at Missionary Ridge, November 24 and 25. It wintered near Dalton and was in the Georgia campaign till the fall of Atlanta and then followed the fortunes of Hood through Tennessee at Franklin and Nashville. At Franklin Gen. Strahl was killed. The regiment passed through Columbia, Pulaski and across the Tennessee to Corinth where the men were furloughed. In February the men were sent to North Carolina and were at the final struggle at Bentonville and surrendered at Smithfield on April 26.

Thirteenth Regiment was organized at Jackson, Tenn., on June 3, 1861, under call of Gov. Harris. Company C, the secession guards from Germantown under Capt. J. H. Morgan and E. W. Douglass, was the only company from Shelby County. (A sketch of this regiment is given on page 572 of the State history in this volume.)

The Fifteenth Regiment was organized at Jackson, June 7, 1861.

The regimental officers were C. M. Carroll, colonel; H. R. Taylor, lieutenant-colonel; J. W. Hamilton, major; several changes occurred from resignations. At the reorganization at Tupelo, R. C. Tyler became colonel, Capt. Brooks lieutenant-colonel, and Dr. Wall, major. The companies from Shelby County belonging to this regiment were the companies of Capts. A. C. Ketchum, Dr. Frank Rice, Chas. E. Ross, Ed. S. Pickett, J. F. Cameron, E. M. Cleary, Joseph Kellar and O. Carroll. Capt. Pickett and his company withdrew from the regiment in a short time and Capt. J. F. Cameron and the Young Guards withdrew at Union City. The places of these were filled by the Washington Rifles from Memphis under Capt. Nick Freck and a company from elsewhere. After the battle of Perryville the Fifteenth was consolidated with the Thirty-seventh. (A fuller history of the Fifteenth may be found on page 573 and 576 of this volume.) The officers of the Young Guards at first were J. F. Cameron, captain; J. Bain, first lieutenant; W. F. Burne, second lieutenant; O. H. Smith, third lieutenant. This company returned to Memphis in June and re-enlisted for "three years or during the war." It was attached to Hindman's legion and served with distinction during the war.

Ninth Tennessee, Companies E and I, were from Memphis. These companies were organized in May, 1861, and each numbered about 100 men. The officers of E were Thomas Apperson, captain; John Brown, first lieutenant; J. N. Hughes, second lieutenant, and Fred Battle, third lieutenant. H. R. Rodgers was captain of Company I. The regiment was organized at Camp Beauregard, Jackson, Tenn., May 22, 1861. H. L. Douglass was elected colonel; C. S. Hurt, lieutenant-colonel and S. H. White, major. The regiment was reorganized in May, 1862, when C. S. Hurt was elected colonel; J. W. Burford, lieutenant-colonel and G. W. Kelso, major. At the surrender, April 26, 1865, the regiment had but forty men, eight of whom belonged to E and nine to I. (See pages 569 and 570 of State history.)

The Thirty-eighth was organized in September, 1861. Its regimental and field officers were Robt. L. Looney, colonel; J. C. Carter, lieutenant-colonel; H. W. Collier, major; H. S. Jones, surgeon; E. A. Shryock, quartermaster and R. L. Caruthers, adjutant. The Shelby County companies were A, H. W. Coulter, captain; B, C. H. Holland, captain; D, H. H. Abbington, captain; I, J. C. Thrasher, captain; G, J. J. Mayfield, captain; H, J. G. Cook, captain; J, W. B. Wright, captain; K, A. B. Lovejoy, captain. (A fuller history of this regiment may be found on page 585 in this volume.)

First Cavalry, Company F, of this regiment, was from Shelby County.

This company was commanded by Capt. M. V. Gray. It was organized into a battalion commanded by Maj. H. C. King in April, 1862. Later it helped to form a regiment, the officers of which were Thomas Claiborn, colonel; James Pell, lieutenant-colonel; M. J. Wick, major; H. C. Bate, adjutant. The operations of this regiment were confined mainly to Tennessee and Kentucky.

The nucleus of the Seventh Cavalry was Logwood's battalion, which was composed of the Memphis Light Dragoons, T. H. Logwood, captain; Shelby Light Dragoons, captain, J. G. Ballentine; Tennessee Mounted Rifles, captain, Joe White. This battalion was organized in the fall of 1861, with T. H. Logwood, lieutenant-colonel; C. H. Hill, major; J. W. Somerville, adjutant. This body of men operated in Kentucky and near the State line for some time. On June 10, 1862, this was formed into a regiment, with the following regimental officers: W. H. Jackson, colonel; J. G. Stock, lieutenant-colonel; W. L. Duckworth, major. The following companies were also added: From Shelby County—Company K, W. F. Taylor, captain; J. W. Sneed, first lieutenant; H. W. Watkins, second lieutenant. Company C, S. P. Bassett, captain; J. T. Lawler, first lieutenant; John Albrecht, second lieutenant. A company (partly from Tipton County), J. A. Anderson, captain; Alex. Duckworth, first lieutenant; John Trent, second lieutenant. The regiment was engaged at Bolivar and again at Medon in August; at Britton's Lane, near Denmark, in September; then at Corinth. On October 4 it assisted in cutting Grant's base at Holly Springs, and destroying $5,000,000 worth of stores. It was with Van Dorn in a raid to Bolivar, and then returned to Grenada. It was engaged with Loring and Tilghman at Yazoo. Col. Jackson was made a brigadier-general, and J. C. Stock became colonel, and W. L. Duckworth lieutenant-colonel. Company A, under Capt. W. F. Taylor, became escort to Gen. W. H. Jackson, and Company B, under J. B. Russell, became escort to Gen. Loring. J. B. Lawler became captain of Company C, on the death of Capt. Bassett at Medon. Companies were stationed at different parts of the country. Col. Stock resigned, and W. L. Duckworth became colonel. In a dash upon Collierville, October 11, the regiment came near capturing Gen. Sherman. His horse, sword and a part of his staff were captured. The regiment then retired to Holly Springs. The Seventh assisted in the defeat of Smith and Grierson in their raid into Mississippi. At a new organization W. L. Duckworth was retained as colonel; W. F. Taylor was made lieutenant-colonel; C. C. Clay, major, and W. S. Pope, adjutant. In March, 1864, the Seventh assisted in the capture of Union City, with 700 prisoners, without loss. In the summer of 1864 it assisted in the defeat of Gen. Sturgis at Guntown, Miss., and in the fall joined in the raid through West Tennessee, through Paris and to Johnsonville, where fifteen boats and twenty-one barges were destroyed, the whole amounting to $3,000,000. This was a preliminary step to Hood's raid into Tennessee. The Seventh passed by way of Henryville, Mt. Pleasant, Columbia, Spring Hill and to Franklin November 30, and on to Nashville, where the regiment occupied a position on the Charlotte Pike, within two miles of Nashville, where it was engaged December 15 and 16. When the army had reached Tupelo the men were allowed a furlough, but reassembled again at West Point, Miss., whence they were taken to Selma, where they were opposed by Gen. Wilson, to whom they surrendered at Gainesville, Ala., in April, 1865. The regiment lost in killed and wounded 207 men.

Forrest's old regiment was organized at Memphis in October, 1861. N. B. Forrest was elected lieutenant-colonel, D. C. Kelley, major, and C. A. Schafer, adjutant. This regiment was made up from both Mississippi and Tennessee. Company C, containing ninety men, was from Memphis, of which company T. H. May was chosen captain. The regiment originally contained eight companies, and followed the various fortunes of its indomitable leader. It won its first laurels in its escape from Donelson, and was connected with every success of its leader, including the capture of Murfreesboro, with the capture of Col. Streight and the capture of Johnsonville. Before the close of the war the commissioned officers of the companies and the regiment were largely from Memphis and Shelby County.

Bankhead's battery, a body of men 100 in number, was raised by S. P. Bankhead and W. T. C. Humes. It was organized in April, 1861, at Memphis. The commissioned officers of the company were S. P. Bankhead, captain; W. T. C. Humes, first lieutenant; J. C. McDavitt, W. L. Scott and W. B. Greenlaw, second lieutenants. They first saw service at Fort Pillow, in the heavy artillery service, but returned to Memphis in the summer, and were organized as light artillery, having four guns. They were at New Madrid, Columbus, Island No. 10 and at Shiloh, where the battery lost twenty men. On May 14, 1862, the battery was reorganized, and later Capt. Bankhead was made brigadier-general of artillery and W. L. Scott was made commander of the battery. Henceforth it was known as Scott's battery. The battery fought at Murfreesboro, Chickamauga and Missionary Ridge. At the latter place the battery was nearly annihilated. The guns were lost and nearly all the men were killed. There being so few left, the men were attached to Marshall's battery, where they served to the close of the war. A portion of Jackson's battery, also some of Carnes' battery, were from Memphis, but it is believed no regularly organized body joined either. Company A, and Company H, from Memphis, joined a regiment composed of Tennesseans, Alabamians and Mississippians. The officers of Company A were Joe Barbiere, captain; T. J. Brooks, first lieutenant, and T. J. Spain, second lieutenant. The officers of Company H were J. R. Farabee, captain; G. F. Pillow, first lieutenant. The regiment was organized February 26, 1862. After the capture of Island No. 10 the companies were assigned to some of the older regiments.

Shelby County furnished at least fifty-three full companies; these with the recruits would doubtless aggregate 6,000 men. The voting population in 1860 was only about 6,000.

The evacuation of Forts Pillow and Randolph in June, 1862, left the river open for the advance of the Federals. The concentration of all the Confederate forces at Corinth stripped the country of men. Brig.-Gen. Villepigue was then commander of the forces about Memphis and Col. Thos. H. Rosser of the post. The Federal fleet arrived above the city on Thursday night, June 5, and at 9 o'clock anchored within about one mile and a half of the place. It consisted of the rams Queen, Monarch, Lancaster and Switzerland all under command of Col. Charles Ellet. The gunboats were the Benton, Commodore Davis' flag-ship, St. Louis, Mound City, Louisville, Cairo and Carondolet, all under Commodore C. H. Davis. The Confederate consisted of the Gen. Van Dorn, Gen. Price, Gen. Bragg, Gen. Lovell, Gen. Beauregard, Jeff Thompson, Sumpter and Little Rebel, all under command of Commodore Ed. Montgomery By direction from Richmond M. Jeff Thompson, who witnessed the battle, was made general commander with Montgomery. Before the engagement began Commodore Montgomery made the Little Rebel his flag-ship instead of the Van Dorn owing to a large amount of stores on board that vessel. Thompson says he held a consultation with Montgomery as to the defense to be made. Two companies of soldiers were asked for to help man the boats but before they could be brought from the depot, the battle had begun. According to his statement the action commenced much sooner than was expected. Col. Ellet says he was not expecting to encounter a Confederate fleet at all, as it was understood that it had retreated, and that the action was a surprise to him. By the official report of both Col. Ellet and Commodore Davis, the battle began at 5:30 A. M. and ended at 7 A. M., lasting one hour and a half. The battle was opened by Commodore Montgomery, who advanced to meet the enemy as far as Wolf River. After some wild firing the Queen and Monarch advanced boldly. The Queen aimed a blow at the Beauregard but missed her mark and was herself struck by the Beauregard and so damaged that she ran ashore on the Arkansas side. Col. Ellet who commanded the river fleet, was on board the Queen as his flag-ship, and was himself wounded in the leg by a pistol shot, the only casualty on the Federal side. The Beauregard and Price made for the Monarch, but a blow by the Beauregard at the Monarch missed its aim and tore off the wheel-house of the Price, which drifted and sank on the Arkansas shore. The Little Rebel struck the Monarch but did no damage and in turn the Monarch struck the Beauregard and crowded her on her side. The Federal gunboats were now closing in and a shot from one penetrated the boiler of the Beauregard which sank opposite Fort Pickering. A Federal tug rescued the crew. The Gen. Lovell was penetrated early in the action and she careened and sank in deep water. Captain Cabell was killed by a sharpshooter, but Capt. Delacy and most of the crew swam ashore and escaped. The boiler of the Little Rebel was exploded by a shot, but she drifted ashore and most of the crew escaped. The Sumpter, was captured in a damaged condition. The Jeff Thompson was fired by a shell and burned to the water's edge, when her magazine exploded with terrific force. The other vessels attempted to make their escape, but were pursued and all captured except the Van Dorn. The vessels returned from the pursuit at 10 o'clock. According to Commodore Davis, the Federal loss was, Col. Ellet wounded, and the ram, Queen or Queen of the West disabled. He also reported four prisoners captured, and about 100 killed and wounded of the Confederates and seven vessels. M. Jeff Thompson in his report to Beauregard, thinks the battle was ill-advised, that the boats were poorly handled and that the result was unavoidable under the circumstances. He speaks further of the work of the Federal sharpshooters as being particularly fatal. At 10 o'clock Commodore C. H. Davis sent Medical Cadet Chas. R. Ellet, son of Col. Ellet, Lieut. Crandall of the Fifty-ninth Illinois, and ten boatmen bearing a flag of truce, demanding the surrender of the city to the authority of the United States, to which Mayor John Park replied: "By the force of circumstances the city is in your hands." The Federal officers and men then proceeded to place a flag upon the courthouse, also one upon the custom house. They were met by the mayor and leading citizens with their characteristic courtesy, but they were surrounded by a hooting and howling mass who showed their contempt for the invaders not only by hurling invectives but shots and other missiles. In a short time Col. Fitch, with detachments of the Forty-third and Forty-sixth Indiana Regiments landed, and at 3 o'clock P. M. the mayor met him and arranged for the government of the city. Order was issued for business, except saloons, to proceed, and for citizens to return to their homes. Capt. John H. Gould was appointed provost-marshal. The majority of the leading citizens, officers, bankers, etc., left the city and went south. The Federal commander issued rigid orders to the citizens; he also ordered any soldiers pilfering or straggling from ranks to be shot.

A singular feature of the battle was that it was witnessed by almost the entire population of the city, at that time estimated at 5,000. There was more or less friction between the civil and military authorities till July 2, 1864, when martial law was declared. On May 11, 1866, a conflict occurred between the police, citizens and the negro soldiery stationed at the forts. Bad feeling was existing between the police and soldiers, some of whom were of a very disreputable class, and Gen. Stoneman says some of the police were not of the best. The soldiers were used to execute the orders of the Government agents, marshals, etc., and were frequently brought in conflict with the police. A deadly feud grew up, which was encouraged by agitators and demagogues. A reign of terror existed from the 1st to the 3d of May, which was only suppressed by Gen. Wallace and the leading citizens. About twenty-four negroes were killed, and property estimated at $120,000 was destroyed. These disturbances have long since passed away.

In Elmwood Cemetery is set apart a portion for the repose of the Confederate dead. In this are buried 117, who were residents of Memphis and vicinity. Besides these there are nearly 1,000 from Arkansas and other States. There is now in course of erection a monument, whose towering shaft is to perpetuate the memory of the fallen.

The National Cemetery was established in 1867. The land was selected and purchased by Rev. W. B. Earnshaw, Lieut.-Col. A. W. Willis and Maj. G. W. Marshall. It was first called the Mississippi River National Cemetery, but has since been named the Memphis National Cemetery. There was purchased forty-four acres of ground for which there was paid $9,817.56. A space about 800x1,800 feet, about thirty-seven acres, is enclosed by a brick wall; the remaining seven acres are enclosed by a wooden fence. In the main enclosure are buried the remains of the soldiers. This enclosure also contains the house of the superintendent and such other buildings as are necessary. Sections are set apart for the regular army, the navy, and each of the States whose soldiers are buried there. There is also the "Fort Pillow Section," containing 248 dead. The cemetery contains the remains of all who died from Kentucky to Mississippi, including both sides of the river. It is the fourth cemetery in size in the United States. The order and size are as follows: Vicksburg, 16,588; Nashville, 16,538; Arlington, 16,260, and Memphis, 13,932.

In 1874 there had been expended upon the cemetery $249,556.66. It is beautifully shaded and has nice drive ways. Capt. Hess is the present superintendent.

But little, if anything, was done for public education in Shelby County before 1870. During this year, in accordance with the code of Tennessee, and an act of the Legislature, passed July 7, 1870, the scholastic population of the county was enumerated in part, but as the school records are incomplete a full history of the schools is unattainable. So far as those records show, the school population was as follows: In the First Civil District, white 424, colored 296; in the Sixth District, white 415, colored 422; in the Seventh, white 293, colored 508; in the Ninth, white 432, colored 420; in the Thirteenth, white 126, colored 388; in the Seventeenth, white 53, colored 49. This enumeration included the youth between six and twenty-one years of age. In 1871 the enumeration was continued and based upon the ages from six to eighteen. In the Third District, white 165, colored 235; Tenth, white 401, colored 340; Twelfth, white 159, colored 246. In the Ninth District 513 attended school and in the Tenth 351, 268 white children and 83 colored. In 1872 the following additional districts made reports: the Second, white 207, colored 251; Fifth, white 236, colored 82; Eighth, white 204, colored 218; Sixteenth, white 128, colored 270. In 1873 the Fifteenth District reported white children 305, colored 125.

During the succeeding years the work of organizing the schools went slowly forward, and even of what was done reports are meager. Turning backward and going over the same ground, January 14, 1871, the school commissioners made a report to the effect that they had found some difficulty in carrying out the provisions of the law on account of the general apathy of parents and guardians with regard to the schools and the want of suitable buildings for schoolhouses. They had, however, succeeded in organizing one school which would commence operations January 16, 1871, and another was in process of organization. In the Fourteenth District, school commissioners were elected February 20, 1871, and in the Eleventh and Twelfth on the 25th of March. On the 1st of the following July the school commissioners of the Seventeenth District reported that they had received from the county trustee $554.20, and that the second school had been organized, that school had been in session five months, that seventy-three scholars had been in attendance and that the amount paid out for school purposes had been $501 and for furniture, $21.70. On October 12, 1871, the total amount of funds in the Fourth District was reported to be $480.17, and that Mrs. Hamilton had received $152.85 and Mrs. Amelia Templeton, $100. In the Second District the commissioners reported for the year ending June 30, 1872, having received from the county trustee $566.25, and having paid out for instruction $432, for house rent $6, for two loads of wood 75 cents and for a water bucket 50 cents, and in the Sixteenth District for the same year the commissioners reported that school had been taught four months for the white children, with an average attendance of forty-three, for which $314.16 had been paid, but that there had been no free school for the colored children for want of a house in which to hold it.

These facts and figures are given merely as illustrative of the work attempted during the early years of the school's existence. The superintendents paid praiseworthy attention to the duties of their office, and the people generally, not having seen the advantages free public schools confer upon a community, could not appreciate those advantages. Previous to 1882 some of the county superintendents were a Mr. Tyler, George Fleece, Judge G. P. Foote, C. H. Stein and Dr. W. L. Henderson. In 1882 Mrs. W. H. Horton was elected by the county court and since then the schools have made steady and commendable progress. During the first year of her incumbency she held three teachers' institutes; during 1883, four; during 1884, five; during 1885, five, and during 1886, five. The West Tennessee Institute was held in Collierville in June, 1886, by the State superintendent of common schools. There were in attendance about eighty-five teachers, fifty of them from Shelby County. There were present four instructors of the teachers, Prof. Frank Smith, Prof. A. B. Bourland and Mrs. Horton.

The progress the schools of the county have made is shown by the following statistics from the report of Mrs. Horton for the year ending June 30, 1886. At the beginning of the year there was on hand $12,769.60; there was received from the State during the year $7,660.91; from the county, $55,381.77; total school fund for the year, $75,812.29. The scholastic population was, white males, 7,591; white females, 6,781; total white children, 14,378; colored males, 9,813; colored females, 9,777; total colored children, 19,590; a grand total of 33,968. The number of schools in the county was for white children 69, for colored children 79, total number of schools, 148; the number of schoolhouses was 148, one stone and 147 frame; 7 frame schoolhouses were erected during the year. The number of white male teachers employed during the year was 17; white females, 58; colored males, 59, and colored females, 20; a total number of 154 teachers. There are 19 school districts in the county and 12 graded schools. The number of pupils enrolled during the year was 10,556, of which the white males numbered 1,829; white females, 1,778; colored males, 3,270; colored females, 3,679. The average daily attendance was, white children, 4,166; colored, 6,338; total, 10,504. The average number of days taught during the year was 120, and the average compensation was $35 per month. The schoolhouses are valued at $37,517.50, and the apparatus at $1,640; total value of school property $39,157.50. At the election held January 3, 1887, Dr. W. L. Henderson was chosen to succeed Mrs. Horton.

Great interest attaches to the public schools of Memphis. Generally they have been ably managed, and they have attained a high degree of efficiency. But it would be very difficult without great effort in the way of investigation to accurately apportion to those responsible for their establishment the credit due to each. It is believed, however, that J. W. A. Pettit was the first to urge upon the Board of Aldermen of Memphis to establish a system of free schools for the city. This was early in 1848, and in accordance with his advice the members of the board had schools opened each in his respective ward. Col. Pettit, as alderman, opened the first school at the northeast corner of Third and Overton Streets, in the house of Mrs. Moore, whom he employed as teacher. Subsequently he opened a second school, the teacher of which was Mr. Walker, near the corner of Main and Overton Streets. Subsequently it was moved to the Methodist Church, east of Center Alley and south of Concord Street. Later schools were opened in the Second and the Third Wards. On the 1st of April, 1848, a resolution was adopted by the Board of Aldermen that an assistant teacher be employed by the alderman of the First Ward for the school in that ward, "provided the compensation of such assistant shall not on any account exceed one-half allowed the teacher ($30 per month) now employed, and that said assistant shall at any time be discontinued by the board with no compensation except for the time he or she may have been employed as such assistant." On the 13th of May, 1848, a committee was appointed to examine into the progress of the Third Ward school, and on the 20th J. Wright and Col. Pettit offered separate reports in relation to the adoption of a system of free schools. A resolution was offered on June 3 to reinstate Thomas J. Pearson as teacher of the Third Ward school, to which an amendment was offered to discontinue the whole of the ward schools, both amendment and original resolution being voted down, showing that there was some dissatisfaction with the working of the free school system. But it had too many friends to permit of its overthrow, and on the 19th of June, 1848, an ordinance was introduced and passed concerning the free school system. This ordinance consisted of selections from two ordinances previously proposed but not passed, one of them having been introduced by Mayor G. B. Locke, the other by Mr. McGeveney.

From Mr. McGeveney's proposed bill were selected Sections 1, 2, 8 and 9, and from Mayor Locke's, Sections 3, 4, 5, 6 and 7. Section 1 of the ordinance as adopted divided the city into school districts; Section 2 provided that the school tax should be one-eighth of the city revenue as provided by the charter, and that the schools were to be equally free to all white children between the ages of six and sixteen; Section 3 said that all that part of the city north of Poplar Street should be the First District, and all that part of the city south of Poplar Street should be the Second District; Section 4, that the Board of Education, then called the Board of Managers, should consist of the mayor, two aldermen and two citizens, one from each school district; Section 5, that there should be two school houses in each district, and Section 7 required the Board of Managers to report to the Board of Mayor and Aldermen. On the 1st of July the Board of Managers was increased by two members, and a superintendent of schools provided for. Col. J. W. A. Pettit was elected to this position, and was the first superintendent of schools of Memphis. On the 18th of this month the duties of the superintendent were prescribed, and the responsibility for the success of the schools was laid upon his shoulders. Supt. Pettit opened schools on Market, Poplar, Adams, Court, Madison, Gayoso, Main, Hernando and Third Streets, and Brown Avenue. Among the early teachers besides those mentioned above were Misses Cochran, Cook, Root, Pettit, Gayle, Creighton, Porter and Davis, Mesdames Margaret Doyle, Creighton, Sappington, Erwin, Barnett and Jenkins, and Messrs. Davis, Creighton, Kilpatrick, B. R. Trezevant, Carroll, Bell and Ring. The progress of the schools under the Board of Managers, constituted as already recited, not being satisfactory a change was proposed by Mr. Barry in the following ordinance:

"Be it ordained by the mayor and Board of Aldermen of the city of Memphis that hereafter the Board of Mayor and Aldermen be the sole board for conducting and controlling the public schools of the city, and that the present Board of Managers be discontinued," which was passed on the same day. The old Board of Managers had found it necessary to act irregularly and had not reported the irregular action to the Board of Mayor and Aldermen at their first meeting after such irregular action had been taken. Dr. Fowlkes on the 21st of October proposed an ordinance, which was passed, providing for the establishment of a high school as nearly as practicable in the geographical center of the city in the Third Ward.

The Board of Mayor and Aldermen passed a resolution on the 1st of August, 1850, in which they approved of having a general superintendent for the schools, and fixed his salary at $600 per year. At the same time they appointed J. W. A. Pettit superintendent, "subject to removal at any time." Up to this time Col. Pettit had served without pay. According to his annual report for the school year ending June, 1851, the number of schools had increased to twelve, with 580 pupils, the cost for the year being $4,891.50. Had Col. Pettit's advice with reference to the purchase of lots for schoolhouses been followed, thousands of dollars would have been saved to Memphis in the expense of her schools. He remained superintendent of the schools until June, 1852, when he removed to Germantown, where he died August 24, 1863. Col. Pettit has been called the "father of the Memphis public schools."

The next superintendent after Col. Pettit was Dr. Ebbert, for the year ending June, 1853; then J. F. Pearle, for the year ending June, 1854, and for the year ending June, 1855, Mr. Tarbox, and S. H. Tobey after Mr. Tarbox went to Nashville. Mr. Tobey was succeeded by Dr. A. P. Merrill, who served two years, until June, 1857. During his first year, on May 4, 1856, the city schools were incorporated by an act of the Legislature. Previous to this incorporation some of the principal teachers otherwise than as named were the following: Miss Black, now Mrs. Boyd, of Memphis; Miss Mary E. Woods, now Mrs. C. A. Richardson, of Memphis; Miss Wood, now Mrs. George W. Fisher, of Memphis; Miss Emily Bowdoin, now Mrs. E. B. Armour, of Memphis; Miss Fannie Gayle, now Mrs. Jobe, of Memphis; Miss Florida Pettit, now Mrs. Dr. Thompson, of Germantown, and Mrs. Henrietta Hampton, who commenced teaching in October, 1852, has been so engaged ever since, and is still a valuable teacher in the schools.

By the act of incorporation referred to above, the Board of Mayor and Aldermen was required to appoint a suitable person from each ward of the city and one for the city at large as visitors of the city schools. This board of visitors was given power to choose one of their own number president, to employ and dismiss superintendents, teachers, etc., to fix salaries, rent school-rooms, buy furniture, and to have full control of the schools. No one was to be admitted as a pupil except white persons residing within the city limits, and between the ages of six and twenty, except upon payment of tuition, and the board was authorized to prescribe higher branches of study than those usually taught in the city schools, charging therefor a suitable tuition fee if the ordinary school revenue was not ample to pay the extra expense attending the introduction of these higher branches. The first board of visitors under this act was composed of Dr. L. Shanks, Dr. J. W. Maddox, J. B. Kirtland, Leroy Pope, H. L. Guion and Robertson Topp for the wards, and Dr. A. P. Merrill at large. A new act of incorporation was passed March 20,

1858. During the war the schools were conducted without much interruption, but it was very difficult for the city to pay expenses, these expenses being from necessity paid in scrip. On the 5th of July, 1864, the following resolution was passed by the Board of Mayor and Aldermen: "That the warrants issued by the School Board shall be received and cashed as all other city warrants;" and in this way the schools were maintained. In the scholastic year of 1861-62 there were seventeen schools, with 1,495 pupils; in that of 1864-65 there were twenty-seven schools, with 2,419 scholars. In 1865 the superintendent said in his report that without suitable buildings, with an empty treasury, and with all the excitement and feeling aroused by civil war, the schools had been successfully conducted through the storm. The tuition of each pupil in daily attendance upon the schools had been $4.30, and the total cost of conducting the schools for that year had been $45,473.88.

The following table comprises more information with reference to the schools of the city than can otherwise be presented in the same space, and corrected as it is by the preceding sketch it will prove especially valuable:

YEARS.	Scholastic Population.	Enrollment.	Average Number belonging.	Average Daily Attendance.	Expenses.	No. of Months in Session.	Total Cost per Pupil attending.	Presidents.	Superintendents.
1850-51					$		$		
1851-52									
1852-53		584							Dr. Ebbert.
1853-54		1,298						A. P. Merrill	J. F. Pearle.
1854-55	2,000	1,599	1,006		17,152			A. P. Merrill	Tarbox & Tobey.
1855-56		1,578	998	867	16,239		18 73		A. P. Merrill.
1856-57								J. H. McMahon	A. P. Merrill.
1857-58		1,555	912	736	21,586		29 32	G. R. Grant	Leroy Pope.
1858-59		1,501	824	691	20,469	10	29 62	T. W. Preston	Leroy Pope.
1859-60	3,568	1,682	964	798	23,896	10	29 94	John A. Nooe	Leroy Pope.
1860-61		2,073	1,187	1,019	29,977	10	29 41	John A. Nooe	Leroy Pope.
1861-62		1,791	863	755	20,038	10	26 54	G. R. Grant	A. P. Merrill.
1862-63		1,495	774	607	20,078	10	33 07	James Elder	Richard Hines.
1863-64		2,216	1,129	902	23,707	10	26 28	S. T. Morgan	Richard Hines.
1864-65		2,418	1,259	1,036	54,330	10	52 44	S. T. Morgan	Richard Hines.
1865-66	3,865	2,523	1,361	1,209	51,212	10	42 35	J. J. Peres	W. Z. Mitchell.
1866-67	4,505	2,597	1,417	1,276	87,011	10	68 19	H. H. Higbee	W. Z. Mitchell.
1867-68	5,555	2,884	1,740	1,573	52,867		33 60	H. D. Connell	W. Z. Mitchell.
1868-69	9,427	2,362	1,585	1,383	43,329	5	31 32	J. T. Leath	W. Z. Mitchell.
1869-70	10,667	3,307	2,500	1,659	54,026	10	32 56	Thos. R. Smith	J. T. Leath.
1870-71	9,909	5,005	2,891	2,599	54,858	9	21 10	R. B. Maury	J. T. Leath.
1871-72	9,909	5,120	2,783	2,556	72,194	10	28 24	W. Z. Mitchell	H. C. Slaughter.
1872-73	13,393	5,240	2,583	2,522	74,935	10	29 71	Chas Kortrecht	H. C. Slaughter.
1873-74	10,381	5,823	2,968	2,749	71,538	8½	26 02	Chas. Kortrecht	A. Pickett.
1874-75	10,400			2,927	70,261	9	24 00	Chas. Kortrecht	A. Pickett.
1875-76	10,419	5,506	2,660	2,392	47,181	9	19 72	R. W. Mitchell	A. Pickett
1876-77	9,091	5,687	3,097	2,457	49,478	9	20 13	W. A. Goodman	J. T. Leath.
1877-78	9,011	5,174	3,131	2,822	58,951	8	20 88	W. A. Goodman	J. T. Leath.
1878-79	9,141	4,105	2,611	2,389	31,434	8	13 15	W. C. Folkes	W. H. Foute.
1879-80	9,141	4,134	2,565	2,365	38,942	6½	16 46	W. C. Folkes	W. H. Foute.
1880-81	9,745	4,367	2,887	2,578	41,559	8	16 12	G. V. Rambaut	Chas. H. Collier.
1881-82	11,242	3,948	2,030	2,671	44,265	8	16 57	G. V. Rambaut	Chas. H. Collier.
1882-83	11,200	4,323	2,991	2,814	45,023	8	16 00	G. V. Rambaut	Chas. H. Collier.
1883-84	13,169	4,226	2,981	2,729	47,390	8	17 36	G. V. Rambaut	Chas. H. Collier.
1884-85	13,169	5,143	3,333	3,016	47,643	8	15 80	R. D. Jordan	Chas. H. Collier.
1885-86	13,808	4,920	3,903	3,591	56,845	8	15 83	R. D. Jordan	Chas. H. Collier.

Referring briefly to the colored schools it may be stated that among the first efforts made with reference to their establishment was in September, 1864, when a special order was issued that the control and discipline of the educational interests, school and teachers of the public schools for the colored people of the city of Memphis, "is hereby entrusted to the municipal government of the city, and the committee on public schools is hereby constituted a school board with full power for the efficient management of the same." Subsequently the colored schools were incorporated with the white schools, and in 1869 J. T. Leath, president of the board of education, said he had heard no complaint because of this joint incorporation. President Leath then expressed himself in the following language: "Imbued and clothed as our colored friends are with all the immunities of citizens, they should be qualified by education and moral training to perform all their duties to society, to their country and to their Maker."

Commendable progress has been made in the public schools for colored children. In March, 1874, the Clay Street schoolhouse was completed. At this time there were 3,902 colored children of school age in the city, 1,565 of whom were enrolled. At the close of the school year 1878-79 there were seven schools for white children and three for colored. In 1882 there were five schools for colored children, as was also the case in 1885. The subjoined table is of great interest as comparing the work of the two classes of schools for the year 1885.

SUMMARY.

SCHOOLS.	Number different Pupils enrolled.			Number of Days Present.	Number of Days Absent.	Number of Times Tardy.	Per cent of Attendance.	Average Enrollment.	Average Number Belonging.	Average Number Attending.	No. remaining at Close of Session.
	Boys.	Girls.	Total.								
Smith School—senior dep't	24	116	140	15,892	1,185	381	93.	109	105	100	96
Intermediate and prim. dep'ts.	205	279	484	50,676	3,626	1,318	93.3	355	335	315	329
Leath	247	290	537	63,314	6,409	1,738	90.	427	415	380	406
Peabody	237	255	492	48,863	5,143	1,809	90.5	356	326	294	325
Merrill	187	207	394	41,250	3,033	711	93.3	288	274	256	258
Jefferson	156	161	317	30,808	2,504	918	92.5	210	197	183	177
Pope	143	145	288	30,404	2,626	541	92.5	208	200	185	197
Total white	1,199	1,453	2,652	281,207	24,526	7,416	92.	1,953	1,851	1,713	1,788
Kortrecht	406	553	959	100,579	6,805	1,434	93.	648	637	597	574
Monroe	252	314	566	48,191	5,403	826	90.	348	331	298	310
Winchester	200	239	439	36,225	1,037	532	97.	240	256	224	267
Saffarans	148	175	323	22,527	1,592	262	93.4	168	146	136	143
Seventh Street	93	111	204	15,780	1,770	491	90.	112	112	100	99
Total colored	1,099	1,392	2,491	223,302	18,607	3,545	92.3	1,516	1,482	1,305	1,393
Grand total	2,298	2,845	5,143	504,509	43,133	10,961	92.	3,469	3,333	3,016	3,181

The Highbee School is located at the intersection of Beale, Lauderdale and Jessamine Streets and fronts on each street. It was established in

1875 as the Presbyterian Grammar and High School, with Miss Jennie M. Higbee, principal. Miss Higbee had been for ten years principal of the Memphis Female High School, and it was thought by her friends that her sphere of usefulness would be enlarged by placing her at the head of this school. In 1879 the name was changed to "Miss Higbee's High School," and in 1882 to "The Higbee School." The building in which this school is kept is a three-story brick with seventeen rooms devoted to study and recitation. The grounds are beautifully shaded with oaks, elms and magnolias. In addition to the above described a new building has just been completed. It is an imposing structure and so arranged as to meet all requirements. It is the result of a conference of Miss Higbee's friends, who recognizing the great good she had accomplished in a long series of years by her unaided efforts, furnished the means for its erection and equipment. Besides the common branches of an English education, the course of study comprises the higher English branches, natural sciences, literature, ancient and modern languages, music, phonography, painting and wood carving. The object of the principal of this school is expressed in her motto, "Not many things, but much." Following are the names of the faculty of this school: Miss Jennie M. Higbee, principal; Miss Laura Shortt, higher mathematics, Latin and Greek; Miss Helen Marion Quinche, natural sciences; Mrs. P. E. Phillips, history, mathematics and languages; Mrs. W. R. Johnson, intermediate classes; Mrs. Mary Shouse, principal of primary department; Mlle. Marie Jost, French; Prof. Bignon, French; Prof. Leon Lausberg, German; Miss Martha Tradeau, principal of school of music; Miss Jonnie Winston Fall, phonography and type writing; Miss Carrie Deslonde Dobyns, principal of art school, and Miss Aurelia Lane, resident governess. This school has had over 2,000 students and 193 graduates.

The Clara Conway Institute was founded in September, 1877, "for the purpose of affording Southern girls the opportunity of acquiring a broad and liberal education, such as would fit them for independent living for honor and usefulness." The school is located at 259 Poplar Street. Since its establishment it has had in attendance 1,843 pupils. There are in the school four courses of study: English, literature, classical and special. The classical course requires eleven years for its completion; the English course, which includes the classical except the last year, requires ten, and the literary course requires ten years. The special course is optional. As showing the limit of study in the classical course the eleventh year's branches are given as follows: Trigonometry, Horace, Herodotus, the history of philosophy, political economy, English literature, the history of art, civil government and a course of historical reading. One object of education is expression which, as defined by Miss Conway in her tenth annual catalogue, is as follows: "Every thought and feeling writes itself upon the plastic body of the little child, and the face and body at sixty are but the history of the soul, that has either beautified it or disfigured it. It is thus in every woman's power to be beautiful in old age." The school was chartered in May, 1885. The following are the officers of its board of twenty-one trustees: John K. Speed, president; T. J. Latham, vice-president; John H. Shepherd, secretary, and T. H. Milburn, treasurer.

The Le Moyne Institute was established in 1871 through the American Missionary Association, a Congregational benevolent organization deriving its funds from individual contributions and from the Congregational Churches of the North. For some years previous to the establishment of this institution the American Missionary Association had sustained a number of common schools for colored youth in Memphis. In 1870 Dr. F. Julius Le Moyne of Washington, Penn., a life-long, earnest and active friend of the colored people, gave $20,000 to be used by the association in founding an English school for colored youth in Memphis. After the cost of erecting the necessary buildings had been taken out of this fund, there remained about $11,000 as an endowment fund and the school was opened in September, 1871. Since this time the institution has been fostered by the association, the money necessary to its maintenance, over and above that received as tuition from the pupils, being furnished by it.

The school is divided into primary, intermediate, grammar and normal grades. The two latter departments provided thorough instruction in the branches taught in the public schools of the State. Approved methods of teaching and the proper management of classes and schools are likewise thoroughly taught. One very important feature of the work in this school is its department of manual training. It consists of an experimental kitchen and sewing rooms, in which are taught household duties. In the wood-working department the boys are duly taught the use of various kinds of tools, including the turning lathe, etc. Three years are spent in the primary grade, two in the intermediate, three in the grammar grade, two in the elementary normal course, at the completion of which students are presented certificates, and two in the advanced normal grade, at the end of which they are given diplomas. Thus twelve years are spent in this institution. The enrollment for the year 1886–87 is as follows: First primary grade, 72; second primary, 69; intermediate grade, 85; grammar grade, 68; normal department, 151, a total enrollment, 445; names counted twice, 18; net enrollment, 427. The instructors in this school are as follows: Andrew J. Steele, principal and professor of natural science; Rev. Benjamin A. Imes, pastor and instructor in Christian work; Esther A. Barnes, grammar and English literature; Rebecca M. Green, mathematics and drawing; Ruth E. Stinson, geography and history; Sarah C. Bateham, grammar grade; Celestia S. Goldsmith, intermediate grade; Zulu E. Fellon, second primary grade; Fannie A. McCullough, first primary grade; Margaret A. C. Stewart, vocal and instrumental music; Minerva A. Kinney, girls' industrial work and matron of teachers' home; C. M. Stevens, boys' industrial work, and Ella A. Hamilton, missionary and night school teacher.

In 1864 efforts were made to secure the establishment by the Christian Brothers of the Christian Brothers' College in Memphis, and September 21, 1865, a lot was purchased on Wellington Street between Linden and Vance Streets, by Rev. Thomas L. Power, O. P., the pastor of St. Peter's Church; but owing to pressing demands in other portions of the United States, it was not until after 1871, when the great Chicago fire destroyed several of their institutions that a few brothers could be spared to found this college in Memphis. Most Rev. Patrick A. Feehan, bishop of Nashville, aided by his clergy and parishioners, raised the first subscription toward paying for the college property and the institution was formally opened November 19, 1871, since which time its patronage has been very liberal and its success exceedingly gratifying. Extensive additions and improvements were completed in 1886 at a cost of more than $20,000.

The object of this institution is to afford the means of acquiring a liberal and refined education, and the curriculum embraces a preparatory, commercial, collegiate, literary and scientific course. Of the scientific and literary courses, the Greek and Latin classics and English literature constitute an essential part. The junior members are required to devote special attention to mathematics, logic, literature and the philosophy of history, and the senior members to political and moral philosophy and the doctrine of ontology.

By its revised charter this institution is authorized to confer the degrees of A. B. and A. M. and such other degrees as are usually conferred by similar institutions in the United States. Following are the names of the executive officers of the institution: Brother Maureham, president; Brother Abban, vice-president; Brother John of the Cross, secretary, and Brother Nicholas, treasurer.

St. Agnes Female Seminary was established in 1851 by Father T. L. Grace, and incorporated in 1852. It was immediately taken in charge by six sisters of the order of St Dominic from St. Catharines, Ky. The names of these sisters were Veronica Ray, who was the first Mother Superior; Magdalen, Frances, Vincent, Catharine and Vincentia, the latter of whom is the only one now living. The property, which is on the south side of Vance Street, near Orleans Street, was purchased by Father Grace, and at the time was known as the "Coe place." In addition to the building then standing the sisters have erected others as required. At first there were but very few students, but the number steadily increased and it is remarkable that there was no diminution in attendance during the war, and no cessation of instruction on account thereof. There were then about 100 students in attendance, which is the present number, although there are accommodations for 175. In May, 1878, the buildings were destroyed by fire as also was an excellent and choice library valued at $6,000. New buildings were erected in 1879 and the library has been to some extent replaced, having now about 1,500 volumes. Pupils are in attendance from all the adjoining States, varying in age from six to nineteen. They are taught by eleven teachers and ten others are engaged in household duties about the institution. The Mother Superiors have been as follows: Mother Veronica Ray, eleven years; Mother Ann, three years; Mother Mary Joseph, three years; Mother Mary Bernard, two years; Mother Mary Louisa, seven years; Mother Mary Alphonso, one year (died of yellow fever); Mother Mary Thomas, four years; Mother Mary Josephine, three years, and again Mother Mary Thomas, commencing in 1885.

The First Presbyterian Church was organized with five members—three females and two males—June 7, 1828, by W. C. Blair. L. Henderson was chosen ruling elder and Rev. W. P. Alrich acted as stated supply from December 13, 1829, to February 12, 1830. In the following November Rev. S. M. Williamson became stated supply and remained until November, 1833. Services were conducted in the log schoolhouse on Court Square up to 1834, when a lot was presented as a building site upon which a frame building was erected. Rev. Samuel Hodge became stated supply in February of this year, remaining only a few months, after which there was no regular pastor until March, 1837, when the Rev. J. Harrison was installed, remaining until July, 1843. The Rev. George W. Coons was engaged in December, 1843, and installed in November, 1844, when the South Memphis Church was organized. In October, 1852, the Rev. Mr. Coons was succeeded by the Rev. S. Kay, D. D., of London, who served as stated supply until January, 1854, when the Rev. J. O. Stedman was elected pastor, remaining until March, 1868, when the Rev. F. H. Bowman of Virginia came and remained until his death, October 6, 1873, of yellow fever. The church was then without a pastor fourteen months, when the present pastor, the Rev. Eugene Daniel, was engaged as stated supply and installed April 18, 1875. The church building erected in 1834 was used until 1852, when a new one was commenced and completed in 1854. This was used until destroyed by fire in 1883. The brick church now used was then commenced and completed in 1885, at a cost of $30,000. The present membership is about 350. The Bible class and the Ladies' Benevolent Society connected with this church are the means of accomplishing much good.

The Second Presbyterian Church was organized Friday night, December 26, 1844. Following are names of the original members: Alexander S. Caldwell and wife, Martha; Dr. Joseph N. Bybee and wife; T. Pritchett; M. F. Prichett; Misses M. A., M. C., P. C. and M. L. Patillo; Mrs. Eliza Houston, James D. Goff and wife, Miss L. C. Boyd and her slave, Scipio; Dr. R. H. Patillo and wife and J. S. Levett. The first elders were Joseph N. Bybee and R. H. Patillo, and the first deacons A. S. Caldwell and J. S. Levett. Rev. John H. Gray was unanimously elected pastor on Monday, the 29th of December, on which day the session was constituted and Joseph N. Bybee elected its clerk. Seven additional persons were admitted to membership that morning. The church edifice, standing at the corner of Maine and Beale Streets, was soon afterward erected, and dedicated April 2, 1848. The Rev. R. C. Grundy was elected to the pastorate February 22, 1857, and remained until 1861, after which the Rev. J. N. Waddell and Rev. J. H. Gray were each stated supply for a short time, and in August, 1865, the Rev. T. D. Witherspoon became pastor, remaining until   , when Rev. W. E. Boggs was chosen and remained until 1879. The pulpit was filled by supplies until January, 1881, when Rev. J. M. Rose became pastor and remained until 1882, when he was succeeded by the Rev. J. F. Latimer, who remained two years. In May, 1885, the present pastor, Rev. Dr. Boggs, returned to the church. The membership is now about 350, and the Sunday-school, of which R. E. Wilcox is superintendent, has about 220 scholars.

The Third Presbyterian Church, standing at the corner of Seventh and Chelsea Streets, was organized October 7, 1856, with fourteen members. The Rev. Edward Porter, having served the church from the time of its organization as stated supply, was installed pastor October 20, 1860, and on the next day the brick church which had been in process of erection about eighteen months was dedicated by the Rev. John H. Rice, D. D. On the 27th of April, 1862, the pastor resigned and entered the Confederate Army and was succeeded by the Rev. William A. Sampler, who was installed October 13, 1866. Rev. E. M. Richardson, D. D., the present pastor, was chosen November 10, 1868, and installed June 13, 1869. The church is situated in what is known as Chelsea and is a most attractive and comfortable structure, with a seating capacity of 500. The present membership is about 150, and both the Sunday-School and ladies' society are in an energetic and flourishing condition. The Church meets its obligations promptly, and liberally contributes to benevolent objects.

The Alabama Street Presbyterian Church was organized in 1868 by a colony of about thirty from the First Presbyterian Church, who chose the Rev. Dr. J. O. Stedman, a native of Fayetteville, N. C., and a graduate of Princeton College, pastor. A temporary church edifice was erected standing at the corner of Alabama Street and Jones Avenue, the lot upon which it was built having been donated for that purpose by J. C. Johnson. This, a frame building, cost about $1,500, and was occupied until the present brick church was completed in 1880 at a cost of about $9,000. The Rev. Dr. Stedman remained pastor until this year, when on account of failing health he resigned and was succeeded by the Rev. E. E. Bigger, who remained about a year and was followed by the Rev. William Johnson in 1882, who died within a year and was followed by Rev. William Darnall, who also remained about a year. In July, 1885, the present pastor, Rev. J. L. Martin, was chosen. The present membership of the church is about 140, and the Sunday-School, of which Carrington Mason, Jr., is superintendent, has about the same number of scholars.

Lauderdale Street Presbyterian Church was established as a mission on Union Street during the pastorate in the Second Presbyterian Church of the Rev. T. D. Witherspoon. A chapel was erected and dedicated by the Rev. John H. Gray, and a Sunday-school was conducted for some years by members of the Second Presbyterian Church. The first preacher at this mission was the Rev. Mr. Wykoff, who was succeeded by Rev. J. F. Latimer, now professor in Union Theological Seminary, Virginia. In 1874 the church was established by the name of the Union Street Presbyterian Church with the Rev. A. Shotwell pastor about a year. He was succeeded by the Rev. John A. Waddell, at present chancellor of the Southwestern Presbyterian University at Clarksville. Subsequently a lot was purchased at the corner of Lauderdale and Beale Streets and the present building commenced in June, 1876, and dedicated in October following when the name was changed to the Lauderdale Street Church. In 1879, upon the election of Dr. Waddell to his present position, the Rev. N. M. Long was engaged and in 1881 the Rev. R. A. Lapsley became the pastor, remaining until 1882. The present pastor, Rev. Samuel A. Caldwell, was then chosen. In connection with this church is a large and flourishing Sunday-school of which Judge B. M. Estes is the superintendent.

The Cumberland Presbyterian Church was organized August 1, 1840, or a few days thereafter at a protracted meeting held by the Revs. Samuel Dennis, Reuben Burrow, D. D., with eighteen members. Rev. Samuel Dennis remained pastor of the church one year during which time nine more members were admitted. Soon afterward a lot was purchased for $1,100, and on September 3, 1844, the corner-stone of the new church was laid with imposing Masonic ceremonies by Memphis Lodge, No. 91. Rev. Robert Donnell accepted a unanimous call to the pastorate and began his labors February 9, 1845, remaining until June, that year, and was followed by Rev. Mr. Dennis who remained until March 16, 1851, and was succeeded by the Rev. Herschell S. Porter, of Philadelphia, a very able preacher and author, who died in 1855 of yellow fever. The Rev. A. M. Bryan, D. D., began his labors in April, 1856, but resigned to return to his former congregation in Pittsburgh, Penn., in April, 1859; Rev. A. C. Davis, of Lexington, Mo., succeeded and remained until his death in 1867. On January 1, 1868, Rev. L. C. Ransom, of Murfreesboro, entered upon his duties, also remaining until his death in October, 1874. Rev. G. W. Stainback began his ministry in January, 1875, and resigned in January, 1879, when he was succeeded by the present pastor, Rev. H. A. Jones, of McMinnville, Tenn.

The church building is a large, two-story brick structure, with Sunday-school and other rooms in the basement, and auditorium capable of seating 1,200 persons above. Here is a very large, fine pipe-organ, one of the largest, if not the largest, in the Southern States. The Sunday-school was organized March 23, 1845, and is in a flourishing condition.

The First Methodist Episcopal Church was organized as a society in February, 1826, by Rev. T. P. Davidson. The society consisted of three members: Elijah Coffee, Mr. Dickens and Mrs. Paulina Perkins, who afterward married Dr. Dudley Dunn. Mr. Coffee withdrew from the Methodists and united with the Primitive Baptists because the Quarterly Conference would not license him to preach. In 1830 Revs. T. P. Davidson, J. E. Jones and Moses S. Morris were in the circuit with Thomas Smith, presiding elder. In 1831 Joshua Boucher was presiding elder with Pleasant B. Robinson and Ashley B. Rozell as circuit riders. In 1832 Memphis was made a station with Rev. Francis A. Owen, preacher, appointed by the conference in response to the petition of the Methodists residing at Memphis. Upon his arrival there was but one available male Methodist in Memphis, John Manning. After preaching at a private house and one Sunday in the upper room of a store, the dining-room of the old "Blue Ruin Tavern" was chosen for an auditorium. Becoming tired of having no church home Mr. Owen made an earnest appeal to the congregation, and especially to the ladies, who are always foremost in religious work, to build a church edifice. A lot was purchased of Maj. Winchester, a church building commenced, and the first sermon delivered in it as yet incomplete on the first Sunday in June, 1832. A revival commenced, resulting in sixty converts; when the church was organized by Rev. Mr. Owen there were but eleven, the organization taking the name of Wesley Chapel. Following is a list of the preachers of this church, together with the year in which their respective pastorates commenced: Revs. Robert Alexander, 1832; W. Phillips, 1833; T. P. Davidson, 1834; S. S. Moody, 1835; W. D. F. Sawrie, 1836; Isaac Heard, 1837; T. C. Cooper, 1838, remaining but a few months, his appointment being filled out by Rev. Joab Watson; Rev. Samuel Watson, 1839, who returned a membership of 387; A. T. Scruggs, 1841; S. S. Moody, 1842; Dr. Thweat, 1843; S. G. Starks, 1844; Wesley Warren, D. D., 1845, in which year a new church building was completed; M. J. Blackwell, 1847; S. J. Henderson, 1848; James L. Chapman, 1850; W. C. Robb, 1852; J. W. Knott, 1853; Thomas A. Ware, 1855; James E. Temple, 1856; J. T. C. Collins, 1857, during which year 150 joined the church; A. H. Thomas, 1858; W. T. Harris, 1860. Rev. Mr. Harris entered the Southern Army and was followed by Rev. Samuel Watson, and he in 1862 by Rev. J. W. Knott, "who, considering that the city was filled with Yankee soldiers, did about as well as could be expected;" D. J. Allen, 1863. But he had no sooner commenced his work than the Methodist Episcopal Church, by order of the Secretary of War, occupied the building through chaplains, and after a short time the Rev. Mr. McMullen, of Indiana, was selected to be the permanent pastor of the church; finding, however, that the members were disinclined to attend, Mr. McMullen retired. After the Methodist Episcopal Church gave up the building, Rev. J. W. Knott again took charge, and was succeeded in the fall of 1865 by Rev. A. H. Thomas; A. P. Mann, 1866; E. C. Slater, D. D., 1869; S. B. Suratt, 1873; E. C. Slater, D. D., 1877, who died of yellow fever in September, 1878; R. H. Mahon, 1878; S. A. Steel, 1882, and R. H. Mahon again in 1886. The present church-building, a two-story brick standing on the east side of Second Street, near Poplar Street, was erected in 1850. In 1886 the lot on the corner of Second and Poplar Streets was purchased and plans and specifications for a new stone church to be erected on this lot, were prepared by Jacob Snyder, architect of Akron, Ohio, which when completed will be the most elegant and complete edifice in Memphis.

Asbury Church stands on the corner of Hernando and Linden Streets. It was first regularly organized in 1843 by Nathan Harcott and John

Brown. Previous to this time, however, there had been religious services in the vicinity in private houses, and in John Brown's carpenter shop, standing on the corner of Hernando and Vance Streets, fitted up for such services by Mr. and Mrs. Brown. Upon the advice of Rev. Moses Brock the lot upon which the present church stands was purchased. The first house built upon this lot was exceedingly primitive, and a description of it is worthy of preservation: "It was a shanty. Holes were dug in the ground, posts set up, and rough planks nailed on the sides. It was covered with planks. Scantling laid on the ground and planks laid on them made the floor." Enlarged a little, the congregation continued to use it as a house of worship until 1847, when a plain frame building was erected which lasted until 1882. This frame building then gave way to a one-story brick Gothic structure which will seat about 450 people and which cost $15,000. Following is a list of the pastors of Asbury Chapel, named after Bishop Asbury, the founder of Methodism in America, as Wesley Chapel, now the First Methodist Episcopal Church South, was named after John Wesley, the founder of Methodism in the world: Revs. Benjamin A. Hayes, commencing in 1843; D. W. Garrard, 1845; L. D. Mullins, 1846; W. C. Robb, 1847; A. H. Thomas, 1849; S. J. Henderson, 1850; Joseph H. Brooks, 1852; James W. McFarland, 1853, who died before his year had expired and was succeeded by B. M. Johnson; J. T. C. Collins, 1854; Philip Tuggle, 1856; W. H. Leigh, 1857; J. T. Meriwether, 1858; E. E. Hamilton, 1859; Robert Martin, 1860; Guilford Jones, 1861, who in 1862, not wishing to add to his experience at Paducah, Ky., with the Federal Army, left for Arkansas, D. J. Allen filling out his appointment; Guilford Jones, 1865; F. S. Petway, 1867; L. D. Mullins, 1869; J. H. Evans, 1871; E. E. Hamilton, 1873; J. C. Hooks, 1875; Guilford Jones, 1877; Warner Moore, 1879; David Leith, 1882; J. M. Spence, 1886. In 1850 the membership of this church was 235 whites and 43 blacks; in 1854, 153 whites and 104 blacks; in 1865, owing to the war, the membership was very low. Both church and Sunday-school are now in prosperous condition.

Central Methodist Episcopal Church South was started not long before the war, their small frame church edifice, at No. 187 Union Street, being dedicated in 1860. This congregation was organized by the Rev. J. T. C. Collins, and the building dedicated by Bishop George F. Pierce. For some time the church was served by temporary supplies. The small frame church lasted until 1868, when the present brick building was begun. It cost $40,000, will seat 750 people, and was finished in 1883. Since 1869 the pastors have been Revs. W. M. Patterson, 1869;

A. L. Pritchett, 1871; P. T. Scruggs, 1873; S. B. Suratt, 1873; E. C. Slater, D. D., 1874; J. A. Heard, 1875; W. T. Harris, 1877; S. W. Moore, 1879; S. B. Suratt, 1880; J. H. Evans, 1881; R. H. Mahon, 1882, and R. W. Erwin, 1886.

Besides the above Methodist Churches there are two small congregations, one called the Georgia Street Methodist Episcopal Church South, and the other the Saffarans Street Methodist Episcopal Church South. All of the Methodist Churches in Memphis belong to the Southern connection. The colored Methodists have Collins' Chapel, on Washington and Orleans Streets, and Avery Chapel, on De Soto Street, the latter being one of the most elegantly finished edifices in Memphis.

The first Baptist Church was organized April 6, 1839, with eleven members, at McGeveney's schoolhouse, standing near where the fountain now is in Court Square. The first pastor was Rev. L. H. Milliken, who remained though the years 1839–41. During 1842 Rev. Mr. Eager and Rev. B. F. Farnsworth served as pastor or supply, the latter gentleman resigning in September. In 1843 Rev. S. S. Parr was pastor. In 1845 a lot was purchased on Second Street, between Adams and Washington Streets, on which there was a small frame building which was fitted up as a temporary place of worship, and in February, 1846, Rev. P. S. Gayle was elected pastor, remaining three years. During his pastorate a church costing $7,000 was erected, the membership being about 175. February 14, 1849, Rev. John Finlay was elected pastor, remaining until 1852, when he was followed by the Rev. C. R. Hendrickson. He was succeeded in 1857 by the Rev. T. J. Drane, who remained until 1862, when Rev. S. H. Ford began preaching, and remained until the occupation of Memphis by the Union Army, June 6, when he left for the South, and the church building was taken possession of by the military authorities for hospital purposes, the damage to the church caused by such occupancy being afterward made good by the United States Government. In the spring of 1863 the American Baptist Home Mission Society of Philadelphia advised the church that unless a minister were secured a preacher would be sent to take charge of the church, and in order to avoid having a foreign minister, not of their own choosing, a call was extended to Rev. A. B. Miller, of Owensboro, Ky., who became pastor in June, 1863, and remained until January, 1868. The subsequent pastors have been the Rev. D. E. Burns, commencing in 1868; Rev. I. T. Tichnor, April, 1871; Rev. Dr. G. A. Lofton, May, 1872; Rev. R. B. Momack, 1876; Rev. Dr. W. A. Montgomery, 1878, and the present pastor, Rev. R. A. Venable, October 6, 1880. The present membership of the church is about 350. R. G. Craig has been the superintendent of the Sunday-school for twenty-one years.

The Central Baptist Church was organized December 3, 1865, at the First Church, standing at the corner of Adams and Second Streets. Before the war the Beale Street Church and the mission at Fort Pickering were doing the work of the Baptists, but at its close the Beale Street Church had no pastor, no house of worship, no regular meetings, and to all appearances had gone to pieces, as was the case with the Mission at Fort Pickering. South Memphis was thus without Baptist services, and the only Baptist Church was in the extreme northern end of the city. A considerable number of members of the First Baptist Church, however, lived toward the south end of the city, and it was inconvenient for them to attend their own church. After consulting with old members of the Beale Street Church, a new organization was effected and named the Central Church, composed of forty-three members of Beale Street Church and seventy-five of First Church. The Beale Street Church conveyed their lot to the new organization, and the First Church allowed its retiring members $10,000, as their share of the property. On December 3, 1865, at a meeting presided over by Rev. S. H. Ford, D. D., the Central Baptist Church was organized, and Dr. Ford immediately chosen pastor. For six months the new church and the First Church used the building of the First Church on alternate Sundays, and in the meantime the Central Church leased a lot on Court Street, upon which they erected at a cost of $3,000, a frame building known as the Tabernacle. The Tabernacle was used from June 24, 1866, to December, 1868. In the fall of 1867, the Central Church bought the ground upon which the present church stands, paying therefore $22,500. Times were then prosperous, everybody had plenty of money and was confident of the future. An architect was employed whose plan was approved and accepted, and work on the building commenced, but on account of business depression which was felt throughout the country from 1868 to 1873, but little could be done except to complete the basement story of the building containing the lecture room. This was used first on February 21, 1869, and continued to be used nearly seventeen years. The walls of the second story, the roof and tower which is of the Swiss order of architecture, and designed when erected to be only of temporary utility, were all completed in 1876, and imposed upon the organization a debt of $10,000, most of it bearing ten per cent interest. The existence of this debt made it impracticable for the organization to finish the structure until 1884, when work was resumed and the building completed by and dedicated on December 6, 1885. At this time the membership was about 300, and at the present time (January 1, 1887) it is 369. The building is a two-story brick, with lecture room in the basement seating 400, and the auditorium in the second story containing 600 opera chairs. The extreme length of the building is 150 feet, and the extreme width 80 feet and the tower 150 feet in height. The total cost of the building has been about $130,000. The Sunday-school has about 150 scholars and twenty officers and teachers. The Rev. Dr. S. H. Ford was pastor until July 1, 1871; the Rev. Sylvanus Landrum, D. D., from October 1, 1871, to July 1, 1879; the Rev. Thomas J. Rowan from January 1, 1880, to July 29, 1882, and the present pastor, Rev. A. W. Lamar, from Macon, Ga., commenced his pastorate November 1, 1882.

The colored Baptists have a very fine church on Beale Street, which is massive in construction and well attended.

St. Peter's Church was organized in 1840, the building standing at the corner of Adams and Third Streets. In 1841 the Rev. Michael McAleer was placed in charge and remained until 1845, when he resigned, when Bishop Miles placed the parish in charge of the Dominicans, whose mother house was then as now at St. Rose, near Springfield, Washington Co., Ky. The first Dominicans in charge were the Rev. James S. Alemany, O. S. D., afterward archbishop of San Francisco, and the Rev. Thomas L. Grace, O. S. D., present bishop of St. Paul. From 1845 to 1853 in addition to these two priests Fathers J. H. Clarkson, Anthony O'Brien, Aloysius Orengo, Francis Cubero, R. A. White, J. A. Boekel, Sr., and J. R. Cleary ministered in turn to the Catholics in West Tennessee and eastern Arkansas. In 1853 the population of Memphis had reached 11,000, and the Catholics had so increased in numbers that the little brick church was far too small for their accommodation; hence in the beginning of this year the Rev. Father T. L. Grace with the aid of his assistant pastors began the work of building the present St. Peter's Church edifice, which was completed in 1857. It is a fine structure, 80x150 feet, cruciform in shape, of the Gothic style of architecture, capable of seating 1,500 people and cost $150,000. As an ecclesiastical structure it stands unrivaled in the South, and the organ in this church procured through the exertions of the Rev. Father Clarkson, is also one of the remarkable instruments of the kind in the Southern States. It was procured in 1864, having been originally built for a church in Atlanta, Ga., but the closing in of the lines of the Federal Army around that city prevented its being erected in its originally designed position. Accordingly negotiations were entered into with Henry Erben, of New York, then the foremost organ builder in the United States, as the result of which the magnificent instrument was set up in St. Peter's in the spring of the year mentioned. Its original cost was to have been $13,000, but it was secured for St. Peter's for $9,000. It has three manuals and a pedal of twenty-nine keys.

In 1856 Rev. Father Grace established St. Peter's Orphan Asylum, placing it in charge of the Sisters of the Third Order of St. Dominic, and for the last thirty years this asylum has been sustained by the efforts of the Dominican Fathers. During the last forty-one years forty different priests have been stationed at St. Peter's, those in charge at the present time being Pastor Very Rev. M. D. Lilly, O. S. D., and the Rev. R. M. Bloomer, O. S. D., and Rev. J. P. Moran, O. S. D. During the yellow fever epidemics of 1873, 1878 and 1879 no more heroic sacrifices were made in attempting to relieve the sufferings of the sick than were made by the priests of this church. As soon as one priest died another came from the North to take his place, when to do so was almost certain death. At the close of terrible epidemics St. Peter's had furnished eight victims as follows: In 1873—Rev. J. R. Daley, O. S. D.; Rev. D. A. O'Brien, O. S. D.; Rev. B. V. Carey, O. S. D., and Rev. J. D. Sheehy, O. S. D.; in 1878—Rev. J. A. Boekel, Jr., O. S. D.; Rev. J. R. McGarvey, O. S. D., and Rev. P. J. Seawell; in 1879—Rev. Dalmatius Reville, O. S. D. All of these voluntary victims to the dread epidemic lie buried in Calvary Cemetery, where a fitting monument commemorates their heroic deeds. About 400 families belong to the church. A parish school was established soon after the church was built. It is under the control of the pastor and taught by the Sisters of the Third Order of St. Dominic. At present there are about 120 pupils in attendance. Tuition is free.

St. Mary's Church is the only German Catholic Church in Memphis. It was established as a mission of St. Boniface in 1852, the object being to build up a charge for the Germans, who had hitherto been members of St. Peter's Church. Among the Dominican Fathers at St. Peter's were some German priests who had cared for the German Catholic members of the congregation. The last of these was the Rev. Father J. A. Boekel, who with the German Catholics of St. Peter's purchased a lot on Union Street, which they sold in 1856 and purchased one on the corner of Market and Third Streets for $9,000. A small frame building on the lot was fitted up for a church and the Rt. Rev. James Whelan, bishop of Nashville, sent in 1860 a secular priest to take charge of the new congregation, the Rev. W. J. Repis, who died in 1885 at Feehanville, near Chicago. In 1862 the Rev. Father Thoma took charge. The war coming on then materially checked the growth of St. Mary's, but in 1864 a new and substantial brick church was erected, having been begun by the Rev. Cornelius Thoma. The Rev. L. Schneider succeeded Father Thoma in 1867, and nearly finished the church outwardly and purchased the adjoining lot at a cost of $9,000. Petitions of the German Catholics of Memphis for the Franciscan Fathers were at length answered by the appointment of

Father Eugenius Puers from Teutopolis, Effingham Co., Ill., in 1870, who on account of poor health was superseded in August of the same year by the Rev. Kilian Schlosser, at present rector of St. Peter's in Chicago. In September, 1871, Rev. Ambrosius Jansen built a fine new monastery near the church. In 1873 Rev. Father Buchholz built a new entrance to the monastery on Market Street. Being called back to Germany in 1879 Rev. Aloysius Wiener became rector and remained until 1885, when he was succeeded by Rev. Father Nemesius Rohde, who came here from St. Peter's in Chicago. During the epidemics in 1873, 1878 and 1879 the Franciscan Fathers were very much devoted to the sick, especially Father Aloysius Wiener, who lived and labored successfully through all the fever years, though three learned assistants fell victims to the scourge: Rev. Fathers Lee Rinklage, Maternus Mallmann and Chrysostom Reinke, and also the good Fathers Amandus and Erasmus. Besides these four Franciscan Sisters died of the yellow fever, as also some sisters of St. Mary's from St. Louis. In connection with St. Mary's Church is St. Mary's School, which was kept by Franciscan Sisters from Joliet, Ill., until after the fever of 1873, when, having lost so many Sisters, the General Sister Superior gave up the school, and for six years the girls were taught by the Dominican Sisters of Memphis and the boys by male teachers secular and regular. After the epidemic of 1879 the Ursuline Sisters from Louisville accepted the oft-repeated petition to take charge of the school at Memphis, and since that time the school has steadily improved. Plans are now completed for the erection of a new school building.

The Very Rev. Martin Riordan, V. G., under Bishop Feehan, came from St. Louis to Tennessee with the Bishop in 1865, and also Father Martin Walsh, who built St. Brigid's Church. Rev. M. Riordan was appointed to labor among the Catholics in the northern part of Memphis, and he at first established a school in a rented building on Wellington Street. Rev. M. Riordan also at this time attended the Catholic Missions throughout West Tennessee. In 1866 he built the parsonage at St. Patrick's, in which he held services on Sundays pending the erection of the brick church now used as a schoolhouse, which continued to be used as a school until 1869, when the present frame church building at the corner of De Soto and Linden Streets was erected, costing the enormous sum of $11,000, the parsonage having also cost $11,000, and the brick schoolhouse when up one story costing $5,000. The explanation of this great cost is in the flush times in which they were built, carpenters and bricklayers then receiving $7 per day for their labor. In 1867 a cemetery containing eighty acres was purchased at a cost of $500 per acre. This purchase was made by Rev. M. Riordan, after consulting some of the best business men of Memphis, who pronounced the price not by any means too high. The purchase was made wholly on credit, $5,000 to be paid annually at six per centum if paid at maturity, otherwise eight per centum was to be paid, and in some cases ten per centum. While Rev. M. Riordan paid for all the buildings he erected and for the ground upon which they stand he found it impossible to meet the annual payments on the cemetery (Calvary) grounds as they came due, and there still remains to this parish as a legacy, including, however, the floating debts, about $30,000 of debt. In 1877 Calvary Association was formed consisting of six laymen, with the bishop of the diocese an ex-officio member, and the pastors of St. Patrick's and St. Brigid's Churches, directors. Rev. Mr. Riordan, a very excellent man, died of the yellow fever in 1878, and was succeeded by Father Edward Doyle, who died of the fever in 1879. Father Quinn then took charge of the parish and remained until June, 1881, when the present pastor, Rev. Father J. Veale, commenced his labors here. He has added the second story to the brick school building and has improved both the church building and the parsonage at a cost of from $5,000 to $6,000. The present membership of the church is about 300 families and the school which is taught by Sisters of Charity from Nazareth, Ky., contains about 240 pupils.

St. Brigid's Church, standing at the corner of Third and Overton Streets, was opened for worship December 25, 1870. The building is about 103 feet long by 55 wide, and will seat 750 persons. It has five altars. Over the high altars is an artistic stained glass window representing the Crucifixion and Sts. John and Luke, the evangelists. The other windows are adorned with the statues of the patrons of the church: St. Brigid, St. Joseph, the Blessed Virgin and of the Sacred Heart of the Redeemer. Attached to the church is a convent of the Sisters of Charity from Nazareth, Ky., and a two-story brick schoolhouse erected in 1873, the school having on an average 200 scholars in attendance. At first this school was conducted by the Franciscan Sisters and subsequently by the Sisters of St. Dominic and lay teachers. In 1879 it was taken charge of by the Sisters of St. Joseph and then by lay teachers until June, 1882. Since September, 1882, it has been conducted by the Sisters of Charity. From 1879 to 1883 it was a free school, but now, as at the beginning, it receives contributions toward its expenses by such pupils as are both able and willing to pay. The priests in charge of this church have ever since its foundation been particular in the matter of education. The first pastor was the Rev. Martin Walsh. In 1873 the congregation suffered severely from the yellow fever. About 800 of the Catholic population who died that year were attended chiefly by Rev. Fathers Walsh and Quinn. But notwithstanding the great suffering of the church on account of this epidemic the congregation contributed liberally toward the upbuilding of the church, pastoral residence and brick school, all occupying a half-square of ground. In 1878 Father Matthew Camp originated here, organized at the suggestion of the present rector by the Father Matthew, Total Abstinence Society attached to St. Brigid's Church. A camp of refuge was established for all persons worthy of relief who could be reached by the camp's officers. Both Father Martin Walsh and Michael Meagher died August 29, 1878. Father Walsh was succeded by Rev. William Walsh, who has been assisted by the Rev. Michael Ryan and Rev. John J. Walsh, the latter of whom died of small-pox in February, 1882. In 1878 the pastors of this church received as contributions from various parts of the United States, $29,000 toward the relief of the distressed. Father Matthew Camp was established in 1879 with similar success.

The Rt. Rev. Patrick Feehan, then bishop of Nashville, and the Very Rev. Martin Riordan, his vicar-general, were originators of the project of forming a new congregation in the southern part of Memphis, otherwise called Ft. Pickering. It was entrusted to the care of Rev. Antonio Luiselli, then assistant pastor of St. Patrick's, having served seven years in that capacity. The corner-stone of St. Joseph's Church was laid March 17, 1878, in the presence of a large concourse of people. The address of the occasion was delivered by the Rev. Mayer of Nashville. The church building was dedicated June 23, 1878, though yet unfinished. A beautiful and exquisitely sweet-toned organ has recently been imported from Europe by the pastor, at a cost of $2,000. The membership of this church is composed mostly of Italians, of whom there are about 1,000 in the parish, though some of the Italians belong to other parishes in Memphis.

The Stranger's Church was organized as the First Congregational Church in 1863. Meetings were held in various places, as in the Odd Fellows' hall, Greenlaw's Block on Union Street, etc., until 1864, when the church received from Massachusetts assistance toward the purchase of a lot, and from F. H. Clark a gift of $1,000 toward the same object. The present church edifice on Union Street was erected at a cost of about $5,000, and was dedicated June 20, 1865, by the Rev. T. E. Bliss, the first pastor. During the war there were very large congregations because of the large number of northern people in the city. After the retirement in 1868 of the Rev. Mr. Bliss, the pastor was Rev. A. E. Baldwin, from Lincoln, Ill., who remained until 1875, and was succeeded by Rev. W. D. Millard, who was pastor two years and was succeeded by Rev. N.

M. Long, who had been for some time pastor of the Landerdale Street Church, but who was compelled to retire from the Presbyterian Church on account of a trial for heresy, in which, however, he was three times acquitted by the presbytery, synod and general assembly. Rev. Mr. Long commenced his labors in the old First Congregational Church building in December, 1881, with eight members, the name Stranger's Church being adopted. One year afterward there were thirty-four members, and at the present time about 100. The Ladies' Aid Society is very active, having paid out $935 during the past year.

The Linden-Street Christian Church was organized in 1846 by Mr. and Mrs. Egbert Wooldridge, Mr. and Mrs. E. W. Caldwell, Mary McIntosh and Ann McGuire. A lot on the southeast corner of Linden and Mulberry Streets was purchased, on which stood a small frame dwelling which was immediately remodeled and fixed up for a church. This church building was used until 1860, when the present large brick church edifice was erected, but which was finished after the war. It is a two-story structure with Sunday-school room and pastor's study below and auditorium above. A massive tower stands on each front corner of the building, which is itself about 45x100 feet in dimensions, and which cost the remarkably low sum of about $20,000. The parsonage, a two-story frame building at the rear of the church, was erected in 1877 and cost $4,000. The organ used in the church is of Mason & Hamlin manufacture and cost $1,000. The pastors of this church have been as follows: From its organization to 1853, Elder B. F. Hall, who in that year was succeeded by Elder R. E. Chew. In 1855 Elder W. J. Barbee became the pastor and remained until the war, during the continuance of which there was no regular preaching. Since the war the following elders have filled the pulpit: R. A. Cook, commencing in 1864; T. W. Caskey, in 1866; Curtis J. Smith, 1869; David Walk, 1870; J. M. Trible, 1879; G. W. Sweeney, 1882, and J. B. Briney, January, 1886. The church organizaation was chartered about the year 1850. The present members of the incorporation are Tom Gale, president; D. C. Jones, secretary; J. J. Lovin, W. H. Bates, T. J. Latham, W. C. Griswold, J. H. Smith, J. N. Jones and R. C. Lane. S. C. Toof is the treasurer. The policy of this organization is to avoid debt, which is one secret of its success, and its affairs are managed on strictly business principles. The minister is relieved from all labors except those legitimately belonging to pastoral work and preaching. The church thus has the benefit of his maximum efficiency, and its whole work, including business management and Sunday-school work, is accomplished with a minimum friction. Its membership is now about 220, and the Sunday-school, of which S. C. Toof has been superintendent most of the time for the last twenty-three years, has about 110 scholars.

St. Mary's Cathedral (Episcopal) is located on Poplar Street at the junction of Orleans Street. The church was founded in 1857, during the episcopate of the Rt. Rev. James H. Otey, D. D. It stands on a lot fronting 100 feet on Poplar Street and extends through to Alabama Street; this lot, together with the one on which stands the Episcopal residence, was donated by the late Robert C. Brinkley. The church was originally built as a mission chapel by members of Calvary Parish, under the rectorship of the Rev. Dr. C. T. Quintard. The late Rev. Richard Hines, D. D., held the rectorship fourteen years, and at the close of his rectorship the parish was made a cathedral or church of the bishop of the diocese. The Rev. George C. Harris, S. T. D., was installed as dean in 1871, holding the position until 1881. The Very Rev. William Klein was installed dean immediately after the resignation of Dean Harris, and is the present incumbent. During the past year there were 109 baptisms and seventy-one persons presented for confirmation. There are connected with the cathedral the following organizations: Sunday-school, teachers twelve, scholars 148; choir of men and boys; cathedral school for girls; St. Mary's mission to the poor; the Cathedral Guild for women; St. Mary's Guild for women; St. Timothy's Guild for Sunday-school teachers; St. Martha's Guild for the children of the cathedral school; the Ministering Children's League; a Ward of the Confraternity of the Blessed Sacrament for the deepening of spiritual life.

The parish school of the cathedral is in successful operation. Adjoining the cathedral is St. Mary's School, a boarding and day school for young ladies and children, in charge of the Sisters of St. Mary, containing about 150 pupils. These Sisters also have charge of the church home, an orphanage located on the Old Raleigh Road, which provides for fifty or sixty orphans.

A part of the work of the cathedral is the parish of Emanuel Church for colored people. The church edifice, located on Third Street between Jefferson and Court Streets, originally built for a German Lutheran congregation, was purchased in 1884. Dean Klein has entire charge of the work, the Rev. D. R. Anderson, a colored deacon, serving under him. Connected with this colored mission is a parish school of about 100 pupils, taught by the Rev. Mr. Anderson.

Calvary Parish was organized in 1835. The first building was erected near Court Square, and the present structure standing on the corner of Adams and Second Streets, in 1841. This building was enlarged and improved in 1880, and is now worth about $25,000. It will seat 750 people. The membership of the parish is about 900, and the communicants number 352. The altar and the organ in the church cost about $6,000. It is believed that the first rector of this parish was Dr. Page, who was followed by Dr. Philip Alston before the war. Bishop Otey and the present bishop of Tennessee, Dr. C. T. Quintard, both served this church, and were followed by Rev. Dr. George White, who was rector nearly twenty years, is now rector *emeritus*, and was succeeded by Rev. Davis Sessums in 1883. Rev. Mr. Sessums, in the latter part of 1886, resigned to accept a call to New Orleans. Calvary Parish has been very liberal to the venerable Dr. White, having paid him during the three years and nine months prior to January 1, 1887, $7,300, while at the same time it has paid its rector, Rev. Mr. Sessums, $6,475. This extreme liberality to its rector *emeritus* has militated seriously against the prosperity, and while it is creditable to the hearts of the parishioners, yet it reflects little credit upon their judgment.

The Congregation of the Children of Israel was formed in 1854 by a few Israelites, who obtained that year a charter for the congregation. The incorporators were J. I. Andrews, Moses Simons, John Walker, D. Levy, Julius Sandac, T. Folz, M. Bamberger, M. Bloom, Joseph Strauss and Reinach. From a large sum bequeathed by Judah Touro of New Orleans, toward assisting small congregations in building synagogues, $2,000 was set aside to this congregation. A lot was purchased on Second Street, and a building at the corner of Main and Exchange Streets, formerly occupied by the Farmers and Merchants Bank, rented and dedicated as a house of worship in February, 1858, by the Rev. Dr. Wise. Shortly afterward this property was purchased and used as a synagogue until January 18, 1884, when the present elegant building on Poplar Street was erected at a cost of $50,000. At this dedication the Rev. Dr. J. M. Wise, H. Sonneshein and M. Samfield officiated. The congregation at present numbers 176, and the Sunday-school, of which Rev. M. Samfield is superintendent, has 120 pupils, taught by a staff of eleven teachers. A new cemetery was dedicated in 1885 and a mortuary chapel built on it in 1886.

July 1, 1860, the Rev. S. Tuska was elected rabbi of the congregation, and served until his death, December 30, 1870, when he was succeeded by the present learned rabbi, Rev. M. Samfield. The Congregation of Beth El Emes was formed from members of this congregation about 1863, but it was reincorporated into this congregation in 1883, since which time it has been very strong in members and in means.

The German Lutheran Church of Memphis, was organized in 1855, and had religious services and preaching by Rev. W. Fick, of New

Orleans, who also attended his own congregation in New Orleans. Toward the latter part of the year Paul Beyer, a student of theology at St. Louis, was sent to Memphis and preached a short time. In 1856 he was called to the ministry of this church and remained until 1858, when he was succeeded by Rev. G. M. Gotsch, D. D., who remained until his death in 1876. He was succeeded by his pastor, Rev. H. Lieck, who remained until the breaking out of the yellow fever epidemic of 1878, when he left the city, and was followed by Rev. Thomas Bensen, who died in 1881. In September of this year Rev. T. G. Plautz became pastor and was followed by the present pastor, Rev. Wilhelm H. Th. Dau, in 1886. The congregation now numbers thirty members.

The parochial school in connection with this church has always been under the direction of pastors of the congregation, who have been assisted by various teachers. At the present time there are about forty pupils. After worshiping and teaching at No. 110 Main St. for several years the congregation bought Lot No. 98, Washington St., in 1874, and upon it Mr. Stoltz of Washington, D. C., erected the first story of the present building. The second story which is not yet finished inside was added in 1883. The congregation have recently agreed upon the following name: "The German Evangelical Lutheran Trinity Church and School."

The city of Memphis is on the Mississippi River in north latitude 35° 6′ and in 13° west longitude from Washington and on the fourth Chickasaw bluff. About the time of the treaty with the Chickasaws, by which the western district was opened up to settlement by white people, there were but a few white settlers at this point and none in the surrounding country. These few were the families of Patrick Meagher, Joshua Fletcher, Quimby, John Grace, William Irvine, John B. Moore, Anderson B. Carr, Thomas D. Carr and Tillman Bettis. All but the last three had lived here for a considerable number of years, trading with the Indians. In the spring of 1819 M. B. Winchester, accompanied by William Lawrence, came down the Mississippi in a flatboat from Cairo, Ill., to the fourth Chickasaw bluff. Upon their arrival, after a trip of twenty days, Mr. Winchester formed a copartnership with Anderson B. Carr and established a trading house, making the third house of this kind then at the Bluff, although the entire trade at this point at that time did not exceed $25,000 per annum.

The original proprietor of the town site of Memphis was John Rice, to whom North Carolina had granted 5,000 acres of land at this point by grant No. 283, as fully explained elsewhere in this sketch. This grant was devised by him to his brother, Elisha Rice, and sold by Elisha Rice to John Overton in 1794 for $500. This is a very remarkable thing,

John Rice having paid £500 in specie to North Carolina for the same land. John Overton conveyed one-half of the tract to his personal friend, Gen. Andrew Jackson, who at various times sold portions of his interest, until finally the ownership of this tract settled down as follows; John Overton, one-half; Gen. James Winchester, one-fourth; Gen. Andrew Jackson, one-eighth and William Winchester, one-eighth. In 1819 Judge Overton and Gen. Winchester came to Memphis and laid out a town which they thus named, Front, Main, Second and Third Streets being laid out from Bayou Gayoso to Union Street, not being extended farther south because the proprietors did not know where the survey would locate the south line of the grant. In 1820 it was thought by the most sanguine that Memphis was destined to become a populous city, and there were 362 lots laid off on the plat. The streets were designated as running to the four cardinal points, which they do very nearly, and are wider than is customary in southern cities. There were at first four public squares, Court Square being one of the four, and between the front lots and the river an ample promenade was reserved. The place was described as being the only site for a town of any magnitude on the Mississippi River between the mouth of the Ohio and Natchez, no other place on either side being sufficiently high and dry, level and extensive and the country back of it was seen to be comparatively elevated, level and dry, of great extent and well drained, well adapted to the growth of blue and herd grass and clover and to cotton, corn, wheat and tobacco. The superiority of the bluff on which Memphis stands, over the few other situations of high lands along the Mississippi, had not been overlooked by La Salle, who in 1736 selected it for a trading fort and garrison. Spain also recognized the value of the position as a healthy and commanding place for a similar establishment. A fort and garrison had been built by the latter many years previous to the surrender of the place in accordance with the treaty of St. Ildefonso.

At this time, 1820, Memphis had fifty inhabitants, the following being some of the principal heads of families besides those already named: Isaac Rawlings, who came here originally about 1813 as a sutler with Gen. Jackson. He was also Indian agent up to the time of their removal. For a number of years he had a large quantity of Indian and army stores in the block-houses at Fort Pickering. He was in addition a kind of magistrate by popular consent, without the formality of an election or an official appointment, from which fact he was honored with the title of "Squire Rawlings," and it is written of him in "Old Times Papers," that "it is questionable whether justice was not more equally administered then than it has ever been since." It is also said that after the extinguishment of the Indian titles he was appointed by the Legislature one of the magistrates, but did not give the satisfaction when administering justice by a written system as when governed by the dictates of his own honest heart; somewhat on the principal probably that a violinist accustomed to play by rote cannot play equally well by note. But he became a great student of law, especially of the decisions of the most distinguished judges, and if he were not one of the most learned men of the day, he was certainly one of the most mistaken men of the day.

John C. McLemore was another of those heads of families. He purchased Gen. Jackson's interest in the town site, and thus became one of the proprietors of the town, as also one of its most active and liberal friends. It was through his exertions that a large number of settlers was induced to make the Bluff their home. Isaac Rawlings, as has been before stated, was an Indian trader years before the establishment of the town of Memphis, and after its establishment he continued still in the commercial line, his principal competitor being Maj. Marcus B. Winchester, one of the handsomest and courtliest of men, whose stock of goods was far more extensive and valuable than anything that "Ike" had ever had. Maj. Winchester's place of business was on Front Street just south of Jackson Street, where he erected the finest house in the town. Rawling's establishment was at Anderson's bridge, a favorite camping-ground, particularly with the Indians, in consequence of which he had carried on the most extensive trade; but after Winchester's fine store was put up on the Bluff, the trade was gradually transferred to the latter place, and to change this condition of affairs, Rawlings determined to change the location of his store. He selected a lot on the west side of Second Street, between Jackson and Winchester Streets, for which he paid some $10 or $15. The selection of this position was considered by him a fine strategic movement, as the place was high, overlooking the camping-ground at the bridge and also Winchester's store at the Bluff, and would, he thought, enable him to retain all of his trade at the former place and draw off a good deal of that of his rival, Maj. Winchester. But in order to secure the full benefit of his new position it would be necessary to have the alley on which his new store stood widened, but this he could have done without going to Winchester, who represented the proprietors, and asking him to have it done. Putting a bold face upon the matter, as is usually the better way, the haughty Rawlings made the proper request of the proper party, and much to his surprise the request was readily and politely granted and he himself given the privilege of conferring a name upon the widened street. Rawlings, therefore, named it "Commerce Street." The new store, erected at greater expense than would have been the case had not Winchester had such a fine store, is still standing with a basement added on account of the grading down of the street. A large stock of goods was put in, a portion of which remained on hand unsold in 1844, eighteen years later, because of his resolute resistance to marking down his prices in order to compete with his rivals. The fact that everybody else was underselling him, and that his custom was for this reason steadily leaving him, was in his judgment no reason for taking the only practical method of retaining his trade. His store therefore at length became little else than a magistrates office, in which he delighted to sit for hours every day arguing legal questions and giving advice upon all subjects pertaining to agriculture, commerce or law, while the simple principles upon which to conduct his own little business of merchandising, were either entirely ignored, or were as profound a mystery as was the origin of the pyramids or of the Sphinx. It was thought then by some, and it must have been true, that the retrograding movement which Memphis then underwent was due in great part to "Ike" Rawlings' persistent opposition to everything in the way of improvement, although it is also said that the general impression abroad that Memphis was a very unhealthy place very much retarded her growth. Like all new towns in the South and West, her citizens were subject to malarious fevers, which nothing can prevent but the improvements gradually introduced by civilization. The larger part of the sickness afflicting Memphis from her origin to the present time, except the special epidemics of yellow fever and small-pox. have doubtless been caused by the existence of large areas of unclaimed wild lands, ponds, and lakes across the Mississippi River in Arkansas.

When the town of Memphis was laid out the proprietors of the original plat were John Overton, Andrew Jackson, Gen. James Winchester, of Tennessee, and the devisees George and William Winchester, of William Winchester (deceased), of the city of Baltimore. In the sale of lots which went on from time to time in Memphis from 1819 to 1829, John Overton and Andrew Jackson were represented by their attorney, John Overton; James Winchester acted for himself, and M. B. Winchester was attorney for the devisees of Winchester. The first sale of lots by the proprietors through their attorneys was made in March, 1822. Lots No. 1 and No. 2 were sold to Patrick Meagher, the followlowing being the form of deed in each case:

WHEREAS John Overton, Andrew Jackson, James Winchester, of Tennessee, and the devisees of William Winchester, deceased, of the city of Baltimore, owners of a 5,000-acre tract of land upon the Chickasaw Bluff at the mouth of Wolf River, have laid off said tract into a town known by the name of Memphis, and

WHEREAS the aforesaid John Overton and Andrew Jackson, by John Overton, their attorney, and James Winchester, for himself and the devisees of William Winchester, deceased, by their several powers of attorney, dated the 22d day of April, 1822, and registered in the office of the register of Shelby County, Tenn., did authorize and appoint William Lawrence and Marcus B. Winchester, their respective and joint attorneys, for them and in their names, to execute conveyances to purchasers of lots in said town of Memphis, which have been or may hereafter be sold by direction of the aforesaid attorneys, therefore

Know ye that we, William Lawrence and Marcus B. Winchester, as aforesaid, by virtue of the powers and authority aforesaid, in consideration of valuable improvements put upon Lot No. 1, in said town, by Patrick Meagher, citizen of said town, etc., do give, grant, enfeoff and convey unto the said Patrick Meagher, all the right, title and interest of the aforesaid owners of Lot No. 1, lying at the intersection of Jackson and Chickasaw Streets, beginning at a stake marked N. 1, the southeast corner of said lot, at the intersection of said streets; thence running north $9\frac{1}{4}°$ east, with the west line of said Chickasaw Street 37 feet $1\frac{1}{2}$ inches to a stake, the south corner of Lot No. 2; thence north $80\frac{1}{2}°$ west with the south boundary of Lot No. 2, $148\frac{1}{2}$ feet to a stake the southwest corner of Lot No. 2; thence south $9\frac{1}{4}°$ west 37 feet $1\frac{1}{2}$ inches to a stake; thence south $80\frac{1}{2}°$ east, fronting on the public promenade, $148\frac{1}{2}$ feet to the beginning.

Lot No. 2 was also sold to Patrick Meagher for $140, the deed to both being dated February 6, 1823, and signed by William Lawrence and M. B. Winchester for John Overton and Andrew Jackson, and by James Winchester for himself and the devisees of William Winchester. Lot No. 53 was sold to Benjamin Fooy (Foy) of the Territory of Arkansas. This lot was at the intersection of Winchester Street and Mississippi Row, and the consideration was valuable improvements made upon the lot, the deed being dated October 13, 1823. Lots Nos. 50, 185 and 186 were sold to Anderson B. Carr, February 13, 1825, the consideration for the three lots being $612. Lot No. 50 was on the corner of Mississippi Row and an alley, and Lot No. 186 at the corner of Main and Jackson Streets. Lot No. 49 was sold to Marcus B. Winchester June 30, 1824, for valuable improvements made thereon, services as agent and $1 in hand paid, at the corner of Jackson Street and Mississippi Row. Lot No. 148 was sold January 5, 1825, to John R. Kent, in consideration that he erect a good frame or brick house with two comfortable rooms, each room to be at least fifteen feet square, within eighteen months. One-half of Lot No. 40 was sold September 3, 1825, to Charlotte Fordan for $94, and the other half of the same lot was sold to Anderson B. Carr, on the same day for the same amount. Lot No. 32 was sold January 6, 1826, to E. Coffee for $25, and Lot No. 147 was sold May 3, 1826, to S. Rosebrough for $140.50.

The sale of lots went on slowly in this way until 1829 when the attorneys for the proprietors made application to the county court for a division of their different undivided interests in sundry unsold lots in Memphis and a tract of 1,200 acres of land. In this petition which was dated April 20, 1829, the petitioners state their respective interests to be as follows: John Overton's, one-half; John C. McLemore's, one-eighth; the heirs of Gen. James Winchester, one-fourth, and the devisees of William Winchester, one-eighth. It was signed by William Lawrence, attorney in fact for John Overton and John C. McLemore, and by M. B. Winchester, attorney in fact for George and William Winchester. The court in accordance with this petition ordered that Anderson B. Carr, Nathaniel Anderson, John Ralston, David Dunn, Tilman Bettis, James H. Lawrence and William Lawrence, or any five of them, be appointed commissioners to set apart to the petitioners their several portions in severalty of said town lots and land and report to the next court. The next court of pleas and quarter sessions was held at the courthouse at Raleigh July 20, 1829, to which the commissioners reported that they had made a particular examination of the unsold lots and of the 1,200-acre tract, lying northeast and south of the town of Memphis and usually known as the town reserve, and had parcelled the said lots, etc., into eight divisions as nearly equal in value as they could make them, and that John Overton was entitled to four of said eight divisions, John C. McLemore to one, George and William Winchester, together, to one, and that the estate of the late Gen. James Winchester was entitled to two of the said eight divisions. The particular division which should belong to each interest was determined by ballot, and the entire proceedings of the commissioners signed by Tilman Bettis, John Ralston, William Lawrence, Anderson B. Carr and James H. Lawrence.

In December, 1826, as is elsewhere stated, the Legislature passed an act incorporating the town of Memphis. This took the citizens generally by surprise. Some were pleased, others were indifferent, and still others were very much opposed to having to support an incorporation. At a public meeting at which "Ike" Rawlins presided, the incorporation was denounced as a trick of the proprietors, and the chairman of the meeting himself made a strong speech against it, showing how severe it would be on several of the poor people living in the outskirts of the proposed town. Speakers on the other side as strongly favored the incorporation as being a necessity and proposed, in order to satisfy Rawlings' temporary prejudices, to leave out the poor people in the outskirts. Notwithstanding the opposition to the incorporation it was a success. After two years of charter life, Memphis having experienced meantime considerable improvement, the charter was amended so as to give to the town all the powers of Nashville, and providing that the mayor should not hold any office under the Government of the United States. This without anything else in his favor would have elected Isaac Rawlings mayor of the town, M. B. Winchester being at the time both mayor and postmaster, and he was elected and re-elected a number of times, serving in all many years.

For the first few years of the town's existence its growth was quite slow. From the nature of the soil on which it was built the streets were very muddy, at times almost impassable. Trade was light and confined almost exclusively to river craft. The first receipts of cotton in this market were in 1826, when 300 bales were sent in from Fayette and Henderson Counties. In four years the growth of this business was so rapid that in 1830 the receipts were 10,000 bales. In 1836 they were 50,000 bales; in 1845, 75,000 bales; in 1850, 150,000 bales; and in 1854, 180,000 bales. The population of the place which in 1820 was 50, was in 1830, 704; in 1840, 1,700; in 1850, 6,427; in 1854, 12,687. The increase of population during these earlier years was so steady and great that enthusiastic prophets ventured to predict in 1854 that at the end of the next thirty-five years, the population would be over 800,000. In 1845 proper measures were taken to improve the streets, and since then large sums have been expended, especially since the yellow fever epidemic of 1878-79, and as a consequence the streets are at this time (1887) in a better condition than are those of most other southern cities. In 1834, when W. A. Bickford came to Memphis, there were but two physicians, M. B. Sappington and Wyatt Christian. In 1838 Mr. Bickford made a list of the adult male white citizens, containing 209 names, which was thus the first directory of Memphis. Not more than nine of this number are now living.

After the failure of numerous special projects to build up the city, the navy yard project came up in 1843. In 1841 Congress had appointed commissioners to locate a navy yard somewhere in the Mississippi Valley, and after a careful examination of the Mississippi River throughout its entire length, from the mouth of the Ohio to New Orleans, these commissioners reported that at the mouth of Wolf River was the best location. When this subject was first broached it was regarded by many as a huge joke; but it was as necessary then as now for congressmen to do something for their constituents. Helena, Ark., had a Government Hospital, and Vicksburg had a lighthouse, which was, it is believed, actually lighted up during one entire month, and Memphis, to stand on a par with her sister cities of the valley, must have a navy yard, though hundreds of miles from the sea. It was however a much more easy matter to get through Congress the bill providing for its establishment, than it was afterward to secure appropriations for its support. In 1843 three young officers of the navy visited Memphis for the purpose of examining into its adaptability for a naval depot and dock yard. The space of ground devoted to the navy yard was bounded on the north by Auction Street ; on the east by Front Street ; on the south by Market Street and on the west by the Mississippi River.

This tract of land was in part or wholly donated to the United States Government for the purpose of securing the location of the navy yard. The first action taken by the board of mayor and aldermen looking to this end was on September 23, 1841, when the following preamble and resolutions were adopted.

WHEREAS the Government of the United States has passed an act promising the establishment of an armory on the western waters, and believing the local situation of Memphis is advantageously situated for such an establishment, therefore

Resolved, That the mayor be authorized to appoint a committee of five citizens to draw up a memorial to the President of the United States setting forth the claims of Memphis and the advantages she possesses for such an establishment.

On May 1, 1843, the board received from the commissioners of the General Government a plat of a survey made by them with a view of reporting to Congress on the practicability of establishing a naval dock yard and depot. The plan included a part of the Promenade and Batture, lying north of Market Street, and also town lots belonging to private individuals from No. 1 to No. 24 inclusive. A committee was appointed to act with the mayor to obtain from the owners of said lots by purchase or otherwise the right and title to the same with a view to transferring them to the General Government if the national works should be located at this point. On the 4th of May succeeding an act was passed by the board of mayor and aldermen enacting that for and in consideration of the sum of $20,000, when paid, the mayor would under the authority of the act they were then passing make a deed conveying to the General Government of the United States the ground surveyed by the committee for a navy yard and depot, if the same should be required within three years, for the establishment of such navy yard and depot. After some difficulty over the title to the property, on the 23d of December, 1844, the committee appointed to close up the titles to the property was instructed to take the deed of Seth Wheatley for twenty-three lots, and the corporation would then make a deed for the whole, including streets and Batture, to the General Government, and that the committee should go on to perfect the titles excluding the twenty-four lots west of Chickasaw Street. After the completion of the transfer to the Government, a wall was erected, twelve feet thick at the base as also a rope walk, a large store, a commandant's house, a blacksmith shop, a carpenter shop, a sawmill, an office building resembling the Coliseum at Rome, with columns all around. Commodore Shields and Commodore Lavalette were the successive commandants at this famous naval depot. After struggling along for a number of years with increasing difficulty to secure the necessary appropriations for its support, the navy yard and its buildings were abandoned, the amount of money spent theron having been from $1,200,000 to $1,500,000. The only creditable piece of work turned out of this novel navy yard, was the great iron steamship of war, "Alleghany," which was entirely built and equipped here with the exception of her hull. This was a most wonderful war vessel! Her speed is said to have been four miles per hour down stream, that being about the ordinary rapidity of the current, and four hours to the mile up stream, and after a brief but entirely unsatisfactory history, having cost the Government nearly $500,000, she was totally condemned. The navy yard itself was overtaken by a similar fate. In 1853 Senator (ex.-Gov.) James C. Jones, incensed at the parsimony with which Congress made appropriations for the support of the Memphis navy yard, made a demand that the property be returned to the city. The Senate, as if hoping some such way would present itself to get the elephant off its hands, instantly took the senator at his word, and thus ended one of the greatest failures in the shape of a navy yard this country has known.

In 1841 the city extended but little below Poplar Street, and there was but one brick house in town. It was not until 1844 that much business was transacted below Madison Street. In 1842 and 1843 the Gayoso House was built, and in 1844 a store was erected at the corner of Front and Union Streets, and South Memphis was built up after 1840. In 1847 W. A. Bickford erected at the corner of Front and Poplar Streets, extending to Exchange Street, a large business and office block, known then and ever since as the Exchange building. It contained the City Hall, 52x106 feet, besides a number of smaller halls for various public purposes, such as the mayor's office, the council's office, and a lecture hall. In 1849 the large building on the corner of Main and North Court Streets was commenced, and completed in 1850. In 1853 the city contained the following numbers of business houses: nineteen groceries; four hat, cap, boot and shoe stores; thirty-seven dry goods stores; fifteen clothing merchants; four auction and commission merchants; two book stores, one musical instrument store, two dentists, five merchant tailors, three millinery establishments, three saddleries, seventeen foundries, plumbers, etc.; one flouring-mill, five hardware stores, eight drug stores, two real estate agents, nine hotels, among them the Gayoso kept by J. M. Fletcher, three factories, two daguerreotypists, three printing offices, six painters, ten furniture stores, etc., three banks, forty law firms, thirty-two physicians, three livery stables, three jewelers, Memphis Medical College with eight professors, and four newspapers. The population, as has been seen, was 12,687 in 1854.

Previous to laying out the town of South Memphis there was considerable strife and hard feeling between the two sections, a complete history of which however is not deemed appropriate in this work. The north part of the town or rather Memphis was known by the not very euphonious designation of "Pinch," and South Memphis was in retaliation named Sodom. The feeling went so far that the names of Sodom and Gomorrah were applied to the Methodist Churches in the two places. In the north part there was a bend in the bayou, which constituted a considerable lake, one known by the name of Catfish Bay. The abundance of fish in its waters and the cheapness of lumber in the vicinity induced a number of poor families to build shanties and settle upon its banks. One group of very poor houses, noted for the destitution of its occupants, was named by Craven Peyton "Pinch Gut." This name was of course distasteful to the occupants of the row, and they insisted that it belonged to the other side of the bay. The latter people were much displeased at the attempt to fasten upon their locality such an opprobrious epithet, and the feud thus created was much enjoyed by those living outside of both localties. However, their enjoyment was to be only short-lived, as the application of the name continued to expand until it finally took in the entire north end of town. But the extension of the name was of great value to those people as it served to bind them together with a common tie, and caused them all to work together for the advancement of the locality known as "Pinch." The bitterness of feeling however had a lasting effect upon the destinies of South Memphis. A glance at the map of Memphis as now incorporated shows that the most of the north and south streets in the city are not continuous below Union Street, the object of the people of South Memphis being to restrict as much as possible communication with the detested residents of Pinch.

During the early history of Memphis great trouble was experienced in collecting wharfage. Wharfage could not, in fact, be collected previous to 1841. There being no railroads the products of the Southern and Western States were carried down the Mississippi River in flatboats, which frequently came in fleets. The managers of these flatboats were opposed to paying wharfage, and when they banded together in resistance to the wharf-master it was only discretion which he exhibited when he abandoned all attempts to collect it, and retreated with becoming celerity up the hill. The income from wharfage for several years was out of all proportion to the trouble and annoyance of the wharf-master, who, together with some of the best citizens of the place, was frequently assaulted and shamefully abused by the boatmen. But this state of things could not last forever. In 1841 a reform board of mayor and aldermen was elected, William Spickernagle being elected mayor. Mr. Spickernagle attempted a thorough reform in the kind of men elected to office. Two voluntary military companies, known as the Guards and the Blues, were encouraged to organize and equip themselves; and upon the completion of their organization they offered their services to the mayor, to assist in the enforcement of the laws. The board of mayor and aldermen was placed in a particularly trying situation. The three towns of Memphis, South Memphis and Fort Pickering were doing what they could to injure each other, and in this way it was hoped to build up themselves. The board was fully impressed with the necessity of selecting a good man for wharf-master, as they were well assured that some hard fighting must be done, and to encourage the wharf-master to do his work thoroughly they offered him twenty-five per cent on all collections. His administration proved to be a success, but not without some severe tussles with the boatmen. Since then wharfage has been a considerable item in the revenues of the city, but the victory was not won until May, 1842. At this time—when the water in the river was low—about 500 boats were lying at the Memphis landing at one time. Among them was one commanded by a noted desperado named Trester. He was going to see whether the wharf-master at Memphis was to have his own way, and to test the matter armed himself with a big club, which he trimmed so that the limbs stuck out about one-half an inch from the stem. When the wharf-master appeared before him in the regular performance of his duty Trester exclaimed: "Who are you?" "The wharf-master," was the reply. Grasping his stick Trester exclaimed: "Do you see this? I cut this on purpose for you and I am going to use it on you if you show yourself here while I remain, and if you don't leave quickly I will give it to you now. I am the master of this wharf." As Tester was cheered on by a considerable crowd, the wharf-master thought it prudent to withdraw. Obtaining a warrant from the mayor, he got the town constable, G. B. Locke, to attempt to serve it. "I have a warrant for you," said the constable. "And I have one for you," said Trester, advancing with his big stick. A crowd of boatmen soon collected, and the two officers thought it best to again withdraw. They soon returned, however, with Capt. E. F. Ruth of the Guards with ten or twelve of his men, well armed. Trester and his men now attempted to escape, but as his two boats were heavily loaded he could not keep out of the way of the small flat which carried the small company of Guards in pursuit. An attempt was made to board Trester's boat, but his heavy club came down with such force on the wharf-master as to lay him sprawling on the flat. Capt. Ruth, Constable Locke and another man tried to board the boat, but were each knocked down, when some one called out to the Guards: "Fire! fire!" which order was obeyed by four of the soldiers, and Trester fell dead upon the deck. After this, though with considerable difficulty, the rest of the boatmen were taken prisoners. In course of time a board of magistrates upon investigation fully justified everything that had been done to enforce the law, and this was the last resistance to the collection of wharfage.

The unhealthfulness of Memphis previous to 1880, or rather the frequent recurrence of severe epidemics previous to that time, and its comparative healthfulness since then, have attracted wide attention throughout the country. So far as official records show, the first epidemic from which Memphis suffered was in 1851, when ninety-three deaths occurred from cholera. Yellow fever visited the city in each of the four following years, but from 1856 to 1865 inclusive there are no official records. In 1866 there were over 400 deaths from cholera. In 1867 yellow fever and cholera both prevailed, the number of deaths from the former being 259. In 1873 yellow fever was officially announced in Memphis on September 14, though a number of deaths had previously occurred from the disease, which was not recognized by the physicians until that date. The last case occurred in November, and the entire number of deaths from the fever that year was officially reported as 1,244.

But the most terrible experience from this dread scourge was reserved for the city to undergo in 1878, when 17,600 persons suffered from the disease, of whom 5,150 died, the ratio of mortality to cases being one to three and three-tenths of those taken sick. The population of the city was believed then by those best informed to be 19,600. There were three patent causes for this great epidemic: First, the filthy condition of the city; second, the extreme heat of that summer; and third, the feverish excitement of the public mind which had existed through a period of twenty years because of the changing conditions of political life. Notwithstanding the previous epidemics the controlling authorities of the city either had not learned wisdom, or were not in a position to render practical the wisdom they had learned. The first case of yellow fever which occurred in 1878 was that of a colored man, on July 21. A young man, Willie Darby, was taken sick July 25, but neither of these cases proved fatal. The first case officially recognized was on August 2, and the first death appears to have been that of Mrs. Zack, on August 5. The following cases were reported on August 12: A son of G. B. Clarke, Mattie L. Isaacs, Roger Jones, J. W. Kearnes, George Mitchell (colored), Katie Neighbors, Mrs. Jennie White and Jung Yung Tah. Twenty-two new cases were reported on the 15th, and the fear of the plague, already great, received a new impetus, and caused large numbers to seek relief in flight. Thirty-three new cases were reported on the 16th, and the entire population was precipitated into an indescribable panic. In numerous cases self preservation proved in reality to be the first law of nature. In the first forty-eight hours fifty-five victims fell, and considering the experience of 1873, it is not to be wondered at that almost every one who could do so, by any and all means of conveyance, and even on foot, in all directions and to all conceivable points, sought safety in flight. By the 24th of August 25,000 people had left the city, and in two weeks more 5,000 additional ones were in camp in the vicinity. But the panic was over by the last week in August. All had gone who could get away, and there were in the city about 3,000 cases of fever. The temperature during August averaged 82.2°; in September, 72°; in October, 60.8° and in November 57.8°, being from 1° to 8° higher than during the same months in 1873. This long continued heat, combined with the fearful strain upon the nervous system, drained the vital energies of the citizens to such an extent that it was next to impossible for any human being to escape the dread disease.

Not more than 200 white people escaped the fever, and most of them had had it before. If there were, as there were, many cases of apparent and real selfishness, there were also many, and perhaps many more, cases of noble self-abnegation and devotion, in the face of almost certain death, every one of which is worthy of perpetual remembrance. Of the resident physicians who died at the post of duty and of honor were the following: V. W. Avent, A. J. Armstrong, P. D. Beecher, S. R. Clarke, S. R. Dawson, P. M. Dickerson, John H. Erskine, W. R. Hodges, H. R. Hopson, Dr. Ingalls, W. R. Lowry, Paul H. Otey, J. M. Rogers, W. H. Robins, John C. Rogers, P. K. Watson and J. W. Woodward. Volunteer physicians from abroad who died were the following: From Tennessee—T. W. Bond, Brownsville; O. D. Bartholomew and T. W. Menees, Nashville; John B. Hicks, Murfreesboro; T. H. McGregor, Tipton County; R. B. Montgomery, Chattanooga. From Alabama—J. S. Stevenson, Bankson. From Ohio—R. Burcham, Hiram M. Pierce, P. Tuerk and R. H. Tate, Cincinnati. From Georgia—L. A. Chevis, Savannah. From Arkansas—E. T. Easley, Little Rock; F. H. Force, Hot Springs, and L. B. Harlan. From Texas—J. G. Forbes, Round Rock, and — Heady, Sherman. From Indiana—J. O. G. Gorrell, Ft. Wayne, and J. G. Renner, Indianapolis. From New York—M. T. Keating. From St. Louis—J. W. McKim, Dr. Nelson and P. G. Nugent. From Kentucky—W. C. Mead, Hopkinsville and R. B. Williams, Woodburn. From Louisiana—Dr. Smith, Shreveport and R. B. Fort.

The priesthood, both Catholic and Protestant, was characterized by most admirable earnestness and devotion, as were likewise the sisters of the various orders. The names of the Catholic clergy who died were the following: Revs. Martin Walsh, M. Meagher, Father Asinus, Father Maternus, J. R. McGarney from Harrodsburg, Ky.; J. A. Boekel, Baltimore; Rev. Vantroostenburg, Kentucky; J. P. Seawell, Louisville, Ky.; Rev. M. Riordan and Father Marley. The nuns who died were Mother Alphonso; Sisters Rose, Josepha, Bernardine, Mary Dolora, Mary Veronica, Wilhelmina, Vincent, Stanislaus, Gertrude and Winkelman, the latter of St. Louis. The Protestant ministers who died were Revs. Mr. Parsons, Mr. Schuyler, Mr. Thomas, Mr. Moody, A. F. Bailey, E. C. Slater, David R. S. Rosebrough, P. T. Scruggs, Victor Bath and S. C. Arnold with his wife and child.

The Citizens' Relief Committee, the Howard Association and the police all labored heroically in the performance of the most unpleasant but the most sacred duty—the nursing of the sick and the preservation of order and of life. The Citizens' Relief Committee was burdened with the greatest responsibility, in caring for and distributing the supplies sent with such a prodigal hand from all parts of the world. As showing the magnitude of the work entrusted to their hands, which was performed with the most scrupulous honesty and fidelity, the following summary of donations to Memphis is introduced:

Arkansas contributed $6,690.37; Arizona, $5; Alabama, $6,281.45; California, $29,047.30; Colorado, $3,950.95; Connecticut, $5,070.28; Dakota, 663.50; Delaware, 41.02; Florida, $1,516.83; Georgia, $11,414.34; Illinois, $52,307.60; Indiana, $13,787.69; Indian Territory, $5; Iowa, $6,407.58; Kansas, $6,559.67; Kentucky, $8,810.52; Louisiana, $1,427.15; Maine, $817; Maryland, $495.98; Massachusetts, $3,964.28; Minnesota, $2,651.77; Mississippi, $727.65; Missouri, $16,891.37; Michigan, $11,200.43; Montana, $987; miscellaneous sources, $9,607.18; Nebraska, $4,509.41; Nevada, $1,374.94; New Hampshire, $1,607.50; New Jersey, $3,983.67; New Mexico, $134.30; New York, 56,804.16; North Carolina, $7,190.76; Ohio, $26,020.72; Oregon, $2,514; Pennsylvania, $11,770.33; Rhode Island, $6,513; South Carolina, $6,039.66; Texas, $11,400.30; Tennessee, $23,847.97; Utah Territory, $2,774.70; Virginia, 9,524.55; Vermont, $829.31; Washington, D. C., $1,775.30; West Virginia, $2,990.55; Wisconsin, $10,592.57; Wyoming, $875.75; a grand total of $400,412.54. .The entire amount received by the South in 1878 from all parts of the world on account of the yellow fever was $4,548,703.

Under the new form of government called the "Taxing District," the board of health was organized in February, 1879, which as soon as practicable commenced the work of sanitation, though for various reasons much valuable time was consumed without accomplishing much for the city's good. Upon the subsidence of the epidemic of 1878 the sanitary condition of the city was worse than it had ever been, and as six months had been suffered to pass without anything being done, the new board found its hands more than full, though in five weeks from the time of commencing the work the surface cleaning of all the streets, alleys and public grounds had been completed at a cost of $2,449 and a garbage service instituted to prevent similar accumulations. The citizens themselves also accomplished more sanitary work than they had ever done before, impressed with the necessity of doing something to prevent the return of the plague. But in July, 1879, the fever reappeared in spite of all that had been done, which seemed to demonstrate the possibility of its holding over from one summer to another despite the cold of the intervening winter. The first case occurred on the 9th of the month, known as the Mulbraden case, and the Ray, and Tobin cases occurred very soon afterward. The exodus of the people for the next few days was very large, not more than about 1,500 unacclimated remaining; and when the Hester cases were reported the flight began again. It was considered with apparently the best of reason, by Dr. T. J. Tyner of Memphis, in a paper read by him at Nashville, on the "Etiology of Yellow Fever," that the chief causes for its appearance in Memphis were the privy vault system, many of which, dug to the depth of forty feet, had not been emptied of their accumulated excreta for from ten to forty years; and he also said that the cistern water was contaminated by seepage from these vaults. The work of emptying the vaults went on very slowly. There were 6,000 of them in use, 3,668 of which were in a very foul condition, and a very large number of unused vaults, the contents of which only imperfectly covered with a thin layer of ashes. Three thousand five hundred and eight cisterns were within contaminating distance of these vaults, and the cisterns furnished the most of the water consumed.

The first death in 1879 occurred July 9, at No. 204 De Soto Street. Three cases occurred at one house, No. 425 Wellington Street, and two at No. 55 Bradford Street, the latter being about a mile from either of the other two. One death occurred at each place about the same time. At the outbreak of this epidemic the population of the city was estimated at 40,000, and at the close of the month of July there were living in the city but 16,110 persons. Two thousand two hundred and fifty-four went to the various camps in the vicinity, and the rest to various points at a distance by rail, river and other means of transportation. In order to prevent the spreading of the disease, every article of baggage was fumigated with sulphuric acid gas for three hours in a close room, and the mails were subjected to a similar treatment. In this work, including the infected houses, rooms, etc., there were consumed thirty-four barrels of sulphur, and about 1,200 pounds of sulphate of zinc. Nine thousand privy vaults were disinfected during the continuance of the epidemic, one or more times, 19,581 visits being made. In this work, 9,343 barrels of lime, 135,250 gallons of zinc solution, and 212,000 pounds of sulphate of iron were used. Of the sixty or more laborers, mostly colored, employed in this disinfecting process, but few had had the fever, not one was attacked with the disease. The disinfection of infected houses, bedding and wearing apparel was also pursued to such an extent that 2,383 articles, embracing one flatboat, three houses, two bedsteads, and every description of bed clothing and wearing apparel, were consumed by fire. On the 29th of July a census of the people showed 4,283 white people, and 11,287 colored people, of whom 9,743 had had the fever before. An important feature of sanitation was the emptying and filling up of privy vaults, 1,644 of which were thus treated, and the destruction of houses and other buildings which were in an unsanitary condition, 138 of these being destroyed in 1879. The expense of this work was $21,584.62. The deaths from yellow fever in 1879 were as follows: whites 391, colored 106, total 497. The number of cases was 860 whites, 680 colored, total number of cases 1,540.

Commencing in 1875 the death rate for five years for Memphis, excluding mortality from yellow fever, was 34 per 1,000, estimating the population at 35,000. In 1880 the death rate for the whites was 20.38, and for the colored people was 32.55. In 1881 the death for the whites was 30.22 and for the colored 44.77. In 1882 it was for the whites 14.85, and for the blacks 39.45. In 1883, estimating the population at 62,335, the death rate for the whites was 15.19 and for the blacks, 35.83. In 1884 it was for the whites 18.80; for the blacks, 41.66; and for 1885, it was for the whites 16.56, and for the blacks, 36.96. But this excessive negro mortality is not peculiar to Memphis. The same general facts are noticeable in Nashville, Chattanooga and other southern cities. Investigation by the best physicians into the causes for this excessive mortality among the negro population, shows that consumption and pneumonia play an important part toward the production of this high death rate as do debility, marasmus, dentition, inanition and premature births. Lung diseases are accounted for by the exposed and improvident life led by the colored people. And it is further noticeable that both the young and old among them are more liable to die than the same classes among the whites. This is fully accounted for by the general poverty of the race as yet, and the want of care in many cases where such proper care might be given, but is not, because of the looseness of family ties among them. The wonderful improvement made since 1879, in the sanitary condition of Memphis, is summarized under the head "Taring District," elsewhere.

South Memphis was incorporated January 6, 1846, and an election for mayor and eight aldermen was held on the third Saturday of the same month, resulting in the election of Sylvester Bailey, mayor, and A. B. Shaw, H. H. Menus, George W. Davis, W. Howard, J. E. Merriman, John Brown, J. P. Keiser and James Kennedy, aldermen. The boundaries of South Memphis were defined as follows: On the east, south and west the boundaries are the same as the South Memphis tract, and on the north the boundary line commences in the center of the Mississippi River, opposite the rise of Union Street; thence east with the center of Union Street, as at present laid off until the same intersects with the Pigeon Roost road; thence with the south side of Pigeon Roost road to the east line of the South Memphis tract of land. On September 4, South Memphis was divided into four wards. The treasurer for the first corporate year made a report showing that the revenue amounted to $6,266.17, and licenses, etc., to $3,750.50. John T. Trezevant was mayor in 1847–48 and A. B. Taylor in 1849. The last meeting of the mayor and aldermen of South Memphis took place December 31, 1849.

Memphis was incorporated by act of the Legislature of Tennessee, December 9, 1826, as the town of Memphis. The substance of this charter was as follows: Section 1 incorporated the town and conferred upon it its name as above. Section 2 gave the town authorities power to pass all kinds of needful legislation for the government of and the preservation of the health of the town. Section 3 required the sheriff of the county to hold an election on the first Saturday of March, 1827, and on the same day in every subsequent year, for members of the board of aldermen; at which election any person holding a freehold in the town, who was entitled to vote for members of the General Assembly, should be qualified to vote for mayor and aldermen. Section 4 is rather curious in its grammatical construction. It reads "that the seven persons having the highest number of votes at any election shall be taken to be elected, and the sheriff of said county shall within two days thereafter, and a majority being present, shall proceed to elect a mayor from their own body for said corporation for the time the aldermen were elected."

This charter did not reach Memphis until after the first Saturday of March, 1827, and the election for aldermen, which according to its provisions should have been held on that day, was not held until April 26 following. The members of this first board, elected on April 26, were Joseph L. Davis, John Hooke, N. B. Atwood, John R. Dougherty, George F. Graham, William D. Neely and M. B. Winchester. The first meeting of this body was held May 9. The certificate of election was presented as follows:

> We, the undersigned, being judges of an election, opened and held at the old courthouse in the town of Memphis, on the 26th day of April, 1827, for the purpose of electing seven persons to serve as aldermen for the said town of Memphis, do certify that upon counting out the votes M. B. Winchester, Joseph L. Davis, John Hooke, N. B. Atwood, George F. Graham, John R. Dougherty and William D. Neely were duly elected.
>
> NATHAN ANDERSON.
> ISAAC RAWLINGS.
> S. R. BROWN, *Sheriff*.   A. RAPEL.

At this first meeting M. B. Winchester was elected mayor by the board in accordance with the requirements of the charter, and the first resolution passed was that it was important to the interests of Memphis that ordinances be passed. Notice was given that on May 12 an election would be held for treasurer, recorder and town constable, the election when held resulting in the choice of Isaac Rawlings for treasurer; Joseph L. Davis, recorder and John K. Balch, town constable.

On the 30th of May the Board of Mayor and Aldermen had some difficulty over the question of the legality of their organization. They had been elected on the 26th of April, instead of on the first Saturday of March, as required by the charter. But after a sufficient amount of discussion and subtle logic had been brought to bear upon the question, the board themselves finally decided the question in their own favor, by the following process of reasoning: That the charter did not reach Memphis until after the first Saturday of March; it was evidently the intention of the Legislature that the corporation should be organized during the current year; that the judges held the election legal and the sheriff had so certified; hence it was declared proper on the part of the board that they consider themselves a legal body and proceed to business to pass the ordinances needed by the new town.

The first ordinance passed related to the classification of property, into taxable and non-taxable, the following being ordained to bear their proper share of the public burdens: All town lots; all free males between the ages of twenty-one and fifty; all slaves between the ages of twelve and fifty; wholesale and retail stores, including medicine stores; peddlers and hawkers; members of the learned professions, who practice the same for profit; tavern-keepers; retailers of spirits; stud horses and jacks. Taxes were levied in the following proportions: improved lots with buildings, 10 cents on the $100; unimproved lots, 10 cents; each free male inhabitant,

25 cents; each slave, 25 cents; each wholesale and retail store, $8; each trading boat, peddler, or hawker, $10; each lawyer or doctor practicing for profit, $2; each tavern-keeper $3; each retailer of spirits without tavern license, $10.

The limits of the corporation were fixed by the ordinance as follows: "Beginning at the intersection of Wolf River with the Mississippi River; thence with Wolf River to the mouth of Bayou Gayoso; thence with said bayou to the county bridge; thence with the line of the second alley east of and parallel with Second Street to Union Street; thence at right angles to Second Street to the western boundary of the tract of land entered to John Rice by grant No. 283, dated April 25, 1789; thence with the said western boundary up the Mississippi River to the Wolf River."

The editor of the Memphis *Advocate* was then chosen public printer and the recorder elect was required to give bonds in the sum of $500 and the treasurer in double the sum liable to come into his hands during the current year. Other ordinances were passed which the curious may find in the public records, and all were signed by all the members of the board, including M. B. Winchester, mayor.

On October 17, $80 was set apart for the improvement of Chickasaw Street and $120 for a wharf from high to low water mark at the lowest steamboat landing. On May 19, 1828, David Banks was elected constable, and the office of town surveyor established. January 16, 1829, a superintendent of the graveyard was provided for. At the second election for mayor, M. B. Winchester was again selected, the other aldermen being Samuel Douglass, William A. Hardy, John D. Graham, Augustus L. Humphrey, Joseph L. Davis and Robert Fearn. On the 4th of March, 1829, Isaac Rawlings was elected mayor, by a vote of four to three of the board, and he was again elected in March, 1830. On the 16th of August following, the town was divided into three wards as follows: Ward No. 1 comprised all that part of Memphis northeast of a direct line from the Mississippi River to Overton Street, thence with said street to the Bayou Gayoso: Ward No. 2, all that part of Memphis south of the aforementioned line to Overton Street, to Bayou Gayoso, and northeast of a direct line from the Mississippi to Winchester Street and thence with Winchester Street to the eastern boundary of the town; Ward No. 3, all that part of Memphis south of the last mentioned line.

In March, 1831, Seth Wheatley was elected mayor, and Robert Lawrence in 1832. Isaac Rawlings was then elected mayor for three consecutive years. Enoch Banks was elected in 1836 and 1838, John H. Morgan intervening in 1837. On August 6, 1838, a board of health was appointed as follows: Drs. Christian, Sappington, Frazier, Hickman, Dewitt, Mabry and Shanks. The extent of the business transacted by the corporation at this time is indicated by the receipts and disbursements of the treasurer for 1838, the former being $5,957.48, and the latter $5,452.95. In March, 1839, Thomas Dixon was elected mayor, and on the 4th of March, that year, a list of the taxable property of the town and the taxes thereon was as follows: 471 town lots, valued at $587,400, taxes thereon $2,950; 152 slaves, value $91,800, taxes $223.50; five carriages, taxes $20, and 231 white polls, taxes $231. The reader of the general history will remember that the constitution of 1834 disfranchised the free colored men, hence at this time there was no poll tax except upon white polls. Thomas Dixon was again elected mayor in March, 1840, and on the 25th of April the Legislature passed an act changing the title of the place from the town of Memphis to the city of Memphis. The tax list for this year was as follows: 499 lots, value $552,425, taxes $4,143.18¾; 221 slaves, value $107,500, taxes, $268.75; 324 white polls, $324; 6 carriages, $24. In March, 1841, William Spickernagle was elected mayor. All the previous incumbents of this office appear to have served their city without a salary, but now the town having become a city, the aldermen at last began to think that his duties had become sufficiently valuable and onerous to deserve a pecuniary compensation, and to learn whether this sentiment was also entertained by the people, it was resolved on the 15th of September, that the recorder be required to ascertain as nearly as possible the sense of the people on the subject of giving the mayor a salary and to inform the board at the next meeting. The sense of the people appears also to have been in favor of the salary, for on the 12th of November 1841, it was resolved that the mayor be paid a salary of $500 per annum, "from the 15th of September last."

On the 5th of February, 1842, an act was passed to amend the charter of the city of Memphis, by which the city was divided into five wards and each ward entitled to elect two alderman, who, with the mayor, were required to prescribe the limits of the wards. The power to elect the mayor was now conferred upon the people. In March, 1842, Edwin Hickman was elected mayor, and also in 1843 and 1844; in 1845, J. J. Finley; in 1846, Edwin Hickman; in 1847, Enoch Banks, and in 1848, Gardner B. Locke. At the popular election held on March 4, the candidates and votes for the office of mayor were Enoch Banks, 356; Gardner B. Locke, 356; E. Hickman, 87; James Seawell, 80, and W. F. Fannehill, 61. On the 11th of March, Mayor Banks still presiding, the salary of the mayor for the twenty-second corporate year was fixed at $1,000, and on the 13th the board went into an election for mayor on account of the tie in the popular vote, on the second ballot electing Gardner B. Locke, he receiving six votes, a majority of the entire board.

An act was passed January 21, 1848, reducing all the charters of Memphis into one act or charter. By this charter the limits of the city were thus defined: Beginning at a point in the middle of the Mississippi River opposite to the center of Union Street; thence eastwardly with a line passing through the center of Union Street, to the western bank of Bayou Gayoso; thence down said bayou with the western bank of the same to the point of its intersection with Wolf River; thence down Wolf River with its northwesterly bank to its intersection with the Mississippi River; thence down the Mississippi River to a point opposite the north side of Market Street; thence to a point in the main channel of the Mississippi River opposite to the said north side of Market Street, and thence down the said main channel of the said river to the beginning." The mayor and aldermen, two from each ward, were to constitute a city council, each alderman to be a *bona fide* resident of Memphis, and all to be elected by the qualified voters of the city. The tax levy was limited to three-fourths of one per cent upon all property taxable for State purposes, and the city council was given authority to borrow money to the amount of the annual revenue of the city, and no more in any one year, to establish hospitals, to establish a system of free schools and to regulate the same in such manner as to avoid sectarian influence, and to create an annual fund not exceeding one-eighth part of the annual revenue of the city for their support.

On the 21st of February, 1849, the ward boundaries were rearranged as follows, because the city was growing more toward the south, and the southern portion was not adequately represented: Ward one—all north of Jackson Street; Ward two—all between Jackson and Market Streets; Ward three—all between Market Street and Market Place alley; Ward four—all between Market Place alley and Carr's alley; Ward five—all between the Fourth Ward and Finley alley; Ward six—all the remainder of the city north.

An election for mayor and twelve aldermen was held March 5, 1849, at which Enoch Banks received 462 votes, "more than was received by any other candidate." The corporate year lasted from March, 1849, to July, 1850. On May 22, the city council passed an ordinance defining taxable property and levying taxes as follows: Taxable property—real estate, slaves, pleasure carriages, piano fortes, gold and silver plate, watches and jewelry, and capital loaned or deposited at interest; taxes to be three-fourths of one per cent for general purposes, and an additional annual tax of one-eighth of three-fourths of one per cent for the support of schools; upon all free white males qualified to vote in the city of Memphis a poll tax of $1.50 for general purposes, and an additional tax of 19 cents for school purposes. Exemptions were as follows: property used for religious, educational or hospital purposes; that belonging to the United States, to Tennessee, to Shelby County and to Memphis, to any regular organized fire company, all slaves under twelve and over fifty years of age, and all others incapable of rendering service to their masters. Ministers of the Gospel and free white persons in the army of the United States were exempt from poll tax. Privilege taxes were provided in various sums according to the business followed, and an additional tax of one-eighth of the privilege tax was levied in each case for the benefit of the free schools.

E. Hickman was elected mayor in 1850 and 1851, and A. B. Taylor in 1852, 1853 and 1854. In 1855 A. H. Douglas was elected over James Wickersham by 745 votes to 607. In 1856 Thomas B. Carroll was elected, receiving 973 votes to 583 for A. H. Douglas. In 1857 R. D. Baugh was elected, receiving 827 votes to 619 for Samuel F. Magen. In 1858 Mr. Baugh was again elected by 1,187 votes, to 843 cast for George Dixon and 307 for John Martin. In 1859, R. D. Baugh received 1,139 votes, John Park 1,039, and J. B. R.----563. Mr. Baugh was again elected in 1860, but the record of the vote is missing. John Park was chosen mayor in 1861, 1862, and 1863, receiving in the latter year 1,553 votes to Charles Kortrecht's 670, but previous to the time for the qualification of officers chosen at an election in 1864 the city was placed under martial law. Following are the several orders under which the civil government was for the time being set aside.

HEADQUARTERS DISTRICT OF WEST TENNESSEE,
MEMPHIS, TENN., July 2, 1864.

Special Order No. 70:

I. The utter failure of the municipal government of Memphis for the past two years to discharge its proper functions, the disloyal character of that government, its want of sympathy for the Government of the United States, and its indisposition to co-operate with the military authorities have long been felt as evils which the public welfare required to be abated. They have grown from bad to worse, until a further toleration of them will not comport with the sense of duty of the commanding general. The city of Memphis is under martial law, and the municipal government existing since the armed traitors were driven from the city has been only by sufferance of the military authorities of the United States. Therefore, under the authority of General Orders, No. 100, dated War Department, Adjutant-General's office, April 24, 1863,

It is ordered, that the functions of the municipal government of Memphis be and they are hereby suspended until further orders.

The present incumbents are forbidden to perform any official acts or exercise any authority whatever; and persons supposed to be elected officers of the city at an election held on June 30, 1864, will not qualify. That the interests and business of the city may not be interrupted, the following appointments of officers are made:

Acting mayor, Lieut.-Col. Thomas H. Harris, assistant adjutant-general United States Volunteers; recorder, F. W. Buttinghaus; treasurer, James D. Davis; comptroller, W. O. Lofland; tax-collector, F. L. Warner; tax-collector on privileges, John Logue; chief of police, P. M. Winters, and wharf-master, J. J. Butler, who will be fully respected in the exercise of the duties assigned them; and all records, papers, moneys, and property in any manner pertaining to the offices, government and interests of the city of Memphis, will be immediately turned over by the present holders thereof to the officers appointed to succeed them, etc.

The officers herein named and appointed will constitute a board, which shall discharge the duties heretofore devolving upon the board of aldermen, and [the acting mayor shall be chairman thereof, and their acts, resolutions and ordinances shall be valid and of full force and effect until revoked by the commanding general of the district of West Tennessee, or superior military authority.

By order of   Maj.-Gen. C. C. WASHBURN.
                                                        W. H. MORGAN, *Asst. Adj.-Gen.*

Official: W. H. MORGAN, *Asst. Adj.-Gen.*

XIII. L. R. Richards is hereby appointed register of the city of Memphis and a member of the board, constituted by Special Order No. 70, part I, of this date from these headquarters.

By order of   Maj.-Gen. C. C. WASHBURN.
                                                        W. H. MORGAN, *Asst. Adj.-Gen.*

To Lieut.-Col. Harris, *A. A. Gen. and Acting Mayor.*

On the 16th of July, 1864, Special Order No. 83 were issued, so far modifying Special Order No. 70, as to constitute a council to discharge the duties of the board of mayor and aldermen. They were to be known as the Provisional Mayor and Council of the city of Memphis. Following are their names:

First Ward—J. P. Foster, Andrew Renkert.
Second Ward—G. D. Johnson, S. T. Morgan.
Third Ward—B. F. C. Brooks, A. J. Miller.
Fourth Ward—I. M. Hill, J. G. Owen.
Fifth Ward—W. S. Bruce, William W. Jones.
Sixth Ward—J. E. Merriman, C. C. Smith.
Seventh Ward—G. P. Ware, Joseph Tagg.
Eighth Ward—Patrick Sherry, H. T. Hulbert.

On the 28th of July, E. T. Morgan was appointed city attorney for the city of Memphis, and on the 12th of August, J. P. Foster was appointed chief of police, *vice* P. M. Winters, relieved; Henry G. Smith was appointed councilman, *vice* J. P. Foster, and J. B. Wetherill was appointed councilman, *vice* W. S. Bruce, resigned; on the 6th of September W. M. Farrington was appointed alderman in place of A. J. Miller, deceased. This was the last order issued here by Maj. Gen. C. C. Washburn, and on the 4th of October, Brig.-Gen. Morgan L. Smith issued Special Order No. 159, by which W. R. Moore was appointed councilman *vice* H. G. Smith, resigned. On the 19th of October Lieut.-Col. Harris was relieved as acting mayor, and Capt. Channing Richards, of the

Twenty-second Ohio Volunteers appointed, and on July 3, 1865, Special Order No. 70, and Special Order No. 83, were revoked, the officers appointed by them were commanded to cease to exercise their functions, and to turn over to the officers elect all books and papers pertaining to their several offices. This revoking order was signed by Maj.-Gen. John E. Smith.

The officers elect referred to above were in part as follows: mayor, John Park, who had received 1,356 votes to W. O. Lofland's 835; recorder, John C. Creighton, 1,049, to Sam Tighe's 368, and chief of police, B. G. Garrett, 1,021 to Dan McMahon's 920. By default of an election John Park continued to serve as mayor until October 15, 1866, when W. O. Lofland, elected October 13, 1866, was qualified and served until January 1868. John W. Leftwich was then elected and served until 1870, when John Johnson was elected and served through the years 1870-73. John Logue was elected in 1874 and served two years, when he was succeeded by John R. Flippin, who was elected in 1876 by 5,909 votes to John Logue's 1,564, and was the last mayor Memphis has had.

In 1879 Memphis was in a very bad shape financially as well as otherwise. Her credit was entirely gone and she was bankrupt. This state of things had been brought about in part by very bad management on the part of her municipal government, and in part by the terrible scourges to which she had been subjected. By the yellow fever epidemic of 1878, following close on the heels of that of 1873, the city had been almost depopulated of its white citizens, and she was encumbered by an enormous debt, a statement of which is here introduced: 6 per cent Post Bonds, $2,426,000; 6 per cent Paving Bonds, $743,500; 6 per cent School Bonds, $95,000; 6 per cent Mississippi River Railroad Bonds, $80,000; 6 per cent Funding Bonds, $341,000; 10 per cent School Bonds, $20,000; other 10 per cent bonds, $5,000; total bonded debt, $3,710,500; floating debt, embracing innumerable items, $2,074,872.67; total debt, $5,785,372.67. The assets of the city at the same time amounted to $2,194,639.07, leaving the city's net indebtedness, supposing the entire assets to be available, $3,590,733.60. Most of the citizens felt sure, and in fact knew, that much of this enormous indebtedness had been unjustly created, and were desirous of devising some means by which they could be relieved of its payment. The idea of a "taxing district" was conceived and put into operation as an experiment. It was not because of anything intrinsically corrupt in the old form of municipal government, that a change was sought and effected. No form of government can be in and of itself corrupt. But one form of government may furnish opportunities for corruption and be of necessity more expensive and burdensome than another, and this is really the difference between the old form of government of Memphis and the taxing district. The taxing district has no authority to levy taxes, this authority being vested in the Legislature. Then under the charter granted in 1869, a council was created, consisting of ten aldermen and twenty councilmen, a form of government almost cumbersome enough for a State. The act creating the taxing district was passed January 29, 1879, and approved January 31. It consists of twenty-five sections, providing that cities might form taxing districts in certain cases. It said that the several communities embraced in the territorial limits of all the municipal corporations in this State, which had or might have their charters abolished, or such as might surrender them, under the provisions of that act were by it created taxing districts, in order to provide local government for the peace, safety and general welfare of such districts, and that the necessary taxes for the support of such local government should be imposed by the General Assembly of the State and not otherwise. This act provided for:

1. A board of fire and police commissioners. 2. A legislative council of the taxing district, consisting of the commissioners of the fire and police board, and the supervisors of the board of public works. 3. A board of health to consist of the chief of police, a health officer, and a physician. 4. A board of public works.

The board of fire and police commissioners was to consist of three commissioners at least thirty years of age, and tax-paying citizens of the district, for at least five years. One of these was to be appointed by the governor of the State, and to be president of the taxing district, and was to devote his entire time to the duties of his office at a salary of $2,000 per year. In the act a wharfage tax was provided for as follows: All steamboats, barges, and hulls used as barges, were to pay 5 cents per ton, which should entitle them to the privilege of the wharf and landing for six days, and 2 cents per ton per day for each day they remain after the expiration of the six days, the county trustee to collect the tax.

The first government of the taxing district was composed of D. T. Porter, president, John Overton, Jr., and W. W. Gay, until the death of Mr. Gay, when M. Burke was appointed to fill the vacancy which lasted from 1879 until the end of the first half of 1881. From this time until January, 1882, the government was composed of John Overton, Jr., president, M. Burke and R. C. Graves. In January, 1882, the officers of the taxing district were all elected as they have been ever since, being David P. Hadden, president, M. Burke and R. C. Graves. In 1883 they were. David P. Hadden, president, M. Burke and James Lee, Jr. The third government consisted of David P. Hadden, president, James Lee, Jr., and H. A. Montgomery, and the fourth elected in January, 1886, was the same.

The first board of public works of the taxing district was composed of C. W. Goyer, John Gunn, R. Galloway, J. M. Goodbar and M. Burke, until Mr. Burke was appointed to the city government, when W. N. Brown was appointed to this board. The present board is as follows: R. F. Patterson, J. E. Randle, Q. J. Graham, Charles Kuey and Symmes Wallace.

The president of the board of health has been G. B. Thornton, M. D., ever since the organization of the district. P. R. Athy was chief of police up to 1880, when he was elected sheriff; since then W. C. Davis has been chief of police. M. McFadden was chief of the fire department until his death in 1882, since when J. E. Cleary has filled the position. The city attorneys have been C. W. Heiskell, 1879–84, and S. P. Walker, 1884–1887. Niles Meriwether has been city engineer from 1879 to the present time, and P. Kallaher, wharf-master. The registers have been W. A. McCloy, 1879; A. P. Tack, 1880; B. K. Pullen, 1881 to September, 1886, and B. K. Pullen, Jr., from September, 1886, to the present time. The inspectors of weights and measures have been G. J. Mallory, S. B. De Groat and J. C. Mhoon, from 1884 to the present time, and as hospital physicians have served A. A. Lawrence, 1879 to February, 1883, and J. E. Black from February, 1883, to the present time.

At the time the taxing district government went into operation the streets were in a very bad condition. Since then there have been paved miles of street as follows: In 1879–80, 5.28 miles, costing $158,456.45; in 1881–82, 5.22 miles, costing $190,554.26; in 1883–84, 6.85 miles, costing $200,853.89, and in 1885–86, 5.37 miles, costing $150,028.84, making a total of 22.72 miles, at an aggregate cost of $699,893.44. Besides this street pavement the following work has been done at an expense of $324,398.30:

New sewer lines .... (miles)	39.38
Old private sewer lines (bought by T. D.) added .... "	4.1
Sub-soil drains .... "	35.9
Water closets	6844
Privy sinks (latrines)	51
Slop sinks	4811
Urinals	365
Bath tubs	568
Wash basins	476
Elevators	11
Cellars and house drains	74
Flush tanks	198
Man holes	67
Observation openings	445
Catch basins	6

The first bank organized in Memphis was the Farmers and Merchants Bank, in 1834. It was located on the corner of Main and Winchester Streets. About 1840 this institution erected the building on the corner of Main and Exchange Streets, afterward used as a synagogue, and about 1850 the same bank erected another building on Jefferson Street nearly opposite the present Priddy Hotel.

The Branch Union Bank was started in 1839, in a brick building on the northwest corner of Exchange Square. In 1852 it removed to the northeast corner of Madison Street and Front Alley, and in 1853-54 it erected a building on the opposite corner of the alley, at present occupied by the First National Bank.

The Branch Planters Bank occupied the building south of Cochran Block on Main Street, about 1842. It afterward moved into a building on the southwest corner of Main and Jefferson Streets. There were also other banks here prior to the war: the Southern Bank of Tennessee, established Sepember 1, 1853; the Mechanics Bank, started December 1, 1853; the Branch Bank of Tennessee, the Bank of West Tennessee, the Bank of Memphis, established September 1, 1853; the Commercial Bank, established March 1, 1844, and the Citizens Bank, started December 1, 1853.

The First National Bank was organized in April, 1864, with a capital of $100,000. F. A. Davis was the first president and C. P. Norris the first cashier. The capital now is $150,000, and surplus $50,000. Since it commenced business it has declared $556,000, in dividends. At different times it has carried accounts with all the business men of the city. Up to 1872 its deposits generally averaged over $1,000,000. Since then they have been about $500,000 and now they are $800,000. The bank has always been at its present location, No. 14 Madison Street. N. M. Jones succeeded F. A. Davis as president in 1882; N. W. Thatcher became cashier in 1869, and C. W. Schulte in 1882. One remarkable fact about banks in Memphis is that since this bank was started nineteen other banks have failed, three of them national banks. The strength of this bank is accounted for by the fact that such firms as the following are stockholders: Brown & Jones, Brooks, Neely & Co., Hill, Fontaine & Co., and Oliver, Finnie & Co.

The German National Bank was organized under national charter in 1864, John A. Ainsley being the first president, succeeded by T. M. Apperson, Louis Hanauer, Horace E. Gorth and Thomas H. Milburn. The bank was reorganized in 1885 under the State law, and its name became the German Bank of Memphis. Its officers at present are John W. Cochran, president; W. C. McClure, vice-president; Edward Goldsmith, cashier; Louis Hanauer, J. T. Pettit, R. C. Graves, J. J. Jenny, George Arnold, D. P. Hadden, Jacob Weller, J. T. Frost, J. S. Robinson, R. H. Vance and William Katzenberger. The capital stock of the bank is $250,000 and surplus $140,000. The deposits amount to $872,144.28 and the undivided profits $28,253.56.

The Union and Planters Bank was organized and commenced business September 1, 1869, with the following directors and officers: William M. Farrington, president; William A. Williamson, vice-president; S. P. Read, cashier; J. J. Rawlings, C. B. Church, John Johnson, C. W. Goyer, W. B. Greenlaw, W. B. Galbreath, Napoleon Hill, A. Vaccaro, Joseph Bruce, Z. N. Estes, M. L. Meacham, James A. Rogers and Nathan Adams. The present [directors and officers are Napoleon Hill, president; William A. Williamson, vice-president; S. P. Read, cashier; A. Vaccaro, Joseph Bruce, R. Dudley, John R. Pepper, E. Ensley, Benjamin Barr, Isaac N. Snowden and James H. McDonald. The paid up capital stock is $600,000, dividend on hand $121,377, deposits, October 26, 1886, $1,074,125.15.

The State National Bank was organized August 27, 1873, with the following directors and officers: R. C. Daniel, president; I. B. Kirtland, vice-president; J. J. Freeman, cashier; T. N. Nelson, J. J. Busby, H. T. Lemmon, H. Cloth, A. J. White, Hugh Stewart, John P. Hoffman, B. Lowenstein and N. Malatesta. The present directors and officers are W. B. Bethel, president; A. B. Gwynn, vice-president; M. S. Buckingham, cashier; W. J. Chase, R. H. Vance, H. T. Lemmon, Thomas J. Latham, W. M. Sneed, Gen. Colton Greene, John K. Speed, R. L. Coffin and Z. N. Estes. The capital stock of the bank is $250,000, and surplus $80,000.

The Mercantile Bank commenced business May 21, 1883, with a cash capital of $200,000. It has eighty stockholders, all of them representative business men of Memphis. In selecting stockholders it was careful not to place itself outside of those who had business to give it, hoping in this way to make its stock self-supporting, and the success of the institution is a sufficient justification of the wisdom of this policy. During the entire period of its existence it has distributed to its stockholders each six months a five per cent cash dividend, and has besides accumulated a surplus of $30,000. The bank is a depository of the State of Tennessee. Following are the names of its directors and officers: J. R. Godwin, president; J. M. Goodbar, vice-president; C. H. Raine, cashier; D. T. Porter, A. W. Newson, F. M. Nelson, C. B. Bryan, J. M. Smith, W. S. Bruce, W. N. Wilkerson, T. B. Sim, John Armistead, H. E. Coffin, R. T. Cooper, J. W. Falls, M. Gavin, R. J. Black, W. P. Dunavant and Charles Kuey.

Manhattan Savings Bank and Trust Company was organized in July, 1885, with the following officers: David P. Hadden, president; Edward Goldsmith, vice-president; James Nathan, cashier. The present board of trustees are L. Hanauer, M. Gavin, L. Levy, Napoleon Hill, A. Kenkert, J. A. Omberg, J. G. Handwerker, Thomas Boyle, David P. Hadden, J. S. Robinson, John W. Cochran, Sol. Coleman, Hardwig Peres, Edward Goldsmith. This bank receives sums of $1 and upward, and allows interest at stated periods, executes orders in stocks, bonds and securities, sells drafts on all parts of Europe, and executes cable transfers. The capital stock is $20,000, and surplus $5,000.

The Mechanics Bank was first organized in 1856, with F. M. White, president. The charter having been kept alive the bank was reorganized in 1886 with $100,000 capital. The present directors and officers are M. H. Katzenberger, president; Napoleon Hill, vice-president; J. Katzenberger, cashier; W. H. Carrol, J. H. Biscoe, A. S. Myers, A. Cohn, J. M. Schorr, A. F. Tobin and John A. Denie.

The Security Bank of Memphis was organized February 1, 1886. It is a safe deposit trust company and savings bank, located at No. 42 Madison Street. The first directors and officers were C. C. Graham, president; W. M. Wilkerson, vice-president; R. J. Black, cashier; W. D. Bethell, Thomas H. Allen, S. I. McDowell, J. R. Godwin, John Overton, Jr., R. Dudley Frayser, S. P. Read, W. F. Taylor, William A. Williamson and R. B. Snowden. With the exception of the president, who is now R. Dudley Frayser, the officers are the same. This bank does a general banking business, pays interest on deposits, has a safe deposit vault, and is a depository of the State.

The Bank of Commerce was established in 1873 with a capital of $200,000, at No. 12 Madison Street. The presidents of this bank have been E. McDavitt, from 1873 to 1876; J. T. Parkerson, 1876 to 1880; S. H. Dunscomb, 1880 to present time. Vice-president, John Overton, Jr., for one or two years at first, and then from 1886 to the present time. Cashiers, R. A. Parker, 1873 to 1879; J. A. Omberg, 1879 to the present time. The capital of the bank is at present $200,000 with a surplus of $80,000.

The Hermando Insurance Company, 22 Madison Street, was incorporated in 1850. It does a fire and marine insurance business, and has a paid up capital of $150,000. Its assets, including capital, amount to $182,000. S. H. Dunscomb is president; Joseph Bruce, vice-president; J. S. Dunscomb, secretary, and its other directors are R. L. Cochran, J. H. McDavitt, F. M. Nelson, L. Hanauer, A. Vaccaro, J. R. Pepper, W. B. Mallory, N. Fontaine and J. T. Willins. Originally only ten per cent was paid in. After the war the company reorganized and ten per cent more was paid in, and the stock was all paid up by July 1, 1874, since which time it has paid from eight to twenty-four per cent to the stockholders annually.

The Planters Fire & Marine Insurance Company, 41 Madison Street, was incorporated in 1867, and has a capital of $150,000. Following are the names of the directors and officers: D. T. Porter, president; John Overton, Jr., vice-president; J. H. Smith, secretary; F. B. Hunter, assistant secretary; S. H. Brooks, R. L. Coffin, J. R. Godwin, J. M. Goodbar, J. C. Mills, Harding Peres and J. M. Phillips. This company does a large and conservative local business, and is agent for the Georgia Home Insurance Company, the Springfield (Mass.) Fire & Marine Insurance Company, the Mountain City Company of Chattanooga, Tenn., and of the Anglo-Nevada Insurance Company of San Francisco, Cal.

The People's Insurance Company, 16 Madison Street, was organized in 1867, and has met with well deserved success in a safe and conservative career of twenty years. It does a general fire insurance business, making a specialty of dwellings and good business property. It has a cash capital of $200,000. Its directors and officers are as follows: William M. Farrington, president; H. T. Lemmon, vice-president; W. L. Parker, secretary; W. S. Bruce, Enoch Ensley, John Overton, Jr., and Thomas B. Turley.

The Home Insurance Company was organized in 1870 with a capital of $100,000. It has conducted a successful fire and marine insurance business from the beginning. This business is steadily increasing, indicating the possession of the fullest confidence of the public. Its officers are on the floor of the building at the corner of Front and Madison Streets. This company represents the Phœnix of London, the Fire of England, the Washington of Boston, and the Crescent of New Orleans. The officers of this company are E. L. McGowan, president; John K. Speed, vice-president, and Bun F. Price, secretary. The other directors are H. Wetter, James Yonge, H. Luehrmann, P. McIntyre, R. B. Snowden, L. Hanauer, Louis Erb, John N. Harbin, W. D. Bethell and A. Vaccaro.

The Memphis City Fire & General Insurance Company, 19 Madison Street, was incorporated January 24, 1870, and commenced business May, 1871, on a subscribed capital stock of $250,000, of which there was called in and paid up $50,000. The company has done a careful and conservative business from the beginning; by June 30, 1883, had earned the eighty per cent required to make the paid up capital $250,000. Since that time it has paid regular cash dividends to the stockholders, and has used its funds in commercial loans. Its directors and officers are Napoleon Hill, president; W. N. Wilkerson, vice-president; Henry J. Lynn, cashier; W. D. Bethell, R. E. Semmes, William I. Cole, James Reilly, John Logue, S. Mansfield, D. B. Myers, and G. Harrington, soliciting agent.

The Bluff City Insurance Company, 285 Main Street, was established in 1871, with a paid up cash capital of $150,000. This company occupies a prominent place in insurance circles, and is established on a solid basis. Its directors and officers are J. C. Neely, president; David P. Hadden, vice-president; W. H. Moore, secretary; J. T. Frank, H. M. James, W. A. Gage, M. Gavin and J. W. Falls.

The Factors Mutual Insurance Company, No. 18 Madison Street, was organized in 1881, with a guarantee fund of $130,000. Its assets amount to $171,424.72. Its operations are confined to marine inland risks. Its board of trustees is composed of seventeen of the most prominent business men of Memphis, and its officers are Noland Fontaine, president; Colton Greene, vice-president, and James E. Beasley, secretary.

The Vanderbilt Mutual Insurance Company, No. 3 Madison Street, was organized in August, 1881. It has a capital of $100,000, and does a large and conservative fire insurance business, in Memphis and other large cities of the United States, but has no soliciting agents. Its board of trustees is composed of thirteen of the most enterprising and substantial business men of Memphis, and its officers are John Overton, Jr., president; Thomas H. Chilton, vice-president, and Phil B. Jones, secretary.

The Factors Fire Insurance Company, No. 18 Madison Street, was incorporated in September, 1882. Its capital stock is $250,000 and its reserve and surplus fund is $20,729. The business of the company, which is largely local, extends also to all the principal cities of the South and West. Its safe conservative methods inspire the fullest confidence of the community. Its board of trustees is composed of twenty-one of Memphis' most prominent business men, and its officers are Noland Fontaine, president; Colton Green, vice-president, and James E. Beasley, secretary.

The Arlington Insurance Company, No. 43 Madison Street, was organized September 1, 1883, with a subscribed capital of $100,000. The paid up capital was 20 per cent of this sum. Three dividends have since been made aggregating 15 per cent. The directors and officers are as follows: T. B. Sim, president; J. M. Smith, vice-president; W. H. Kenneday, secretary; W. P. Dunavant, A. Kenkert, J. W. Richardson,

W. T. Stone, George Arnold, Otto Schwill, B. H. Carbery, I. M. Hill, D. Canale, Alston Boyd, L. Lawhorn and John A. Denie.

The Citizens Insurance Company, No. 43 Madison Street, was organized July 1, 1886, with a subscribed capital stock of $200,000, $10,000 of which was paid in. It does a general fire and marine insurance business, and guarantees the lowest rates. It makes a specialty of country stores and residences and solicits gin houses and insures steamboats. Losses are promptly adjusted and paid at Memphis. This is the only home company making a specialty of this class of business. The directors of the company are T. B. Sim, George ———, T. F. Duffin, John Armistead, J. W. Richardson, W. N. Nickerson, W. P. Dunavant and W. H. Kenneday, secretary.

The Phoenix Fire & Marine Insurance Company, No. 10 Madison Street, has the following directors and officers: H. M. Neely, president; W. S. Bruce, vice-president; John Johnson, secretary; J. S. Day, L. B. Suggs, John K. Speed, W. J. Crawford, R. J. Black, W. N. Brown and C. B. Oliver. The company has a cash capital of $150,000, and on December 1, 1886, its total assets were $171,529.48.

The Memphis Board of Fire Underwriters was organized in 1871, for the purpose of adopting and establishing general rules and regulations for the management of fire insurance business in Memphis, and suburbs within ten miles of Court Square. Any person representing a fire insurance company in Memphis may become a member of the board. The officers consist of a president, vice-president and secretary, elected by a majority of the members, of whom there are now twenty, including individuals and firms. At the present time J. J. Murphy is president, Thomas Wellford, vice-president and Jere Sullivan, secretary.

The Signal Service Observatory was established in Memphis, February 28, 1871, in accordance with a joint resolution of Congress, approved February 9, 1870. The following have been the observers in charge: Thomas J. Brown, February 28, 1871, to August 28, 1871; S. W. Rode, August 28, 1871, to September 14, 1874; H. M. Ludwig, September 14, 1874, to July 22, 1876; W. McElroy, July 22, 1876, to his death from yellow fever, September 1, 1878; F. M. Neal, September 1, 1878, to January 24, 1879; R. R. Martin, January 24, 1879, to July 31, 1879; R. L. Dabney, July 31, 1879, to January 11, 1880, and D. T. Flannery, January 11, 1880, to the present time.

According to certain authorities the first postmaster at Memphis was James Stewart, who served from 1820 until M. B. Winchester was regularly appointed, April 22, 1823. Mr. Winchester served continuously until 1849, on the 17th day of April of which year F. S. Latham was appointed. The postoffice was then on Madison Street where the Bank of Commerce now is. On the 5th of April, 1853, Gen. William H. Carroll, son of Gov. William Carroll, was appointed and served until June 3, 1860, on which day Col. M. C. Galloway was appointed and held the office until the United States Army came down, on July 6, 1862, when it went into the hands of the military authorities and remained with them two years; Col. Robert C. Gist was then appointed June 7, 1864, and served until April 5, 1869, when Col. Josiah De Loach became postmaster and served until June 8, 1877. Robert A. Thompson succeeded and served until his death from yellow fever, September 3, 1878. The affairs of the office were then managed a few days by L. S. Knowlton, and then by the bondsmen of Mr. Thompson, with W. J. Chase in charge. During the continuance of the fever there was great trouble connected with the office on account of the quarantine against the city. The accumulation of through mail, the lack of money to pay money orders, etc., created great embarrassment. The First National Bank cashed the money orders to the extent of $30,000 and thus rendered great assistance to the citizens. On September 28, 1878, Mrs. Anna D. H. Thompson was appointed and early in 1879 the office was moved to the Masonic Temple. Mrs. Thompson remained in the office until September 10, 1882, when she was succeeded by James H. Smith. The present postmaster, Jeptha M. Fowlkes, was appointed July 6, 1885, and assumed charge of the office August 1 of that year. In December following, it was removed to its present quarters in the United States Custom House, at the foot of Madison Street.

The charter incorporating the Memphis Merchants Exchange being dated January 11, 1885, it is the successor of the old Chamber of Commerce, which was disorganized in 1878. Following are the names of the incorporators: John K. Speed, M. C. Pearce, E. C. Buchanan, John R. Pepper, James Lee, Jr., John S. Toof, M. Cooper, L. Erb, W. J. Chase and E. A. Keeling, The object of the incorporation was "to afford better facilities for the transaction of general mercantile business; to increase the privileges of buying and selling merchandise, produce and various other commodities; to acquire, preserve and disseminate useful information concerning the commerce of the country; to adopt standard classifications; to establish just and equitable principles of trade; to maintain its rules, regulations and usages, and to adjust controversies between its members." The capital stock of the Exchange was limited to $250,000.

The presidents of this organization have been John K. Speed, 1883; W. W. Schoolfield, 1884; A. B. Treadwell, 1885; W. J. Chase, 1886;

vice-presidents, N. Cooper, 1883 and 1884; W. J. Chase, 1885, and J. H. Martin, 1886; secretary, E. A. Keeling, 1883 to 1886, inclusive; treasurers, W. J. Chase, 1883-84; W. D. Bethell, 1885-86.

During the first and second years of the existence of this exchange comparatively little interest was manifested in its proceedings and welfare, and it was thought by some that the institution was on the wane. When organized it had ninety-five members; at the beginning of 1885 it had but 139, among whom there was much indifference and the institution was in debt. On the 5th of February, it was decided to inaugurate a call board, and on the 21st the certificate of membership plan was inaugurated, limiting its membership to 350. During the year the entire membership was taken up. At first the certificates of membership were held at $25 each. They soon increased to $50 and by the beginning of 1886 they were $125. On September 1, 1885, the board moved into its present elegant hall, which was dedicated on the 15th of October. In the ten months succeeding March 1, 1885, the value of goods sold on call was $484,800.50. According to the annual statement of the Merchants Exchange, there were received for the season of 1880-81 (the season commencing September 1, and ending August 31), 470,267 bales of cotton; for the season of 1881-82, 339,240 bales; for that of 1882-83, 510,789; for 1883-84, 450,077; and for that of 1884-85, 430,127. For the season of 1885-86 they were 478,770* bales and for the first four months of 1886-87, they were 491,459 bales, making the aggregate number of bales of cotton received in Memphis, from 1826 to January 1, 1887, 11,000,000. At $60 per bale this would amount to $660,000,000.

The Memphis Cotton Exchange was incorporated April 20, 1874 by the following charter:

STATE OF TENNESSEE.
BE IT REMEMBERED, That on to-wit, April 20th, 1874, in the Second Chancery Court of Shelby County, Tennessee, Hon. Sam'l P. Walker, Chancellor, the following proceedings were had and appeared of record, to-wit:

No. 1041.
SCHOOLFIELD, HANAUER & CO., and others, Petitioners,
EX PARTE,
To incorporate "The Memphis Cotton Exchange."

Be it remembered, That this cause came on to be heard before the Hon. Sam'l P. Walker, Chancellor of the Second Chancery Court of Shelby County, Tennessee, on this the 20th day of April, 1874; it appearing that a majority of the petitioners reside in Shelby County, that the petition sets forth the purposes and objects of the corporation prayed for, that immediately upon the filing of said petition the Clerk and Master of this Court caused publication to be made for thirty days in the *Memphis Appeal*, a newspaper published in this State, that said publication gave the names of the petitioners and nature

*Estimated.

of the corporate rights prayed for, and by it all persons were notified to appear and show cause why letters of incorporation should not issue; no one appearing to show cause, the statements and allegations of the petition are taken as confessed, and the Court proceeds to a hearing of the cause *ex parte*. It further appearing that the objects of the corporation prayed for are not in conflict with the laws of the land, nor detrimental to the public interests or morals, it is therefore ordered, adjudged and decreed, that Schoolfield, Hanauer & Co., W. B. Galbreath, A. G. Tuther (Agent Star Union Line), Hill, Fontaine & Co., Pettit & Simpson, Guy, McClellan & Co., R. M. Bradford (for B. & O. R. R.), B. Bayliss & Co., A. M. Agelasto, Shane, Harris & Co., Martin & Hillsman, Day & Proudfit, J. W. Jefferson & Co., Stratton & Wellford, Ford, Porter & Co., Louis Ranger & Co., G. Falls & Co., Fargason & Clay, Sledge, McKay & Co., C. F. Smith, O. B. Parker, E. Hobart & Co., Busby, Johnson & Co., Brooks, Neely & Co., Hartmus & Co., T. B. Dillard, Benj. Babb, S. M. Anderson, Wm. Bath, A. M. Scarbrough & Co., Katzenberger's Sons, S. M. Gates, A. A. Paton & Co., Ely, Harvey & Richardson, J. R. Miles & Co., C. T. Curtis, A. C. Treadwell & Bros., W. Tracy Eustis, Hugh Torrance & Son, Estes, Fizer & Co., S. B. Carver & Co., Gage & Fisher, J. J. Rawlings & Co., Rutland, Freeman & Co., Pearce, Suggs & Co., J. R. Godwin & Co., Cochran, Cirode & Co., Philip R. Durfee, P. S. Jones, Goodlett & Co., Furstenheim & Co., Ad. Storm (Agent M. & St. L. P. Co.), Ralph Wormeley & Co., F. M. White & Co., A. J. Roach & Co., Thos. H. Allen & Co., T. B. Haynes & Co., Robt. Gibson (for L. & N. R. R. Co.), R. C. Daniel, Jones, Brown & Co., Dillard & Coffin, Taylor, Radford & Co., J. F. Frank & Co., Herron, Connor & Co., E. E. Clarke, Harris, Mallory & Co., W. W. Thacher, Cashier (for First National Bank), M. Gavin & Co., Jno. S. Toof and E. B. Webber & Co., be, and they are hereby incorporated, with all the powers and privileges of a corporate body, under the name and style of "The Memphis Cotton Exchange," with perpetual succession, and power to use a common seal and alter the same at pleasure, to sue and be sued, to take and to hold by grant, purchase or devise, for the purposes of said corporation, real and personal property to an amount not exceeding one hundred and fifty thousand dollars, and to sell, convey, lease and mortgage the same, or any part thereof and with full power to issue capital stock to an amount not exceeding one hundred and fifty thousand dollars, under such rules and regulations as may be prescribed by said corporation.

It is further ordered, adjudged and decreed, that said corporation have full power to adopt a constitution for its government, and to make all proper and needful by-laws necessary or incident to the purposes of its organization not inconsistent with the Constitution and laws of the State of Tennessee or of the United States.

STATE OF TENNESSEE, }
   SHELBY COUNTY.

I, M. D. L. STEWART, Clerk and Master of the Second Chancery Court of Shelby County, Tennessee, do hereby certify that the above and foregoing is a true and perfect copy of the final decree granting charter to "The Memphis Cotton Exchange," as the same appears of record in my office, on the day and date set forth in the caption of this decree.

               Given under my hand and seal of office, at office in the City of Memphis, Tennessee, this April 27th, 1874.

{ SEAL. }   M. D. L. STEWART, C. & M.
                       By GEO. MALLORY, D. C. & M.

The purposes of the Cotton Exchange are set forth in the second article of its constitution, as follows:

SECTION 1. The purposes of this Association shall be to provide and maintain suitable rooms for a Cotton Exchange in the city of Memphis; to adjust controversies between members; to establish just and equitable principles, uniform usages, rules and regulations, and standards for classifications, which shall govern all transactions connected with the cotton trade; to acquire, preserve and disseminate information connected therewith; to decrease the risks incident thereto; and generally, to promote the interests of the trade, and increase the facilities and the amount of the cotton business in the city of Memphis.

Following is a list of presidents, vice-presidents, treasurers, secretaries and assistant secretaries from the organization to the present time:

Presidents—W. B. Galbreath, 1873-76; J. T. Petfit, 1877-78; David P. Hadden, 1879-80; Napoleon Hill, 1881-82; C. P. Hunt, 1883-84; W. J. Crawford, 1885-86; L. B. Suggs, 1887.

Secretaries—John S. Toof, 1873-79; Sam. M. Gates, 1879-80; Henry Holter, 1881-86.

Treasurers—R. C. Daniel, 1874; F. S. Davis, 1875-76; S. P. Read, 1877-80; S. H. Dunscomb, 1881-84; J. R. Godwin, 1885-87.

The officers of the Cotton Exchange Building Committee have been since 1885 the same as those of the Cotton Exchange.

These two exchanges meet in the most elegant building in Memphis. It is situated on Second Street and extends from South Court Street to Madison Street. The purchase of the site was made in 1883 at a cost of $60,000. The Cotton Exchange Building Committee was formed in 1883, and consisted of J. W. Fulmer, J. M. Fowlkes and W. W. Schoolfield. The capital stock of this committee was fixed at $99,000, of which the Cotton Exchange was to take $50,000, the $49,000 being distributed. The following description of the building, which was taken possession of September 1, 1885, and which cost $145,000, is taken from the Memphis *Avalanche* of that date:

"Viewed from the outside one is deeply impressed with the grandeur of the building that to-day will be taken formal possession of by the sister exchanges. It is at once solid and ornamental in appearance. The skill of the architect and the conscientiousness of the builder are plainly apparent in every feature of the structure. It is four stories high and of the Gothic style of architecture. The frontage is resplendent with artistic ornamentation. An air of elegance pervades the entire building and there is not the slightest suggestion of gingerbread work anywhere. The frontage abounds with heavy French plate windows, encased in massive frames of stained wood. The lofty archway of the main entrance on Second Street, the substantial double iron stairways leading to the Cotton Exchange on Madison Street and Merchants Exchange on Court, all are worthy of more than a casual glance. The basement is protected by heavy iron rails, supported by massive posts. The transoms of all the windows are of stained glass, containing many unique and beautiful designs. Above the third story is the attic, surmounted by four slate covered domes ornamented with the design of an open cotton boll in galvanized iron. The material used in constructing the building is the finest Zanesville (Ohio) pressed brick. The moldings generally are composed of the same excellent and durable material."

The Memphis Water Company was organized in February, 1870, with John Cubbins, president; Charles J. Phillips, treasurer; W. L. Cameron, superintendent; T. M. Mahan, financial agent; O. P. Lyles, solicitor; A. R. Ketchum, consulting engineer; G. W. Pearsons, constructing engineer; M. J. Riley, superintendent of street mains; W. L. Cameron, secretary; and other directors, John S. Toof, B. C. Brown, J. H. Humphreys and John E. Randall. At the annual meeting of 1872 no report could be made, except that a contract had been made for machinery with the Holly Manufacturing Company, of Lockport, N. Y., and another contract for hydrant service and rents with the city. About this time bonds to the amount of $600,000 were placed upon the market. By the annual meeting, April 30, 1873, the works were complete and in running order, with seventeen miles of pipe laid. The site of the works is on the east side of Wolf River, about two miles north of Court Square, and comprises about four acres of land. The bank here is 36 feet above high-water mark. The suction-pipe is 20 inches in interior diameter; the pump-well is a tube of boiler-iron 18 feet in diameter and 60 feet long. The machinery consists of 8 lifting and force pumps, each 20 inches in diameter and 24 inches stroke. Up to the date of the secretary's report for April 30, 1873, the entire expenditure for construction was $472,278.39. At present the board of directors consists of T. J. Latham, president; W. S. Bruce, vice-president; W. L. Cameron, secretary; C. C. Graham, C. B. Bryan, J. R. Godwin, G. W. McCrae, S. H. Dunscomb, W. D. Bethell and S. M. McCallum. The assistant secretary is Lawrence J. Simpson.

The Brush Electric Light and Power Company was organized in March, 1883, with the following officers: H. A. Hamilton, president; S. T. Carnes, vice-president; George W. Woodruff, secretary and treasurer. The works are at the foot of Jefferson Street, in a two-story brick building. At first the company had but one engine of 150-horse power, but about the 1st of March, 1887, a second engine of similar strength was set up. There are four dynamos in these works, which at first supplied electricity for 50 lights; this number has been increased to 155 arc lights. Incandescent lights were first introduced by this company in March, 1885, of which they have now in use about 100, varying in intensity from 16 to 150 candle power. The present officers are S. T. Carnes, president; H. A. Hamilton, vice-president; and John L. Kerr, secretary and treasurer.

The Thompson-Houston Electric Light Company was organized in May, 1886, under a charter granted March 30, 1886. The incorporators were M. Burke, T. F. Duffin, R. A. Speed, M. Coen and E. B. McHenry. Upon organization, M. Burke was elected president and E. B. McHenry secretary. The capital stock of the company is $25,000. On the 7th of May, 1886, their lights first shone upon the city, fifteen lamps then being the number. The works are located in the rear of No. 381 Main Street, where they have two engines, of 80-horse power each, and five dynamos. On the 1st of January, 1887, they had 140 arc lights burning, and 100 incandescent lamps from the same circuit. The distinguishing feature of this arc light is that it is at the same time brilliant and steady. No lamp has yet flickered or gone out except when the entire circuit was broken.

Elmwood Cemetery lies two and a half miles southwest of Memphis. The Elmwood Cemetery Association was organized September 11, 1852, stock having been subscribed on the 28th of August, premiums to the amount of $25,000, $500 each having been subscribed by fifty shareholders, whose object it was to establish a proper cemetery near Memphis. At the first meeting of these shareholders, Dr. A. P. Merrill was made chairman, and E. P. Stewart, secretary. Dr. A. P. Merrill, J. W. Fowler, J. M. Williamson, William Ruffin and D. M. Leatherman were authorized to purchase land for cemetery uses. These gentlemen as a committee reported September 25, 1852, that they had bought forty acres, lying between the old Fort Pickering & La Grange Railroad and Walker Avenue. The permanent organization of the board was effected October 9, 1852, with the following officers: D. M. Leatherman, president; J. W. Fowler, treasurer; J. N. Williamson, secretary. The association was incorporated February 13, 1854, by the following persons: D. M. Leatherman, J. M. Williamson, John W. Fowler, Wilie B. Miller and William Ruffin, and such other persons as might sign the indenture of December 14, 1852, setting forth the principles of the association. The property of the association was exempted from taxation by the Legislature, February 15, 1869. From 1859 to 1862 President Lenow, of this Association, labored to remove the bodies of the dead in the old Morris Cemetery to Elmwood, the Morris Cemetery being in a rapidly growing section of the city, and the work, after completion, gave great satisfaction to all concerned. One hundred and seventeen Confederate soldiers and a few Union soldiers lie buried in Elmwood Cemetery. "If the dead deserve praise, and they who read epitaphs owe a debt of gratitude, it will be most cheerfully paid when most modestly exacted."

The Leath Orphan Asylum was established in 1855, by a bequest of

Mrs. Leath of fifteen acres of land, and by a donation by citizens and others, a building was erected. Under the charge of Mrs. Jane Ward, it accomplished great good to the orphans in the vicinity of Memphis. Mrs. Ward died in 1876, and was succeeded by the present matron, Mrs. Ida Peabody. Previous to 1875, in which year a new building was erected, Mrs. Leath donated to the asylum twenty acres more land. The institution is on the New Raleigh road at the edge of the city, and is managed by a board of trustees, which board at present consists of W. S. Bruce, president; Judge J. R. Flippin, secretary; S. H. Dunscomb, treasurer; Dr. D. T. Porter, I. N. Snowden and W. W. Schoolfield. The building is capable of keeping 200 inmates.

The Young Men's Christian Association, after a somewhat checkered career in 1870-71-72 and 1873, was reorganized April 26, 1883. It has had rooms in the Odd Fellows' building, in Ayres Block, and finally in the Lee Block, No. 207 Main Street, into which it moved August 1, 1886. At present the officers are, president, R. G. Craig; vice-president, Judge L. H. Estes, Jr.; secretary, C. Mason, Jr., and treasurer, George S. Fox. Services are held in the hospital, jail and mission home, and free concerts and lectures are given occasionally. The membership is now about twenty-five and the association is growing and doing much good.

The Old Folks' Society was organized May 9, 1857, when the following officers were elected: Nathaniel Anderson, president; William D. Ferguson, vice-president; J. B. Moseley, secretary; Eugene Magevney, historian. The purposes of the Society were " to rescue from the oblivion into which it is rapidly sinking the past history of our city and county; to collate and preserve the memories and incidents of the earlier and the late lives of the hardy and revered pioneers, who came hither to woo from the wildness of the unbroken wilderness, our present heritage; to transmit from son to son, in authoritative and reliable records, the events to which the progress of our city and county have given birth, and the names of those who have devoted their lives and talents to the development of their resources, and to cultivate amongst the survivors and descendants and successors of these worthies of the past, the general good feeling which should characterize those who were the common sharers of the privations of an early border life."

The society, continued up to the beginning of the war, 1861, and was reorganized in 1866, with Col. Chas. D. McLean as president and John B. Moseley as secretary.

This society, having been reorganized on its former principles, proved very imperfect. While the "Old Folks" had to "foot the bills," the young folks, and especially strangers, crowded them out, monopolized the grounds and everything else. The consequence was that the members lagged in interest and the Society went down. In 1870, October 8, a meeting was held for a second reorganization of the Old Folks at Home, and the following members were enrolled: J. R. Abernathy, T. C. Bleckley, B. Bayliss, M. C. Cayce, S. H. Dunscomb, Newton Ford, H. L. Guion, C. W. Goyer, H. E. Goodlett, A. J. Hayes, W. F. Hardin, C. J. Hargan, Hon. John Johnson, Chas. D. McLean, Michael Magevney, Eugene Magevney, W. P. Mitchell, E. McDavitt, R. A. Parker, Frank W. Royster, Sr., E. F. Risk, Sr., John T. Stratton, John T. Trezevant, John S. Toof, W. F. Taylor, A. Vaccaro, J. J. Worsham, James S. Wilkins, J. C. Ward and J. D. Williams.

January 15, 1884. Officers elected: John Beamish, president; W. J. Smith, first vice-president; Tom Gale, second vice-president; E. O. Milton, secretary; J. S. Wilkins, treasurer; C. F. Vance, historian. At this time there are 147 members in the society.

The manufacturers of Memphis are an important element in her prosperity. Of these she has over 300 establishments of various sizes. Foremost in the list are the cotton-seed oil mills, of which there are eleven—the Panola, Gayoso, Globe, Hope, Memphis, Hanauer, City, Valley, Planters, De Soto and Star. The manufacture of cotton-seed oil, cake and meal has been inaugurated since the war, but although thus young has grown to large proportions, and is constantly adding to the wealth of the valley of the Mississippi and to Memphis in particular.

There are seven saw and planing-mills in operation, giving employment to about 500 hands; are based upon a capital of $500,000, and producing about 60,000,000 feet of lumber annually.

Of iron manufactories there are the Chickasaw Iron Works, the Livermore Foundry & Machine Company, the Milburn Gin & Machine Company, the Bluff City Stove Works, the Memphis Metal & Wood Manufacturing Company, and the Variety Agricultural Works.

Of wagon and carriage manufacturers there are W. S. Bruce & Co., the Lilly Carriage Company, the Woodruff-Oliver Carriage & Harness Company, and the James & Graham Works.

The Chickasaw Cooperage Company is an important industry, as are the three cracker and candy manufactories, the Pioneer Cotton Mills, the two ice factories, the six flour and corn-meal mills, the broom factory, the brick manufactories, the soap factory, the trunk manufactories, and the hundreds of other miscellaneous establishments and industries which can not be even named in this work. The entire number and value of manufacturing industries in Shelby County in 1880 may be found in another place in this brief sketch.

The first paper established in Memphis was the Memphis *Advocate*, by Thomas Phoebus in January, 1827, the eleventh number appearing March 27 of that year. The *Advocate* was published several years as a weekly, as was also the *Times*, both of which papers were consolidated and named the *Times and Advocate*, this name being afterward changed to the *Gazette*, with O. P. Gaines, editor. After the *Gazette* came the Memphis *Enquirer*, Vol. III, No. 295, appearing December 13, 1849. The *Daily Express* was started in 1850, No. 176 of Vol. I appearing September 11 of that year, published by J. C. Klinck & Son. The *Western World* was published by Solon Borland, afterward for many years the United States senator from Arkansas. The full name of this paper was the *Western World and Memphis Banner of the Constitution*. In 1840 the paper was purchased by Col. Henry Van Pelt and its name changed to the *Appeal*, the first number of which appeared April 21, 1841, and was dressed in mourning on account of the distinguished President of the United States, William Henry Harrison. John R. McClanahan was associated with Col. Van Pelt until 1851, when the colonel died, and William Hutton became a partner and remained until 1857, when his interest was sold to McClanahan and Leon Trousdale, the latter gentleman having become a partner in 1854. Mr. Trousdale sold his interest in 1859 to W. F. Dill, when the firm became McClanahan & Dill. This firm erected the *Appeal* building on Union Street, where the paper was published when the Union Army entered the city, June 6, 1862. Early that morning the press and material were started south to Jackson, Miss., where the paper was published until the spring of 1863, when, as Gen. Grant's forces entered West Jackson, the last of the *Appeal's* material was crossing Pearl River. The wagon carrying part of it being too heavily loaded, the proof press was thrown into the river, whence it was recovered in a few days. From Jackson the paper was carried to Atlanta, where it was published until the early spring of 1865, when it was again forced to move on by the victorious forces of the Union Army. It was finally overtaken by Gen. Wilson at Columbus, Ga., April 16, 1865, when the material was destroyed and Mr. Dill, then with the office, put under bond not to publish the paper again during the war. After the close of the war McClanahan and Dill returned to Memphis, the former during the summer of 1865 falling from the Gayoso House and being killed. The publication of the *Appeal* was resumed November 5, 1865, by W. F. Dill, and J. H. McMahon soon became connected with it. Mr. Dill dying shortly afterward his widow continued its publication until February 1, 1867, when it became the property of J. S. C. Hogan & Co., composed of J. S. C. Hogan, Albert Pike and John Ainslie. After the lapse of about two years Ainslie, Keating & Co. became the proprietors, and then Keating, English & Co., which firm published the paper until December, 1870, when it was sold at chancery sale to the *Appeal* Publishing Company, by whom it was published until January, 1876, when it passed to Gallaway (M. C.) & Keating (J. M.). Both the daily and weekly *Appeal* circulate largely in West Tennessee, Alabama, Mississippi and Arkansas. It has always been a Democratic paper, and in the bitter contests of party it has been thoroughly identified with the majority of the people among whom it has circulated, that majority having usually been Democratic.

The *Morning Bulletin* was founded by J. H. McMahon in the fall of 1855, the publishers being H. D. Bulkley and John Hitchler, and was continued under the same management until May, 1861. In politics it was a conservative Whig, not advocating in 1856 the election of any particular candidate. In 1860 it advocated the election of John Bell to the Presidency, and Edward Everett to the Vice-Presidency. In May, 1861, the *Bulletin* was purchased by P. B. Wills & Co. (J. B. Bingham) and by them published until the Federal occupation of the city in 1862, when Mr. Wills withdrew, Mr. Bingham continuing the publication until after the war. Mr. Wills soon afterward resumed his interest and the two published it for several years before it was suspended. The *Memphis Sun*, by W. A. McCloy & Co., succeeded the *Bulletin* for a few years.

The *Commercial* was started late in the war by J. M. Keating and associates, and the *Argus* by Priddy & Brower. Both were consolidated under the name of the *Commercial and Argus*. After being published a few years it was suspended. J. R. Bingham published the *Daily Herald* during 1877–79.

The *Memphis Daily Avalanche* was started in 1858 by M. C. Gallaway, who remained with the paper until the breaking out of the war, when the paper was suspended. After the suppression of the Rebellion the *Avalanche* was resumed, Mr. Gallaway remaining with it until 1872 or 1873, when he sold out to Col. J. R. Kellar. He, in 1876, formed a partnership with R. A. Thompson, the latter being business manager, and the former, editor. In 1878 Mr. Thompson died of yellow fever, and in 1880 a stock company was formed, Mr. Kellar retiring. During the latter part of the Kellar and Thompson proprietorship, D. A Brower, now of the Little Rock *Gazette*, was editor, and was succeeded in 1879 by F. S. Nichols, who upon his death in 1884 was succeeded by H. M. Doak, who retained his editorship until December, 1886, when he was succeeded by A. B. Pickett, late city editor of the *Memphis Appeal*. In politics the *Avalanche* is mildly Democratic, and is an excellent newspaper.

The *Public Ledger* was started September 1, 1865, by E. and W. Whitmore under the firm name of Whitmore Bros., and named after the Philadelphia *Public Ledger*, Mr. William Whitmore having then recently paid a visit to Philadelphia and been highly pleased with the office of that paper. The Memphis *Public Ledger* was the outgrowth of a job printing office established in 1856, by William Whitmore & Co., and was established after the war, upon the return of E. Whitmore from the Confederate Army, as an afternoon paper. It is now the oldest afternoon paper in the Southern States that has been continuously published. The first editor was F. Y. Rockett, an experienced journalist before the war. He was succeeded by Col. J. J. Du Bose in 1868, who held the position two or three years, and was succeeded in 1872 by the present editor, J. Harvey Mathes, who had been city editor two or three years. In 1870 E. Whitmore became sole proprietor, and so remained until May, 1886, when, retaining the job printing office, he sold the *Ledger* to J. Harvey Mathes and W. L. Trask, Mr. Trask having been engaged on the paper eight years as commercial and city editor. The weekly edition of the *Ledger* has been published since 1869. The *Ledger* has always been conservatively Democratic. The policy of the paper is expressed in the following extract from its columns of August, 1886: "It is our aim to treat all men, of whatever creed, color or politics, fairly, justly and courteously. The gospel of tolerance and honest difference of opinion in regard to affairs of state, society, morals and government, is destined to be the secular gospel of the near future."

The *Southern Post-Journal* is a consolidation of two papers, the Memphis *Journal* and the Memphis *Post*. The *Journal* was started in 1875 by Charles Weidt and conducted by him until 1878 when, on account of the yellow fever, he left the city, returning, however, after the epidemic had spent its force, and in the fall he sold the paper to J. B. Huehlefeld. In 1880 the *Post* was started by a stock company with Carl Koch manager, in opposition to the *Journal* and was run about nine months when it was purchased by Zimmerman & Bro., who in 1882 purchased the *Journal*, consolidated the two and changed the name to the Southern *Post-Journal*. Since 1883 Louis G. Fritz has been editor of this paper. It is a weekly, nine-column folio, is published in the German language and is devoted to the interests of the Germans of Tennessee, Mississippi and Arkansas.

The *Union Triangle* was started in 1884 by August Hitzfeld as the *Universal Triangle*, for the purpose of advocating the cause of the Universal Brotherhood. It remained true to the interests of that order until the establishment of the *Columbic Union*, which was incorporated

June 24, 1886, under the laws of Ohio, the incorporators being Thomas J. Harcourt, Samuel B. Lowenstein, Julius Kahn, Edward J. McBride and Sarah Durward. The purpose of this incorporation is benevolence toward the members thereof and their families. The officers of the society are superior president, A. Hitzfeld, Memphis; superior vice-president, Mrs. Sarah Durward, New Orleans; superior secretary, T. J. Harcourt, Cincinnati, Ohio; superior treasurer, E. J. McBride, St. Louis, Mo. By the first anniversary of its existence its present membership of 1,000 is confidently expected to be 2,000, when a $2,000 insurance policy will be worth its face. The *Union Triangle* is issued monthly and has a circulation of 5,000.

The Memphis *Sunday Times* was first issued on the first Sunday in December, 1884, by Walker Kennedy and O. P. Bard, is a seven-column folio, and was devoted to local, social and literary matters. In August, 1885, C. L. Pullen bought the interest of Mr. Bard, since when the *Times* has been conducted by Kennedy & Pullen, the former gentleman being the editor and the latter, business manager. The form of the paper was changed in September, 1885, to a six-column quarto, and its scope enlarged at the same time by adding Talmage's sermons and a continued story. In March, 1886, the paper was again enlarged to a seven-column quarto. On November 8, 1886, the office was transferred from No. 15 Union Street to the rooms formerly occupied by the Young Men's Christian Association in Odd Fellows' building on the corner of Main and North Court Streets. About the 1st of January 1886, the proprietors commenced illustrating the *Times* by the photo-engraving process, and it now is a handsomely illustrated home paper.

The Memphis Daily *Scimitar* was started January 15, 1882, by G. P. M. Turner, as the Memphis Monday Morning *Scimitar*. It was a nine-column folio and its office was at 65 Adams Street. The *Daily Scimitar* was started September 11, 1883, and named the Memphis *Evening Scimitar*. At this time the office was moved to 15 Jefferson Street where it still remains. The editor, Mr. Turner, was assisted by Miss Hattie A. Paul, who had full charge of the business department until the sale of the paper on January 3, 1887, to S. P. Barinds and his associates, with N. Picard in editorial charge, Mr. Barinds himself assuming the business management. The city editor under the new *regime* is H. P. Richetts. The *Monday Morning Scimitar* is still published as a weekly paper, and has a circulation of nearly 3,400, while the evening *Scimitar* has a circulation of about 3,000. In connection with this paper is an excellent job printing office fully equipped with the most improved printing machinery, including a two-revolution Campbell press. The *Scimitar* has always been the consistent champion of the labor cause, and is very popular with the industrial classes, but it is not in any sense the advocate of anarchy or socialism.

The *Southern Record* was started in July, 1885, by H. P. Hanson and M. F. Blalack, as a weekly workingmen's paper. At first it was named the Memphis *Weekly Record*, and was a six-column folio. Its publication commenced on Jefferson Street, between Main and Second Streets. It moved to 295 Second Street in March, 1886, and was sold August 21, 1886, to J. P. Hanson and C. E. Gebhardt, who now conduct it at 20 Jefferson Street. They enlarged the paper to a six-column quarto and placed the editorial department in charge of T. E. Hanson. The circulation of the *Record* is about 4,000, the subscription price being $1 per year.

The *Watchman* was started in 1876 by C. C. Dickinson as the *Missionary Baptist*. In 1882 T. Nightingale joined Mr. Dickinson, and they ran the paper a year, when they sold it to the present company, who changed the name to Memphis *Watchman*. It is a four-column, eight-page paper, and is devoted to the interests of the colored race. In politics the paper is Republican. It is edited by J. T. Turner, and has a circulation of 1,200.

The *Living Way* was started February 10, 1884, under the auspices of the Tennessee Baptist Educational Convention, with W. A. Brinkley as editor and R. N. Countee, business manager, at its present location, 161 Beale Street. It is a weekly paper, and has always been the fearless foe of secret societies as they have existed among the colored people of Memphis, such societies having in many cases been established merely for purposes of fraud. The circulation of the *Living Way* is about 1,000, and it was one of the first papers to employ colored men as compositors. The entire outfit of the paper is worth about $2,500.

Adam is a "weekly journal for the Christian home." It was founded in March, 1885, by Rev. William Walsh, pastor of St. Brigid's Church. The reason given for the choice of this singular name was that the editor purposed speaking through its columns to all who claimed Adam as their great ancestor. It was originally a thirty-two column paper, and has since then been doubled in size. It was conducted solely by the Rev. William Walsh until June, 1886, when the Adam Publishing Company was established with a capital limited to $30,000, and with its office at 12 Jefferson Street. The officers of this company are John S. Sullivan, president; P. McCadden, vice-president; Rev. William Walsh, secretary. The other directors are John Walsh, Patrick Boyle and Col. H. R. Bate. This paper represents the Catholic elements of the population of Memphis.

The *Mississippi Valley Medical Journal* was founded in January, 1880, by Dr. Julius Wise, as a forty-eight page octavo pamphlet. Dr. Wise published it about eighteen months, at the end of which time Dr. Sim purchased it and became sole proprietor and editor in July, 1881. Dr. E. A. Neely became associate editor in March, 1886. The magazine is devoted to medical science and to the discussion of sanitary measures. It favors the allopathic school of medicine, and has for its proper field the territory surrounding Memphis and bounded by the fields occupied by similar journals published at Nashville, St. Louis, Fort Worth and New Orleans.

The *Tennessee Baptist* was started in 1834, in Nashville, by the Rev. R. B. C. Howell, D. D., who was its first editor. For the first ten years of the paper's existence its circulation was quite limited, but in 1846 it passed into the control of Rev. J. R. Graves with a list of 1,005. The circulation increased slowly but steadily, and its name was changed to the *Tennessee Baptist*. Soon after Mr. Graves became the editor the *Baptist* became the advocate of "Old Landmarkism," and its circulation then rapidly increased. In May, 1858, its editors were announced as J. R. Graves, J. M. Pendleton and A. C. Dayton. When the war broke out the circulation was larger than that of any other Baptist paper in the world. Its publication was suspended during the war, but resumed upon the return of peace, the place of publication being transferred to Memphis and the name changed to its original, the *Baptist*. In 1876 Mr. Graves, still retaining its editorial management, leased its publication to J. S. Mahaffy and G. W. Cranberry, the latter gentleman retiring in 1881 and Mr. Graves assuming his interest in the publication. The firm name has since been Graves & Mahaffy. In 1876 Mahaffy & Cranberry established the Baptist Book House, which has become the headquarters for Baptist literature in the South. Among the books published by this house are "The Seven Dispensations," a revised edition of "The Great Iron Wheel," "The Trilemma," "Middle Life," "Old Landmarkism," "Inter-communion," and a series of denominational tracts averaging sixty pages.

The local secret societies of Memphis are the following: Master Masons—Penn Chapter, No. 22; Memphis Chapter, No. 95; R. & S. M. Eureka Council, No. 6; Knights Templar, Memphis Commandery No. 4; St. Elmo Commandery, No. 15; Masonic Board of Relief, No. 1.

Independent Order of Odd Fellows—Memphis Lodge, No. 6; Chickasaw Lodge, No. 8; Schiller Lodge, No. 140; Banner Lodge, No. 147; Gayoso Encampment, No. 3.

Ancient Order of United Workmen—Equity Lodge, No. 20; Johnson Lodge, No. 21; Bluff City Lodge, No. 22; Chickasaw Lodge, No. 40.

Independent Order of Berna Breth; Euphrates Lodge, No. 35; Hiddekel L dge, No. 10; Simon Tuska Lodge, No. 192.

K. S. B.—Ezra Lodge, No. 39; Noph Lodge, No. 137.

I. O. F. S. of I.—Memphis Lodge, No. 108.

Knights of Honor—Memphis Lodge, No. 196; Chelsea Lodge, No. 280; Diamond Lodge, No. 583: Esperanza Lodge, No. 3105: Fountain Lodge, No. 296; Germaina Lodge, No. 369; Unity Lodge, No. 217; Pearl Lodge, No. 92; Knights and Ladies of Honor, Teutonia Lodge, No. 25; Knights and Ladies of Honor, and Rose Lodge, No. 405.

Knights of Pythias—Tennessee Division, No. 1; Roland Division, No. 2; Lodges Pythian, Castle, Constantine, No. 23; Jonathan Woods, No. 30; Memphis, No. 6; Roland, No. 25; Progress, No. 39; Endowment Rank, Section 36, and Section, 370.

American Legion of Honor—Chickasaw Council, No. 789; Memphis Council, No. 1183.

Grand Army of the Republic—Memphis Post, No. 3.

Raleigh is historic not for what it now is but from what it has been. The place was named in respect to Joseph Graham, the first circuit clerk of the county, who was from near Raleigh, N. C., and who assisted the commissioners James Fentress, Benjamin Reynolds, William Martin and Robert Jetton in locating the county seat in December, 1824. The land upon which Raleigh was built was obtained from Wilson Sanderlin and James Freeman. The first settler in the neighborhood of Raleigh is said to have been a man by the name of Tapp, who came from North Carolina to that place in 1816. Here he lived and died in the land of his adoption at the age of nearly eighty years, not, however, until such a change had been wrought over the county as if done by the magician's wand. Among the early settlers of Raleigh and vicinity may be mentioned John Only, Benjaman McAlpin, Wilson Sanderlin, James Wilson, W. P. Reaves, J. R. King, Elias Pharr, Abram Bayless, Dr. Benjamin Hawkins, Thomas Taylor, William Sanders, E. H. Porter, Jesse M. Tate, J. E. Martin, Jefferson Messick, S. M. Allen, A. B. Taylor, T. B. Smith, —— Reinhurst, Benjaman Duncan and Dr. David Coleman. After the courts began to meet at Raleigh the growth of the place was rapid. It reached its maximum prosperity about 1836. At this time it did an extensive business, perhaps exceeding that of Memphis. The leading business firms at that time were Abram Bayless, Jessee M. Tate, Taylor & Sanderlin, Rawlings & Wren. A saw and gristmill was built on Wolf River by Wilson Sanderlin. At the time of its greatest prosperity Raleigh contained from 1,200 to 1,500 inhabitants. The only grown person who was living in Raleigh in 1836 who still lives is J. J. Rawlings of Memphis. The only ones of any age who lived there at that time are Squire J. M. Coleman and Dr. Duncan. In 1829 provision was made for the erection of an academy at Raleigh by the election of Wm. Battle, Daniel Dunn, J. S. Lemaster and James Rembert as trustees. This was done under the law of 1806 for building academies in the various counties of the State. In a few years the funds of the institution had so increased that a new academy was erected. They were then known as the Raleigh Male and Female Academies. At one time these institutions contained 400 pupils. Courts continued to meet at Raleigh till they were broken up by the war and were soon after moved to Memphis. Such distinguished men as Tapp, Brown, Dunlap, V. T. Barry, Henry Berry, Yerger, Small, Scruggs and Coe were familiar to the citizens of Raleigh. Amusing stories are told of the sudden and unceremonious adjournment of court at this place on the supposed approach of the Federal Army. Owing to muddy roads and the great commercial interests of Raleigh, a great deal of money was expended in the vain attempt to improve the navigation of Wolf River. Raleigh now contains only about 300 inhabitants. There are two or three business houses, two churches, a Methodist and a Presbyterian, and a good school. The town is surrounded by a rich farming country. From the manuscript report of Dr. Enno Sander, analytic chemist of St. Louis, in 1866 it is learned that geologically the formation around Raleigh is of the tertiary period and of the La Grange group, consisting of layers of sand with clay, and containing beds of lignite and marl and sand colored with iron oxides, the depth of the whole amounting to about 200 to 400 feet. The elevation of the place is 127 feet above Memphis. Tapp's Hole, a place containing some peculiar natural physical features is the source of some excellent medicinal springs whose virtues were accidentally discovered by Dr. Coleman in 1842. The following is the analysis of each of the four springs made by Dr. Sander in 1866.

MARBLE SPRING.

Protocarbonate of iron	.193
Chloride of sodium	.146
Sulphate of soda	.214
Sulphate of potassa	.356
Sulphate of alumina	.086
Carbonate of lime	.060
Free carbonic acid	.450

FREESTONE SPRING.

Chloride of sodium	.182
Chloride of potassium	.078

Chloride of calcium... .135
Chloride of magnesium... .003
Bicarbonate of magnesium.. .143
Protocarbonate of iron... .042
Sulphate of lime... .175
Free carbonic acid... 1.005

BOX SPRING.

Chloride of sodium .... .190
Sulphate of soda... .142
Sulphate of potassa.. .077
Bicarbonate of magnesia.. .044
Protocarbonate of iron... .296
Carbonate of lime.. .201
Sulphate of alumina .... .153
Free carbonic acid 1.793

BEACH SPRING.

Protocarbonate of iron... .421
Chloride of magnesium .... .083
Chloride of calcium.. .235
Chloride of sodium .... .275
Chloride of potassium.. .015
Free carbonic acid... 2.003

The specific gravity of each of these springs is 995. The temperature of Marble Spring is 68° with a range of 10°; the temperature of Freestone is 66°, and each of the other two range from 72° to 74°. A railroad seems to be the main thing needful for the development of these springs into a great health resort. In 1873 a narrow gauge road was begun from Memphis to Raleigh. The road was graded to the national cemetery by private subscription. In addition to the amount of private subscriptions $50,000 in county bonds were issued to aid the enterprise. The contract for the completion of the road was undertaken but the contractor failed in the financial stagnation of 1873-74. A new charter was issued for the Memphis & Raleigh Springs Road on March 18, 1885. This was chartered by D. H. Porter, John Donnelly, J. M. Coleman and others.

Arlington, lying on the Louisville & Nashville Railroad, twenty-five miles from Memphis, was located as a depot about 1856. The grounds of nearly five acres were donated by Gen. Sam'l J. Hays. It was called Withe Depot on account of its being the principal shipping point from Old Hickory Withe of Fayette County. Capt. Henry Pittman, who was the first depot agent, built the first dwelling-house in the place. He used the depot building for a schoolhouse during the war. John Dwyer, an Irishman, built the first storehouse in the place. His stock consisted mainly of bad whisky, as it is said the whisky came near drowning out the fire when his house was burned. The second store was built by Alexander Donelson, a planter, who lives about four miles south of Arlington. This house was occupied by Ike Berlin, a Russian Jew, during the war. All the land surrounding Arlington belonged to the estate of Gen. Hay until 1868, when the executor of the estate laid off the town and sold the lots at public sale. The village began to grow. The place was called Haysville in honor of Gen. Hays, but as no postoffice could be established in that name it was called Withe, until 1883, when it was changed to Arlington. The village now contains 500 inhabitants, and has a steam saw and grist-mill, steam cotton-gin, stores, livery stables, shops, etc., also a Methodist and a Presbyterian Church, and two negro churches. In 1883 the Methodist Church located the Memphis District High School at Arlington. The building is situated on a commanding site overlooking the town and surrounding country. This is a flourishing institution and is known as the college. The following were pioneer settlers in the neighborhood of Arlington, each of whom assisted in opening up the country: Joel Herring came from North Carolina in 1836, John Poore from north Alabama in 1833; Alex Cothran, North Carolina, 1830; Jacob Peck, South Carolina, 1830; Squire Wm. Battle, a very prominent man from North Carolina, 1830; J. Gray, North Carolina, 1845; G. L. Douglass, 1832; W. M. King, Georgia, 1828; J. M. Thomas, South Carolina, 1830; Jacob Kirkendal, Georgia, 1828; J. E. Kelley, Alabama, 1830; Jessee Osborn, Alabama, 1829; Lewis Herring, North Carolina, 1830; Alexander Donelson, Middle Tennessee, 1830; C. A. Starr, Virginia, 1830; George Cherry, 1842. Other well known men were Wm. Exum, E. E. Greenlee and J. Royster.

The second town or city in Shelby County is Collierville, which was named in honor of one of the pioneer settlers. A small business was done as far back as 1840 at the place. In 1848 it had two stores, one owned by S. B. Buford and the other by J. B. Williford. There was no church there at that time and but one schoolhouse, a small, log building. A saloon took prominence among the early enterprises, while cock-fighting and horse-racing became the common amusements of its devotees. The war destroyed most of the business houses and left but few of the residences. Two small engagements were fought at this place during the war. Since the war new life has been instilled into the place. It now boasts of 1,200 inhabitants, good brick business houses, nine dry goods stores, eight grocery stores, two drug stores, two hardware stores, two furniture stores, three livery stables, two hotels and shops, grist-mill, saw-mill, etc. Among the oldest business men are Dr. Stratton, J. K. Waddy and J. T. Briggs. There are two colleges, Bellevue and Miss Holdens' school. The two have an enrollment of over 300. The churches are the Methodist Episcopal South, Christian, Missionary Baptist and Presbyterian.

The postmasters before the war were M. F. Robinson and J. L. Jones. Then since that time have been G. H. Davis, R. W. Ramsey, M. S. Say, Mrs. E. M. Bleckley, Thomas Bleckley, S. H. Russell and the present incumbent, J. T. Williams. Collierville was incorporated by an act passed February 17, 1870. J. B. Abbington was the first mayor with the following aldermen: J. Lynch, John Moore, S. D. Mangum, A. S. Stratton and J. R. Waddy. The town is located near the southeast corner of Shelby County, within four miles of the Mississippi line, from which State it receives a large trade. The present mayor is R. F. C. Moss; the aldermen are John W. Houston, F. M. Gilliland, Jr., W. C. Coopwood, T. H. Humphreys and J. E. Harrell. Magnolia Cemetery, near Collierville, is a striking feature of the place. It receives great care and is a chartered institution of which J. R. Waddy is president.

Bartlett lies about eleven miles from Memphis, on the Louisville & Nashville Railroad. It was formerly called Union Depot and was a mere station on the railroad at its first construction. In 1866 it was incorporated and the name was changed to Bartlett in honor of Maj. G. M. Bartlett, who was one of the pioneer settlers in the neighborhood of the place. Maj. Bartlett was not only a pioneer settler, but at one time a magistrate, a member of the Legislature and a business man of Memphis. Bartlett is situated at the corner of three large tracts of land—Pruden's, Ward's and Bartlett's tracts. Joseph Walker was one of the first business men of the place. Bartlett had little growth until after the war. One of the most active men in building up the place was I. B. Mercer. The village now contains about 300 inhabitants. The principal business firms are Small & Massey, W. O. Edwards, W. R. Cross & Co., A. B. Lurry and F. J. Warner. These are all general stores. There are two grist-mills, each having a gin attached, one mill owned by J. M. Davis, the other by M. Gotten. Bartlett contains three churches; Methodist, Baptist and Cumberland Presbyterian; the Methodist formerly worshiped at Pisgah but since a class was organized in Bartlett, and about 1870 a new house was built in the town. The membership of the church is about 100. The Baptists formerly worshiped in a log house, but have since erected a nice frame building. The Cumberland Presbyterians have a church, but do not maintain regular church services. A very pleasant feature of Bartlett is her excellent school. The school was chartered in 1885, by Dr. John McBrooks as president of the board; John F. Cochran, secretary and treasurer, with S. Williford, M. Jones, J. A. Arbuckle and others as directors. The school is managed by Neuhardt & Neuhardt, assisted by Miss Lizzie Pope. The schools are carried on about ten months in the year and have an enrollment of about 100 pupils.

The board owns a good schoolhouse in what was formerly the Bartlett courthouse. The country surrounding Bartlett has a soil of moderate fertility, but some of it is much worn by continuous growth of cotton. This land, however, is easily reclaimed and yields excellent fruits and vegetables.

The pioneer settlers in the vicinity of Bartlett include Maj. Bartlett, above mentioned, Drs. Samuel and Washington Bond and John Bond. The three Bonds were brothers and came to the county from North Alabama. They all opened up plantations in the virgin forests. Joseph Ward settled a part of the land on which Bartlett now stands. Joseph Blackwell settled in the same neighborhood. S. L. Berryhill has been living in the vicinity for half a century or more. He is one of the few pioneers still living. Joseph Locke, a pioneer and a good man, left a family and a good name. Besides these the Crenshaws, Pulliams and Prudens might be mentioned. Bond Station, four miles east of Bartlett, is a station on the same road. It contains a store, postoffice and gin. Cedar Grove is a station one mile west of Bartlett.

Germantown, comprising about 200 inhabitants, is situated about fifteen miles southeast of Memphis on the Memphis & Charleston Railroad. It took its name from the fact that a large number of German families settled in that vicinity in an early day. The land where the village stands was owned by Nancy Shepherd. The first business in the place was done about 1830. Among the first merchants was a man named Rash. Soon after came Lucker and Schieley, two Germans. This village, being near the line of the old Memphis & La Grange Railroad, it was a place of great commercial activity from 1840 to 1850 and even some time later. The place was incorporated about 1854 but the charter was allowed to lapse during the war. It was reincorporated, however, in 1880, on petition by R. T. Anderson, E. M. Cole, J. A. Thompson and seventeen others. Cotton and the usual farm products are handled extensively at Germantown. The principal business firms of the present time are C. M. Callis, G. W. Thomas, W. E. Miller, E. W. Gorman, Hatcher & King and Tuggle & Kimbrough. Germantown was terribly scourged by the yellow fever in 1878. About fifty per cent of those taking the disease died. The disease was imported from other plague stricken sections. Germantown is well supplied with churches, Methodist Episcopal Church South, Presbyterian and Baptist. Each of these denominations have good houses of worship. The Presbyterian Church alone escaped the ravages of the war. The membership of these churches is about 50, 75 and 125, respectively. The most distinguished divine in this vicinity is Rev. Evans, of Germantown, who has been administering to the spiritual interests of his flock for more than a quarter of a century. Two very distinguished physicians of this place were Drs. Morgan and Cornelius. Present physicians are Drs. Williams and Yancy. Germantown Lodge, No. 95, was instituted by dispensation in April, 1841, and was regularly chartered October 7, 1841. The officers were Joseph Collis, W. M.; B. Duke, S. W.; Jas. Kimbrough, J. W.; W. Evans, Tyler; Chas. D. McLean, Treas.; J. D. White, L. Henderson, Sec. A hall was erected by this order in 1852, which still stands. The present officers of the lodge are A. J. Wight, W. M.; J. S. Weir, S. W.; A. G. Kimbrough, J. W.; E. W. Gorman, Sec.; R. T. Anderson, Treas.; N. F. Harrison and N. J. Ulander, Deacons; G. W. Randoll, Tyler. Present membership, 34.

Caro Lodge No. 1664, Knights of Honor, was organized June 28, 1879, with thirteen members. The present membership is forty-seven. The officers are Robt. Payne, S. W., and Wm. Evans, J. W. This lodge also meets in the Masonic Hall.

The public schools of Germantown are taught in the Masonic Hall, first floor. The enrollment of pupils amounts to about 100. The school term lasts about five months. They are under control of Prof. B. J. T. Moss, with Mrs. Moss as assistant, and Miss Jessie Williams primary. Other stations or villages are Buntyn, White, Ridgeway, Forrest Hill, Bailey, Ray's Station and Holly's Crossing.

Few if any settlers located in the vicinity of Germantown previous to the year 1825. Wm. Twyford came from Kentucky in 1825 and settled beyond Wolf River. He is said to have assisted in building the first store house in Memphis. The Ecklins—Joshua and Robert—came from North Carolina in the fall of 1833 and settled on a plantation almost entirely in the woods. Frances Wright's Nashoba settlement was entered mainly in 1824. The history of this settlement is related elsewhere. Wesley and Winfred Cole came to the county about 1833. The Masseys, Benjamin Robbins, Eppy and J. D. White were in the county before 1835. John Gant was from Middle Tennessee, but afterward moved to Texas. Squire Henry T. Jones came to Shelby County the last of 1835, and still lives near Germantown, hale and hearty, at eighty-six. Mrs. Lucy Coghill has lived in the county since 1825. Others who deserve mention are the Bonds, E. Pulliam, B. Willett, E. Amonett, E. Clark, Thomas Davison and Thomas Allen. Thomas Davison was one of the first circuit riders ever in West Tennessee. The majority of these persons opened plantations out of the virgin forests and were men of the highest character.

Lucy is a pleasant little village on the line of the Chesapeake & Ohio Railroad. It is a fine business point.

SHELBY COUNTY.

William A. Albright, a farmer by occupation, was born in Haywood County, Tenn., September 30, 1838, and was the second child in a family of two sons and two daughters born to Jonathan and Mary (Marr) Albright, and is of German-Scotch descent. The father was born in North Carolina, December 30, 1812, and moved to Haywood County, Tenn., where he married and lived until 1845, when he moved to Shelby County, and settled near the present home of our subject. He was a member of the Cumberland Presbyterian Church the greater part of his life and died at his home April 18, 1863. The mother was born in Virginia, October 1, 1810, and died at the homestead in Shelby County, December 1, 1861. Our subject was raised on the farm, and has always given his time to agricultural pursuits. He enlisted in the Confederate Army and belonged to Col. Baker's regiment. He was captured at Island No. 10, and taken North where he was held first, at Camp Randall, at Madison, Wis., then at Camp Douglas, at Chicago, for four months and was then exchanged at Vicksburg, Miss. He was married at Marshall County, Miss., September 25, 1866, to Miss Sallie E. Ford, a daughter of Rev. Miles H. Ford, of the Methodist Episcopal Church South, and a native of Tennessee. Eight of the nine children that were the issue of this marriage, are living. The mother of this family was born at Oxford, Miss., June 8, 1848. Mr. Albright is a Mason and a Democrat. He owns 514 acres of land four miles northwest of Collierville, and raises grain and cotton, making the latter the chief market product. Mr. and Mrs. Albright are worthy members of the Methodist Episcopal Church South. He possesses fine business qualifications, and is justly entitled to the respect and confidence accorded him by all who know him.

C. H. Albright, agent of the Southern Express Company for Memphis, was born in Alamance County, N. C., October 9, 1846. His parents are still living at the old homestead. His father, John G. Albright, who is postmaster at Graham, N. C., is over seventy years of age. Our subject received a fair English education, and at the age of fifteen enlisted as a soldier in the Confederate Army, serving under Magruder at Yorktown and in front of Richmond till after the hard fighting around that city in 1862, when he was mustered out of service on account of his youthfulness. In 1864 he re-enlisted in Gen. Wade Hampton's cavalry corps and served till the end, at Appomattox. After the war he remained at home engaged in business till January, 1866, when he went to Vicksburg, Miss., where he engaged in the hotel business for two or three years, leaving it to go to merchandising, which he followed till 1871, when he sold out and entered the service of the Southern Express Company. He has continued with that company since, filling various positions with credit to himself and profit to his company in Memphis, Jackson (Miss.), St. Louis, Mo., and just prior to assuming the duties of his present position, was route agent west of the Mississippi River. He has been agent at Memphis about two years. He has a family consisting of wife and two bright little boys, and lives in his own home, a beautiful cottage in a large yard, within easy reach of his office. He and his wife are members of the Presbyterian Church. She was the daughter of an old Presbyterian minister of Memphis—Rev. James O. Stedman, D.D., who died several years ago.

James P. Alexander, grocery and drug merchant at 380 Beale Street, Memphis, established the business in 1886. He is the son of John D. and Emma (Pirtle) Alexander. The father was general passenger agent for a railroad corporation. Our subject was born and reared in Rutherford County, Tenn., and was educated at Sweet Water, E. Tenn.; also at Woodbury and Tiptonville, of the same State. Soon after completing his education he engaged as clerk in the drug business in Tiptonville, and here continued for three years. He then purchased the stock of his employer and remained in business at this place for four years, after which he went to Little Rock, Ark., and established a drug business there. After a short time he sold out and came to Memphis, where he established his present business, in which he has been quite successful. In 1880 he married Emma Whitford, daughter of A. S. Whitford, a cotton factor of Memphis. This union resulted in the birth of three children, all of whom are living. Mr. Alexander is a Democrat in politics, and a pleasant, social gentleman.

Rev. J. D. Anderson was born in Tippah County, Miss., March 22, 1852, and is the son of James Anderson, who was born in Jackson County, Tenn., in 1809, where he was raised and educated, and in 1834 moved to Mississippi, where he married Miss M. J. McGill, who was born in the year 1823, and is still living at the old homestead in Tippah County, Mississippi. Seven sons and two daughters were born to this marriage, our subject being the fifth child. The father was a farmer all of his life, and an old line Whig in politics, and was strongly opposed to secession, using his vote and his influence to keep his State in the Union; but when the war commenced he went with his State, and while on a trip to Louisiana to procure supplies for himself and neighbors, he contracted the disease from which he died in May, 1862. Our subject was raised on the farm, and received his preparatory education in the common schools of the county, and afterward spent two years at the Mississippi College, then two years at the Southern Baptist Theological Seminary at Greenville, S. C., and two years at the University of Mississippi, from which he graduated in five departments, and two years later received the honorary degree of A. M. from the Southwestern Baptist University at Jackson, Tenn. Mr. Anderson has been in charge of the Baptist Church at Germantown for four years. December 29, 1874, he was married at Blue Mountain, Miss., to Miss Maggie E. Lowrey, daughter of Gen. M. P. Lowrey, who held the rank of brigadier-general, under Hood, during the war. Four daughters have blessed this marriage: Florence Modena, Mary Rolly, Janie Sanford and Agnes Brooks. The mother was born in Corinth, Miss., January 29, 1852. Mr. Anderson is a Democrat, and strongly in favor of prohibition. He is a prominent Mason. Mrs. Anderson is a devout member of the Baptist Church. They have a pleasant home in the central part of Germantown. Mr. Anderson is a minister of fine ability, possessing rare oratorical power and being an unusually well read man. He has been very earnest and very successful in his work, and has the respect and affection of all who know him.

David O. Andrews is a native of Mississippi, and was born June 8, 1854, and was brought by his parents to Memphis when a child, and was here reared and educated. He first engaged in the grocery business as clerk for C. R. Ryan and finally became a member of the firm, and is now the active manager of the establishment. February 18, 1879, he was joined in matrimony to Miss Lula Betts, of Mississippi, and by her has two living children, both daughters. Mr. Andrews is a Democrat, a member of the K. of H. and of the I. O. O. F. and of the Methodist Episcopal Church. The firm of C. R. Ryan & Co., wholesale and retail grocers, is composed of Frank T. Ryan and D. O. Andrews. The business was established by the late C. R. Ryan in 1876, Mr. Andrews becoming a member in 1884, and Frank T. Ryan taking an interest in November, 1885, upon the death of C. R. Ryan. The firm has one of the largest retail trades in the city, and employs four commercial travelers and twenty-eight men to do the business in this city. Their trade extends over Tennessee, Mississippi, Alabama, Arkansas and Missouri.

E. M. Apperson, senior member of the firm of E. M. Apperson & Co., first came to Memphis in 1838, and located here in 1840, selecting this place from many he had visited throughout the South. In 1841 he formed the partnership, Allen & Apperson, which existed until 1847 when he bought Allen's interest and formed the present firm, though his associates have been often changed. His partners have been as follows: C. D. Loach, David Adams, W. A. Jones, G. B. Rambeau, and J. D. Crigley, the latter being the present partner. Mr. Apperson is a native of Virginia, and was born near Richmond on July 13, 1814. At the age of ten years he was left an orphan, and went to live with a relative in North Carolina. While living here he helped to build the first bridge over the Roanoke River and to construct the Wilmington & Welston Railroad, the third road built in the United States. His parents were John and Susan (Morecock) Apperson, natives of Virginia and agriculturists by occupation. The father died in 1825 and the mother in 1827; the former was of Scotch descent and the latter of English. In 1831. our subject married Miss Susan B. Morecock, who bore her husband nine children, only three of whom are now living. Mr. Apperson is an ex-president of the German National Bank and of the Memphis City Fire Insurance Company. Before the competition in trade became so strong, he sold annually as high as $1,500,000 worth of goods and handled annually as high as 43,000 bales of cotton. His annual trade is now about $200,000. Before the war he owned as high as 300 slaves. He is a member of the Masonic order.

T. B. Armistead, of the firm of Armistead Bros., dealers in staple and fancy groceries, dry goods, etc., is a native of Mississippi, and came to Tennessee in 1879, locating in Lauderdale County. Here he remained till 1884, when he came to Shelby County, located in the village of Arlington, and in partnership with his brother established his present business. Mr. Armistead received a limited country school education in the State of Mississippi. His parents, T. R. and Drucilla (Baird) Armistead, are natives of Georgia and Alabama, respectively. The father follows agricultural pursuits and is now a resident of De Soto County, Miss. The mother of our subject died in August, 1886, and was well esteemed and respected by her acquaintances. Mr. Armistead is a member of the K. of H.

Spencer F. Armour, farmer of Shelby County, is a son of Arthur and Susan (Shelton) Armour. The father was a native of Ireland, born about 1800, and came to America, settling in Mecklenburg County, N. C., where he met and married Miss Shelton. Both passed the remainder of their days in that county tilling the soil. Their family consisted of seven children—four sons and three daughters. Our subject was the fifth child of this family. He was born in Mecklenburg, N. C., May 28, 1832, and received a very limited education. At the age of twenty-one he went to Mississippi and farmed till 1871, when he came to this county. In 1862 he entered the Confederate service on detached duty, having volunteered five times and each time rejected on account of ill health. He served throughout the entire war, being detailed as deputy sheriff of Rankin County, Miss., which position he held the last nine months of the war. In 1856 he married Sarah Frances Ashley, of Mississippi, and the result of this union was seven children. As a farmer Mr. Armour has been very successful. When he came to Shelby County in 1871 he had nothing; now he owns 162 acres of the best land as the fruits of his own exertions. For fifteen years he has been a resident of this county, and has succeeded in gaining the reputation of a good farmer and an honest, upright citizen. He is a Master Mason, and his wife is a member of the Missionary Baptist Church. He is a Democrat in politics.

Dr. W. T. Arrington, of Memphis, Tenn., was born in Weakley County, Tenn., in 1836. There were six children in his father's family, three living. The parents were James H. and Mary W. Arrington, both natives of North Carolina. The father was born in 1801, and was educated at Chapel Hill College, North Carolina, and moved to Weakley County, Tenn., at an early date, where he was a farmer and where he died in 1862. The mother was a Miss Spruill, a daughter of Dr. Benjamin Spruill, who was an eminent physician; her mother was a Miss Blount a relative of William Blount. Mrs. Arrington was born in December 1804, and died in 1861. Dr. W. T. Arrington was educated in this' State, then commenced the study of medicine, but afterward abandoned, it for that of dentistry, and in 1856 graduated at the Philadelphia College of Dental Surgery; he then located at Trenton, Tenn., and practiced until 1860, when he moved to Memphis. In 1859 he married Miss Emma C., daughter of Archibald and Christiana Levy. Mrs. Arrington is a native of Gibson County; they have two sons: William T. and Guy. Dr. Arrington served some time in the Confederate Army, in the quartermaster's department, but owing to ill health was compelled to resign, and after the war returned to Memphis. Dr. Arrington is a man of energy and perseverance, and has done a great deal for the profession in Tennessee; was one of the organizers and the first secretary of the Tennessee Dental Association, also took a prominent part in organizing the Southern States Dental Association at Atlanta, Ga., in 1868, and was unanimously elected its first president; was elected to a professorship in the Cincinnati College of Dental Surgery in 1867, which position he resigned after serving one term. He also during that year became a member of the National Dental Association. He is a great lover of science and devotes much of his leisure time to study and scientific research and is a man of broad and advanced views. He served for a number of years on the public school board of Memphis, where he did much to correct abuses and bring about reform. Having secured and retained the confidence and esteem of his community, he has ever enjoyed a large and lucrative practice, commanding as he does the highest fees for his professional services. Dr. Arrington is justly regarded as one of the leading members of the dental profession.

Miss Cora H. Ashe. Among the prominent names in the history of North Carolina appears that of Ashe. Samuel was a distinguished lawyer of that State, its chief justice, and finally its governor. His son, John B., served through the Revolutionary war, reaching the position of lieutenant-colonel. He was a member of the First Continental Congress, and later yet, governor. Samuel P., son of John B., was a member of the North Carolina Legislature. He came to Tennessee about 1830 and settled in Haywood County. One of his sons, Shepherd M., married Martha Rogers, also a native of North Carolina, and this union resulted in the birth of ten children, two sons and six daughters now living. The two sons, Haywood S. and Henry M., are physicians. Maggie L. and Annie A. are students of art in Paris, France; Cora H. follows the profession of teaching. Having received her education in the private schools of Memphis, she began in the lower grades. Gradually she arose from this to teacher in the high school and such was the tact and ability displayed that she was promoted in 1884 to the principalship of one of the city schools.

J. A. Austin, the leading wholesale clothier of this section, is a native of Brownsville, Tenn., and a son of Robert S. and Margaret B. Austin. Both were Virginians, but, at time of death, residents of Brownsville, where the father had been farming with great success for some time. The subject of this sketch served four years in the Confederate Army. He enlisted in the Thirty-first Tennessee Infantry, of which he was promoted to the rank of adjutant. In 1865 he went to New York, and engaged in the wholesale dry goods and woolen trade, in which line he continued until he came to Memphis. The firm of "Grubbs & Austin" was established in 1872, in the wholesale clothing business. In 1879 the partnership ceased to exist. It was succeeded by J. A. Austin & Co., with our subject as sole owner and proprietor. He carries a fine and extensive stock of clothing and furnishing goods, transacting annually about $250,000 worth of trade. He is known and liberally patronized all through Arkansas, Mississippi, Louisiana, Tennessee and Alabama. Eight traveling salesmen are kept on the road, and about thirty hands constantly employed in the manufacture of certain lines of goods. Mr.

Austin is a gentleman of ability and enterprise, and one of Memphis' most substantial and respected residents. In 1871 he wedded Miss Azalia Fowler, of Memphis, with whom he had three children, all of whom are living. The mother died in 1879, and in 1881 Mr. Austin married Miss Lillie Martin, of Mississippi, to whom one child was born, but which they had the misfortune to lose.

Benjamin Babb & Co. are cotton brokers who established their business in 1881, the firm being composed of B. Babb and Dennis Smith. Mr. Babb, the senior member of the firm, is a native of Virginia, and came to this city in 1844. He is the son of John and Elizabeth (Pope) Babb. After coming to Memphis our subject spent several years clerking for different cotton establishments until 1859 when he was admitted as junior partner in the firm of Harris, Hunt & Co., and has since that time directed his attention exclusively to the brokerage business. June 9, 1859, he married Mrs. Mary (Smith) Kennedy, of this city. She is a member of the Catholic Church. Mr. Babb has always been a good citizen, and has been for several years, and is still a director in the Union & Planters' Bank.

A. R. Barret & Son are merchants in the First District of Shelby County, dealing in general merchandise, and carrying a stock of goods valued at $18,000. The business was first established in 1869 under the firm name of Barret & Witherington, and in 1873 A. R. Barret purchased his partner's interest, and in 1882 took his son, J. H. Barret, as a partner. The firm has done an extensive business, the yearly sales having averaged $100,000. A. R. Barret was born in Henderson County, Ky., and moved to Tipton County, Tenn., when young, and to Shelby County in 1857. He married Miss Rebecca Hill, a native of Virginia. They have had five children; four of them are living. Mr. and Mrs. Barret are active members of the Cumberland Presbyterian Church, and he is a Mason, and in politics a Democrat. J. H. Barret, the son, was born in Shelby County in 1860. He was educated at Lebanon, Tenn., and as soon as he left college went into business with his father, as above stated. He is a young man of fine moral character, and belongs to the Cumberland Presbyterian Church. He is an enthusiastic Democrat, anticipating a brilliant future for the New South under Democratic rule.

Thomas Barrett is the vice-president and general manager, and largest stockholder of the Citizens' Street Railroad Company, of Memphis. His parents, Edmund and M. Ford Barrett, were natives of Ireland, but came to the United States at an early day and located at New Orleans, where they died, his mother in 1849, and his father in 1855. The subject of our sketch, full of ambition and energy, went to California in 1857, where he remained until 1862, and was very successful during his five years in California. When the war broke out he returned to the States and took the position of chief clerk in the quartermaster's department at Baltimore, with Capt. P. T. Turnley, and afterward at St. Louis, Mo., which position he resigned to take the office of secretary to a military commission under Gen. P. H. Sheridan, which was appointed to examine war claims at St. Louis in 1862. When Gen. Sheridan was assigned to other duties, Mr. Barrett resigned and removed to Memphis in 1862, where he took charge of the quartermaster's office, under Capt. H. S. Fitch, as chief clerk, and during the time he was connected with the quartermaster's office at Memphis, he made a great many friends by the many acts of kindness he did in getting their property restored to citizens from whom it was taken by the provost marshal and other officers, and since the war he has assisted several parties to get paid for property used by the Government during the war. In 1863 he invested in real estate at Memphis, where he permanently located, and has since then become closely identified with its commercial and railroad enterprises. Politically, Mr. Barrett is a Democrat, and always has been. He served for a short time as councilman, and was the man who introduced in the council the resolution to wind up the old city government so as to vacate all the offices, and make room for the new government, known as the Taxing District. He is considered a very substantial, enterprising citizen, and a bold financier. In 1876 he married Miss Maria J. Frost, a very bright, intellectual young lady, formerly of Chicago, but who removed to Memphis in 1871. They have three bright, promising sons, T. Frost, Hosmer J., and Dover J. Barrett.

G. T. Bassett, secretary and treasurer of the Cole Manufacturing Company, came to Memphis in 1857 and engaged in the lumber business until the commencement of the war. He was connected with Baxter & Rose. In 1861 he enlisted in the One Hundred and Fifty-fourth Senior Tennessee Regiment, Confederate States Army, and served with credit until the cessation of hostilities, when he returned to Memphis and accepted a clerkship with M. E. and J. W. Cochran in the lumber trade, and continued until 1870 and then became agent for the Memphis Wood-works Manufacturing Company, but quit in 1874 when that company was burned out. January 1, 1875, he formed a partnership with C. B. Moore, under the style of Moore, Bassett & Co., which partnership expired January 1, 1880, when a connection was formed with the Cole Manufacturing Company, which still continues. Our subject was born February 5, 1837, in Delaware County, N. Y., and is one of a family of fifteen children of Cornelius and Elizabeth (Cushing) Bassett, the mother being a niece of Hon. Caleb Cushing. They were married at Schenectady, N. Y. The father was a participant in the battles on the lakes during the war of 1812, and was a member of the State Legislature in 1836–37. He died in 1864 and lies buried in the same cemetery as Washington Irving. The mother died when our subject was a child. The latter graduated at Columbia College, New York, in 1854, and was for a short time engaged in the grain trade in the Upper Mississippi Valley. July 3, 1866, he was married to Miss Lucretia Lockwood, a native of Iowa, and to these parents eight children have been born, one son and two daughters still living. Mr. Bassett is a Democrat, and is a member of the F. & A. M., K. of P., K. of H. orders, and he and family are members of the Episcopal Church.

George H. Battier, a citizen of Memphis, is engaged in the drug business at No. 120 Beale Street. The business was established by his father, R. Battier, in 1866, and the father managed it very successfully until his death in 1883, when it passed into the hands of George H. Battier. During the most trying times of the yellow fever epidemics the firm were never known to leave their posts. To the marriage of R. and Alice (Donnell) Battier, were born two children, George H. and R. C. George H. was married to Miss Mary Burton, who was born in Memphis, and is a daughter of Andrew Burton. Three children have been born to this marriage. Mr. Battier is a member of the A. O. U. W., Chickasaw, No. 40. He is a sound Democrat, and is well known throughout the city, and regarded as one of Memphis' most correct business men.

W. D. Beard, a member of the legal firm of Beard & Clapp, is a graduate of the law school at Lebanon, Tenn., class of 1859, and immediately after graduation began the practice of this profession at Memphis, continuing until 1862, when he enlisted in the Confederate service, and was placed on the staff of Gen. A. B. Stewart, where he remained for one year, and was then transferred to the command of Gen. Jackman, of Shelby's division, and served here until the close of the war. He then resumed the practice of law in Memphis as one of the firm of Wilson & Beard, but in 1879 became associated with J. W. and W. L. Clapp, under the firm name of Clapp & Beard. In 1885 J. W. Clapp withdrew, and the present firm was formed. Our subject was born at Princeton, Ky., in 1835, and remained at home until he began the study of his profession. In 1860 he married Miss Amelia Henderson, of Lexington, Mo., and they have two children—R. H. and Lee. R. H. was born April 23, 1861, and upon reaching early manhood attended the Kentucky Military Institute, and the University of Michigan at Ann Arbor. In 1885 he was elected secretary and treasurer of the Woodruff Lumber Company of this city in which capacity he is yet serving. He is one of the most promising young business men of the city. (See elsewhere for a sketch of the Woodruff Lumber Company.) Lee, the youngest son, was also educated at the Kentucky Military Institute, and graduated in his eighteenth year. Immediately thereafter he took a position with Fulmer, Thornton & Co., one of the leading wholesale houses of Memphis, and for several years past has occupied the responsible place of cashier of this firm. The father of W. D. Beard was a minister of the Cumberland Presbyterian Church, at Princeton, Ky., where he resided until 1853, when he moved to Lebanon, Tenn., and became professor of theology in the Cumberland University, continuing until his death in 1880. Rev. Dr. Beard was a man of deep piety and profound learning, and was born in Sumner County in 1799, and in 1834 married Miss Cynthia Castleman, a native of Davidson County, where she was born in 1806. W. D. Beard is one of the most successful and prominent members of the Memphis bar.

Julian Bedford (deceased), who was a farmer by occupation, was born in Nashville, Tenn., March 5, 1825, and was the third child of nine sons and three daughters, born to B. W. and Martha A. (White) Bedford, and was of English descent. His father was a native Virginian, and immigrated to Tennessee. When our subject was six years of age he moved to Fayette County, and two years later to Panola County, Miss., where our subject was raised and educated, afterward graduating at the Nashville University, and was a man of superior information, well known and greatly respected in the county. He settled in Shelby County in 1851, and married at the present homestead August 5, 1851, Miss Virginia Kenney, a daughter of Col. Edward Kenney, who was formerly a farmer of Virginia, but was born in Dublin, Ireland, June 11, 1802. He came to America when twenty-one years of age, and settled in Virginia. He was educated in Edinburg, Scotland, for the ministry, but not liking the profession, in order to avoid it, he joined the English Navy. After arriving in Virginia he taught school, and married Miss Lucy Ruffin. Mrs. Bedford, our subject's wife, was the only issue of this marriage. Her father moved in 1830 to Hardeman County, and in 1837 to Memphis, where he went into the commission business under the firm styled Ander, Carr, Walker & Co. He died at the present home September 25, 1857. His wife was born in Mecklenburg County, Va., and died March 25, 1861. Our subject's family consists of two daughters and two sons— Rosa (McDonald), Ellen, Willie H. and Julian. Mrs. Bedford was born in Hardeman County, Tenn., January 27, 1832. Mr. Bedford was an old line Whig. He was opposed to secession, but went with his State. He died September 3, 1879. He left his family 1,800 acres of land, 640 acres being in the home tract, four and a half miles west of Collierville, on the Memphis & Charleston Railroad. Mr. Bedford was a man of fine ability and sound judgment, sincere in his friendships and devoted to his family.

Hugh L. Bedford was born in Fayette County, Tenn., June 11, 1836. His father was B. W. Bedford, who was born in Mecklenburg County, Va., June 8, 1794, and when six years of age was brought by his parents to Middle Tennessee, and settled on Stone River, where he was raised and educated, but before he attained his majority he accepted a clerkship in Nashville, where he married Miss M. A. Whyte, daughter of Judge Robert Whyte, who was on the supreme bench of Tennessee for twenty-four years. After the close of the war of 1812, he commenced merchandising in partnership with his brother, William H. Bedford—for whom the county of Bedford, Tenn., was named—and they continued the business for several years. On account of the cholera in Nashville in 1834, the family moved to Fayette County, where they settled temporarily. After this they moved to Panola County, Miss., as he owned large plantations in that State. The last few years of his life were spent in Shelby County, Tenn. He was a man of extensive information, sound judgment and fine business qualifications. A short time before his death he made arrangements to move to Florida, and died at Tampa, Fla., while on his way to his new home, October 23, 1883. Our subject's mother was born at Nashville, Tenn., March 4, 1804, and died in Shelby County, Tenn., May 17, 1872. Hugh L. Bedford was raised on a plantation in Mississippi, and had the finest educational advantages. He graduated from the University of Mississippi, the Kentucky Military Institute, and from the law department of the Cumberland University at Lebanon. He practiced law three years in Memphis before the war, then enlisted in the Confederate Army, and rendered valuable service in the engineer's department at Fort Donelson. During the engagement at the above named place he was in command of the ten-inch columbiad, and was made a prisoner of war, and was held at Johnson's Island for six months. After being exchanged, he received a field appointment as commander of a battalion, which he held for four months, and was then made lieutenant of artillery on ordnance duty, which was soon followed by provisional rank of captain. He served until the close of the war, and was surrendered at Jackson, Miss., in May, 1865. May 23, 1867, he was married at Grenada, Miss., to Miss Louisa McLean, daughter of Judge Robert D. McLean. Two sons, Benjamin W. and Hugh R., were born to this union. Mrs. Bedford was born in Granada, Miss., March 8, 1845.

Mr. and Mrs. Bedford are influential members of the Presbyterian Church. Politically he is an active and ardent Democrat, and has done a great deal for the party in his section of the State. He owns 1,100 acres of land, 755 acres being in the home place, twenty miles east of Memphis. Mr. Bedford is a man of great force of character, a lawyer of marked ability, and a man of broad culture.

William D. Bethell—president of the State National Bank, director of the Security Bank of Memphis, director of the Memphis Cotton Press & Storage Company, director of the Chickasaw Cooperage Company, director of the City Oil Mills, director of the Bluff City Stove Works, director of the Memphis Water Company, and also of several insurance companies of the city—was born in St. Mary's Parish, La., in 1840, and is the only survivor of a family of four children born to Pinkney C. and H. E. (Smith) Bethell, natives of North Carolina and Mississippi, respectively. The parents were both taken to Louisiana in childhood, and there grew up and were married, but moved to this city when our subject was a child. They accumulated valuable property in this city, which at the father's death our subject inherited. The father was a man of more than ordinary character and capacity, and died in February, 1884, but the mother is still living. At the age of eight years our subject entered the preparatory department of Baltimore College, with which institution he remained several years. He also attended other popular institutions of learning, concluding with the Western Military Institute, at Nashville. He was here when the war broke out, and immediately enlisted and was made captain in the Twenty-Second Tennessee Regiment, which position he retained until placed on Gen. Pillow's staff. Later he was placed on Gen. Biffell's staff and served thus until the close of the war. After the war he located in Louisiana, but in 1873 moved to Maury County, Tenn., and engaged in stock raising, agricultural pursuits, etc., continuing until 1883, when he came to Memphis, and has since been interested with the State National Bank. In June, 1861, he married Cynthia S. Pillow, niece of Gen. Pillow, and daughter of Jerome B. Pillow. They have the following children: Bessie P., wife of Dr. Foster, of New Orleans; J. Pillow, Pinkney C., Jennie W. and William D. Mr. Bethell is a Mason and he and family are members of the Presbyterian Church.

William A. Bickford, a pioneer citizen of Memphis, was born in Madison, Carroll Co., N. H., June 15, 1808, and is the son of Moses and Lydia (Richards) Bickford, both natives of New England and of English descent. Our subject was reared in his native State and was educated at the New Hampton Institute, at New Hampton, N. H., where he studied civil engineering and afterward taught a public school in Bridgewater, N. H., in 1829-30. In 1833 he went to New Orleans, and was engaged in contracting and building until May, 1834, when he came to Memphis, and continued the same occupation about seventeen years, accumulating a handsome property, notwithstanding considerable loss during the late war. He is one of the most substantial citizens of the city, and his character is above reproach. He was one of the earliest public school visitors of the city, was trustee in the first medical college, and vestryman of Calvary Church, and continued to serve in these institutions for many years. He never had any political aspirations; was formerly an old line Whig, but since the dissolution of that party he has affiliated with the Democratic party. He is conservative in all things and liberal in his opinions. In 1838 he married Miss Louise Howland, a native of Boston, Mass. These parents have two living sons: William A. and Henry H., the latter a practicing physician of this city. They have been constant attendants of Calvary Church (Episcopal) since 1844, and are now the oldest members of that congregation living.

Henry H. Bickford, M. D., is a native of this city and a son of W. A. Bickford, a well known pioneer citizen of Memphis. Our subject was born September 16, 1848, and was reared to manhood in this city. He received his literary education in the University of Toronto, Canada, and in 1872 entered the medical department of the University of Pennsylvania, from which institution he graduated in 1875. He then entered the Jefferson Medical College of Philadelphia, where he graduated in 1877, after which he accepted a position as resident physician of the Protestant Episcopal Hospital of Philadelphia, and remained there until 1880. He then received a diploma from the institution, and the same year located in St. Louis, where he soon established a good practice, which, however, he was compelled to abandon on account of ill health. After sojourning at different times in Colorado he came, in the fall of 1885, to Memphis, where he has since remained, engaged in the practice of his profession, meeting with satisfactory results. In 1872 he married Elizabeth, daughter of George Winchester, the well known cotton merchant of this city, and a lineal descendant of Wm. Winchester, of Baltimore, Md., one of the original proprietors of Memphis. By this union they have two children living. Dr. Bickford and family are members of the Episcopal Church.

B. J. Bicknell, salesman for John E. Randle & Co., is a native of New York who emigrated to the South in 1857, and in 1865 located in Memphis. He was very prosperous in early life, and at one time was engaged in a lucrative wholesale dry goods business in this city. For the last twelve years he has directed his attention principally to machinery. He was twice married while in New York, his second wife dying in 1860. In 1866 he married Miss Thompson, of Mississippi, and this union resulted in the birth of two children. Mr. Bicknell took an active part in the late war between the North and South, and was a gallant soldier. He is a member of the Masonic fraternity, and also of the K. of H.

R. J. Black, cashier of the Security Bank, of Memphis, vice-president of the Memphis Abstract Company, a member of the firm of R. J. Black & Co., real estate dealers, vice-president of the Woodruff Lumber Company, and a director in the following boards, viz.: Mercantile Bank, Phœnix Insurance Company, the Workingmen's Building & Loan Association, and the Memphis Bethel; is a native of Fayette County, Tenn., where he remained until his parents removed to Haywood County prior to the late war. He was principally educated in Fayette County, but attended one term at New Salem Academy, in Shelby County, and one term at a school at Olive Branch, Miss. At the commencement of the late war he enlisted in Hill's cavalry, a company organized in Tipton County, Tenn., which became a company in Logwood's battalion; afterward merged into and designated as Company B of the Seventh Tennessee Cavalry Regiment, with which branch of the service he remained until the close of the war in April, 1865, said regiment having been with Gens. W. H. Jackson, J. R. Chalmers, E. W. Rucker and Lieut.-Gen. N. B. Forrest. Soon after the war he moved from Haywood County to Memphis, accepted a clerkship in a dry goods house, but about one year later he received the appointment of deputy chancery court clerk and served in that position until 1878, when he was appointed clerk and master of the chancery court, continuing in that office until 1884, when he engaged in the real estate business in the firm of R. J. Black & Co. and is thus connected at present. In 1886 he was elected to his present position in the Security Bank. Mr. Black was born November 27, 1841, and is one of three survivors of a family of five children. His parents were William and Jane (Teas) Black, natives of Virginia. They were married in Humphreys County, Tenn. The mother died in our subject's childhood, but the father is yet living in Haywood County, and is following agricultural pursuits. In 1869 our subject married Miss Fannie M. Somerdell, of Tipton County, who has presented her husband with the following children: Robert J., Fannie M., Joseph S. and Janie, the last one dying in infancy.

Dr. Nicholas Blackwell, is a prominent physician of Bartlett, Shelby County, Tennessee, and is the son of Gen. Nicholas and Sarah (Baldwin) Blackwell. The father moved to Alabama when our subject was quite young, afterward moved to northern Mississippi, where Dr. Blackwell attended the school in Pontotoc County (now known as Union County), and completed his education at Union University, at Murfreesboro, Tenn. March, 1860, he graduated in medicine at the Jefferson Medical College, at Philadelphia, and located for one year at New Albany, Miss., when he enlisted in the Forty-third Mississippi Regiment under Col. Harrison, and a month afterward was made captain of the company, fighting gallantly under this rank until the war closed. He was in the battles of Corinth, Franklin, Nashville, and at Atlanta was slightly wounded in the head and knee. When the war closed, he returned to his home in Mississippi, and, though only twenty-seven years of age, was identified with the leading citizens of his State, and was a delegate in the State convention. December, 1865, he located in Shelby County and resumed the practice of medicine, where he is regarded as a skillful physician, and well posted in his profession. He married Miss L. V. Ward, a daughter of Mr. J. P. Ward, and granddaughter of Col. Alexander, who was one of the earliest settlers of this section of the State, and an opponent of the renowned Davy Crockett in the race for Congress. One daughter, Miss Willie, was born to this union. Mrs. Blackwell died in January, 1870. She was a true Christian, and a member of the Baptist Church. Dr. Blackwell is a Mason and Odd Fellow, and in politics a Democrat. He is a cultured gentleman and a fine physician.

George H. Blood was born in Worcester, Mass., June 9, 1822. He is the son of Joshua and Caroline Blood, natives of Massachusetts, and of English descent. Our subject was reared and educated in the Empire State. He worked for a few years in the mercantile business in Hamilton, Ontario, but left there in 1859 and came direct to Memphis and engaged in the wholesale and retail hardware and stove business, and conducted one of the largest institutions of the kind in the city or the Southwest until 1873, when he engaged in the cotton-seed oil trade here and at Pine Bluff, Ark., in which business he has since been engaged, having met with more than ordinary success. Mr. Blood is a Republican and a Mason, and is connected with the largest oil company in the United States. In 1843 he married Miss Margaret Thompson, a native of Scotland, and by her has four living children: Henrietta, wife of E. Urquhart, vice-president of the American Oil Trust Company, of New York; Emma A., the wife of C. W. Schulte, of this city; Margaret, the wife of Frederick Heakes, manager of the oil-mills at Pine Bluff, Ark., and Charlotte, wife of William R. Moore, of Memphis.

J. P. Bone, M. D., was born in Hopkins County, Ky., in 1831. He is the son of Andrew M. and Mary A. (Alexander) Bone. The father was a farmer by occupation, and lived in Hopkins County, Ky., at the time of his death, which occurred in 1857. The mother died previous to this in 1852. Our subject was reared on a farm, and realized but little benefit from schools. He was, however, very studious at home, and is a self-made man. By his own efforts he earned the means to pursue his medical studies, and entered the medical department of the university at Louisville, Ky., in 1856, where he graduated in 1859. He located at Nebo, Hopkins Co., Ky., and practiced until 1861, when he enlisted in Company B, Forrest's cavalry, as a private, serving both in the field and hospital. After the close of the war he practiced in Fayette County for twelve years, and in 1878 came to the village of Arlington, where he has had a large and lucrative practice up to the present time, serving through the yellow fever epidemic in 1878. In 1867 he married Mrs. Nettie (Thompson) Clary, daughter of Squire George Thompson and widow of Dr. J. W. Clary. Four children were the fruits of this union, three daughters and one son. His son, George A., at the age of eighteen graduated in the Cumberland University at Lebanon, Tenn. The Doctor is a Mason and a K. of H.

George C. Borner, dealer in staple and fancy groceries, established his business in 1868 at No. 97½ Beale Street. He was born in Memphis in 1849 and is the son of Herman G. and Mary W. Borner. The father is a native of Germany and came to the United States in 1837, locating in Memphis in 1839. He was the father of three children, of whom our subject is the eldest. The mother died in 1867 and the father in 1873. George C. was educated in the city of Memphis and in 1872 was united in marriage to Mary E. Passmore, of Olney, Richland County, Ill., who bore him eight children, six of whom are living. Mr. Borner is engaged in business on the same lot that the house stood on in which he was born. His children were also born on the same lot. He is a member of the I. O. O. F. and from present prospects expects to pass the remainder of his days in Memphis.

Thomas Van Brady was born in Huntsville, Ala., October 13, 1828. His father, Edward Brady, was born in Halifax County, Va., and immigrated to Alabama when thirteen years of age. After attaining his majority he married Elizabeth Van, daughter of Bryant Van, and by this marriage had four sons and a daughter, our subject being the second child. The father moved to Marshall County, Miss., in 1835, where he engaged in farming, and died in 1875, at the advanced age of eighty-eight. The mother was born in Marshall County, Ala., and died in Marshall County, Miss., at the age of forty-two. Thomas Van Brady was raised on a farm and educated in the common schools. At the age of seventeen he went into the mercantile business as a clerk at Tullahoma, with Eckles & Howze, remaining with them three years, and was then employed by Strickland, Sanders & Co. for three years, when he became a partner in the firm of Howze & Brady, at Wall Hill, where he continued five years. He was married in Marshall County, Miss., December 13, 1853, to Miss Catherine H. Wilson, daughter of Rev. LeGrand W. Wilson, of Virginia. She was a native of Virginia, and died April 15, 1878. Eight children were born to them; five are living. Mr. Brady was an old line Whig, but is now an independent Democrat. He is a Royal Arch Mason of thirty-five years standing, and a worthy member of the Baptist Church. Mr. Brady is a farmer and mechanic, and was at one time a magistrate in Marshall County, Miss. He has always been an energetic man, upright in all business transactions and generous in disposition.

Eugene L. Brown, a member of the firm of Manfield & Co., wholesale druggists, was born in Jefferson County, Ala. After attending the common schools, he finished his education at the University of Alabama, and then engaged in the drug business in Mississippi for about three years. He then moved to St. Louis, and soon after to Louisville, Ky., and from 1869 to 1881 he acted as traveling salesman for R. A. Robinson & Co., one of the largest drug firms of that city. At the close of his service there he went to Little Rock, Ark., and engaged in the wholesale drug business under the title of Lincoln & Brown. In 1883 he came to Memphis, and the following year joined the firm of Manfield & Co., where he has since continued. In 1883 he married Annie Green, of Alabama, by whom he has one child, Eugene L. Mr. Brown has followed mercantile pursuits all his life. His father was also a merchant, which business he carried on in connection with farming. Our subject is a member of the Knight Templars of Louisville Commandery, and he and wife are members of the Methodist Episcopal Church.

M. S. Buckingham, cashier of the State National Bank, is a native of Memphis, and was born in 1846 and has all his life resided in this city. He was educated here and began business life as collector for the Jackson Insurance and Banking Company, and since that time has risen to his present position through all the intermediate steps of the banking business. He is well qualified for his important trust. December 29, 1876, he was united in marriage with Miss Annie Gifford Nash, a native of New Orleans, to whom these children have been born: Miles Gifford, Theophilus Nash and Cornelia Beckwith. Mr. Buckingham and family are members of the Episcopal Church and he is a Democrat. He is one of four survivors of a family of seven children born to Henry G. and

Eliza (McIntosh) Buckingham. The father is of the well known Buckingham family, of Connecticut; was for many years of the firm of William C. Tompkins & Co., wholesale jobbers of dry goods in New Orleans, La. He retired from business some years ago on account of bad health and resides in Memphis. The mother was a native of Nashville, but married her husband in Memphis, and here her death occurred in October, 1886.

Dr. R. E. Bullington, dentist, is a native of Mississippi, born September 2, 1847, and the only child reared by D. E. and Caroline (Stubblefield) Bullington. He received his literary education at the Kentucky Military Institute. In 1870 he began the study of dentistry, and graduated from the New Orleans Dental College in 1872. He then located at Huntsville, Ala., where he successfully practiced his profession for one year, after which he returned to his old home, Hernando, Miss. He here continued the practice of dentistry until 1885, when he came to Memphis. December 30, 1869, he married S. A. Peete, of Mason, Tenn., and the daughter of Dr. John S. and Ann E. Peete. Seven children were the result of our subject's marriage—six daughters and one son. Since coming to this city the Doctor has built up an extensive practice and is one of the leading dentists of the city and is prominently connected with the Southern Dental Association. He is a Democrat in politics, a member of the I. O. O. F., the K. of H. and the K. of P. He and wife are members of the K. and L. of H., and are also members of the Baptist Church. His father was born in Richmond, Va., about 1813 and was a dentist by profession. He moved to Nashville, Tenn., about 1838, and from that city to Franklin, where he remained some time. He then moved to Hernando, Miss., and here died, October 24, 1878. The mother of our subject was born in North Carolina, in 1829, and her earthly career ended in 1884.

Michæl Burke, general superintendent of the Mississippi & Tennessee Railroad, is the son of Michæl Burke, a native of Ireland, who came to Vermont when young and here married Catherine Lane, who bore him a family of seven children, three of whom are now living. The father was a Democrat in politics and followed the occupation of a farmer. Both parents lived to a good old age. Our subject was born in Crittenden County, Vt., March 24, 1834, and received a good academic education. At the age of sixteen he served an apprenticeship as a machinist and then was fireman on an engine a short time. From 1854 to 1861 he served as machinist, being foreman in the Nashville & Chattanooga Railroad machine shops. In 1861 he enlisted in Company F, First Tennessee Infantry, as first lieutenant. After the battle of Fort Donelson he was on detached railroad duty till the close of the war. In 1865 he came to Memphis as master mechanic of the Memphis & Charleston Railroad and in 1872 was elected to his present position. In 1867 he married Annie Baker, of Memphis. Mr. Burke is a stanch Democrat and takes an active part in politics. He and Mrs. Burke are members of the Presbyterian Church.

C. L. Byrd & Co., the most extensive jewelry establishment in the South, dates its origin back to 1841. The business was established by Merriman & Clark, by whom it was conducted for seven years. It then took the firm title of James E. Merriman & Co. About 1865 it assumed the title of Merriman, Byrd & Co., and in 1870 Mr. W. C. Byrd, of the firm, took charge of the business, which he successfully conducted up to the time of his death in 1874. Our subject became his successor, and the firm became C. L. Byrd & Co. C. L. Byrd is a native of Ohio, as were also his parents, Charles and Mary Byrd. Of their family only two sons, both residents of Memphis, are now living. Our subject came to Memphis in 1867, and for many years was a bookkeeper. In 1875 he married Alice Bruce, daughter of W. S. Bruce. Mr. Byrd's establishment at Memphis is a perfect wonder in completeness of arrangement, in magnitude and in richness of stock.

P. Callahan & Co., plumbers, gas-fitters, etc., are located at 217 Second Street, Memphis. Mr. Callahan, the principal member of the firm, is a native of Ireland, and immigrated to the United States with his parents when but an infant. He is the son of John and Mary (Sweeney) Callahan, and came to this city in 1859, serving for three years as an apprentice with Kennedy & Smith. He worked at his trade in St. Louis, and in 1878 returned to this city, where he established his present business. In 1876 he married Mary Gloreing, who died in 1880, leaving three children. In 1885 Mr. Callahan married Mary Gallager, of Memphis, and this union resulted in the birth of one child. Our subject and family are members of the Catholic Church.

William D. Cannon, sheriff of Shelby County, was born in Fayette County, Tenn., April 29, 1843, and is the son of Henry J. and Sarah S. (Peebles) Cannon, both parents being natives of North Carolina. His father came to Tennessee in 1843, and located in Fayette County, where he very successfully followed agricultural pursuits. He was an exemplary citizen, and in 1861 moved to Memphis, where he died in January, 1862. Early in life he had prepared himself for the practice of law, but relinquished it for the life of a planter, which pursuit better suited his tastes. He was active and prominent in politics, but was not an aspirant for office, and on one occasion refused the nomination to Congress.

William D. passed his youth without noteworthy event, and in 1861 came with his parents to Memphis. He entered the Confederate service in 1865, and continued to serve until the final surrender. After the war he followed agricultural pursuits in Shelby County until 1870, when he was elected constable of the Eighteenth Civil District. He served thus until September, 1874, when he became a deputy sheriff under Charles Anderson. He served as deputy eight years, and was then (April, 1882) elected sheriff to fill the vacancy caused by the death of Sheriff Athy. At the general election of 1884 he was elected sheriff by the largest vote cast for any one on the ticket. He is one of the most popular sheriffs the county has ever had. Early in the seventies, while farming, he served two terms as Master of Melrose Lodge, P. of H. August 1, 1870, he was united in marriage with M. Florence Jackson, a native of Fayette County, and by her is the father of four children—two sons and two daughters. He is a Knight Templar of the Masonic Order; is a member of the K. of P. and the K. of H. In 1886 he was nominated by acclamation by the local Democracy, and was supported by the Republicans for the office of sheriff, and was elected by a handsome majority, a noticeable indorsement of his popularity.

Rev. John B. Canada, a talented minister of the Missionary Baptist Church, was born in Halifax County, Va., June 19, 1817. His parents were Willis C. and Annie (Wilkes) Canada, and were also natives of the above named country and were married in Virginia in 1814. They were of Irish and English descent. Our subject was the second child of a family of five sons and a daughter. The father enlisted in the war of 1812, and was stationed at Norfolk, Va. He was a farmer and died in his native country in 1843. Our subject was reared on a farm, receiving a limited education. In 1843 he became a licensed preacher in the Missionary Baptist Church, but realizing the necessity of a more thorough education he devoted the next six years to earnest study. The first three years were passed at Botatott Seminary and the last three in the Columbian College, at Washington, D. C., where he graduated with high honors. December 1, 1849, he went to Memphis, Tenn., and in 1850 was an ordained minister. Mr. Canada has been an earnest and conscientious minister and has been rewarded with great success in his work. He has preached to the congregation at Bartlett, Tenn., for twenty-four years, and Beaver Creek Church nineteen years, and to other churches from ten to fifteen years. He was married at Germantown, October 17, 1850, to Miss C. J. Dennis, daughter of J. S. Dennis, a merchant and a native of Maryland. Ten children have blessed the union, seven of them living. Mrs. Canada was born in Baltimore, Md., September 15, 1831. Mr. Canada is a Democrat and a prominent Mason. His wife and most of the children are members of the Baptist Church. Mr. Canada owns 376 acres of land in Fayette County and 150 acres six miles south of Memphis. He resides in Collierville, where he is loved and esteemed as a true Christian and a cultured gentleman.

Richard S. Capers, Clerk of the Shelby County Criminal Court, was born in Haywood County, Tenn., June 21, 1847, and is the son of Benjamin H. and Rebecca J. (Greaves) Capers, both parents being natives of Abbeville District, S. C. In January, 1850, Richard S. was brought by his parents to Memphis, and in this city he was reared to manhood. His education was finished at St. Thomas Hall, Holly Springs, Miss., and at Urnes College, Clinton, Miss. Upon the breaking out of the war in 1861 he enlisted in the Confederate service, but was discharged on account of his youth; but in 1863 he again enlisted in Company F, Forrest's old regiment of cavalry, and served faithfully until the close of the war as a private. In May, 1865, he accepted a position as deputy clerk of the criminal court, which position he held continuously through all the various official changes of this court until August, 1886, when he was rewarded for his long and faithful execution of court duties by election to the position he now holds. He is recognized as a conscientious, trustworthy and obliging officer, and is one of the substantial citizens of Memphis. February 3, 1883, he was united in marriage with Miss Alice J. Tapscott, of Marshall Institute, Mississippi. The issue of this marriage is one son, Richard T. He is a member of the orders, K. of P. and Commander of Progress Division.

A. T. Chambers, an influential citizen of Shelby County, was born in Virginia, and in 1854 went to Texas, where he was engaged in farming and stock raising until 1860. He then came to Tennessee, and in 1861 enlisted in the Fourth Tennessee Regiment Infantry as a private, but upon the reorganization in 1863 he was elected third lieutenant, which office he filled until the close of the war, receiving his parole at Greensboro, N. C., in April, 1865. He then returned to Tennessee and located in Shelby County, and has been identified with the best interests of the people up to the present time. His parents, J. P. and Rebecca (Farro) Chambers, were living in Virginia at the time of their death, which occurred about 1846 and 1880, the mother dying first. In 1867 our subject married Mrs. Henrietta (Polk) Bolten, widow of Leonidas Bolten. Two children were born to her first marriage, and six were born to her union with our subject. In 1867 Mr. Chambers located on his present farm, and has tilled it up to the present time. The Chambers family are originally of Scotch lineage, and have made honorable, law-abiding citizens. Mr. Chambers is a Democrat in politics, and he and wife are members of the Methodist Episcopal Church South.

Maj. John A. Cheatham was born in Davidson County, in the suburbs of Nashville, June 6, 1826, and was a son of Col. Leonard P. Cheatham, a soldier with Jackson in the war of 1812, and a native of Virginia. He came to Tennessee at an early age. The Cheatham family were among the earliest settlers of Robertson County, and were recognized as leading men in that part of the State. Anderson Cheatham, the grandfather of our subject, was sheriff of Robertson County, and instrumental in forming the society and establishing the civilization of that locality. Gen. Richard Cheatham, who represented that district in the Legislature for a number of years, and was also a member of Congress, and Col. Edward Cheatham, who had been a member of both houses of the Legislature, and for whom the county of Cheatham was named, and who did a great deal toward the construction of the Nashville & Edgefield Railroad, were numbered among the prominent members of the Cheatham family. The present member of Congress from that district, Hon. Joseph E. Washington, is a descendant of the Cheatham family; his father, the Hon. George A. Washington, formerly vice-president of the Louisville & Nashville Railroad, and one of the wealthiest and most prominent citizens of the State, was descended from the Cheathams on the mother's side. The father of our subject married Elizabeth Robertson, a granddaughter of Gen. James Robertson, for whom the county was named. He was the pioneer, and the acknowledged leader of the colony that settled the locality around Nashville. His life and virtues have been well portrayed by Col. Putman, in his "Life of Robertson." It was from this source that the late Gen. Cheatham, a brother of our subject, inherited his bravery during the late war, and his ability to command. Our subject's parents both died in Nashville, the father in March, 1863, and the mother December 23, 1881. The father was a lawyer and a politician of wide reputation, and held the position of postmaster under President Polk. The family consisted of eleven children, our subject being the fifth child. He was raised on a farm, and has made a business of farming and merchandising. He enlisted in the Confederate Army, belonging to an Arkansas regiment, but was afterward transferred to Gen. Cheatham's staff, and served from 1862 until the war closed, and was surrendered at High Point, N. C. January 17, 1882, he was married in Memphis, at the First Methodist Episcopal Church, to Mrs. Charlotte W. Cheatham. Mr. Cheatham has always been a Democrat, and cast his first presidential vote for Cass. He has a beautiful home three miles from Memphis, and a fine plantation in the Mississippi bottom, sixteen miles south of Memphis. He is well known in Middle and West Tennessee.

Hon. W. L. Clapp, speaker of the House of Representatives and member of the law firm of Beard & Clapp, graduated at the University of Mississippi in 1872, after which he read law with his father in Memphis, and was admitted to the bar in 1874. He practiced his profession in the firm of Clapp & Meux until 1879, when the firm of Clapp & Beard was formed, our subject's father being senior member. In 1883 the elder Clapp became silent partner, and so remained until 1885, when the firm name was changed to Beard & Clapp. The father was a native of Abingdon, Va., and the mother, whose maiden name was Lucas, of Sumner County, Tenn. They were married at Holly Springs, Miss., where the father practiced law. During the war he was chief of the Produce Loan for the Confederacy, receiving his appointment from President Davis. Since 1867 he has practiced law in Memphis. He was elected to the State Senate in 1878 without his knowledge that he was a candidate. He was several terms a member of the Mississippi Legislature, and was a member of the Confederate Congress. Our subject is one of nine children, four girls and four boys yet surviving. In November, 1874, he was joined in marriage to Miss Lamira Parker, a native of this city, who has borne her husband the following children: Jerl, Lucas, Robert, Parker and Aubrey B. Mr. Clapp has been first lieutenant of the Chickasaw Guards since 1880, and has been president of the Tennessee Club two years. He was elected to the speakership of the House in 1886-87 over some of the strongest and most popular men of the State, and presides with exceptional skill and urbanity.

James E. Clary, chief of the Memphis fire department, is a native of Ireland, where his birth occurred in 1845. About a year later his father, Patrick Clary, came to the United States and located in Memphis, and here James E. was reared to manhood. He secured a limited education in youth, and upon the breaking out of the war ran away from home and school and enlisted in Company H, One Hundred and Fifty-fourth Senior Tennessee Confederate Regiment, and served as a private throughout the entire war. Returning home he accepted a position as a horseman in the city fire department, and has remained in this service ever since, having filled every official position. He was elected chief in 1881, and in this trying and responsible position has given excellent satisfaction. Under his supervision the fire department is more efficient than ever before. In 1874 Mr. Clary was united in marriage with Miss Ellen Corbett, a native of South Carolina. To this union are six living children—one son and five daughters. Mr. Clary is a Democrat, and is a member of the orders K. of I., K. of H. and A. F. & A. M., being a Knight Templar of the latter.

J. W. Cochran, president of the German Bank, and of the Panola Oil and Fertilizer Company, of the Hanauer Oil Works, and trustee in the American Cotton Oil Trust, is a native of Virginia and is of Irish descent, and is the son of Conley and Nancy A. (Cassady) Cochran. The parents were natives of the "Emerald Isle." Upon coming to the United States they first located in Virginia, but in 1844 came to Shelby County, and followed agricultural pursuits until their respective deaths—the father in 1852 and the mother in 1847. Our subject was born May 24, 1835, and at the age of nine years began life for himself. He followed various occupations until his majority, then became clerk for a lumber firm of this city. In 1869 he embarked in the oil business, the nucleus of the present oil industry. He was treasurer and manager of this company—Memphis Oil Company—until 1875. He has also been largely interested in oil-mills in Arkansas, and in 1883 he and others founded the American Cotton Oil Trust, of this city, with which organization he is yet engaged. He was for several years one of the directors of the German Bank, and June 15, 1886, became its president. December 20, 1866, he was united in marriage with Miss Ida C. Williams, a native of Fayette County. They have these children: John Knox (deceased), Ida (deceased), ——— (deceased), and Mabel and Maggie living.

R. L. Cochran, dealer in lumber, shingles, doors, sash, blinds, packing boxes, etc., and senior member of the firm of R. L. Cochran & Co., is a native of this city and was born in 1850. Since he began in business for himself, except two years when he was in the grocery trade as a member of the firm of Cochran & Barton, he has been engaged in the lumber trade. He has been quite successful in his business undertakings. In youth his education was finished at Emory and Henry College, Virginia, and at the Kentucky Military Institute. In 1875 he was joined in marriage to Miss Anna E. Gates, who bore him one child, Richard L., still living. This lady died in 1876 and in 1879 he married Mamie Taylor, who has borne him the following children: William T., Marcus E. and Henry L. By appointment of Gov. Bate, Mr. Cochran served an unexpired term as commissioner of Memphis. He is a member of the board of directors of the Bank of Commerce. He and family belong to the Methodist Episcopal Church and he belongs to the following secret orders: F. & A. M., I. O. O. F. and K. of H. His father, M. E. Cochran, established the lumber business here in 1844 and controlled it until his death in 1873. The firm then assumed its present name, the members being R.

L., C. A. and M. A. Cochran. The parents were both natives of Virginia, but came to this county at an early day and were here married. The mother, Sophy (Leake) Cochran, is still living.

Joseph L. Cody was born in Alabama and came to Tennessee in October, 1867, locating in Fayette County, but subsequently in 1874 came to Shelby County. His parents, Miles F. and Minerva Cody, were natives of Tennessee and Mississippi respectively. The father was a farmer by occupation and resides in Marion County, Ala. The mother died in 1862. In 1865 the father married Jane Duke. In 1861 our subject enlisted in the Confederate service, Sixteenth Alabama Regiment, Infantry, and remained in service until the battle of Murfreesboro, which rendered him unfit for duty for about three months. He again returned to the army and was the second time wounded at the battle of Shiloh, which disabled him about two months. After recovering he again joined the army, and in 1864 was commissioned captain in Col. Hetherington's regiment. In 1865 he was again wounded, while in battle near Mobile, Ala., and this disabled him from active duty the remainder of the war. He was paroled at Columbus, Miss., in May, 1865. In January, 1868, he married Harriet A. Cody, of Fayette County, and daughter of Thomas and Jane (Thomas) Cody. Four children have blessed this union, three of whom are living: Maude, Ola and Elsie. Mr. Cody resides in the village of Arlington and is engaged in farming and running a cotton-gin. He is a Mason and a K. of H.

A. E. Cole, of the firm of Hughes & Cole, dealers in staple and fancy groceries, general merchandise, and who established their business in 1880, is a native of Shelby County and the son of Winfield and Frances A. (Massey) Cole, both natives of Virginia. After living a few years in Alabama they came to Shelby County, where the father followed agricultural pursuits until his death in 1860. The mother, too, passed away in 1877. Mr. Cole, the junior member of the firm, was reared on a farm and followed agricultural pursuits until 1874, when he was elected constable of the First District of this county, which office he held for six years. One year previous to the time he engaged in his present business, he was employed as traveling salesman for J. R. Godwin & Co., of Memphis. In 1871 he married Mattie Douglas, of this county, and the daughter of G. L. and J. Douglas. Five children blessed this union, four of whom are living. Mr. Cole is a member of the K. of H. F. M. Hughes, the senior member of this firm, is a native of Lincoln County, Tenn., and the son of Joshua and Temperence (Gunter) Hughes, both natives of North Carolina. They came to Tennessee about 1825 and here the father followed the occupation of a farmer. He died in 1878 in his eighty-first year, and the mother preceded him in death about two weeks. Our subject's father, mother, sister and brother-in-law, all died in the same house within two weeks' time. F. M. Hughes was reared on a farm and followed agricultural pursuits until about five years since. He came to Shelby County with his parents about 1854. In 1861 he enlisted in the Confederate service, Ninth Tennessee Regiment Infantry, and remained until the close of the war. He was twice taken prisoner, and after being released the second time was attached to Forrest's cavalry. In 1863 he married M. E. Stewart, of this county, and daughter of James T. and Mary Stewart. Two children were born to this union: Luna May and Emma Grace. Our subject's eldest daughter is a graduate in music, and in November, 1884, she married J. L. Mercer, of Memphis. They have one child—Mary Grace. Mr. Hughes has been interested in the mercantile business most of the time since the war. He has taken all the degrees in Masonry, including the Chapter degree, and is also a member of the K. of H.

James M. Coleman, justice of the peace, notary public, and commissioner of deeds, is a native of Louisiana and was born September 14, 1830, to the marriage of Daniel Coleman and Amelia Stutts, natives respectively of Georgia and Louisiana. The father, Daniel Coleman, a skillful physician, came with his family, in 1836, to Tennessee, locating at Raleigh, this county, where he practiced his profession until his death in 1871. It was here that our subject was reared and educated. Upon reaching manhood he engaged in mercantile pursuits, continuing until 1874, when he was elected justice of the peace for the Sixth District and opened his office in Memphis, and has occupied this position by re-election until the present. Squire Coleman was formerly an old line Whig, but for many years has been a stanch Democrat, and has taken an active part in local politics, having served as chairman of the Shelby County Democratic Central Committee, as coroner of the county, as chairman of the poor-house committee eight years, during which last official term he was instrumental in securing the erection of the present poor-buildings. June 1, 1851, he married Miss Susan Bayless, a native of this county, and to this union there are two living sons: George B., deputy register of the county, and James M., deputy sheriff. He was appointed coal oil inspector of Shelby County by Gov. Robert L. Taylor.

Capt. Charles H. Collier, superintendent of the Memphis public schools, is the son of C. Miles and Sarah (Cowles) Collier, both of whom were born, reared and married near Fortress Monroe. In early life the father was an officer of "the line" in the United States Navy and afterward a mail contractor for eastern Virginia. His family consisted of four sons, who took active parts in the late war and at its termination returned home without receiving any wounds or being imprisoned. Two were in the army, one a surgeon, the other a captain. The other two were in the navy, one a midshipman and our subject an engineer. He was a native Virginian, born August 25, 1846, and educated in the Hampton Military School. After finishing there he began to prepare himself for the United States naval service, but the war broke out about this time and he enlisted in a company known as Wythe Rifles. After serving a year as private he was transferred to a naval engineer corps, where he remained until the close of the war, principally under Dozier, Rochell and Tucker. In 1871 he came to Memphis and engaged as assistant teacher in the Memphis High School. He was afterward principal of Market Street and Linden Street schools. In 1875 he married Evelin Belcher, who lived only four months. In 1879 he wedded Julia Bingham, by whom he had four children, three of whom are now living. Our subject is a member of the Episcopal Church, as his parents were before him. In 1880 he was chosen superintendent of the public schools, which position he is now holding. The schools are well organized and in fine working order.

A. M. Cooke, assistant general manager of the Louisville, New Orleans & Texas Railroad, was born in Virginia, October 17, 1850, and received his education at the Virginia Military Institute. He was, for some time, connected with the freight department of the Atlantic, Mississippi & Ohio Railroad, and after the consolidation of the express department he was also connected with that. In 1885 he became purchasing agent for the road with which he is now associated, and in 1886 was promoted to the position he is now occupying. He is one of Shelby County's best citizens and a wide-awake business man.

L. P. Cooper, a member of the law firm of Craft & Cooper, of Memphis, Tenn., was born in Rutherford County, Tenn., January 8, 1830. His father, M. T. Cooper, moved to Bedford County when he was a small boy, where he grew to manhood and lived until he moved to Panola County, Miss., in 1857. He was educated at Union University, Murfreesboro, Tenn., from which he graduated in 1852. After graduating he was engaged in the business of teaching until 1856. In 1857 he attended the law school at Lebanon one session of five months. In the fall of 1857 he moved to Panola County, Miss., where he was engaged in the business of planting until the spring of 1862, when he entered in the Confederate Army as a private in the Forty-second Mississippi Regiment. Soon after he enlisted his regiment was ordered to Virginia. After the regiment arrived at Richmond he was made quartermaster of the regiment with the rank of captain. Late in the war regimental quartermasters were abolished. He, however, was retained as assistant brigade quartermaster and assigned to duty under Maj. Reid, quartermaster of Davis' brigade, in which capacity he served until the close of the war. For several months before the surrender he was acting brigade quartermaster. After the surrender he returned to his home in Mississippi. In August, 1865, he was elected as a delegate from Panola County to the Constitutional Convention of Mississippi, called by President Johnson, to amend and remodel the constitution so as to adapt it to the new condition of things. After the adjournment of this convention he returned to his home and commenced the practice of law in the town of Panola. In 1871 the county site was moved to Sardis, to which place he moved and continued the practice of law there until he moved to Memphis, in 1874. There he practiced alone until 1878, when he formed a partnership with Judge Craft, the senior of the present firm. His father, M. T. Cooper, was born in Rowan County, N. C., in 1806. Henry Cooper, the father of M. T., moved to what was then Rutherford, now Cannon County, in 1816. In 1828 M. T. Cooper was married to Miss Sallie A. Vincent, daughter of Henry Vincent, Esq., of Rutherford County. Of this marriage there were born thirteen children, six of whom are living. When the subject of this sketch was a small boy his father moved to Bedford County, where he grew up to manhood and lived until he moved to Mississippi. His father was a farmer and merchant and did considerable business in trading in produce and stock. L. P. was married January 24, 1854, to Miss Pauline H. Scales, daughter of Robert Scales, of Davidson County, Tenn. Six children were born of this marriage, three of whom are living—one daughter and two sons. He lost his first wife April 10, 1864, and was married to his second wife, Miss Cornelia Battle, a native of Shelby County, on the 10th of December, 1868. She is the daughter of the late William Battle, Esq., of Shelby County, who was originally from North Carolina, and who settled in Shelby County in 1830. L. P. Cooper and his wife are both members of the Central Baptist Church, of Memphis, and he is a Democrat.

Henry Craft, one of the oldest members of the Memphis bar, obtained his literary education at Oglethorpe University, Milledgville, Ga., completing the same in 1839. He then followed various occupations and in 1847 began the study of law at Holly Springs, Miss., with Hon. J. W. C. Watson. He attended law school at Princeton, New Jersey. He was admitted to the bar in 1848, in Holly Springs, Miss., and practiced his profession there ten years as a member of the firm of Watson & Craft. In 1858 he came to Memphis, where he has since resided. In 1862 he enlisted in the Confederate service and was a member of Gen. Chalmer's staff until his health failed. He has since practiced law, part of the time alone, and then as a member of the firm of Kortrecht & Craft, until 1873, and of Kortrecht, Craft & Scales until 1875. The present firm of Craft & Cooper was formed in 1878. His father, Hugh Craft, was born on the eastern shore of Maryland, in 1799, and his mother, whose maiden name was Mary E. Pitts, was born in North Carolina, in 1799. They married in Georgia, in 1819, and his father was a merchant there, residing first in Milledgeville and afterward in Macon until 1839. The family moved to Holly Springs, Miss., in 1839, and his father was land agent there until his death in 1867. His mother had died in 1826, and his father had married Martha Cheney in South Carolina, who soon died, and he married Elizabeth R. Collier, who bore him three sons and five daughters. This lady's death occurred in 1877. Our subject was one of two sons and three daughters of the first wife and was born April 8, 1823, at Milledgeville, Ga. In 1856 he married Miss Ella D. Boddie, daughter of Elijah Boddie, of Sumner County, Tenn. She has borne him the following children: Alfred D., born 1858, died 1884; Mary F., born 1861, died 1885; Henry, born 1866; Charles K., born 1868, died 1873; Paul, born 1870: Hugh, born 1874. Mr. Craft is a Democrat and himself and wife are members of the Presbyterian Church.

Richard G. Craig, wholesale agricultural implement and seed merchant, of Memphis, is a native of Hamilton County, Ohio, and was born in 1837. He was there reared and educated and came South and located in Memphis in 1860, engaging in his present business on a limited scale. He has continued the same to the present time, and now has the largest establishment of the kind in the city or in the South. He has been largely instrumental in inducing the farming community to use more modern and improved agricultural implements, to diversify their crops and to restore worn-out farms. He is president of the Memphis Fertilizing Company, the business of which was established in 1882. Mr. Craig is a conservative Democrat, is a Mason, a member of the Baptist Church, and is recognized as one of the most reliable and well-informed citizens, in agriculture, of the city. In 1858 he married Miss Sallie L. Bruce, of Ohio, and by her has three living children, two being sons.

Thomas B. Crenshaw, deputy county court clerk, is a native of this county and was born September 12, 1848, to the marriage of Thomas B. Crenshaw, Sr., and Miss Grace Booker, both natives of the "Old Dominion." The father came to this county in 1836 and located in the Ninth Civil District, where he conducted a plantation until his death in 1866. He was magistrate of that district twenty-seven consecutive years, and was one of the most useful and substantial citizens of the county. Our subject was reared on his father's plantation and was there educated. He followed agricultural pursuits until 1878, when he was elected clerk of the circuit court at Bartlett, this county, which position he filled in a highly creditable manner. In 1885 the court was abolished, and he was then employed as bookkeeper at the same place, continuing until September, 1886, when he accepted his present responsible position under P. J. Quigley. He is a Democrat, and was candidate for the nomination for county register in 1886. He is a member of the K. of H. and is one of the rising young men of the city.

Mrs. E. J. Crockett, principal of the Memphis High School, is a daughter of Edward and Eliza (Johnson) Belcher. The father was a native of Boston, Mass., and the mother a native of Alabama. From Boston the father went to Virginia, and finally came to West Tennessee, locating at Bolivar, where he became distinguished as a lawyer. After marriage they lived at Bolivar a short time and then went to Oxford, Miss., where they made their permanent home. Both were active members of the Episcopal Church. Their family consisted of seven children—three sons and four daughters. Two of the boys chose the profession of their father. After an active, useful life the father died, but the mother, is now residing in Memphis. Our subject was born at Bolivar, Tenn. but received her education at Oxford, Miss., graduating from the female seminary. In 1862 she and William H. Crockett were married. During the late war he fought bravely for the Southern cause, being a staff officer of Gen. Hindman. At the battle of Shiloh he was severely wounded, from the effects of which he never recovered. To this union were born three children, only one of them now living. This one, Elise B. Crockett, is a member of the high school and partakes of her mother's love for books and learning. After the death of her husband Mrs. Crockett began teaching, and after assisting in the Memphis High School a time assumed the principalship of the same in 1875, and has filled that position ably ever since. She is a member of the Episcopal Church, as was her husband.

William R. Cross is a native of Cross County, Ark., where he was born August 12, 1854. His father, Col. David C. Cross, after whom our subject's native county was named, came to Memphis in 1866, but died in Arkansas, in 1874. Our subject finished his education at the University of Mississippi, and in 1874 engaged in the mercantile business at Bartlett, this county, and has since conducted the same enterprise. In 1882 he was elected a justice of the peace and yet retains that position. He is an able and conscientious officer, and has the highest confidence of the public. In August, 1884, he accepted his present position as clerk to the chairman of the county court, C. E. Smith, and has retained it since. In 1875 Mr. Cross was united in marriage with Miss Loula Person, of this county, and these parents have three living daughters. Mr. Cross is a stauch Democrat, is a member of the I. O. O. F., K. of P., of which latter he is chancellor commander. Himself and wife are members of the Methodist Episcopal Church.

Hugh B. Cullen, real estate agent and notary public, was born in Louisa County, Va., July 12, 1851, and is the son of Hugh M. and Anne (Booth) Cullen, natives respectively of Ireland and Virginia. Hugh B. was reared and educated in his native State and came to Memphis in 1871 and took a position as deputy county court clerk under James Reilly, continuing under Owen Dwyer until 1882, when he was elected to the office of clerk and served one term of four years, at the expiration of which he entered his present business and has met with good success. In 1873 he was united in marriage with Miss Lizzie Gibbs, of this city, and these parents now have five living children—two sons and three daughters. Mr. Cullen is a Knight Templar in Masonry, a member of the Encampment in Odd-Fellowship, and is a member of the K. of P. and the K. of H. orders.

John Cummins, dealer in staple and fancy groceries, liquors, grain, feed, cigars and tobaccos, was born in Memphis, where he passed his youth and manhood. He is the son of William and Bettie (Quintan) Cummins, natives of Ireland and Ohio, respectively. They came to Memphis about 1852, and at the breaking out of the late civil war William enlisted and fought bravely in defense of the Southern cause. He died about 1865. Our subject is one of those wide-a-wake, energetic business men with push and energy enough to succeed in any undertaking. The business that he is now engaged in was established in 1878 and is situated at 216 and 218 Poplar Street.

P. Cunningham (deceased) was a blacksmith and wagon-maker, whose shop was situated on the southeast corner of Monroe and De Soto Streets. He established his business in 1858. After locating in this city he was associated with different partners, and at one time sold out and went to Mississippi, where he was employed in the arsenals at Columbus and at Selma, Ala. When the war closed he returned to Memphis and resumed his former business. From 1878 up to the time of his death, which occurred August 5, 1885, Mr. Cunningham ran the business alone. He manufactured carts, trucks and scales, also always kept on hand seasoned lumber, from which he executed the most finished and difficult work in his line. He served his apprenticeship in Dayton,

Ohio, which is of itself a sufficient guarantee of his proficiency. He was a native of Ireland, and immigrated to Canada in 1842, and from there to the United States in 1850, locating in Memphis in 1855. In the following year he married Mary Welch, of Belfast, Ireland, and eight children were born to them, six of whom are living. Since the death of our subject, his daughter, Fannie, has taken charge of the entire business, with John Fox, an experienced workman, as foreman, and is conducting it successfully.

W. H. Dale & Co., leading farmers and saw-mill men, own 960 acres of the best land of the county. This company is composed of J. C., W. H. and D. M. Dale. The father, J. C. Dale, was born in Sumter County, Ala., 1832, being the first white child born in that county, his parents being Hugh and Catherine (Clanton) Dale. Hugh Dale was a native of Ireland, who came to Quebec in 1820, being nineteen years of age at that time. Soon after he moved to Alabama, where he married. The family consisted of ten children, five now living. He followed farming, and died in 1867. His wife is now living at the advanced age of eighty-two. Our subject had the very best advantages for an education, which he improved, graduating from La Grange College, Ala., in 1851. He then engaged in farming, and the following year married Elizabeth A. Mayes, a graduate of Athens Female Institute. To this union were born ten children—four sons and six daughters. Having lived in Alabama and Mississippi till 1884 our subject and wife came to the plantation, where they now live. Mr. Dale is a Royal Arch Mason, a Democrat in politics, and for about three years has taught school.

Squire Henry E. Cannon was born in Wake County, N. C., July 5, 1840, and is a son of Henry J. Cannon, who was born in North Carolina and moved to Tennessee in 1843, settling near Somerville, Fayette County. He was a graduate of Chapel Hill College, North Carolina, and was licensed to practice law, but preferred farming to the legal profession. He was a well-read man, especially upon agriculture, and a member of the Agricultural Bureau of the State, and president of the district fair, which included Fayette County. Before leaving North Carolina he married Miss Sarah P. Peebles, a native of that State and educated at Raleigh. Five sons and two daughters were born to them, six living to be grown. Our subject was the second child. The father moved to Memphis in 1860, where he remained until his death, in the fall of 1861. Henry E. Cannon was raised and educated on the farm. He enlisted in the Confederate Army in May, 1861, in the Seventh Tennessee Cavalry, under Col. W. H. Jackson, and was at the battle of Corinth, Miss., and on the retreat from Dalton to Atlanta, being wounded while scouting around Lost Mountain, and was disabled for six weeks. He served through the entire war, and was surrendered near Gainesville, Ala. Mr. Cannon was married at St. Mary's Church in Memphis, October 29, 1872, to Miss Susie Virginia Devereaux Dunlap, daughter of Devereaux and S. Virginia (Ragland) Dunlap. The issue of this marriage was Sarah Virginia, Susie Dunlap, Henry Hugh, Mary Dunlap, Elizabeth Love, Charles Devereaux Dunlap and Robert Dudley. Susie D. and Elizabeth Love both died. The mother of this family was born in Shelby County, Tenn., January 20, 1855. Mr. Cannon is a Democrat and a Mason, and himself and family are members of the Episcopal Church. He has 3,000 acres of land, 1,280 acres in Louisiana 1,100 in Washington County, Miss., 80 in Arkansas, and the rest in Shelby County, six miles southeast of Memphis. Mrs. S. Virginia Dunlap, the mother-in-law of our subject and a co-subject of this sketch, was born in the suburbs of Memphis, April 14, 1832. Her father, Dr. Nathaniel Ragland, who was the first druggist of Memphis, was born in Virginia, and moved to Kentucky in 1816. He was a well-informed man, with a strong mind and unbending character, with clear judgment and strict integrity. He was married in Louisville, Ky., to Miss Elizabeth Love, daughter of Matthew Love, a native of Pennsylvania. Mrs. Dunlap was married in 1853, near the present home, to Devereaux Dunlap, son of Gen. Hugh W. Dunlap, a prominent and well-known citizen of Tennessee, and twin brother to Hon. W. C. Dunlap, who served on the supreme bench and was a member of Congress for a number of years. Charles Devereaux Dunlap was educated in Kentucky and at La Grange, Ala., and died when still a young man on his plantation in Madison Parish, La., September 16, 1855. Dr. Ragland's family consisted of three daughters and one son: Louisa A. (Anderson), now living in Texas; M. E. (Rambert), residing in the suburbs of Memphis, and our co-subject, Mrs. Dunlap, and Edward D., a soldier in the late war and a graduate of the law department at Lebanon, Tenn., who is at resent a planter in Lee County, Ark.

William C. Davis, chief of the Memphis police force, is a native of Tipton County, this State, and was born March 25, 1845. He is the son of Lewis W. and Margaret C. (Freeman) Davis, natives respectively of Kentucky and Tennessee. Our subject was reared and educated in his native county, and in 1861 enlisted in the first company raised in the county, called the "Tipton Rifles." It was assigned to the Fourth Tennessee Confederate Regiment. After one year's service he was discharged on account of his youth. In 1863 he again entered the service as a substitute for his father, serving in the First Tennessee Heavy Artillery until the surrender of Vicksburg, when he entered the Fourteenth Regiment Tennessee Cavalry and served as a private until the battle of Franklin, when he was promoted second lieutenant by Gen. Forrest for gallantry in that battle, and served thus until the final surrender. His father was captured by the Federals while at home on sick list and imprisoned at Alton, Ill., where he died, refusing to the last to take the oath of parole. After the war our subject engaged in mercantile pursuits in Tipton County until 1868, when he came to Memphis and in 1870 was appointed a patrolman on the city police force. During the yellow fever scourge in 1878 he was promoted to a captaincy, and in 1880 he was appointed chief, in which capacity he has officiated ever since to the satisfaction of the public. March 15, 1866, he was united in marriage with Miss Nancy H. Sullivan, of Tipton County. To this union there are three living sons and two living daughters. Mr. Davis is a positive Democrat, is a member of the K. of H. and A. O. U. W., and himself and wife are Methodists.

William P. Deadrick was born in Shelby County, Tenn., north of Memphis, September 20, 1826, and is a son of J. G. Deadrick, who was born in Nashville, Tenn., and married Eliza G. Dunn, a daughter of David Dunn, a farmer and a native of Virginia. They had four children who lived to be grown, our subject being the second child. The father moved to West Tennessee before 1825 and settled on Big Creek, in Shelby County, where he died December 24, 1831. The mother was born in Brunswick County, Va., and died near Buntyn Station, Shelby County, November 2, 1845. William P. Deadrick was raised on a farm and after attending the common schools in the county he spent two years at college at Georgetown, Ky. He was married at Jackson, Tenn., in May, 1855, to Miss Rachael J. Hays, daughter of Samuel J. Hays, a planter and a native of Tennessee. One son, Sam Hays (deceased), was born to this marriage. Mrs. Deadrick was born in Jackson, Tenn., in 1833, and died December 13, 1861. Mr. Deadrick was again married December 6, 1866, in Memphis, to Miss Mattie S. Park, daughter of David Park, one of the well known citizens of Memphis. By this marriage he has three daughters: Jennie Barron, Elese Garland and Anna May. The mother was born in Memphis, February 21, 1844. She is a member of the Presbyterian Church and Mr. Deadrick of the First Baptist Church. In politics he is a Democrat. He owns sixty acres of land four miles south of Memphis. He is a man of fine principles and of a frank and generous disposition.

James Degnan, vice-president of the board of education and dealer in wall paper, painters' colors, etc., is a son of Philip and Margaret (Cassarly) Degnan, both natives of County Roscommon, Ireland, and both came to America about 1854, the father settling in Tennessee and the mother in New York. Their marriage occurred at Cincinnati, Ohio, and after living a short time in Mississippi and Paris, Tenn., they came to Memphis in 1862. Both were members of the Catholic Church. In their family were three children—two sons and one daughter. The father was a railroad contractor. He died in 1863, and about two years later the mother married Robert Walsh (deceased) by whom she had one son. The mother is still living. Our subject was born June 1, 1856, in Mississippi. His early educational advantages were very meager, having only attended school a part of three sessions. Having commenced as a newsboy he followed that till about the age of sixteen, when he took an apprenticeship in his trade. In 1880 he began business on his own capital and has since had a good share of patronage, making a specialty of decorative work. In 1883 he was chosen vice-president of the board of education, which position he has held in a highly creditable manner since. He belongs to the following societies: A. O. U. W., K. of H., K. of I. and K. of R. B. In both politics and religion Mr. Degnan is independent.

S. A. Douglas, farmer, of Shelby County, was born in Tipton County, in 1856, and is the son of Andrew J. and Laura (Smith) Douglas. The father was a native of Virginia, and when young came to West Tennessee and married Miss Smith. They made their home in Tipton County, and their family consisted of four sons, of whom our subject was second. He received his early education in the common schools, and subsequently attended the University of East Tennessee, situated at Knoxville. In 1878 he married Carrie T., a native of Shelby County, born in 1862, and the daughter of Rev. Andrew H. Kerr, D. D., a native of Virginia, born in 1812. Mr. Kerr came to West Tennessee about 1854, and the town of Kerrville, which was laid out in 1873, was named in honor of him. He was one of the leading lights in the Presbyterian Church, spending about forty-four years of his life in the ministry. The Newport News & Mississippi Valley Railroad would have run one and a half miles east of where the town of Kerrville now stands, but Andrew H. Kerr offered forty-four acres of land, 100,000 bricks for a depot, and $3,500 to turn it through the town. The population of this village is about 150. They have a two-story school building, a Presbyterian Church, five stores, and adjoining the school grounds is a fair ground of eighteen acres. Our subject and wife are members and active workers in the Presbyterian Church. They have a fine farm of 1,900 acres, on which they settled soon after marriage, and where they have since remained. Mr. Douglas is a thorough Democrat in politics.

G. L. Douglass, a farmer and resident of the First District of Shelby County, was born in Virginia and is a son of John Douglass. The father moved to Tennessee when our subject was eighteen years old, and settled in the First district of Shelby County. G. L. Douglass attended school in Virginia, but left before his education was completed, and acquired a great deal of information from his general reading at home. He has always made farming a business. In 1835 he was married in Georgia to Miss Joanna Sanderford. They have had eleven children; seven of them are living: Bettie, wife of Dr. D. G. Godwin, a physician in the First District of Shelby County; Kate, the wife of Dr. C. M. Stewart, a physician also in the First District; Dr. J. P. Douglas, a physician at Arlington, in the Eighth District; Dr. J. B. Douglass, a physician in the Sixth District; Mattie, wife of A. E. Cole, a merchant at Arlington; G. R. Douglass and A. C. Douglass, both farmers in Shelby County. The children that died were Mollie, the wife of J. A. Stewart, a merchant at Memphis; Anna, Emma, and Alice. The entire family are members of the Cumberland Presbyterian Church. Mr. Douglass is a Mason and is a sound Democrat.

J. P. Douglas, M. D., a prominent physician of Shelby County and a native of that county, is the son of G. L. and J. W. (Sanderford) Douglass. The parents are natives of Virginia and Georgia, respectively. The father followed agricultural pursuits, and he and wife are now residing in this county, the father being seventy years of age and the mother sixty-nine. Our subject received his education in the best school of the county, and his medical education at the University of Nashville, graduating from that institution in 1873. He then located first at this place and has since practiced in Tipton County, but returned to Arlington and resumed practice in 1880. In 1873 he married C. L. Pittman, of this village, a daughter of Capt. and M. T. Pittman. One child, Oscar P., was born to this union. He died September 3, 1883. In 1862 Dr. Douglas enlisted in the Confederate Army, in the Fifty-first Tennessee Regiment Infantry, and at the expiration of twelve months he joined Forrest's cavalry and remained with him until the close of the war, surrendering at Gainesville, Ala., in 1865. He is a member of the K. of H.

Judge A. H. Douglass, ex-criminal judge, was admitted to the bar at Somerville, Tenn., in 1843, and practiced there a few months and then removed to De Soto County, Miss., and followed agricultural pursuits in connection with real estate dealings until 1850, when he came to Memphis and has since resided here. He was a non-participant in the war, and at its close resumed the practice of law. He was mayor of Memphis from 1855 to 1857, and during that time the celebration of the completion of the Memphis & Charleston Railroad took place. In August, 1884, he was elected criminal court judge. Our subject's parents were Burchett and Martha (McGee) Douglass, natives of Smith County, Tenn., and were among the earliest settlers there. The paternal grandmother, in more than one engagement with the Indians at Fort Lick Creek, loaded the guns for the men to disperse the savages. Soon after marriage the parents settled in Wilson County, but in 1836 moved to Fayette County, where they both died. The father served in both houses of the State Legislature from Wilson and Fayette Counties, and was speaker of both the Senate and House. He was a very useful, honorable and prominent public man. He was for many years president of the branch State Bank at Somerville. Our subject is one of seven children, and was born August 28, 1820, in Wilson County. He attended Clinton College, graduating in 1837. In 1843 he married Miss Martha A., daughter of Gen. A. C. N. Robertson, of Hardeman County. They have one child—Margaret—Mrs. John West, of Mississippi. The mother died in 1848, and in 1850 he married Miss Eliza B. Randolph, who has borne him the following children: Eliza A., Richard R., Ida May, Adda H., Eugene B. and Mattie. The mother died April 30, 1886. Judge Douglass is a Democrat and a member of the K. of P. and the A. F. & A. M.

Dr. William H. Douglass, a farmer and retired physician of Shelby County, was born in Smith County, Tenn., June 30, 1826. His father, Ila Douglass, was born in the same county November 17, 1797. He was a farmer and moved to Shelby County in 1850, settling ten miles from Memphis, on the "pigeon roost" road, and died March 20, 1885. The mother's maiden name was Miss Elizabeth Harris, a daughter of John Harris, a native of Virginia. She died in Wilson County, Tenn., four miles north of Lebanon, in 1845. The Douglass family were among the very early settlers of the State. Elmore Douglass, our subject's grandfather, moved to the State when the land where Nashville now stands was unbroken and without a house, and they could only live in forts. He had seven brothers who came from Virginia to this State at the same time, our subject's father being next to the youngest brother. Edward Douglass, who died in Missouri, was a soldier in the war of 1812 and was at the battle of New Orleans, and Burchett Douglass was a representative in the General Assembly of the State, when the statutes of the State were revised by Nicholson and Caruthers, and he afterward represented Fayette County in the Legislature. Our subject was raised on a farm and had fine educational advantages. He spent three years at Irving College, Warren County, Va., then read medicine with Dr. Felix Mc-

Farland, of Haywood County, Tenn., then attended lectures at Louisville, Ky., and commenced the practice of medicine in Shelby County, where he now lives, and continued it with marked success until the close of the war. He was married in Shelby County in 1861, to Miss Ann Eliza Wynne, daughter of W. D. Wynne, a farmer, and a native of Tennessee. He died in De Soto County, Miss., where he had moved some time before. No children have been born to this union. Dr. Douglass owns 600 acres of land, 400 being in the home place six miles southwest of Germantown, where he has a handsome residence. Dr. Douglass is extensively known and very popular in his neighborhood, where he exerts an influence for good, and is one of the leading farmers in the county.

Julius J. Du Bose, judge of the criminal court of Shelby County, was born in this county December 13, 1839, and is the son of the late Dr. A. B. C. and Camilla F. (Dunn) Du Bose, natives, respectively, of South Carolina and Alabama. Dr. Du Bose, in his day, was one of the most successful planters and prominent citizens of Shelby County. His death occurred in 1865. Julius J. was liberally educated in youth, finishing his education in Oxford, Miss., and in Wesleyan University, at Florence, Ala. He then studied law in Cumberland University, Lebanon, graduating in 1860. In 1861 he enlisted in the Ninth Arkansas Regiment (Confederate), and served as ensign twelve months, and was assigned to duty in the trans-Mississippi department. In 1862 he was promoted to second lieutenant and was assigned to duty in Arkansas. About a year later he was made chief of ordnance and inspecting officer of North Arkansas and Indian Territory, ranking as captain of ordnance. Returning home after the war he secured an interest in and edited the *Public Ledger*, of this city, three years. In 1870 he was elected to the State Senate, representing Shelby and Fayette Counties. From 1873 to 1886 he practiced law in Memphis, and was then elected judge of the criminal court, and in this position is yet serving. November 29, 1870, he married Miss Mary M., daughter of Col. George W. Polk, of Columbia, Tenn. They have three sons and three daughters living.

John J. Duffy, one of the wholesale and retail grocers of Memphis, was born in Ireland, in 1849. His father, James Duffy, was teller in a bank in the old country, and died in 1850, shortly after coming to America. Our subject in his youth received his education in the schools of Memphis. For about eight years he was bookkeeper for E. Mulholland & Co., of that city. He was for a time senior member of the firm of Duffy & Cary, but this firm soon dissolved partnership and Mr. Duffy established his present business in 1880. The following year he married Jennie J. Barry, of Memphis, by whom he had two children—

John and Ella M. For about twelve years our subject was a member of the board of education, and two years of that time he was vice-president of the same. He took an active part in introducing the present system of city school laws. During the yellow fever scourges of 1873 and 1878 Mr. Duffy was a member of the Citizens' Relief Association and also a volunteer member of the Howard Relief Association. He holds the position of president of the Security Building & Loan Association and is director in the Arlington Insurance Company. He is also director of the Irish American Building & Loan Association. For two years he was one of the commissioners to provide a sinking fund to discharge the city debt, being appointed by Gov. Hawkins.

P. H. Duffy, grocery merchant at 175 De Soto Street, established this business in May, 1881. Mr. Duffy is a native of Ireland and came to America in 1868. He came direct to Memphis and began clerking. In 1870 he became a member of the police force and in 1873 a member of the fire department, discharging the duties of these offices with credit and satisfaction. In 1878 he again engaged in the grocery business, which he continued until he established the business for himself. He married Bridget Roper, also a native of the "Emerald Isle," and to them have been born five children, only two of whom are living. In June, 1875, Mr. Duffy returned to Ireland, the place of his nativity, on a visit to relatives and friends. He was accompanied by his daughter, Miss Maggie. Mr. and Mrs. Duffy are members of the Catholic Church. He is a member of the K. of H., the K. of I., and a stanch Democrat in politics.

Dr. George K. Duncan was born in Limestone County, Ala., April 24, 1828. His father, Benjamin Duncan, was a native of Virginia. He moved to East Tennessee and settled near Greenville; was a stonemason by trade, but was afterward a merchant at Mooresville, Ala. He was married in East Tennessee to Nancy Ross, and they had six sons and four daughters, our subject being the youngest. The father moved, in 1835, to Shelby County and settled on Big Creek, on the old Jesse Benton farm, and died at Raleigh, Shelby County, June 21, 1860. The mother was a native of East Tennessee, and died at the home on Big Creek in 1838. Dr. Duncan was raised in Shelby County and educated in the common schools. He read medicine under Dr. Samuel H. Lapsley, of Raleigh, and graduated from the Jefferson Medical College, at Philadelphia, in 1851, and has since then practiced medicine in Shelby County. In 1873 he was elected physician of the poor asylum of the county, and in 1876 was made superintendent and physician, and still holds the position. He was married in Shelby County, March 1, 1854, to Miss Annie Lamphier, daughter of John Lamphier, a native of Virginia. They had three children—Edith V., Elizabeth and Albert B. The mother was born in Kentucky, and died July 11, 1881, at Raleigh, and Dr. Duncan was married again in Memphis, March 5, 1884, to Miss Sophia Anderson. He was an old line Whig before the war but is now a Democrat and a member of the A. O. U. W. As a physician he has met with great success, and as a man has been greatly esteemed for his many excellent qualities.

Oliver M. Dunn, superintendent of the Memphis line division of the Louisville & Nashville Railroad, was born in La Grange County, Ind., August 14, 1847; is a son of William B. Dunn and Emma (Hatch) Dunn, natives of Elmira, N. Y., and Great Bend, Penn., respectively, who immigrated to La Grange County, Ind., in 1835, when that country was comparatively a wilderness. Their family consisted of five sons and two daughters. By occupation the father was a lawyer and merchant and took quite an active interest in politics, being a stanch Republican from the organization of that party. Our subject received a fair common-school education; in 1868 he married Hattie Seely, a native of New Jersey and then a resident of Brimfield, Ind. To this union one child was born, Seely, who now holds the position of private secretary to his father. Mr. Dunn entered the service of the Michigan Southern & Northern Indiana Railroad (afterward consolidated with the Lake Shore, and now known as the Lake Shore & Michigan Southern) in 1864, and remained in its employ in various capacities, as warehouseman, telegraph operator, ticket and freight agent, etc., at different points until 1872, when he was offered and accepted a position with the Louisville & Nashville Railroad as agent at Shepardsville, Ky., where he remained until 1874, when he was appointed to the agency at Pulaski, Tenn., from which position he was appointed to the general agency at Owensboro, Ky.; from there to the charge of transportation department, New Orleans division same road, at Mobile, Ala., where he remained over two years, when he was made superintendent of the Owensboro & Nashville Railroad, a line owned by the Louisville & Nashville Railroad Company, and then under construction. After that road was completed he was made superintendent of the New Orleans & Mobile division of the Louisville & Nashville Railroad, with headquarters at New Orleans, La., and in 1886 was again transferred to the position he now holds. The prominent positions Mr. Dunn has held speak well for his efficiency as an officer. He is prompt and courteous in his dealings with the public and his employes, and wins a large circle of friends wherever he goes.

Samuel H. Dunscomb, president of the Bank of Commerce, is a son of Samuel D. and Ann W. (Rayburn) Dunscomb. The father was born in New York City and the mother in Montgomery County, Va. At an early day they removed to Kentucky, where they were married. In their family were four children—two sons and two daughters—of whom only one is now living. The father was a farmer by occupation. During the war of 1812 he went on the campaign to Canada, under Shelby. After his death the mother married William C. Baker, by whom she had two children. Our subject is of English and Irish descent, born December 18, 1822, in Simpson County, Ky. He received his education in the common schools, and at the age of eighteen began as salesman in a mercantile house, where he remained about eight years. In 1846 he came to Memphis and engaged in the commission, cotton and grocery business. In 1854 he married Marietta C. Elder, and by her had five sons, two of whom are in the commission business and one secretary of the Hernando Insurance Company. Mr. Dunscomb, his wife and three children, as well as his mother, are Methodists, he having been steward and treasurer of the First Methodist Episcopal Church about twenty-eight years. Since 1869 he has been in the banking business, having been elected vice-president of the De Soto Bank, which position he held till 1874, when that consolidated with the Bank of Commerce, and in 1880 he was elected president thereof. Besides he holds other places of trust and honor, having been president of Hernando Insurance Company since 1867; was also vice-president of the DeSoto Building & Loan Association; director in the Water Company; treasurer of the Board of Education, and trustee and treasurer of the Lee Orphan Asylum some twenty years. He is a member of the I. O. O. F., was a Whig before the war, but since that time has voted with the Democrats. As a business man Mr. Dunscomb has been very successful, having started on a small capital, and has accumulated all his property by close attention to business and a firm reliance in an over-ruling Providence.

Albert L. Duval, manager of the Memphis & Para Rubber Company, of this city, was born in Philadelphia, Penn., September 10, 1848, being the son of George W. and Margaret (Lavallette) Duval, both parents being of French descent, born respectively in South Carolina and Pennsylvania. They came to Memphis in 1846, the father being a lieutenant in the United States Navy, coming here with our subject's maternal grandfather, Commodore Lavallette, to establish the navy yards. Albert L. was born while his parents were on a visit East, and was brought up and educated in this city. For five years he was in the employ of Bigley, Mellersh & Co., in the coal business, and was then with B. J. Semmers & Co. until 1883, when he engaged in his present business and has been highly successful. January 4, 1882, he was joined in matrimony to Miss Nannie V. Bowles, of this city, and by her has one son, Albert L. Mr. Duval is a Democrat, a Knight Templar in Masonry, and himself and wife are members of the Calvary Episcopal Church, of Memphis.

Hon. Lucien B. Eaton was born at Sutton, N. H., March 8, 1837, and was fitted for college at Phillips Academy, Andover, Mass., class of 1855, and graduated at Dartmouth College, Hanover, N. H., in the class of 1859. After studying law for a time he was principal of a public school in Cleveland, Ohio, which position he resigned to enter the Union Army in 1861. He served throughout the war, holding the commissions of second and first lieutenants, captain, lieutenant-colonel and colonel. While captain he was for a long time brigade inspector on the staff of Gen. Harke. He participated in nearly all the battles and campaigns of the Army of the Cumberland. At the close of the war he settled in Memphis with an interest in a mercantile house, but intending to devote himself to the law; but his brother, Gen. John Eaton, engaging in 1866 in the publication of a Republican newspaper, the Memphis *Daily Post*, he became his assistant editor, and upon the former's election in 1868 as State superintendent of schools for Tennessee, became both the business and editorial manager of that paper until its discontinuance in 1870. In February, 1870, under the appointment of Gen. Grant, he entered upon the duties of United States marshal in the western district of Tennessee. This position he resigned in April, 1877, and entered upon the practice of the law, but devoting much of his time to the purchase and improvement of real estate. He was one of the very few who had the courage to buy real estate after the epidemics of 1878 and 1879. He has amassed a fortune in buying and selling lands and building and renting houses. He is one of the largest planters in Shelby County. He is a member of the firm of L. B. Eaton & Co., the owners of the oldest office, furnishing abstracts of title to all lands in Memphis or Shelby County, and of the firms of L. B. Eaton & Co. and Eaton & Smith, engaged in the lumber business. He has also other large interests in various local corporations. He has been president and director of insurance companies and banks. He has served as a member of the Memphis city school board and of the Tennessee State Legislature at its sessions of 1880 and 1882. He was married on December 26, 1867, to Miss Clara Winters, the daughter of Valentine Winters, a banker of Dayton, Ohio. She died in 1885. Only one child by this marriage survives—Valentine W. Eaton, born November 1, 1870. Mr. Eaton is a member of the K. of H., of the Old Folks' Society, of the Tennessee Historical Society, and in politics has always been a Republican and for years a leader of his party in his section, but is now too busy to give much attention to such matters.

Dr. B. H. Eddins, a well known physician at Bartlett, Shelby County, was born in Wilson County, Tenn., February 9, 1818, and was a son of John Eddins, who was a native of South Carolina and moved to Wilson County, Tenn., when a boy. He married Miss Nancy Hooker, a native of North Carolina. They had eleven children, our subject being the second born. Dr. Eddins was educated in Wilson and Madison Counties, then attended the medical university at Louisville, Ky., and graduated at Wetumpka Medical College, Wetumpka, Ala. He practiced one year at Germantown, Shelby Co., Tenn., then located at Bartlett, where he has been a popular and successful physician, and still has a large practice, though he is now anxious to retire from active practice. He married Miss Susan Cole, a native of Tennessee, and a daughter of Wingfield and Frances (Massey) Cole, natives of Virginia. Twelve children were born to this marriage. Only four are living: John W.; Lucy P., wife of W. B. Alexander, who is postmaster at Pine Bluff, Ark.; Samuel C., and Joseph H., who lives in Texas. Dr. and Mrs. Eddins are members of the Methodist Church. He is a Mason and a sound Democrat, adhering closely to party principles. Dr. Eddins is well known throughout Shelby County and held in great esteem.

T. B. Edgington, attorney at law, is a native of Richland County, Ohio, and was educated at the Ohio Wesleyan University, Delaware, Ohio, graduating from the classical department in 1859. He then studied law and began the practice in Iowa, continuing until the commencement of the late war, when he enlisted in Company A, Twelfth Regiment, Iowa Infantry, as private and served until the battle of Shiloh as orderly sergeant, and was then promoted to first lieutenant, and served thus until his resignation in 1863. He then came to this city, where he has continued the practice of law ever since. He is one of seven survivors of a family of twelve children. His father, at the time of his death in 1842, was judge of the associate court, an intermediate court of appeals in Ohio between the common pleas and supreme court. His mother died in 1843. The father was a native of Virginia and the mother of Ohio. In March, 1865, our subject was united in marriage to Miss Katie V. Baxter, a native of New Orleans but a resident of Memphis. She has borne her husband a family of four children—three sons and one daughter—all living. Mr. Edgington is a member of the F. & A. M. and the K. of P. fraternities.

James W. Edwards, vice-president and general manager of the L., N. O. & T. R. R., is the son of Mordecai and Martha J. (Fulton) Edwards, both natives of Georgia, where they reared a family of ten children. All the family are professors of religion. The parents are still living, aged respectively seventy-seven and sixty-one. The father is an extensive planter and an upright, honorable citizen. Our subject was born November 25, 1849, and educated at the University of Georgia, from which institution he graduated in 1869, especially well qualified as a civil engineer. Since 1870 he has been connected with railroads as engineer of the South & North Alabama Railroad; of the Georgia Western and of the Georgia Railroad; supervisor of the track of Macon & Augusta; general freight agent of the Macon & Brunswick; superintendent of the Northeastern Railroad of Georgia, and of the Macon & Brunswick. He finally came to his present position. In 1871 he married Lizzie Scudder, of Athens, Ga., daughter of A. M. Scudder, joint honor man at Princeton College, New Jersey, with the noted William Reese, of Georgia. To our subject and wife were born four children—two sons and two daughters. Mr. Edwards not only holds an enviable position as a railroad man, but is well respected and esteemed by all who know him.

Dr. T. E. Edwards, physician, is a native of Union City, Tenn., born in 1861, and is one of a family of eight children born to the union of W. A. and M. E. Edwards. The father is a native Tennessean, born in 1826, and is a resident of Union City, of that State. He is an architect and builder by occupation. The mother was born in Virginia the same year as her husband. Our subject received his education at the Southern University of Illinois. In 1879 he entered the medical department of Vanderbilt University at Nashville, and graduated from that institution in 1880. Two years later he graduated from the medical department of the University of Tennessee. He has also spent considerable time studying the eye, ear and throat under a renowned physician of Union City. November 4, 1886, he married Jennie Roseborough, daughter of W. D. Roseborough, of Sardis, Miss. Dr. Edwards came to Memphis September, 1883, and has since resided here, engaged in the practice of his chosen profession, his entire time now being occupied in the treatment of the eye, ear and throat.

John T. Elliott, justice of the peace of the Fourteenth Civil District, was born in Ireland in April, 1831, and came to the United States in 1851, and spent sixteen years in Pennsylvania, where he was interested in the iron industry. In 1867 he came to Memphis and followed mercantile pursuits until 1868, when he was elected magistrate and has served continuously in the same office by re-election until the present time, being the oldest but one in the county. He has been a member of the county jail inspectors for twelve years. During the late war he served in the Federal Army in the Eighth and One Hundredth Pennsylvania Regiments, and at the bloody battle of Antietam lost his left arm, after which misfortune he served in the enrolling department, and later was elected first lieutenant in the Fifty-fifth Pennsylvania Regiment, and served thus until the close of the war. In 1881 he married Miss Sarah Toppin, a native of New York. He is a Democrat in politics, and is a Presbyterian in religious faith.

R. E. Ellis, one of the county's prominent citizens, was born in Shelby County, and is the son of B. R. and R. A. Ellis. The father is one of the pioneer citizens of this county. He is a farmer and is now seventy-three years of age. The mother is also living. In 1879 our subject moved to the village of Capleville and assumed control of a cotton-gin at that place. In 1886 the gin was purchased by a company, one of whom was our subject. In 1876 he married Miss Rosa Lee Mitchell, of Shelby County. She died in 1875, and in 1879 Mr. Ellis married Miss Emmit Mullins, also of Shelby County, and the daughter of L. D. and Martha A. Mullins. The marriage of our subject resulted in the birth of two children, Robert E. and L. D. Mr. Ellis is a member of the Masonic fraternity and is a Granger.

Newman Erb, one of the leading lawyers and railroad attorneys of Memphis, is a son of Adolphus L. and Esther (Peck) Erb, Germans by birth. Having come to the United States about 1852, they moved to the West and were among the first settlers in the State of Kansas. The father has been a successful merchant and manufacturer, but now resides with Mrs. Esther Erb at Little Rock, Ark., and is president of the Union Printing & Publishing Company. The subject of our sketch was born June 16, 1852, and early placed at school in St. Louis, Mo., where he was educated and prepared for the bar, but before arriving at majority, on account of the executive ability, of which he gave abundant promise, was without capital taken into the firm of one of the largest saddlery establishments in the West, doing business in St. Louis, and given charge of its office. When he had accumulated sufficient means he severed his connection with the business firm, and started for Arkansas where he was admitted to the bar in 1872, and began the practice of his profession at Little Rock, where he did a successful law business for ten years, and acquired a wide reputation as a safe counselor and corporation lawyer. In 1881 he became a director of the Kansas City, Springfield & Memphis Railroad Company, and was appointed its chief attorney for Arkansas and Tennessee, a position he still holds. He was married at Little Rock in 1874, and has a family of two children, Edna and Fannie. In 1883 Mr. Erb removed to Memphis, where he now resides with his family, and where he has become connected with many public enterprises. In 1884 he originated the plan for the reorganization of the Memphis, Selma & Brunswick

Railroad, and as receiver built it from Memphis to Holly Springs, being the first railroad in the United States completely built and equipped by a receiver. He is now chief attorney in Tennessee of the Kansas City, Memphis & Birmingham Railroad; vice-president of the Kansas City, Wyandotte & Northwestern Railroad, and the Leavenworth & Olathe Railroad, the Western Union Telegraph Company, besides being interested in many other corporations.

J. T. Fargason, senior member of the firm of J. T. Fargason & Co., wholesale grocers and cotton factors, 369 Front Street, Memphis, came to this city in 1879, and established his present business in 1863, under the firm name of Fargason & Clay. The latter firm did business until 1875, when the present firm was established with our subject, C. C. Hein, R. A. Parker, E. L. Woodson and other members. They have an annual wholesale grocery trade of about $1,200,000, and in addition handle about 30,000 bales of cotton annually. Mr. Fargason was born in Alabama, in 1835, and was reared and educated in Chambers County, of that State. In 1859 he was united in marriage with Miss Sarah A. Marsh, a native of New Jersey, who has borne her husband four children, all of whom are living. His parents were Thomas H. and Mary (Stanley) Fargason, who were natives of Georgia, and were agriculturalists. The mother died in 1855 and the father in 1865. Our subject is a director of the Bank of Commerce and of the Citizens' Street Railway, and is a member of the F. & A. M., K. of H. and A. O. U. W. orders.

H. C. Fisher, superintendent of the Southwestern Division of the Southern Express Company, was born in Nashville, May 11, 1842, and entered the employ of the Southern Express Company of that city in 1865 as check clerk. He was subsequently agent at Hopkinsville, Ky., route agent with headquarters at Guthrie, Ky., assistant superintendent, with headquarters at Nashville, and was made superintendent in 1878, with headquarters at Memphis. About fourteen years ago, Supt. Fisher suggested and aided very materially in developing the present extensive fruit-growing in the State, and the influence of his efforts has been felt throughout the entire State, proving a blessing to the farmers and a corresponding advantage to the company he represents. He is highly esteemed, both as a citizen and as an official.

John M. Fleming, was born in Laurens County, S. C., January 17, 1818, and was the son of James Fleming, who was born in 1772, in Ireland, and was but three years old when his parents brought him to America; he was reared in South Carolina, where he married Miss Nancy McClintock, a native of South Carolina. Our subject and a brother, Samuel C., who died November 23, 1838, were the only issue of this marriage. The father was a farmer, and died December 4, 1837. The mother died in South Carolina, November 24, 1838. John M. Fleming was married in his native State September 8, 1840, to Miss Eliza Moseley; they have had one son and a daughter, Nancy M., born July 18, 1841, and Samuel T., born February 20, 1844; the daughter married J. Boyce Farley, and died May 4, 1866. Mrs. Fleming was born in South Carolina, January 19, 1820, and died May 25, 1860, and our subject was married June 2, 1864, to Mrs. Fannie A. Goode, and she died July 5, 1865; and December 10, 1867, he married Mrs. A. B. Sullivan; no children were born to either of the last two marriages. The son, Samuel T., left school at eighteen years of age and enlisted in the Confederate Army, in the Thirty-fourth Mississippi Infantry, under Col. Samuel Benton, and was in the battles at Perryville, Ky., Murfreesboro, Chickamauga and Lookout Mountain, and was captured at the latter place and held as a prisoner of war for sixteen months at Rock Island, Ill., and was released March 13, 1865. Mr. Fleming is a Democrat, a Mason, and a member of the Old School Presbyterian Church; he owns 400 acres of land three and a half miles southwest of Colliersville. He is highly esteemed by all who know him.

Ford & LeMaster, real estate and rental agents, is composed of J. N. Ford and N. F. LeMaster, who established their present business in September, 1886. They already have a profitable and rapidly growing business. Nathaniel F. LeMaster, was born in Shelby County, Tenn., February 13, 1836, and is the son of James S. and Penelope P. (Field) LeMaster, both parents being natives of Kentucky. The father, a successful planter, came to this county in 1831, and here resided until his death in 1874. Our subject grew up in this county and finished his education at Hanover College, Ind., and at Center College, Danville, Ky. October 21, 1857, he married Miss Olivia Rawlings, and located on a plantation in this county, in the Twelth District, which he still owns and on which he resided until 1883. He then removed to Memphis and accepted a position as bookkeeper for a lumber company and served thus and otherwise until he engaged in his present business. He was deputy county trustee two years under Mr. Rawlings, and for the same length of time under Mr. McGowan. He is a member of the Presbyterian Church. His wife died in June, 1883, leaving three children—two sons and one daughter.

Col. R. Dudley Frayser, president of The Security Bank of Memphis, of the Memphis City Railway Company, and of the Memphis Abstract Company, besides being a director in a number of other corporations, is a member of the law firm of Frayser & Scruggs; was born in this city and was educated here at the public schools and at the Kentucky Military Institute, from which last institution he graduated, delivering the valedictory address. In 1861 he enlisted in Company F, Thirty-seventh Tennessee Confederate Regiment as a private, but was soon promoted adjutant and then lieutenant-colonel, which rank he held until the cessation of hostilities, and was senior field officer in command of the brigade at the surrender in North Carolina in 1865. He returned home after the surrender and began reading law with Judge R. J. Morgan, and was admitted to the Memphis bar in 1866, and began the practice as a member of the firm of Morgan & Frayser, which was afterward changed to Morgan, Jarnagin & Frayser by the admission to the firm of Col. Milton P. Jarnagin, Esq., and in 1880 the present firm was formed. Our subject is one of six survivors of a family of eight children born to the marriage of Dr. John R. Frayser and Miss Pauline Brown. The father was a native of Virginia and the mother of Mississippi. They came to Memphis in 1835 and were here married. The father was a graduate of the Philadelphia Medical College in the class of 1835, and has since practiced his profession in this city, being one of the oldest resident physicians of the city. In 1867 our subject was united in marriage to Miss Mary Lane, a native of this city and daughter of Fletcher Lane, formerly a prominent merchant here. By her he has the following children: Pauline, Florence and R. Dudley. He is a member of the orders, F. & A. M., K. of H., A. O. U. W. and I. O. O. F., in the latter order, being president of the general relief committee and ex-Grand Master of Tennessee. The firm of Frayser & Scruggs commands a fine practice. They are the retained attorneys for a number of banks and other corporations. Col. Frayser is regarded as a man of keen and shrewd judgment as a financier, and whatever he goes into generally prospers and comes out gilt-edged. In politics he is a Democrat and in the wrangle about the State debt he was a zealous "sky blue."

J. A. Fry, a merchant at Memphis, engaged in the grocery business, including fancy and family groceries and liquors, at 136 Poplar Street, corner Fourth, established the business in February, 1884. Mr. Fry is a native of Mississippi, and is a son of Calvin and Emily (Hickey) Fry. The father was a native of Alabama and the mother of Tennessee. The father died in 1883 and the mother is now living in California. Our subject moved to Memphis in 1879 and was at first engaged as traveling salesman and was afterward employed by the express company. He was married in 1876 to Miss Lucy Watkins, of Mississippi. They have had five children, but only two are now living. Mr. Fry has shown judgment and enterprise in the management of his business and has a liberal patronage.

SHELBY COUNTY. 965

Fulmer, Thornton & Co., wholesale grocers, cotton factors and commission merchants, No. 306 Front Street, Memphis, is composed of J. J. Thornton and J. W. Fulmer, who succeeded Sledge, McKay & Co., in 1878, and have conducted a large and growing business since, and have the highest commercial standing. They carry a choice and full line of goods pertaining to the wholesale grocery trade, and find market throughout Tennessee, Mississippi and Arkansas. They do a large cotton business, being among the heaviest dealers in the city. No business firm of the city stands higher in the estimation of the trading public, and no firm of the city possesses greater claim to the confidence of all. Mr. Fulmer, of the firm, is a director in the State National Bank, Memphis National Bank, the Factors' Fire Insurance Company and the Factors' Mutual Insurance Company of Memphis, Tenn. He is also a large land owner in the rich valley of the Mississippi River in the State of Mississippi.

C. B. Galloway, one of the proprietors of the Peabody Hotel, is a native of New Jersey, born in 1835, and at the age of twenty-one he went to Minnesota, and engaged in mercantile pursuits until 1858, after which he came to this city and took charge of the Gayoso Hotel until 1866. He then took charge of the "Worsham" two years and of the "Overton" one year. In 1861 he married Lotta Osterhout, a native of New York, who bore him these children: Lotta (Mrs. R. E. Morris), Charles B. and Emma. In March, 1876, Mr. Galloway took charge of the Peabody Hotel, which is a commodious, five-story structure, 178x178 feet. It has 175 large, elegantly furnished sleeping apartments, with bath and water closets on each floor. It also has three finely furnished parlors and two dining rooms, the dimensions of the main one being 40x100 feet. It has three elevators, is heated by steam and supplied with the electric bell system. The hotel was originally a store-room, and was used as such until December 8, 1867, when it was opened out as a hotel, by D. Cochran & Sons, who conducted it about one and a-half years. A Mr. Goodlow then took charge of it for a few months, after which W. C. Miller assumed the proprietorship for one year. He was succeeded by O'Banner & Mars, who in turn were succeeded by Mr. Galloway. Our subject's parents were Rev. Samuel and Rebecca (Scudder) Galloway, natives of Pennsylvania and New Jersey, respectively. The mother is dead and the father is living in Texas.

Hon. Jacob S. Galloway, judge of the probate court, was born in Bergen County, N. J., February 14, 1838, and is the son of Rev. Samuel and Rebecca (Scudder) Galloway, natives respectively of Pennsylvania and New Jersey. His father, who was a graduate of Princeton

College and Seminary, was an eminent minister of the Presbyterian Church, and for several years a member of the faculty of Lafayette College, Pennsylvania. Jacob S. was educated by his own efforts, and graduated at Princeton in 1858, with the degree of A. B., delivering the philosophical oration of his class. He then came south and began teaching in Georgia, and in 1859 came to Memphis and continued teaching until the war broke out, when he enlisted as a private in Company A (the Shelby Greys), Fourth Tennessee Regiment, Confederate States of America. At the battle of Shiloh he was severely wounded, and was afterward detailed for lighter service, serving as an enrolling officer until the close of the war, ranking as first lieutenant. After the war he began reading law with Col. Luke W. Finlay and Gen. Albert Pike, and was admitted to practice in 1866, and thus continued successfully until 1876, when he was elected magistrate, and thus served until his election to the judgeship. In 1883-84 he represented Shelby County in the State Senate. In 1879 he was elected special judge of the circuit court by the Memphis bar. He served as coroner of the county from 1879 to 1882. His official life is characterized by energy and integrity. May 14, 1867, he married Mary E. Tucker, who died of yellow fever in 1878. November 19, 1879, he married Mrs. Sallie R. (Tucker) Coffee. By his first marriage he has three living children—one son and two daughters. He is a Mason, a K. of P., a K. of H. a member of the A. O. U. W., and is one of the substantial citizens of Memphis.

Robert W. Galloway, junior member of the firm of Patterson & Co., came to Memphis in 1865, where he engaged in clerking on a steamboat for some time. He was afterward engaged as delivery agent for the Memphis & Charleston Railroad, in whose employ he remained till 1870. In that year he became connected with the above named firm. Mr. Galloway is also actively engaged in farming and is one of the wide-awake energetic citizens of the county. He was one of eight commissioners elected to put the taxing district system on foot, which system held good for two and a half years. In 1865 he married Mary Hall of New York and he and wife are members of the Christian Church. Both he and partner organized, and are large stockholders in the Memphis Grain and Package Elevator. Mr. Galloway affiliates with the Democrats in his political views.

Gantt & Patterson, attorneys at law, is a strong firm consisting of Col. George Gantt, Col. Josiah Patterson and M. R. Patterson, and was organized in April, 1878, succeeding the firm of "Gantt, Patterson & Lowe." Col. Josiah Patterson is a native of Morgan County, Ala., where he was reared, educated and admitted to the bar in 1859. Upon the breaking out of the late war, he raised, and was made commander of the Fifth Alabama Cavalry, and served with distinction throughout the war. Upon the establishment of peace he opened a law office at Somerville, Ala., where he practiced one year, and then five years in Florence, Ala. In March, 1872, he came to Memphis and was a member of the firm of Patterson & Lowe until the formation of the firm of Gantt, Patterson & Lowe, which was terminated in a few months by the death of Mr. Lowe. In 1882-83 Col. Patterson was a member of the State Legislature from this county. He is a member of the order of F. & A. M. His parents were Malcolm and Mary (Deloach) Patterson, natives of Maryland, and were of the famous Scotch-Irish descent. They followed the occupation of farming, and died in Morgan County, Ala., the father in 1859 and the mother in 1875. M. R. Patterson is a son of Col. Josiah Patterson and was born in the State of Alabama in 1861. He was educated in the Vanderbilt University, and afterward studied law with his father, and was admitted to the Memphis bar in 1881. He then practiced alone for one year, since which time he has been a member of the law firm of Gantt & Patterson. On the 24th of February, 1886, he was joined in marriage to Miss Lucile Johnson, a native of this city. He is a member of the F. & A. M. order.

Samuel C. Garner was born in Pennsylvania, March 28, 1829, and was the third member of a family of four sons and three daughters, born to Robert and Elizabeth (Dow) Garner, and is of Scotch descent. The parents were born in South Carolina, where they were married in 1818. They then immigrated to Philadelphia, where they remained about eighteen years. The father was a ship-carpenter by trade, but after moving to Philadelphia went into the mercantile business, and died in 1859. The mother died in Ohio in 1860. Our subject was raised chiefly in New Orleans, where he obtained a good education, and in early life learned the trade of brick-mason and plasterer. He moved to Tennessee in 1851, and settled in Memphis, where he carried on the contracting and building business. He was married in Shelby County, Tenn., September 15, 1858, to Miss Matilda A. Molitor, daughter of Francis M. Molitor, who was at one time master mechanic on the Memphis & Charleston Railroad. To this union were born Frank R., Willie A. and Mattie C. The mother was born in Philadelphia. Mr. and Mrs. Garner and the children are members of the Old School Presbyterian Church, and in politics he is a Democrat. He is a man of undeviating honesty, good morals and of a liberal disposition, holding the esteem of all who know him.

Kenneth Garrett, a prominent citizen of Shelby County, was born in North Carolina in 1831, and in 1843 came to Jackson, Tenn., by wagon, with his uncle, K. Garrett. He is the son of John W. and H. Y. (Young)

Garrett. The father was a tiller of the soil and was living in North Carolina at the time of his death, which occurred about 1838. The mother died the year previous, leaving four children, who were reared and educated by their uncle, K. Garrett. In 1848 our subject began clerking in a mercantile establishment in the city of Memphis, where he remained three years. During the years 1851 and 1852 he attended college in Virginia, when during the latter year the death of his uncle occasioned his return. In 1853, he, in partnership with his brother, William, and John Hudson, opened a wholesale and retail clothing and gents' furnishing goods store in Memphis. Our subject sold his interest in 1855, and located on his farm in this county where he remained till 1858. He then returned to Memphis and engaged in the brick business, which prospered until the beginning of the war. In 1861 he enlisted in the Confederate service, Seventh Tennessee Cavalry, as third lieutenant, but at the expiration of one year was appointed quartermaster, and at the time Col. Jeff Forrest was killed our subject was one of his staff, and was also acting as brigade quartermaster. He received a slight wound while on a raid near Nashville, but remained in service until the close of the war, losing only sixty days in four years. He then returned home and resumed the brick business, also in the fall of 1865 he was cotton clerk at the Louisville & Nashville depot, and in 1866 he took a contract for getting out railroad ties. He has been engaged in railroad contracting and farming up to the present time. In 1853 he married Louisa C. Patrick, of Memphis, and a daughter of J. M. Patrick. The result of this union was eight children, three of whom are yet living. One of his sons, a promising young man of twenty-five, died of yellow fever in 1878. Mr. Garrett is largely connected with the fuel business in Memphis. He is a member of the K. of H. having filled the offices from Vice Dictator to Deputy Grand Dictator.

John Gaston, proprietor of Gaston's Hotel, was born near Bordeaux, France, in 1828, and when about the age of twelve went to live with his uncle, who was then doing a small restaurant business in Paris, France. Mr. Gaston afterward became employed as steward on ocean steamers. After crossing the Atlantic about thirty times he concluded to remain in America. He served as waiter with Delmonico, New York, and as steward of several of the first hotels of Macon and Augusta, Ga. During the war he was employed likewise for the Confederacy, and after the war landed at Memphis almost penniless, where he was again employed as waiter; from that he gradually rose and by close economy he was soon able to open a small restaurant, which, with his knowledge of the business, allowed him in a short time to amass a small fortune (which he kept adding to his business). His restaurant was termed by connoisseur's the Delmonico of the South. Rising step by step Mr. Gaston has become one of the wealthy citizens of Memphis and the wealthiest French citizen. In 1867 he was married to Mrs. Julia S. Meier, who had three children by her previous husband. To our subject and wife were born two children: Annie and John Patrick (deceased). Peter and Jean, the parents of our subject resided in France. The father was an energetic farmer and lived to the ripe old age of eighty years. The mother died young. Mr. Gaston has taken an active interest in all public enterprises, and is an enterprising and thorough-going business man. He is now partially retired in a beautiful suburban home in the southeastern portion of Memphis.

Gilchrist & Martin, real estate brokers and general collection agents, is a firm composed of M. M. Gilchrist and J. H. T. Martin. Their business was established in June, 1883, by Taylor & Martin, Mr. Gilchrist succeeding Mr. Taylor the following year. The present firm command a large and successful business in real estate, and also do an equally large business in the collection of rents, etc. Their office is on the first floor of the Masonic Temple, and is one of the finest in the city in this line. Mr. Gilchrist is a native of northern Mississippi, and was educated at Vanderbilt University, Nashville, and came to Memphis in 1879, and accepted a position as bookkeeper and cashier with Meacham & Horton, wholesale grocers and cotton factors, and continued thus until he engaged in his present business. He is unmarried, is a Democrat, and is a member of the Tennessee Club and the Jockey and Athletic Clubs, of this city. Mr. Martin is a native of Memphis, and is the son of H. B. Martin, a well known lawyer of this city, and was reared and educated here. He was collector for W. A. Wheatley three years, and later entered the employ of the Gulf, Colorado & Sante Fe Railroad, at Galveston, Tex., continuing there three years. He returned to this city in 1882 and accepted the position of stenographer for Holmes Cummins one year, and then engaged in his present business. He is unmarried, and is a Democrat in politics.

Dr. D. G. Godwin, physician and farmer of the First District of Shelby County, was born in Maury County, Tenn., in 1837. His father, Seth Godwin, was a native of North Carolina, and came to Tennessee at an early day, engaging in farming. Dr. Godwin was educated in Maury County, and attended the Medical University at Nashville, graduating in 1861. He enlisted in the Confederate Army in the Fifty-first Tennessee Regiment, Company I, and was made lieutenant in Col. John Chester's Regiment; a year later he was appointed assistant surgeon, and served in this capacity until the close of the war and surrendered with Gen. Johnston. He was in the battles of Shiloh, Chickamauga, Perryville, Murfreesboro, and Franklin. After the war he returned to Shelby County and practiced medicine until 1878, when he went to Hot Springs, Ark., and practiced there one year. At the end of this year he returned to Shelby County and went into business at Arlington, with Messrs. Hughes and Cole, the firm style being Hughes, Godwin & Cole. Dr. Godwin continued his business until January, 1887, when he sold his interest, and now devotes his entire time to farming. In 1865 he was married to Miss Bettie S. Douglass, daughter of G. L. Douglass, a well known farmer of Shelby County. Five children were born to them, four now living. The entire family belong to the Methodist Episcopal Church South, and Dr. Godwin has been a steward in the church for many years. He is a Royal Arch Mason, and a K. of H. His vote and influence are always given to the Democratic party. He is a man of ability and of fine moral character, greatly esteemed by all who know him.

I. Goldsmith & Bros., dry goods merchants at 348 Main Street, Memphis, began business at 81 and 83 Beale Street in 1870, where they still have a branch store, which is the largest dry goods house on the street. When they began business in Memphis their capital was limited, but by judicious management and honest dealing they have secured and retained the confidence of their patrons and built up an extensive business. When the yellow fever raged in Memphis they opened a branch house in Helena, Ark., where they were very successful. In 1881 they commenced business at 348 Main Street, and are now enjoying an extensive trade upon a cash basis. Isaac Goldsmith, the senior member of the firm, died in June, 1885, and Elias and J. Goldsmith, the two remaining brothers, who constitute the firm, purchased his interest in the business and continued it under the old firm name. The brothers immigrated to America from Germany in 1867, and since then have been residents of Memphis. Elias Goldsmith was married in 1880 to Miss Belle Stein, daughter of L. Stein, of St. Louis, Mo., and J. Goldsmith was married in 1875 to Miss Dora Ottenheim, daughter of L. Ottenheim, a merchant of Memphis. The brothers are members of several benevolent and relief societies of Memphis, and are among the city's most enterprising and liberal citizens.

Edward Goldsmith, vice-president of the Manhattan Savings Bank and cashier of the German Bank, is a native of Europe, born in 1846, but was reared in Philadelphia, and was there educated, entering the Central High School in the class of 1860. In 1864 he came to Memphis and followed bookkeeping until 1869, from which date until 1873 he continued the same business in the Manhattan Bank. He then became assistant cashier and served as such until 1878, and from that date was cashier until the consolidation of the Manhattan and the German Banks, June 30, 1885, since which date he has been cashier of the latter, and upon the organization of the Manhattan Savings Bank, in 1885, he was elected vice-president. In 1872 Mr. Goldsmith married Miss Mendal, a native of Kentucky, who has borne her husband four children, one son and one daughter still living. Our subject's father, Emanuel Goldsmith, was born in France in 1796, and served in the army of Napoleon Bonaparte, but afterward came to America and engaged in the mercantile business in Philadelphia until his death in 1864. The mother, whose maiden name was Regina Stern, was a native of Bavaria, and died in Philadelphia in 1885. She bore sixteen children, seven of whom survived her.

James M. Goodbar, vice-president of the Mercantile Bank, is a native of Overton County, was born in 1839, moved to White County in 1850 and to Memphis in 1860. Upon reaching the latter city he embarked in the wholesale shoe trade as a member of the firm of Bransford, Goodbar & Co., which firm existed one year. He then enlisted as a private in the Fourth Tennessee Confederate Cavalry Regiment, but was soon promoted to second lieutenant and afterward to quartermaster. At the reorganization of the regiment he was transferred to the commissary department and continued there until the close of the war. He then returned to Memphis and re-embarked in the wholesale boot and shoe trade as a member of the firm of Goodbar & Gilliland, continuing thus until 1876, when the firm was formed of which he is now senior member. The company was reorganized January 1, 1886, and is composed of our subject, W. L. Clark, E. J. Carrington and F. G. Jones, all thorough and enterprising business men. The firm now does an annual business of over $600,000. Mr. Goodbar has been a director in the Planter's Insurance Company for several years, and was elected vice-president of the Mercantile Bank at its organization. In 1867 he was united in marriage with Miss Mary Morgan, a native of Mississippi and sister of Hon. J. B. Morgan, at present a member of Congress from that State, and by her has had the following children: William M., Mamie O., Jennie E. (deceased), and James B. He is a member of the K. of H. and of the Presbyterian Church. His parents were William P. and Jane (McKinney) Goodbar, and both were natives of Overton County and are now deceased. The father was a retail merchant and at one time was president of the Sparta branch of the State Bank. He died in 1878 and the mother in 1867.

A. B. Goodbar, the senior member of the firm of Goodbar, Love &

Co., wholesale dealers in boots and shoes, came from Lebanon, Tenn., to Memphis, October, 1868, and engaged in the boot and shoe trade with Goodbar & Gilliland, and was admitted to an interest in the business of that firm January, 1873. In February, 1876, Goodbar & Gilliland were succeeded by Goodbar & Co., in which connection A. B. Goodbar continued until January, 1886, when he and his brother, J. H. Goodbar, withdrew from the firm of Goodbar & Co., and organized the firm of Goodbar, Love & Co. A. B. Goodbar was born in Overton County, Tenn., May 2, 1849, where he was reared and received a primary education, and in his seventeenth year he entered the Cumberland University, Lebanon, Tenn., where he remained for three years, and in his twentieth year he came to Memphis and began his business career. He is a director in the Bank of Commerce, a member of the Merchants' Exchange, a vestryman in Calvary Parish and a Royal Arch Mason. His parents are J. M. Goodbar, Sr., and Verlinder (Cullom) Goodbar; they resided at Lebanon, Tenn., having moved from Overton County to that place in 1865. His paternal great-grandfather came from England to Virginia about the year 1775, and his grandfather came from Virginia to Tennessee about the year 1800 and was one of the pioneers of this State. Two of his paternal granduncles were soldiers in the war of 1812 and were both killed in battle. His maternal great-grandfather, whose name was Cullom, was also of English descent; the family having settled in Maryland, a branch of it moved into Kentucky and afterward into Tennessee. His maternal grandfather, Hon. Alvin Cullom, was an able lawyer and occupied a prominent place in State and national politics before and during the war of 1861. Other members of this maternal family have been distinguished as soldiers, lawyers and politicians, one of whom, Hon. Shelby M. Cullom, is now United States senator from Illinois. A. B. Goodbar was married September 9, 1879, to Miss Luan Joy, and they have one child, a son, now living.

Edward W. Gorman was born in Fayette County, Tenn., August 23, 1838, and is a son of Patrick Gorman, who was a native of Tipperary County, Ireland, born in 1811, and when twenty-one years of age, came with his six brothers to America and settled in Tuscumbia, Ala. In 1834 he moved to LaGrange, Tenn., and commenced merchandising, and in 1837 married Caroline R. Burns, a daughter of Rev. Jeremiah Burns. The father was a merchant until he died at his home in LaGrange, December 19, 1845. For eleven years he was postmaster at LaGrange. The mother was born near Tuscumbia, Ala., in 1818, and is now the wife of T. M. Moore, of Shelby County, Tenn. Our subject is of Scotch-Irish descent and is the only surviving member of a family of three sons and one daughter. He has made merchandising his chief business. At the age of twenty-one he was appointed postmaster at LaGrange, Tenn., and served until the war, when he resigned to enter the Thirteenth Tennessee Infantry under Col. J. V. Wright, and was in the battles of Belmont, Shiloh, Perryville (Ky.), Murfreesboro, Chickamauga, Missionary Ridge and from Dalton to Atlanta, and was then at Jonesboro and Franklin, Tenn.; he was wounded at Resaca, and again at Franklin, and was taken to Camp Chase, Ohio, and exchanged in March, 1865, at Richmond, Va. After the war he commenced merchandising at Germantown in September, 1865. He was married in Shelby County, September 26, 1866, to Miss Fannie T. Edmonson, daughter of Alexander Edmonson, a farmer. Only two of the seven children born to this marriage are living: P. A. and Patrick. The mother was born in Fayette County, near Somerville, October 15, 1842. Mr. and Mrs. Gorman are members of the Baptist Church. He is a Mason and a Democrat. His residence is in Germantown, where he is engaged in the mercantile business, and is also in the livery business. Mr. Gorman is a man of good business qualifications and of strict integrity, possessing enterprise and energy.

R. C. Graves, superintendent and treasurer of the Bohlen-Huse Machine & Lake Ice Company, came to Memphis at the close of the war, and has since been engaged here in the ice trade. The firm of Bohlen, Wilson & Co. was established in 1850, and existed until Mr. Wilson's death in 1865, when Huse, Loomis & Co. succeeded to Mr. Wilson's interest, and the firm took its present name, with James Lee, Jr., president and P. R. Bohlen, vice-president. The company has a stock capital of $100,000 and $25,000 surplus, is incorporated, and began the manufacture of ice in 1873, but still handles lake ice from near Chicago. The company is just on the eve of greatly increasing their facilities, and intend adding $90,000 worth of improved machinery. The parents of our subject were married in Franklin County, Mass., and were W. M. and Amanda (Root) Graves. The father died in 1859, but the mother is still living. Our subject is one of seven survivors of a family of eight children, there having been no deaths in the family for twenty-eight years. He was born in Massachusetts and lived in Chicago for a short time and then in St. Louis, where he began the ice business in 1865. In 1875 he was married to Miss Laura Belcher, a native of Mississippi. He was appointed police commissioner, under Gov. Hawkins, and was afterward elected for a term of four years, but resigned at the end of the second year. He belongs to the K. of H., and he and family are members of the Episcopal Church.

John R. Greer was born in Shelby County, March 10, 1855. His father, David S. Greer, was a native of Clark County, Ga.; his parents moved to Tennessee and settled in Robertson County when he was but an infant; a few years later they moved to Henry County, and settled within a few miles of where Paris now stands, and he was the first man to go into the mercantile business west of the Tennessee River; he was a civil engineer and surveyed and laid off the town of Paris, Tenn., and assisted in laying off Holly Springs, Miss., where he moved in 1837, and from there to Memphis, Tenn., in 1843. He was an extensive planter, owning large plantations in Mississippi, Arkansas and Tennessee; he was a man of fine executive ability, and acquired the bulk of a large fortune before he was forty years of age; he married Miss Martha Dunlap, a daughter of Hugh Dunlap. Three of ten children, born to this marriage, are living: Col. Hugh D., born near Paris, Tenn., February 4, 1836; David S., born in Shelby County, Tenn., January 6, 1852, and our subject. The father died at the present homestead February 17, 1881. The mother was born in Roane County, April 8, 1815, and is still living at the old homestead in Shelby County. John R. Greer was raised on a farm and received a thorough education in the schools at Memphis, and has fine business qualifications, being at present the business manager of the large and undivided estate belonging to the family, and consisting of over 6,000 acres of land in Mississippi and Arkansas, besides the home place in Shelby County. He has served the county as deputy clerk, and is regarded as one of the rising young men of the county.

Henry L. Guion, real estate agent and broker, is a native of this city and was born January 13, 1852, to the marriage of Henry L. Guion, Sr., and Margaret LeMaster, natives respectively of North Carolina and Tennessee. The father, a man of more than ordinary ability, came when a young man to Memphis and became owner and editor of the *Weekly American Eagle*, one of the first newspapers published in the city. Later he became a member of the firm of Cleaves & Guion, booksellers and stationers. He was one of the most influential and useful citizens of the city and died in 1876 in his sixty-sixth year. Henry L., Jr., grew to man's estate in this city and was educated here and at the Kentucky Military Institute. In 1876 he engaged in the real estate business in this city, and has thus been engaged until the present time, having been successful and prosperous. He is a director in the Factors' Insurance Company and a director in the Mercantile Bank. He is a Democrat, a Master Mason, a member of the Tennessee Club and of the Chickasaw Guards. November 22, 1882, he was united in marriage with Miss Lucy D., daughter of Judge C. F. Vance, of this city. This lady died in February, 1866. They had one child, deceased.

Benjamin F. Haller, secretary of the Hope Oil Mills of Memphis, was born in Smyth County, Va., March 4, 1836, and is the son of George W. and Anna (Johnson) Haller, both natives of Virginia, the father being a physician of prominence. Our subject was reared in Virginia, and given a fair education. He came to Memphis in 1858, and was connected with mercantile houses until the war broke out, when he entered the Confederate service as color-bearer of the Fourth Tennessee Shelby Grays. In August, 1861, he was commissioned to raise a company, which he promptly did, and the same was consolidated with another under the name of the Sumter Grays. He became second lieutenant of this company, and after the battle of Shiloh, first lieutenant. His company was transferred to the artillery service, and was assigned to a siege battery at Corinth, and later to the light artillery service, serving thus under Gen. Forrest until the close of the war. He then for three years engaged in the wholesale grocery business in Memphis, then for a time in the wholesale notion and white goods trade, and in 1874 accepted his present position. October 10, 1867, he was married to Miss Clemmie Fisher, of this city. They have one son. Mr. Haller is a Democrat, a Knight Templar in Masonry (being Past Grand Commander of the State and having held all the offices in his local lodge), a K. of H. and a member of the First Presbyterian Church of this city.

Andrew J. Harris, trustee of Shelby County, was born in Henry County, Tenn., September 5, 1852, and is the son of William R. and Evelina P. (Atkins) Harris, natives respectively of North Carolina and Tennessee. When Andrew J. was six weeks old his father moved to Memphis, where he has since resided. Our subject, upon reaching manhood, served a year as deputy United States marshal, when he resigned and accepted a position in the United States internal revenue service. His work was the dangerous task of suppressing illicit distilling in West Tennessee. He succeeded in a highly satisfactory manner. Returning to Memphis, he was appointed deputy sheriff, and having served two years was reappointed and served two years longer. In 1882 he was nominated and elected county trustee, and in 1884 was renominated and re-elected. He is one of the most popular officials of Shelby County. He gave such satisfaction that in 1886 he was again renominated, without opposition, for the same position and re-elected, and is thus engaged at present. June 7, 1877, he was united in marriage with Miss Emily S. Cummings, a native of Mississippi, and to this union there are four living children—three sons and one daughter. Mr. Harris is a Knight Templar of the Masonic order, and himself and wife are members of the Central Methodist Episcopal Church of Memphis, of which church he is a steward.

Needham F. Harrison, register of Shelby County, was born in Fayette County, Tenn., September 13, 1836, and is the son of Henry and Jerusha (Peden) Harrison, natives respectively of North Carolina and Virginia. In March, 1844, the father moved to Shelby County, where he engaged in agricultural pursuits until his death in 1856. He was a successful planter and a useful and honorable citizen. Needham F. was reared and educated in this county and lived upon a plantation until the war broke out, when, in 1861, he enlisted in Company C, known as the "Secession Guards," Thirteenth Tennessee Regiment, Confederate States Army, and served as a non-commissioned officer and private until after the battle of Chickamauga, when he was promoted to first lieutenant of Company C, and as such served honorably until near the close of the war, when he joined the Henderson Scouts and remained with them until the surrender. At Chickamauga he was seriously wounded in the face by a minie-ball. After the war he resumed farming in Shelby County, continuing until August, 1886, when he was elected by the local Democracy to the office of register, and is yet serving acceptably and efficiently in that responsible position. In February, 1866, he was united in marriage with Miss Fannie E. Neely, of this county, and by her has five living children—two sons and three daughters. Mr. Harrison previously lost a wife by death, having by her no issue. He has reached the Royal Arch degree in Masonry, and is the present Grand Scribe of Tennessee. He is also a member of the K. of H., and himself and family are Presbyterians in religious belief.

Capt. James Harvey Mathes is of Scotch-Irish extraction and was born in Jefferson County, Tenn., June 19, 1841, and was reared on his father's farm. He was educated at the country schools until his sixteenth year, when he entered Westminster Academy, East Tennessee, and remained there three years. He then taught school in Alabama, and at the same time pursued the study of law and prepared himself for college. But the war broke out, and on the day that Fort Sumter fell he left his Alabama school and returned home. He immediately espoused the cause of the South, notwithstanding that his father and many of his relatives adopted Union views. He raised a company for the Confederate service and was made captain, but his company was not accepted and was finally distributed to different branches of the army, and Mr. Mathes enlisted as a private in the Thirty-seventh Tennessee Regiment, and was elected orderly sergeant of his company, and later was made sergeant-major of his regiment. He participated in the battle of Mill Springs, Ky., and upon the reorganization of the army at Corinth was elected first lieutenant of his company. He participated at Perryville, where his regiment lost nearly half its number, killed or wounded. At Murfreesboro he was practically left in command of the regiment by the fall of his superior regimental officers. He did considerable detached duty and special service, and late in 1863 joined his old regiment and was soon after appointed inspector of Tyler's brigade. In the Georgia campaign he was under fire about seventy days out of seventy-five, and during that time wrote for the Memphis *Appeal* under the *nom de plume* of "Harvey." July 22, 1864, he was badly wounded in the left knee by the explosion of a shell, and his horse was killed under him. His leg was amputated just above the knee, but he survived the terrible ordeal, although gangrene set in and his life was despaired of. In May, 1865, he returned to Memphis and was paroled. Soon after the war he secured the position of city editor of the Memphis *Daily Argus*. In 1866 his leg was again amputated, being hastened by a railroad accident. After recovery he connected himself with the Louisville *Courier*, but ill health forced him to resign, and he then acted as special correspondent from Indianapolis and Chicago. March 1, 1869, he became city editor of the Memphis *Public Ledger*, and in 1872 was appointed chief editor, and has thus been engaged since. December 2, 1868, he married Miss Mildred Spotswood Cash, daughter of Col. Benj. Cash, and to this union the following children have been born: Mildred Overton; Lee Dandridge, Benjamin Cash, James Harvey and Talbot Spotswood. Capt. Mathes is a member of the Congregational Church, and belongs to the Masonic, K. of H. and the A. O. U. W. orders. He has served several terms in the State Legislature, and has been State elector to the national electoral college on the Cleveland and Hendricks ticket. He owns a half interest in the *Public Ledger*, and continues to be the leading editorial writer of the paper.

David Hastings, a prominent citizen of Shelby County, was born in the south of Scotland, October 6, 1828, and immigrated to America in 1849, settling in the province of New Brunswick, in the British Dominion. In 1853 he moved to Holly Springs, Miss., where he followed farming and carpentering until 1862; then enlisted in the Confederate Army in Company C, Eighteenth Mississippi Cavalry. He was in the battles of Harrisburg, Hurricane Creek and Franklin, and Selma, Ala.; was taken prisoner at Selma, but escaped and soon after reported to Gen. Armstrong at Columbus, Miss. He was granted a parole of ten days, and during the time the general surrender took place. In 1865 he moved to Memphis, Tenn., and engaged in the hotel business until 1884; since then he has enjoyed a quiet life at his beautiful residence in the suburbs of the city. Mr. Hastings was married in New Brunswick, December

10, 1850, to Margaret Murray, daughter of Joseph Murray. Mrs. Hastings was born in New Brunswick on the Straits of Northumberland, April 30, 1833. One daughter, Janet, now the wife of W. H. Landis, of Belle Buckle, Tenn., was born to this union. Mr. and Mrs. Hastings are influential members of the Old School Presbyterian Church. Mr. Hastings is a Democrat and takes an active interest in the success of his party. He owns the Central Hotel at Memphis and 500 acres of land, fifty acres being in the home place, four miles east of Memphis. Mr. Hastings is a man of strict integrity and fine judgment.

Hatchett & Stratton, real estate agents and brokers, No. 298 Main Street, is a strong firm, composed of Americus Hatchett and B. M. Stratton. They do a large general real estate business, and make a specialty of collecting and paying rents, taxes, etc. The present firm established their business in 1883, and it has now grown to large proportions, an index of the energy and faithfulness of the firm. Mr. Hatchett, the senior member of the firm, was born in King William County, Va., July 4, 1822, and is the son of Rev. William Hatchett by his marriage with Miss Hannah T. Gwathmey, both parents being natives of the Old Dominion. Americus was reared in his native State, and removed to Alabama in his twentieth year, where he engaged in the cotton commission business until 1852; then went to New Orleans and followed the same business in New Orleans two years, and then went to Shreveport, La., where he still was engaged in the same business. From 1856 to 1882 he conducted the same business in Memphis, except a few years during the late war, when he was connected, for a time only, with the quartermaster's department of the Confederate Government, at Memphis. In 1883 he engaged in his present business. He is married and has one son and one daughter. In politics he is a Democrat. He is a Mason, an Odd Fellow, a member of the R. A., and is a member of the Baptist Church.

Haynes, Ellis & Co., cotton factors and commission merchants, located at 260 Front Street, Memphis, Tenn., and the firm being composed of T. B. Haynes and J. T. Ellis, established their business in 1886. Mr. Haynes, the senior member of the firm, is a native of Henry County, Tenn., and a son of Henry G. and Matilda (Butler) Haynes. In 1861 he enlisted in the Fifth Tennessee Regiment (Confederate Army) and remained in service until 1862, when he was discharged on account of ill health and returned home. In 1862 he married Docia Allen, of Henry County, and the daughter of W. B. and Elizabeth Allen. Four children blessed this union—two daughters and two sons. One daughter died in 1868. Previous to this, in 1865, Mr. Haynes came to this city and engaged in the cotton factor and commission business with J. W. Cobb. He has, since that time, had several partners, and a portion of the time has been alone, until the establishment of the present firm. He is a member of the Masonic fraternity. J. T. Ellis, the junior member of the firm, is a native of Shelby County, Tenn., and a son of Robert L. and Mary (Cross) Ellis. He was engaged in business at Bartlett, this county, for six years previous to his engaging in his present business. November 13, 1872, he married Ida E. Crenshaw, daughter of William A. and L. H. Crenshaw, and to this union were born seven children, only three of whom are now living. Mr. Ellis is a Mason and he and wife are members of the Cumberland Presbyterian Church.

F. H. Heiskell is a member of the prominent law firm of Heiskell & Heiskell, his father, J. B. Heiskell, being the senior member of the firm. In 1874 the firm of Heiskell, Weatherford & Heiskell was formed, but in 1883 Mr. Weatherford withdrew, leaving the firm as it is at present. F. H. Heiskell is a native of Rogersville, Tenn., and was educated at Washington-Lee University, Lexington, Ky., and began the study of law in this city in 1872. He was admitted to the bar in 1874, since which date he has been associated with his father in the practice of his profession. In 1880 he was joined in marriage to Miss Gussie L., daughter of Secretary L. Q. C. Lamar, of Mississippi, and this lady has presented him with three children, all of whom are living. Mr. Heiskell is a member of the K. of H. His father is a native of Knoxville, Tenn., where he was educated and admitted to the bar in about 1843. He practiced at Madisonville, Tenn., until about 1850, and at Rogersville with Col. John Netherland until 1860. He was a member of the Confederate Congress, and at the close of the war came to Memphis where he has since practiced his profession. He was a member of the State constitutional convention of 1870. In 1846 he married Miss Sarah A. McKinney, who bore her husband seven children, of whom five are still living. The grandparents of our subject were Frederick S. and Eliza (Brown) Heiskell. Frederick S. Heiskell edited and published the Knoxville *Register* from 1816 to 1836, and was State printer from 1820 to 1836. He was a member of the State Legislature in 1847–48. His death occurred in 1882, his wife preceding him in 1854.

Judge C. W. Heiskell is a native of Knox County, Tenn., was educated partly in Knoxville, but graduated at Maryville College. He studied law while teaching school and was admitted to the bar at Rogersville, Tenn., and practiced his profession there until the commencement of the late war, when he enlisted in the Confederate service, and served with distinction, rising steadily in rank, until at the close of the war he was mustered out at High Point, N. C., as colonel of the Nineteenth Tennessee Regiment Infantry. In 1865 he went to Memphis, and has since practiced law there with the exception of eight years (from 1870 to 1878) when he was judge of the circuit court of Shelby County. From 1878 to 1883 he served as city attorney, being one of the strongest advocates who ever occupied that position. He is at present a director in the Memphis Brush Electric Light Company, and is president of the Memphis Bethel, a charitable organization. He was married October 31, 1861, to Miss Eliza Netherland, a native of Rogersville, Tenn., who has born her husband nine children, of whom seven are still living. His parents were Frederick S. and Eliza (Brown) Heiskell, for sketch of whom see above.

John L. Henderson (deceased) was born in Georgia in 1804 and when young moved with his parents to Lincoln County, afterward to Alabama and finally to Jackson, Tenn., where he married Letitia E. Reynolds, who was born September 3, 1807, and the daughter of William and Mary (Exum) Reynolds. Her father was a native of North Carolina and the mother a native of Virginia. When young they moved to Sumner County where they were married and after moving around considerably he went to Mississippi and here the mother died. He then married Frances Cooper and settled in Shelby County where he died in 1854. Mr. and Mrs. Henderson lived for many years in Madison County and later moved to Mississippi. In 1846 he volunteered as a soldier in the Mexican war, but died at Vicksburg ere he reached the scenes of the field. In their family were seven children, all daughters. In 1848 his widow and children moved to Shelby County, Tenn. She has been very successful as a financier, not only paying off all debts against her husband but has arisen to the ownership of 200 acres of splendid land. Both Mr. and Mrs. Henderson were church members, he of the Presbyterian and she of the Methodist. In the days of militia he held the positions of captain, major and colonel.

Dr. W. L. Henderson, superintendent of public instruction of Shelby County, was born in Panola, Miss., June 2, 1838, and is the son of John F. and Irene M. (Shelton) Henderson, natives respectively of Tennessee and Kentucky. Our subject was reared in Missouri, and after attaining his majority began the study of medicine with the view of making it a profession. In 1864 he graduated from the Jefferson Medical College, Philadelphia, and from the Long Island Hospital the same year. He then attended Bellevue and Blackwell Island Medical Hospitals to study oscultation and diseases of the heart, and secured a certificate from Prof. Austin Flint, Sr. He served in his professional capacity in the Confederate service about two years, but was not regularly commissioned. After the war he practiced medicine in Memphis three years, when he removed to his present residence twelve miles north of the city, and has there conducted his plantation and practiced his profession since, with the exception of two years, when he served as county superintendent from 1881 to 1883. In January, 1887, he was again elected to this position for a term of two years. September 2, 1864, he was married to Miss Margaret J. Steele, of this county, daughter of John Steele, of this city. They have living two sons and one daughter. Mr. Henderson is a Democrat, and a member of the Masonic and K. of H. orders, and of the Episcopal Church.

Dr. B. G. Henning, a finely educated physician of Memphis, and professor of materia medica, and also of the chair of clinical diseases of the rectum, in the Memphis Hospital Medical College, was born in Lauderdale County, Tenn., in 1849, and was one of nine children, only two now living, the parents being Dr. D. M. and Ann B. Henning. The father was born in Georgia in 1813, and received his literary education at Athens, Ga., and graduated in medicine at the Jefferson Medical College at Philadelphia; he then located in Lauderdale County and began the practice of medicine, meeting with marked success. Dr. Henning, Sr., was a man of fine business qualifications, and amassed a large estate; he was prominently connected with the Chesapeake & Ohio Railroad, and was vice-president of it for awhile. He died in May, 1886. The mother was a native of South Carolina; she moved to Brownsville, Tenn., when young, and was educated there. She died in 1879. Dr. B. G. Henning was educated at Covington, Tenn., under Prof. Byars; in 1868 he entered the Jefferson Medical College, and afterward attended the Bellevue Hospital Medical College in New York, where he graduated in 1870; then spent some time in the hospitals of that city practicing, and after this he moved to Memphis and was connected with the Memphis Medical College until 1872, when he went to Europe and spent some time practicing and studying in the hospitals of London, France and Germany. He was one of the founders of the Memphis Hospital Medical College, and the first to fill the chair of principles and practice of surgery, continuing to hold it for four years, when he resigned on account of ill health, and in October, 1886, he was elected to fill his present position. Dr. Henning has always been a zealous worker in the interests of this institution, and has devoted the best energies of his nature to the study of medicine, and justly deserves his position in the front ranks of the profession. In 1874 he married Miss C. L., daughter of Dr. J. R. Frayser, and they have three children living. He is a man of culture, and stands without a peer in his profession in the State.

George H. Herbers, senior member of the firm of G. H. Herbers & Co., wholesale grocers and liquor dealers, 338 and 340 Front Street, was born in this city in 1851. He was reared and educated here, and first began by clerking for Cloth & Kettmann, July 1, 1866, and became a partner of this firm September 1, 1874, and in 1886 the present firm was formed, consisting of Louis Kettmann, son of H. Kettmann, deceased, of the late firm of Cloth & Kettmann, and our subject. The firm of Cloth & Kettmann existed from 1860 to 1883. The present firm does an annual business of about $500,000. They do a wholesale business exclusively. In 1875 Mr. Herbers was joined in marriage to Miss Christina Mette, a native of this city, who has borne four children: Christina, Lizzie, Clara and George H., all living. The parents of Mr. Herbers were natives of Germany and came to this country about 1845. The father, a retail grocer, died in 1861, and the mother in 1874.

F. B. Herron, a member of the firm of Fly, Herron & Hobson, wholesale grocers, cotton factors and commission merchants, 322 and 324 Front Street, is a native of Panola County, Miss., but was reared in Tallahatchie County, of the same State, and educated in the common schools. He was born in 1848, and passed his youth without noteworthy event. Beginning in 1866 he spent several years in a store as a clerk at Coffeeville, Miss., and then embarked in the mercantile business for himself at the same place, and so continued until the present partnership was formed. He still continued to reside at Coffeeville, however, until April, 1886, when he moved to this city to take charge of his interests here. For the year 1886 the firm had a trade of about $800,000. The firm is one of the strongest and most reliable in the city. Mr. Herron's father died in 1861, but the mother is yet living at Milan, Tenn.

A. Bruce Hill, secretary of the board of education of Memphis, is a son of John S. and Henrietta (Dewese) Hill, natives of North Carolina, born in 1808 and 1813 respectively. They were married in 1835, and the same year came to Tipton County, where they engaged in agricultural pursuits. For about eighteen years he was a magistrate, and in politics a Whig till 1836, being from that time up to the time of his death a Democrat. Their family consisted of nine children—seven sons and two daughters. Four of the boys, A. Bruce, James M., J. Sloan, and E. W. Thomas fought nobly for the Southern cause during the late war. The last named died in service. In 1863 while waiting on the sick and the wounded of the battle of Chickamauga the father contracted a fever of which he died ere reaching home. The mother still lives. Our subject was born December 12, 1837, in Tipton County, was reared on a farm and received a thorough academic education. At the age of eighteen he began teaching but soon after engaged in the mercantile business. In 1861 he volunteered in Company G, of the Fifty-first Tennessee Infantry, Confederate Army. He was successively promoted to first lieutenant and captain of his company, holding the latter till the close of the war. During nearly four years of service he was neither wounded nor captured, and at the close of the war returned to Tipton County, where he engaged in merchandising. In 1865 he married Hattie E. Thompson who was born in 1843. The fruits of this union are three children, two sons and one daughter, the eldest son being dead. In 1868 Mr. Hill moved to Memphis and the following year his wife died. In 1872 he married Isabelle R. Vanse, born in 1848, and to this union were born seven children—three sons and four daughters. He and both wives are Presbyterians. Having been engaged in the mercantile business till 1881, he was elected secretary of the board of education. He is a Mason, an Odd Fellow; a member of the A. O. U. W., being recorder; a member of the order of K. of H., being financial reporter, and a member of the K. & L. of H., being treasurer. He is a Democrat in politics.

Dr. J. T. B. Hillhouse, superintendent of the roadway of the L. N. O. & T. R. R., is a son of John and Catherine M. (Van Vranken) Hillhouse. The father was born in New York, and educated at West Point Military School. He held the position of lieutenant in the regular army, and that of assistant adjutant-general on the staff of Gen. Martindale during the late war. The mother was born in Schenectady, N. Y. In the family were three sons. The other two are lawyers. In 1880 the mother died and the following year the father, too, passed away. Our subject was born October 24, 1848, near Albany, N. Y., and was educated at Yale College, graduating in 1869. Subsequently he was employed as civil engineer by the Southern Pacific & Elizabethtown, Lexington & Big Sandy Railroad. In 1876 he graduated from the College of Physicians and Surgeons at New York, and for three years practiced in New York City. Not liking the profession he returned to his former calling. From 1881 to 1884 he was chief engineer of the Chesapeake, Ohio & Southwestern, also the Louisville Short Route, and in 1885 he was called to his present position. In 1877 he married Mary L. Dickinson, of New York City, by whom he has one daughter, Adelaide. The Doctor is a first-class engineer.

Hirsch & Gronauer, general insurance agents, is a prominent Memphis firm composed of Samuel Hirsch and Herman Gronauer, whose office is at 289 Main Street. This business was started in 1869 by A. Loeb, who conducted it until 1873, when he removed to Chicago. He was succeeded by Sturm & Hirsch, who continued until 1880, when Mr.

Gronauer took Mr. Sturm's place, and Hirsch & Gronauer has been the style of the firm since. They are now doing a very large general insurance business and represent the following well known and reliable companies: London Assurance, of London; British America Assurance, of Toronto; Niagara, of New York; American Central, of St. Louis; Boylston, of Boston, and Howard, of New York. Mr. Hirsch was born in Germany, June 25, 1837, and came to the United States in 1853 and to Memphis in 1863. He was engaged in the dry goods trade until he entered his present business. He is married and has four sons and three daughters living. He is a K. of H. and since 1873 has been a member of the Memphis board of underwriters, of which he was vice-president six years and president two years. He is now a member and secretary of the Jewish congregation. Mr. Gronauer is also a native of Germany and was born August 5, 1832. He came to the United States in 1856 and to Memphis in 1858, and followed mercantile pursuits until 1870, when he engaged in his present business. He is married and has four sons and one daughter living. He is a Republican and is vice-president of the Jewish congregation. He belongs to the A. O. U. W. and the I. O. O. F., of which last order he is Past Grand of Schiller Lodge, No. 140, of this city.

Tom Holeman, justice of the peace for the Twelfth District, is a native of Person County, N. C., and was born June 12, 1830, and is the son of James and Mary (Van Hook) Holeman, both parents being natives of North Carolina. Tom was reared and educated in his native State, where he read law, and in 1856 he came to Tennessee and located on a plantation in Shelby County, where he has ever since resided. When the war broke out in 1861, he enlisted in Company C, Thirteenth Tennessee Confederate Infantry, under Col. John V. Wright, and, serving through the grades of private, became lieutenant. He was severely wounded at Shiloh, and was then detailed on lighter duties, continuing thus until the close of the war. He has never fully recovered from the wound in his ankle. After the war he resumed agricultural pursuits, and in 1870 was elected magistrate, which position he has occupied ever since. In 1874 he was elected chairman of the county court, serving thus until 1882, when he declined to act further in that office. In politics he is a liberal Democrat, believing in the principles of governmental aid to education, protection to American industries, etc. February 14, 1866, he married his present and second wife, who was Miss Lizzie Daniel, a native of Halifax County, N. C., daughter of William Daniel, and niece of John Jones Reeves, the latter a noted congressman of that State. By this union there is one living son—Tom, Jr., born December

25, 1868. Mr. Holeman and family are members of the Episcopal Church.

W. D. Horne, M. D., is a native of Shelby County and a son of J. B. and Martha (Griffin) Horne. The father came from North Carolina to this county, where he has resided for more than fifty years. The mother is a native of Virginia. In their family were six children, five of whom died in infancy. J. B.'s second wife was Mary J. Berry, of Shelby County. This marriage resulted in the birth of five children, four of whom are living. Dr. Horne received his literary education in this county and at Cave City, Ky. In February, 1876, he began reading medicine under the well known physician, S. C. Maddox, and in October, 1876, he entered the Vanderbilt University at Nashville, where he graduated in February, 1878. He then came to Brunswick and has been engaged in the practice of his profession at this place ever since with evident success, his practice being large and remunerative. In 1879 he married Rosa L. Pearson, of this county, and the daughter of James L. and Emily Pearson. Four children blessed our subject's union. He is a member of the Masonic fraternity and a Knight of Honor.

Mrs. W. H. Horton, superintendent of public instruction of Shelby County, is a daughter of Judge P. T. and Minerva (Rivers) Scruggs, both natives of Middle Tennessee, the father born in 1806 and the mother in 1808. When young they came to Fayette County, where their marriage rites were duly solemnized. In their family were five children, three of whom are living. One of the boys was killed in the late war. Of the living one son is a lawyer. The father also followed that profession, and, though a self-made man, became prominent in his profession. Having moved to Holly Springs, Miss., he there practiced for a period of about ten years, holding for a time the office of circuit judge. After his return to Memphis he was chosen judge of the criminal court, and was holding that office at the time of his death. Both parents and children are Methodists. In 1860 the mother died, and eighteen years later the father died of yellow fever. The subject is a native of Fayette County and received her education at Franklin Female College, Miss. In 1861 she married W. H. Horton, a commissioner, of Memphis. The same year of his marriage he entered the Confederate service under Forrest, and, after serving some two years, lost a leg while scouting around Memphis. His constitution having been ruined by the hardships of war, he became an invalid. To support the family of one son and three daughters Mrs. Horton began teaching, which she continued till 1882, when she was elected superintendent of public instruction and has held the position since. Under her skillful management the schools of Shelby

County have attained a standard of excellence second to none in the State.

Henry Hotter, secretary of the Memphis Cotton Exchange and Cotton Exchange Building Company, was born May 22, 1857. His father died in 1865, and he was thrown upon his own resources. He attended the public schools of the city in 1864–65, and was employed in December, 1873, as a messenger for the Cotton Exchange. In 1874 he was appointed clerk and in 1878 was promoted to assistant secretary, and served as such under John S. Toof, secretary, and S. M. Gates, secretary, until the death of Mr. Gates in April, 1881. He was then elected secretary, and has been re-elected to the same office every year since. The history of the Cotton Exchange is his own history. He began with it at its birth, when he was a boy, and is now one of its most trusted and faithful servants. He has been with it over thirteen years, and is the only one of the original employes still with it. He was married September 25, 1880, to Miss Emma E. Bollinger, Memphis, Tenn., and by her has two living daughters. Mr. Hotter is a Democrat.

Bernard Hughes, contracting freight and ticket agent for the Memphis & Charleston Railroad Company, is a son of Edward and Mary (Fife) Hughes, natives of "the Ever Green Isle." He was born in County Armagh, and she in County Tyrone. Having married in their native country they came to Louisville, Ky., where they passed the remainder of their days. Both lived and died in the Catholic faith. Our subject was born February 5, 1839, in Louisville, Ky., and while growing up received a limited education. In 1858 he became identified with the Memphis & Charleston Road, and save a short intermission during the war, he has been with them since. Few, if any, have been in the employ of one line as long. Having started as a passenger agent he arose by close application to his present responsible position. In 1861 he went out with a division of heavy artillery but was soon called to headquarters to keep up telegraphic communication, serving throughout the war. At its close he spent two years on the plains. He has the honor of having opened the first telegraphic communication between Montana and the States. In 1871 he married W. E. Ellis, of Henderson, Ky., by whom he had five children. Both Mr. and Mrs. Hughes are members of the Catholic Church. Our subject has gained some distinction as a humorist. He delivers lectures to the public on the following unique subjects: "The Mule," "Sunday Laws," "How men could be taught to cook," etc.

Emmett Howard. As head manager of the Western Union Telegraph officers of Memphis stands Emmett Howard, the son of John and Julia (Duncan) Howard, natives of Davis County, Ky., where they reared a family of four children—three sons and one daughter—two of the sons being telegraphists. The father, a contractor and builder by profession, died in 1853, but the mother still lives in the grand old State of Kentucky. Emmett Howard was born in Kentucky and while growing up learned the useful art of telegraphy and soon took charge of an office. During the war he was on post duty at Meridian, Miss. From 1866 to 1877 he had charge of the office at Humboldt, Tenn., and at the same time was also interested in the mercantile business; from there he went to Columbia, S. C., and had charge of the Western Union office about three years. He then became contracting agent for the company with headquarters at Nashville and in 1881 was transferred to Memphis. In 1873 he married Annie E. Gilbert, of Logan County, Ky., who after a happy wedded life of nine years passed to "that undiscovered country from whose bourn no traveler returns." Mr. Howard has proved an able and trustworthy officer from the fact that he is interested with a position that is of so much moment to the commercial world.

Harrison Irby, an old and valuable citizen of Colliersville, Tenn., was born in Virginia, February 16, 1818, and is a son of William H. and Sarah (Glass) Irby, who were both natives of Virginia; the father was raised, educated and married in that State. Four sons and five daughters were born to this marriage, our subject being the youngest child. The father immigrated to Alabama in 1826, and settled ten miles northeast of Huntsville, on Flint River, where he followed farming until his death in 1841. The mother died in Virginia, when our subject was but a year old. Harrison Irby was raised on a farm, and received but a limited education. In 1838 he enlisted in the volunteer service, whose duty was to collect the Cherokee Indians in northern Alabama, and assist in their transfer to the Indian Territory. He married in Madison County, Ala., December 13, 1838, Miss M. J. Moore, daughter of James C. Moore, a farmer and native of North Carolina; seven of the eleven children born to this marriage are living. Mrs. Irby was born in North Carolina, March 29, 1818. Mr. Irby moved to Tennessee in 1851 and settled two miles northwest of Colliersville. In 1866 he moved to Colliersville and with Dr. Virginius Leake bought ninety acres of land where the town now stands, and divided it into lots in September of the same year; this took the town from its old site on the State line road, as it was called, to the present site on the Charleston & Memphis Railroad. Mr. Irby has served his district as magistrate and constable, and the county as deputy sheriff, from 1853 until a few years ago. He is a Democrat and a Mason, and was a member of the I. O. O. F. until the lodge ceased to exist. Mr. and Mrs. Irby are both members of the

Presbyterian Church. Since the war he has been merchandising under the firm name of Waddy, Revell & Co., but in 1875 placed his son in the business and retired. He owns 1,100 acres of land in the vicinity of Colliersville, the home place of twenty-one acres being within the corporation. Mr. Irby is a man of fine morals and good social position.

C. E. Jackson, M. D., was born in Fayette County, Tenn., in 1844 and is the son of James D. and Frances (Wright) Jackson, natives of Virginia and Massachusetts respectively. The father was a farmer and a school-teacher. He took great interest in temperance, which subject he often lectured upon. He died in Fayette County in 1847 and the mother followed him in 1885. Our subject was educated principally in Fayette County and began reading medicine in 1867. In 1868 he entered the University of Louisville and graduated in 1870, after which he at once located in Shelby County and in 1875 moved to the village of Capleville where he soon commanded a good practice. In 1863 he enlisted in the Confederate Army in the Seventh Tennessee Regiment, Forrest's cavalry, where he remained till the close of the war. In 1874 he married Emma Rivers, of Tipton County, and a daughter of T. M. and E. C. (Tuggle) Rivers, both natives of Virginia. To our subject and wife were born five children, four of whom are living. One died in 1877. Dr. Jackson is a member of the Masonic fraternity and the K. of H.

Benjamin W. Jeter, farmer of Shelby County, is a son of Eliott and Polly (Harris) Jeter, both born, reared and married in Virginia, but came to Haywood County in 1835 where they passed the residue of their days engaged in tilling the soil. In their family were eight children, three of whom are living. The mother died in 1837 and after her death the father married Frances Burroughs of Virginia by whom he had two children. In 1876 the father died, being ninety-seven years of age. Of the first family our subject was the seventh child. He was born in Bedford County, Va., August 18, 1824, reared on a farm and received a rather limited education. At the age of twenty-one he commenced the carpenter's trade, at which he worked nearly fourteen years. In 1854 he married Harriet D. Walker and they had one son (deceased). After the death of his first wife Mr. Jeter married Sarah M. Bucey, of Fayette County, and this union resulted in the birth of seven children, three of whom are living. Having farmed in Haywood County till 1881 he came to Shelby County and settled on the place where he now resides, which consists of 822 acres. As a farmer he has met with extraordinary success; having started with nothing he has made all his property by his own efforts. He is a member of the Missionary Baptist Church as was also his first wife, his present wife being a Methodist. In politics he was a Whig formerly, but is now a Democrat.

C. O. Johnson, division freight agent of the Kansas City, Memphis & Birmingham; Kansas City, Springfield & Memphis; Kansas City, Fort Scott & Gulf, and Kansas City, Clinton & Springfield Railroads is the son of Samuel C. and Mary V. (Orrick) Johnson, both natives of Pennsylvania and of English descent. Father and mother were married in Philadelphia, where the father figured prominently as a stock broker and afterward as president of the Pennsylvania & Western Railroad. In their family were three children—two sons and one daughter. The other son, William P. Johnson, is now master mechanic of the Potomac, Fredericksburg & Piedmont Railroad, with headquarters at Fredericksburg, Va. Both parents were Episcopalians. Our subject is a member of the Catholic Church. The father died in November, 1886. The mother is still living in Philadelphia. Grandfather Samuel C. Johnson was one of thirteen survivors in 1885 in Pennsylvania of the war of 1812. Our subject was born in Philadelphia, August 13, 1852, received his early education in that city and subsequently took a collegiate course. He commenced his career as a railroad man, in 1871, as civil engineer on preliminary survey for the Texas & Pacific Railroad, and in the fall of the same year entered the general office of the International Railroad, Hearne, Tex., under H. M. Hoxie, superintendent. He remained with the International & Great Northern Railroad system several years in various positions of clerk in auditor's and general freight departments and as station agent at prominent frontier points. He was afterward connected with the Morgans, Louisiana & Texas; New Orleans & Mobile; Louisville & Nashville; Mexican Central, and Natchez, Jackson & Columbus Railroads. With the latter he filled the position of general freight and passenger agent and auditor, and organized their through system of freight and ticket rates and accounts. He also filled several important positions with the Southern Express Company, and had entire charge of their business in Memphis during the yellow fever epidemic of 1879. In 1883 he resigned his connection with the Natchez, Jackson & Columbus Railroad to accept his present position. In 1873 he married Miss Bertha Meyer, of New Orleans, by whom he has four children—one son and three daughters.

G. W. Jones & Co. are drug jobbers of Memphis. This house was established in 1854, by G. W. Jones, a native of Petersburg, Va., who came to Memphis in 1850, where for some time he was a member of the firm of Means & Co., also of Ward & Jones, druggists. In 1860 A. J. White was admitted to the firm, remaining until about 1865, when he went out and Mr. Jones was again sole proprietor. The trade was at first retail, but finally merged into a wholesale house. Mr. Jones was for many years the leading druggist of Memphis, and an esteemed and enterprising man, also a prominent member of the I. O. O. F. After his death, which occurred in 1877, his wife and heirs continued the business, admitting Messrs. Van Vleet and G. C. Harbin in 1880. January, 1885, Mrs. Jones died, and April of the same year, the firm was reorganized with George C. Harbin, James A. Matthews and H. W. Leath. The trade is now exclusively wholesale, and amounts to about $350,000 annually. George C. Harbin is a native of Lexington, Ky., where he was engaged in the same line of business, until his removal to Memphis in 1850, since which time he has been closely associated with the commercial interests of Memphis. In 1853 he married Juliet M. Grant, a daughter of Dr. George R. Grant. To their union eight children were born, four of whom are still living. The mother is dead. James A. Matthews is a native of Somerville, Tenn., where he resided until the beginning of the war, when he moved across the line to Mississippi, near Colliersville, and in 1868 he came to Memphis. He accepted a position as clerk with Walker Bros. until 1870. He then entered into the drug business at Colliersville, remaining there three years, at which time he returned to Memphis, obtaining a situation with Schoolfield, Hanauer & Co. He worked for them until 1879, and then with J. T. Ferguson & Co. In March, 1882, he embarked in general merchandise business at Little Rock, where he continued until the formation of the present firm. In 1882 he wedded Ella, daughter of G. W. Jones. Mr. Matthews is a K. of H. and R. A. H. W. Leath is a native of Memphis, and grandson of Col. James T. Leath. In 1870 Mr. Leath went to Vermont, where he finished his education, afterward engaging in business for four years in New York, and later in Denver, Col. He returned to his native city in April, 1885, and the same year was united in marriage to Miss Carrie, daughter of G. W. Jones.

R. L. Jones, of the firm of English & Jones, dealers in staple and fancy groceries, dry goods, etc., is a native of Shelby County, Tenn., and established his business in Brunswick in 1866. In February, 1862, he enlisted in the Confederate service, in Company C, Fifty-first Tennessee Regiment Infantry, and remained in service until wounded at the battle of Chickamauga, which rendered him unfit for duty the remainder of the war. He is a son of Stephen and Nancy (Griffin) Jones, both natives of Virginia. In their family were eight children, six of whom are now living. The father took for his second wife Rebecca Thompson, and their union resulted in the birth of two children. He came to this county about 1826, and passed the residue of his days here. He died in 1886 and was eighty-five years of age. In 1871 our subject married

Luella Griffin of Fayette County, Tenn., and the daughter of George W. and Ann E. Griffin. This union resulted in the birth of ten children, one of whom died in 1878 of yellow fever. Mr. Jones is a member of the K. of H.

Prof. Wharton Stewart Jones, principal of the Memphis Institute, is the son of Elder S. E. Jones, known during his life as a distinguished preacher in the Christian Church, and of Mrs. C. S. Jones (*nee* Stewart) sister of the illustrious Lieut.-Gen. A. P. Stewart, Confederate Southern Army. Prof. Jones was born September 14, 1849, near Nashville, Tenn. His early education was received at Minerva College, of which his renowned father was president, and was completed at Kentucky University. He graduated in 1873, as first honor man of a large class, delivering on that occasion the Greek salutatory. Inheriting as he does from both parents superior mental qualities, which have been directed and strengthened by training in the best schools, he is well qualified for the position he holds. From 1875 until 1881 he was principal of Bourbon College, Paris, Ky. Coming to Memphis in 1881 he established the Memphis Institute, which has grown from two teachers to five, and with a constantly increasing patronage. He is not only a man of pure moral character, but is a working Christian. He is an enthusiastic teacher, thoroughly up in all that pertains to his profession. He is a man of broad and liberal culture, and of great force of character. His school is known as one of the best private institutions in the South. He is a mason of high rank, a Knight Templar, and an active member of the Chickasaw Guards.

N. M. Jones, president of the First National Bank, of the Memphis Gas Light Company, and the Peters & Sawrie Company, and director of the Citizens' Water Company, and member of the coal firm of Brown & Jones—is a native of Youngstown, Ohio, and was born June 9, 1836. The coal firm of Brown & Jones was established in 1865 by our subject and W. H. Brown, but upon the death of the latter his sons succeeded him and the new firm retained the old name. Their business extends along the Mississippi River from Cairo to New Orleans and gives employment to several hundred employes, over twenty tugs and towboats and a large number of barges. Our subject was reared and educated in his native State, and resided at Youngstown until he came to this city in 1865. His father was a brick-mason and contractor, and a native of Ireland, while the mother was a native of Youngstown, Ohio. In 1858 our subject married Miss Ann Pollock, a native of Pennsylvania, who presented her husband with two children—one boy and one girl—both of whom are still living, but the mother died August 12, 1885. Mr. Jones is one of the solid business men of Memphis.

Dr. Heber Jones, physician of Memphis, Tenn., is a native of Phillips County, Ark., born November 11, 1848, and is one of a family of six children born to the union of John T. and S. E. (McEwen) Jones. The father was born in Virginia in 1813, and educated at the University of Virginia. He studied law and was admitted to the bar in early manhood. In 1833 he moved to Arkansas, where he has since resided. Soon after moving to the State was elected circuit court judge and held that honorable position until the war. Since that event he has been engaged in farming. He is a man widely known and a much respected citizen. The mother was a native of Nashville, Tenn. Our subject received his early education at home under a private tutor previous to the war. He afterward attended the "Nottingham Academy" at Somerville, Tenn., and then completed his literary course at the University of Virginia. In 1869 he graduated from the medical department of the same institution and then spent three years in the study of medicine in the hospitals of London and on the European Continent. In 1872 the Doctor came to Memphis, where he has since been engaged in the practice of his chosen profession. In 1873 he married Valeria Wooten, a native of Holly Springs and the daughter of John W. and Mary Wooten.

Philip B. Jones, secretary of the Vanderbilt Mutual Insurance Company, was born in Henderson County, Ky., May 13, 1840, and is the son of William S. and Elizabeth S. (Barbour) Jones, both parents being natives of Kentucky. The father was an extensive tobacco dealer in Kentucky and afterward an extensive cotton dealer here until his death, in 1858. In 1852 our subject was brought by his parents to Memphis, and here was given a good high-school education. Upon the breaking out of the war he left school and enlisted as a private under Gen. Morgan with whom he served throughout the war. He was promoted to captain, and later to adjutant of the regiment, and served thus until his capture with his regiment at Buffington's Island, Ohio. He was then held in Federal prisons until the close of the war. He then returned to Memphis and engaged in the hardware business as an employe and continued thus until 1875, when he assisted in organizing the Clerks' Building and Savings Association, of which he was made secretary, and has since officiated in this capacity. He also followed bookkeeping from 1882 to 1885, and in November of the latter year accepted the position of secretary of the Vanderbilt Mutual Insurance Company, and is yet discharging the duties of that important position. In November, 1865, he was united in marriage with Miss Eliza G. Garth, a native of Todd County, Ky., and to this union there are living three sons and one daughter. Mr. Jones is a Democrat, is a Mason, a member of the K. of P., and himself and wife are members of the Presbyterian Church.

George S. Jordan, surveyor of Shelby County, was born in Richmond, Va., October 22, 1835, and is the son of Rix and Sarah A. (Banks) Jordan, both natives of the Old Dominion. George S. was reared to manhood in his native State and was liberally educated at Hampton Military Institute, near Fortress Monroe. He then followed the profession of teaching and in 1859 came to Shelby County. When the war broke out in 1861 he enlisted in Company H, Thirteenth Tennessee Regiment, Confederate States Army, as brevet second lieutenant, but three months later resigned on account of ill health. In 1863 he entered Forrest's cavalry and served first as private and later in the quartermaster's department of the Twelfth Tennessee Cavalry until the close of the war, acting part of the time as quartermaster of Neely's brigade. After the war he engaged in civil engineering and was engaged in 1881 and 1882 in the relocation and the construction of the Memphis, Selma & Holly Springs Railroad. In 1883 he was elected surveyor of the county, and in 1886 he was re-elected. In May, 1886, he was appointed by the United States Government superintendent of the construction of the customs house, Memphis, to complete the work left unfinished by the sudden death of Col. S. L. Fremont. His education and training eminently fit him for his responsible position. In 1860 he was united in marriage with Miss Sallie F. Cole, of Shelby County. They have three living children—two sons and one daughter. He is a Mason, an Odd Fellow, and a member of the K. of H. and A. O. U. W., and himself and wife are Methodists.

Richard D. Jordan, an able attorney at Memphis, is the son of Rix and Sarah A. (Banks) Jordan. The father was born in Virginia and of English parentage, his parents being natives of the Isle of Wight. The mother was also born in Virginia, and a daughter of Richard G. Banks, a noted attorney of that State. Our subject is one of four children, two sons and two daughters; the other son, G. S. Jordan, is mentioned elsewhere in these pages. Previous to his marriage with our subject's mother, the father had married and reared one son, Alfred B. (deceased), who was an eminent physician of Georgia. Both parents were members and active workers in the St. John's Episcopal Church, of Hampton, one of the oldest and most noted churches in America, its bricks being brought from England. In 1848 the mother died, and in 1857 the father followed her. Our subject was born October 7, 1846, in Essex County, Va., and when young was taken to Hampton, where he received a thorough education in the Hampton Military Institute. He there learned to love and respect the United States Government, but the war came on, his State seceded, his dearest friends espoused the Southern cause, and into the whirlpool of secession he was swept. In 1861 he volunteered in Company G, First Virginia Infantry, and served until the close of the war. He was wounded at Seven Pines, also at Gettysburg, and again at Five Forks. At the close of the war he taught school at Raleigh, Tenn., and studied law in the meantime. He afterward read under some of the most noted attorneys of Memphis, and in 1869 was admitted to the bar. Since that time he has been actively engaged in the practice of his profession, and has held the position of county attorney for four years. In 1880 he was elected president of the board of education, which position he still holds. In 1872 he married Bettie Crawford, a native of Vicksburg, Miss., born 1855. To this union three children were born: Louise C., Laura B. and Elvin. Mr. Jordan is a K. of H., member of the Tennessee Club, and also a member of the Chickasaw Guards Club. Both he and wife are members of the Episcopal Church.

Patrick Kallaher, city wharf-master of Memphis, is a native of the county of Clare, Ireland, where he was born March 15, 1847. In 1850 he was brought by his parents to America, and was reared to manhood in Louisville, Ky., and Nashville, Tenn., and given a good English education. In 1868 he came to Memphis, and was given the position of charge of the cotton sheds of the city, continuing until 1876, when he was elected city wharf-master, and has filled this position continuously and still holds the same to the satisfaction of all, and to his own credit. He is also engaged quite extensively in real estate dealings in this city, and has made his business highly successful, owning at the present time considerable valuable property, and being a stockholder in various incorporated companies in the city, and a director in the People's Insurance Company, and other corporations in the city. When he first took charge of the wharf there were only 300 feet paved; now there is nearly half a mile paved and the wharfage has been reduced from 5 cents to $2\frac{1}{2}$ cents per ton. Mr. Kallaher is a member of the Catholic Church, and is an unswerving Democrat in politics. In 1875 he married Miss Margaret Fleming, who died in 1875 (October), leaving no issue. Mr. Kallaher is regarded by his fellow citizens as one of the most successful young men of the city of Memphis, from a financial standpoint.

Edward A. Keeling, secretary of the Merchants Exchange, is a native of this city and was born March 16, 1849, being the son of Edward A., Sr., and Martha (Armstrong) Keeling, natives, respectively, of Giles County, Tenn., and Pittsburgh, Penn. The father, who was one of the prominent business men of Memphis and New Orleans in *ante bellum* days, died here in 1850. Our subject grew to years of maturity in this city and was here educated and started in life for himself. In 1863 he accepted a position in the office of a steamboat agency in this city, and later accepted a clerkship on one of the Mississippi River boats, continuing until 1867 when he entered the employ of the Memphis & Ohio (now the Louisville & Nashville) Railway as office clerk in this city, and in 1873 was made their agent at Mason, Tenn., and in 1874 was put in charge of the office at Brownsville, Tenn. In January, 1878, he resigned this position and engaged in the general milling business at that place. In the fall of 1881 he returned to Memphis and engaged in a brokerage business, and in January, 1883, upon the organization of the Merchants Exchange, was elected its secretary, and has filled this position in a highly creditable manner until the present time. He is a Democrat; is a prominent Mason, being Worshipful Master of South Memphis Lodge, the pioneer lodge of the city, and Generalissimo of St. Elmo Commandery, K. T. He is also a member of the Central Methodist Episcopal Church. October 15, 1874, he was joined in marriage to Miss Mary Nabers, daughter of Hon. B. D. Nabers, of Mississippi, and by her has four living children, one son.

Kelly, Roper & Reilly, wholesale grocers and cotton factors, is a leading business house of Memphis and is composed of M. J. Kelly, John Roper and James Reilly. The business was originally established in 1866 by James and John Roper, but in 1882 became Kelly & Roper, and December 1, 1885, the present firm was established. They are now doing a very large business over the States of Tennessee, Arkansas, Mississippi, Missouri and Northern Alabama, keep several commercial travelers on the road and have a large number of employes to carry on the business in this city. Hon. Morgan J. Kelly is a native of Clare County, Ireland, where he was born in December, 1849. He came to the United States in January, 1863, and engaged as a clerk in the wholesale dry goods trade in Cincinnati, Ohio, until 1872, when he came to Memphis and in 1877 engaged in the wholesale and retail grocery business which he conducted successfully until 1882, when he entered his present business with Mr. Roper. He is a Democrat and as such represented his county in the State Legislature in 1882–83. He is a Catholic, a member of the K. of H., and is unmarried.

Elias Keck, proprietor of a livery stable at 403 Second Street, Memphis, that he established in 1855, was a native of Virginia and was raised in Shelby County, Ind., where his father moved when he was a small boy. He was educated in the common schools of that county and then engaged in farming until 1851, when he moved to Memphis, and four years later established his present business. Mr. Keck started without means, but has, by judicious management, accumulated a vast amount of city real estate, besides a valuable farm six miles from the city, on Big Creek Plank Road, in the Sixth District. This farm is one of the most valuable and best improved farms in this section of the State. In 1864 Mr. Keck married Miss Mattie Felts, a native of Memphis. Five children were born to them, four living. The death of one was caused from the bite of a dog. Mrs. Keck died January 1, 1876, a consistent member of the Second Presbyterian Church, of Memphis. Mr. Keck was married the second time, in 1882, to Miss Jennie Thweatt, daughter of J. O. Thweatt, a prominent farmer of Shelby County. Mrs. Keck was born near Memphis, but lived near Cuba, in Shelby County, where they were married. One child has been born to this union. Mrs. Keck is a member of the Cumberland Presbyterian Church, and Mr. Keck belongs to the K. of H. In politics he is a Democrat. He is an honest, upright business man, well known in Memphis.

A. J. Knapp, general passenger and freight agent of the Mississippi & Tennessee Railroad, is a son of A. G. and Elizabeth (Martin) Knapp. The father was born in Vermont and reared in New York. When young he went to Cincinnati, Ohio, where he married Miss Martin, a native of Ireland, who came to this country in 1835. They moved to Memphis in 1846, where they passed the residue of their days. In their family were eight children, four of whom are now living—two sons and two daughters. The other son is receiving clerk of the Louisville & Nashville Railroad. The father began as a molder in an iron foundry, and from that arose by his own efforts to the ownership of large interests in the foundry business. He was a Whig in politics and his wife a member of the Presbyterian Church. He died in 1860 and she in 1863. The Knapp family are of German descent. Our subject, the oldest child of the family, was born August 3, 1845, in Cincinnati, Ohio, but was reared and educated in Memphis. At the age of thirteen he began to assist in his father's foundry, where he continued some seven years. In 1865 he began as a warehouseman for the Memphis & Ohio (now Memphis division of the Louisville & Nashville Railroad). From that he steadily arose to clerk, local agent, chief clerk of the passenger and freight department, and general freight and passenger agent in 1876. In 1863 he married Julia C. Rogers, of Germantown, Tenn., by whom he has three children: Mamie R., Edmonds S., and Burke R. In 1883 his first wife died and the following year he married Lucy C. Bierce, a native of Cleveland, Ohio. Politically Mr. Knapp is a Democrat.

Spence H. Lamb, secretary and treasurer of the Mississippi & Tennessee Railroad, is a son of Isaac N. and Sidney G. (Hall) Lamb. The father was born in Camden County, N. C., in 1796 and received a good classical education. The mother was a native of the same State, born in 1810. To their union were born five children, of whom only two are now living. By profession the father was a lawyer, and both he and wife were members of the Episcopal Church. He died in 1831 and she in 1843. Our subject was born November 8, 1823, in Elizabeth City, N. C., and is of English and Scotch descent. He attended Washington College, Pennsylvania, and graduated in 1845. The following year he embarked in the book business in Memphis, where he continued till the war. During that time he was secretary to Col. Minor Meriweather, and in 1866 he was chosen secretary and treasurer of the Mississippi & Tennessee Railroad, which position he has filled ably ever since. In 1849 he married Estelle Avery, a native of Hardeman County, by whom he had eight children, five now living. Both he and wife are Episcopalians. Mr. Lamb has been elected successively each year for twenty years, and though the road has changed hands three times such has been the satisfaction he has given as an official that they were unwilling to dispense with his services. He is a member of the K. of H., the R. A. and the A. L. of H.

Judge T. J. Latham is the son of Edmund P. Latham, a prominent and wealthy citizen of Weakley County, Tenn. He received a thorough education, closing his collegiate course at the Western Military Institute. His political proclivities developed when quite young. Before attaining his majority he was on the county electoral ticket, and on each subsequent one till the late war. He began the study of law in Dresden, Tenn., in 1857 and practiced there eight years, when he moved to Memphis, where in 1861 he had married Miss Wooldridge. He was appointed register in bankruptcy for his congressional district; and in 1867 entered upon the discharge of his laborious duties. In 1870 he was the choice of the conservative party of Shelby County as its candidate for Congress, but immovably declined the use of his name before the nominating convention. He gave up his practice in 1872, desiring a more active life, and was elected president of the Memphis Wood Works, which was a prosperous and well known institution at the time of its destruction by fire. He was appointed by Judge Baxter as receiver, when Memphis became so deeply involved, in which position he served with highest credit. He has been president of the Memphis Water Company since 1880, and director in the State National Bank since its organization; vice-president of the Clara Conway Institute, in which he is much interested, and of which Memphis is so justly proud. The Judge was a Union Whig previous to the war. He was violently opposed to disfranchisement, and severed his connection from the body of the Union men, and presided over the first conservative convention in West Tennessee after the war. Since 1868 he has taken no active part in politics. The Judge is an even-tempered, genial, courteous gentleman who is highly esteemed by all.

A. G. Laxton, a merchant at Kerrville, Shelby Co., Tenn., dealer in general merchandise, was born in Scott County, Mo., May 13, 1819. His father, John Laxton, died when he was between two and three years old. The mother then married George Sullivan, and they moved to Madison County, Tenn. Our subject was raised in Lexington, Tenn., where he was educated and learned the tailor's trade. In 1840 he went to Texas and engaged in merchant tailoring. In May, 1841, he returned to Tipton County, Tenn., and continued the same business for eight years, when he sold out and purchased a farm on Hatchie River, in the same county, and remained on it for twelve years. In 1857 he sold this farm and bought one near Indian Creek, where he lived eight years. He then bought part of the Nelson farm in Tipton County, which is about a mile and a half from Kerrville. Mr. Laxton lived three years here, and made sorghum on a large scale. In 1870 he engaged in brick-making, and furnished nearly the entire section with bricks to build chimneys, and in 1873 built the first brick dwelling-house in Tipton County. It is three stories high, and he made all of the shingles with which it was covered. Mr. Laxton lived at this place twenty-one years. December, 1886, he sold it and bought a stock of goods and commenced business at Kerrville. He was married in December, 1843, to Miss Amanda Turnage, daughter of Isaac Turnage, a farmer of Tipton County. Six of the nine children born to the marriage are living. Mr. Laxton is a Democrat. He has been a very energetic man, and is respected for his many excellent qualities.

James Lee, Jr., vice-president of the First National Bank, and of the Taxing District of Memphis, came to this city in 1858, and located here permanently in 1860. He practiced law with Valentine & Lee; Chambers, Lee & Warinner, and Lee & Warinner, but gave up the law in 1877, to manage the Lee line of steamers, of which line he is president and principal owner. Mr. Lee was born in Stewart County, Tenn., March 8, 1832, and graduated at Princeton, N. J., in 1853, and then practiced law at Dover, Stewart County, until his interests drew him to Memphis. His father, James Lee, was a native of Sumner County, but moved to Stewart County, and there married Miss Peninah Lucinda Gibson, who died in 1853. The father, an old retired boatman, is yet living in this city. In 1858 our subject married Miss Rowena Rayliss, a native of

Montgomery County, Tenn., and by her has a family of ten children. The family are members of the Cumberland Presbyterian Church.

T. L. Lee. In 1882 the Louisville & Nashville Railroad conceived the idea of placing the St. Bernard coal of Kentucky on the market at Memphis. Previous to this but little coal had been brought here by railroads, therefore the price was very fluctuating and detrimental to manufacturing. Their movement has done much to assist this branch of industry and to reduce the price of coal for domestic purposes. They now handle over one and a half million bushels yearly. At the head of this gigantic business stands Mr. T. L. Lee, who has been formerly engaged in the same business at Paducah, Ky. He is a native of the Hoosier State, born in 1836 and the son of James C. and Elizabeth (Christman) Lee, natives of Kentucky. They reared a family of ten children—five sons and five daughters. Three of their boys were boat builders, though the father was a hatter by trade. The father and mother are both dead. Our subject's educational advantages were rather limited, but by his own efforts he succeeded in taking a complete course in Jones' Commercial College at St. Louis. At the age of sixteen he began to work at boat building, which occupation he followed for seven years. From 1859 to 1881 he was interested in wharf boats and packet lines, and in 1882 he took his present position. In 1859 he married Adelia N., daughter of Capt. J. W. Mills, and this marriage resulted in the birth of nine children, seven of whom are now living.

Lemmon & Gale are prominent wholesale dry goods merchants of Memphis, the firm being composed of Henry T. Lemmon and Tom. Gale. They established their business in 1856 and by close and enterprising attention to their interests have steadily grown to their present large profitable proportions. In 1878 they built their present large and commodious structure at 326 and 328 Main Street, and here they carry on a large and valuable trade over a large section of country, employing traveling men to sustain their wide business interests. They are one of the most substantial, reliable and enterprising business houses of the city.

Capt. Joseph Lenow, a well known pioneer citizen of Memphis, was born in Southampton County, Va., December 24, 1813, and is the son of Henry and Frances (Hough) Lenow, natives respectively of Berlin, Prussia, and Southampton County, Va. Joseph passed his youth in his native county and was there educated. In 1837 he came to Tennessee and located at Hickory Withe, Fayette County, where he followed mercantile pursuits until 1848, when he came to Memphis and began dealing in real estate rather extensively. In 1852 he was instrumental in establishing Elmwood Cemetery, with which he has been connected ever since; he has been its president for almost the last thirty years. When the war broke out between the United States and Mexico, he enlisted and commanded Company A, Tennessee Regiment of Cavalry. He is an unswerving Democrat, but takes no active part in politics. He was president of the Bank of Tennessee during its existence, and was a director of the Mississippi & Tennessee Railroad for ten or twelve years. He is one of the most enterprising and public-spirited citizens of the State. January 9, 1845, he was united in marriage with Miss Frances C. Broome, a native of Halifax County, N. C., and to the parents six children were born, three now living as follows: Lizzie A., the wife of Judge W. W. McDowell; Henry J., of the State National Bank of Memphis; Jessie L., wife of Hiram A. Partee, of Fort Smith, Ark.

Lilly Carriage Company was incorporated in 1882 as a stock company, the officers being W. S. Bruse, president; B. B. Rodgers, secretary; James Bruse, treasurer, and Owen Lilly, superintendent and manager. This manufactory is located at 325, 327 and 329 Second Street, and consists of a two-story brick building, 75x150 feet in dimensions. This company employs about forty skilled workmen and makes a specialty of fine carriages, landeaus, phaetons, buggies, etc., their annual sales amounting to $75,000. Mr. Lilly, the superintendent and manager of this business, is a native of Ireland, who was born in 1837 and who came to the United States in 1855, locating in Memphis. He served his apprenticeship at the carriage business until twenty-one years of age. In 1861 he enlisted in the Confederate service, and was put on detail duty in the manufacturing department where he remained till the close of the war. He then returned to this city and, in partnership with his brother, engaged in the family grocery business, which he continued for three years. He then engaged in the carriage business which he has continued up to the present time, having consolidated with W. S. Bruse & Co. in 1882. In November, 1866, he married Kate O'Connor, of this city, who bore him six children, one of whom died in 1884.

Very Rev. Father M. D. Lilly, pastor of St. Peter's Church of Memphis, was born in County Fermagh, Ireland, where he received his rudimentary education. After coming to America he located in Memphis in 1851, and for a time kept books in a mercantile house. From this city he went to Perry County, Ohio and attended St. Joseph's Dominican Convent, where he prepared himself for the ministry. In 1865 he returned to Memphis and had charge of St. Peter's Church until 1868, when he was called to New York City to take charge of Ferrer Church, remaining there until 1886, when he returned to his present pastorate.

He has seen the country almost ruined by political upheavals, but has ever pressed forward with the banner of his church unfurled.

A. S. Livermore, president of the Livermore Foundry & Machine Company, is a native of Kentucky and came to Memphis in 1862, since which date he has been recognized as one of the city's most enterprising and progressive business men. He was superintendent of the Mississippi & Tennessee Railroad for nine years prior to 1871, and from that date until 1874 was superintendent of the Memphis & Little Rock Railroad. Since the latter date he has been connected with the foundry and manufacturing interests of Memphis. Isaac Phelan conducted the old Memphis foundry from about 1856 to 1860, when it was purchased by Wat. Bradford, who in 1864 was succeeded by Cubbins & Gunn, the latter firm in 1877 being succeeded by Gunn & Fagan. In 1881 the entire concern was purchased by the present company, which began with a capital stock of $60,000, and has now a surplus of $12,000. In March, 1886, the company purchased the iron and railway supply depot on Second Street. About one hundred hands are employed, and an annual business of about $225,000 is done. The other officers of the company are H. A. Tatum, secretary and treasurer; Phil. Pidgeon, manager iron and railway supply depot, and R. M. Leech, general agent. Mr. Livermore has a family of five children, his wife being a native of Louisiana.

Col. Robert F. Looney is a native of Maury County, Tenn., where he passed the first quarter of a century of his life, and where he studied law under Hon. Edmund Dillahunty, and later practiced that profession in that city for six years. In 1852 he removed to Memphis and continued the practice until the breaking out of the war. He at first favored unity and peace, but finally went with his State, and was among the most active in this city in raising troops for the Confederate service. He soon afterward raised the Thirty-eighth Tennessee Regiment in this city and county and became its colonel. He moved with his command to Chattanooga, thence to Knoxville and thence joined the army of Gen. A. S. Johnston at Corinth, and was soon after engaged in the great Confederate victory at Shiloh. In a brilliant charge in this great battle, his regiment, led by himself, swept through the hottest of the fight and captured 1,000 prisoners. He is one of the most useful and prominent citizens of the "Volunteer State."

C. L. Loop, recently appointed general auditor of the Southern Express Company, was born in Indiana in 1844, and is a son of a physician. Left an orphan in early childhood, he apprenticed himself to a druggist. In 1855 he was appointed agent of the Adams Express Company at Carlisle, Ind., at a salary of $5 per month. In 1860 Mr. Loop was given a run as messenger on the Illinois Central Railroad, and soon after acted as agent at Cairo, Ill. He was subsequently employed in the Cincinnati office learning all the work of the various departments under W. H. Waters, office cashier; D. F. Raymond, freight clerk, etc., and was for a time in the office of Mr. Joseph H. Rhodes, then the able cashier and auditor of the Western Division of the Adams Express Company, now the well known capitalist of Cincinnati. Mr. Loop was afterward sent to St. Louis, and in 1862 was detailed by manager Gaither to go to Memphis, where he filled the position of cashier until December, 1865, during which time he had charge of all the accounting to the general office at Cincinnati, of all the business in the military subdivisions in charge of the late Charles Woodward. At the conclusion of the war the Adams Express Company retired from Memphis and the Southern Express Company resumed the business. In March, 1866, that company appointed Mr. Loop cashier and auditor of its Western Department, embracing the lines west of Chattanooga and Montgomery, Ala. These positions Mr. Loop has filled continuously until October 1, 1886, when he was appointed general auditor. Since 1869 Mr. Loop has also been secretary and treasurer of the Texas Express Company. He is a man of remarkable abilities as an expressman and is universally liked. He is held in particularly high esteem by the general management of the Southern Express Company.

E. Lowenstein & Bros., importers and dealers in dry goods and notions. In 1858 this firm established a retail store under the I. O. O. F. Hall, and three years later they moved to the corner of Main and Jefferson Streets, where they have an immense, choice stock and an extensive trade, both wholesale and retail. They are patronized by at least a dozen States in the Union. From twelve to fifteen traveling salesmen are employed, and about 250 assistants in the store. E. Lowenstein is a director of the Bank of Commerce and the Memphis National Bank; also of the Pioneer Cotton Mills and Factor Insurance Company. He is one of the most able business men in the section, and highly esteemed wherever he is known. By application to his financial affairs and courtesy to patrons he has risen to affluence. He is a native of Germany and came to America in 1854, locating in Memphis. The brothers came in 1857. January 20, 1864, Mr. Lowenstein married Miss Bobeth Wolf, by whom he has a family of six children. His parents, Leopold Lowenstein and Sarah (Barn) Lowenstein, were natives of Germany, where they died in 1846 and 1869 respectively.

A. B. Lurry, a merchant at Bartlett, Tenn., carrying a large stock of general merchandise, was born in Shelby County, Tenn., in 1850, and is a son of Thomas and Sallie (Allen) Lurry. The parents were natives of North Carolina and Tennessee. The father was a farmer and died in 1854, in Arkansas, and left a large estate. A. B. Lurry was raised and educated in Shelby County, acquiring most of his education from actual business experience. When quite young he commenced farming. In 1871 he accepted a position as clerk at Allenton, Tenn., and remained there until 1878, when he formed a partnership with W. D. Galloway and purchased the stock from his employers, and under the firm name of Lurry & Galloway, continued the business two years. In 1880 the firm built a new house, and one year later Mr. Lurry sold his interest and bought a farm, giving his attention to farming until 1883, when he purchased a stock of goods and began merchandising at Abernathy, Tenn., four miles south of Bartlett, and managed a farm in connection with the store for two years. January, 1887, he bought the store-house and farm he had been renting, the latter being a very noted and valuable place. He married Miss Mary L. Robins, of Shelby County, and has had three children, two now living. Mr. Lurry is a member of the Cumberland Presbyterian Church and his wife of the Methodist. In politics he is a Democrat. He stands well as a correct and enterprising business man, and has the confidence and friendship of all who know him.

John Lynch, farmer and mill owner of Shelby County, was born in Walker County, Ala., and is now about fifty-three years of age. He is the only one living of three sons and a daughter born to G. B. and Polly (McGlathery) Lynch, and is of Irish-Scotch descent. The father was formerly from East Tennessee, but settled in Morgan County, Ala., in 1825, soon after moving to Walker County. In the early military service of the State, in transferring the Cherokee Indians from northern Alabama to the Indian Territory, he held the rank of captain and rendered efficient service. He was a farmer and died away from home when our subject was quite small. The mother was a native of East Tennessee and died when he was but four years old, and was buried on the summit of one of the highest hills in that section, overlooking the Jasper road. John Lynch was raised in Memphis. Being an orphan he had few advantages for obtaining an education. When seventeen years of age he was employed by the Memphis & Charleston Railroad as fireman of a locomotive. When nineteen or twenty he became an engineer and served the road over fifteen years, winning the confidence and esteem of the company, and being regarded as a practical and faithful employe. January 20, 1856, he married in Colliersville, Tenn., Miss A. J. Ramsey, daughter of R. W. Ramsey, a carpenter and farmer. The children born to this marriage were: Joseph F. (deceased), Lillie E.

and Mary Irene. The mother was born in Williamson County, Tenn., in 1838. In politics Mr. Lynch is neutral, though he usually votes with the Democratic party. He is a Mason, belonging to the Chapter, Blue Lodge and Council; also a member of the K. of H. and the A. O. U. W., and with his wife belongs to the Methodist Episcopal Church South. By good management and integrity he has succeeded so well in business as to place his family in comfortable circumstances. His business is in Colliersville, where he owns a steam grist and saw-mill, and a cotton-gin, and owns near the place 180 acres of land. He has served his town as alderman and as mayor, and has been identified with the progress and interests of the place.

Mallory, Crawford & Co., wholesale grocers, cotton factors and commission merchants, No. 254 Front Street, Memphis, began business in 1879, and is one of the strongest and most reliable firms in the city. The firm is composed of Capt. W. B. Mallory and W. J. Crawford, men of high integrity and rare business qualifications. The firm succeeded Harris, Mallory & Co. which did business from 1872 to 1879, and which in turn succeeded Harris, Cochran & Co. The present firm transacts an annual business of about $1,500,000. Capt. Mallory is a native of Virginia, and served during the war as captain of Company A, Nineteenth Virginia Confederate Infantry. In 1869 he came to Memphis and engaged in the insurance business, continuing until the present company was formed. He is a manager of the wholesale and commission trade, while Mr. Crawford has charge of the cotton business. Mr. Mallory's parents were Virginians, agriculturists, and are both deceased. In 1859 he married Miss Harris, who bore him five children, of whom four are still living. This lady died in 1871 and in 1873 he married Miss Newell, of Clarksville, who has presented her husband with five children, all now living. W. J. Crawford is president of the Memphis Cotton Exchange and the Memphis Cotton Exchange Building Company, and is director in the Phœnix Insurance Company, and the Merchants Cottonpress & Storage Company. He was born in Mississippi in 1844, and came to Memphis in 1859, and in 1869 began handling cotton, at which business he has since been mostly engaged. He served three years in the Fourth Tennessee Confederate Regiment. In 1874 he was joined in marriage with Miss Anna Thompson, a native of Mississippi, who has borne him three children, all living. His father died in 1865, but his mother is still living. Mr. Crawford is a member of the K. of P. and K. of H. orders.

Dr. Samuel Mansfield. One of the oldest and most prominent business men of Memphis is Dr. Samuel Mansfield, of the firm of Mansfield & Co.

(wholesale druggists). He was born in 1821 in Kent County, Md., where he received his early education. At the age of seventeen he removed to Knoxville, Tenn., to engage in the drug business as a salesman. From that he arose to proprietorship, but in 1846 he came to Memphis that he might have a wider field in which to operate. From that time to the present, with the exception of a short time during the war, he has been engaged in the drug business. At one time the firm was changed but Mr. Mansfield was always the principal. The other members of the present firm are E. L. Brown and J. M. Wood. Within the last five years the business has been exclusively wholesale. In 1855 Mr. Mansfield wedded Mary B. Robertson of Fayette County, Tenn., by whom he has five children living. He is also extensively engaged in the manufacture of medicines and has by his own study and observation discovered several remedies, for different ailments, all of which he manufactures and sells. Besides he is connected with other business interests, being one of the directors of the Bank of Commerce and also the Memphis City Fire & General Insurance Company.

A. J. Martin was born in Davidson County, Tenn., near the Hermitage, April 15, 1832, and on the maternal side is related to the Donelson family, one of the first families to settle in Nashville, and through them distantly connected with the family of Gen. Jackson. He received a thorough education in one of the leading colleges in Nashville, and afterward graduated from the Law University of Virginia. He was married September 27, 1869, to Mrs. Rosa A. Martin, daughter of Col. C. C. White. Mary, A. J., Shelton W., and Rosadelle, were the children of this marriage. The mother was born in Marshall County, Miss., January 13, 1841. She had previously been married to Dr. John D. Martin, afterward a general in the Confederate Army, who was killed in the charge on the breastworks at the battle of Corinth, October 3, 1862. One son was the issue of this union—John D., a member of the law firm of Young & Martin; he graduated from the State University, at Knoxville, Tenn., and at the Law University of Virginia. Mrs. Martins' father, Col C. C. White, was born in Elbert County, Ga., April 20, 1813, and was of English descent. He immigrated to Mississippi in 1838 and settled in Marshall County where he owned a large plantation; in 1868 he moved to Shelby County, Tenn., locating at Buntyn. He was married in Marshall County, Miss., October 31, 1839, to Miss Mary E. Withers, daughter of Sterling Withers, a native of Virginia. Three sons and two daughters were the result of this marriage: Albert T. (deceased); Alphonsus C., who was *aid* to Gen. Martin during the early part of the war, and afterward a member of Jackson's escort, and died

August 12, 1864; Shelton W., now a planter in Mississippi, and Rosa A., the co-subject of this sketch, and Emily E. (deceased). The father died at his home in Buntyn, Tenn., January 17, 1886, and was buried in Elmwood Cemetery, at Memphis. The mother was born in Sussex County, Va., December 22, 1823, and is still living at the old homestead in Buntyn. A. J. Martin, our subject, resides at Buntyn, and deals in real estate. He is a man of fine social standing and great stability of character, and has the esteem and confidence of all who know him.

E. D. Massey, a merchant carrying a stock of general merchandise at Bartlett, Shelby Co., Tenn., was born in Limestone County, Ala., and is a son of Reuben and Sallie (Wren) Massey, who were both natives of Virginia. The father gave his time to farming and moved to Shelby County in 1836. E. D. Massey was raised in Shelby County and educated in Memphis. After finishing his education, he spent some time clerking in a dry goods store and then commenced business on his own responsibility, but in 1862 was compelled to close out on account of the war, and the capture of Memphis by the army. Mr. Massey then went South and traveled constantly until the war closed, when he returned to Shelby County, and engaged in farming until 1879, when he established his present business at Bartlett. Mr. Massey is a Democrat, and manifests a deep interest in the success of his party. He has been quite successful in his business, and is upright in all his dealings. He is well known in Shelby County and esteemed by all.

James Clare McDavitt, attorney, manager of L. B. Eaton & Co.'s abstract office, was born in Shelby County, Ky., November 25, 1834, and is the son of George and Linnie (Nowlin) McDavitt, both natives of Kentucky, and members of old and distinguished families of that State. James C. was reared in Kentucky, and was liberally educated, finishing at Asbury (now DePauw) University, of Indiana. He studied law under Judge T. W. Brown, of Shelbyville, Ky., and in 1857 came to Memphis to practice his profession. He became a member of the law firm of Kortrecht & McDavitt, and continued thus until the war. He entered the Confederate service and became first lieutenant in Bankhead's battery, light artillery, and served thus the first year of the war. Later he became inspector and adjutant of artillery under Gens. Maury and Polk, and for a short time was in command of the iron-clad floating battery and Battery McIntosh, at Mobile. After the war he resumed the practice of law and for a year was one of the firm with Lewis Bond, then until 1870 was one of the firm of Estes, Jackson & McDavitt, since which date he has given his entire time to the examination of real estate titles, in which important business he has become an expert. He accepted his present position in 1882. In politics Mr. McDavitt is a Democrat, but was formerly an old line Whig. He is a member of the K. of H. and of the Cumberland Presbyterian Church, and is one of the substantial citizens of Memphis. In April, 1866, he was joined in marriage with Miss Flora R. Dobyns, of Haywood County, Tenn., and to this union there is one daughter, Mattie.

Samuel Irwin McDowell, clerk and master of the chancery court of Shelby County, was born in Gibson County, September 4, 1848, and is the son of John D. and Nancy (Irwin) McDowell, both parents being natives of North Carolina. In 1832 the father came to Tennessee and located in Gibson County. Here our subject was reared and educated, finishing his literary education at Andrew College, Trenton. Upon becoming twenty-one years old he went to Arkansas, where he bought a plantation and conducted it until 1872, when he came to Memphis, and a year later engaged in abstracting titles, continuing until 1880, when for three years and a half he served as deputy county trustee, assuming much of the responsibility of that office. November 26, 1884, he was appointed clerk and master of the chancery court, in which position he is yet serving to the entire satisfaction of his constituents. He is at present director of the Security Bank and of the Home Insurance Company, and is recognized as one of the most efficient officers of the city and one of the most useful citizens. December 12, 1883, he was united in marriage with Miss Bessie McGowan of Memphis. In politics Mr. McDowell is a stanch Democrat, and is a member of the K. of H. and the K. of P.

Niles Meriwether, taxing district engineer, Memphis, was born in Christian County, Ky., January 26, 1830, and is the son of Garrett M. and Mary (Miner) Meriwether, natives respectively of Orange and Louisa Counties, Va. Our subject was reared and educated in his native State. In 1850 he accepted an engagement on one of the original surveys of the Nashville & Chattanooga Railroad, with which road he worked for about four years. He then engaged with the Alabama & Great Southern Railroad, and assisted in locating the line from McMinnville to Burksville, Ky., via Sparta, Tenn. He also assisted in locating he road from Winchester, Tenn., to Huntsville, Ala. In October, 1853, he came to Memphis and accepted a position as assistant engineer for the Mississippi & Tennessee Railroad, and from 1857 to 1867 was chief engineer of the road. From 1867 to 1875 he was chief engineer of the Memphis & Charleston Railroad, and from 1875 to 1877 was chief engineer of the line of road from Cairo, Ill., to New Orleans. This is now the Illinois Central Railroad. During 1878 he was chief engineer of the Natchez,

Jackson & Columbus Railroad. In February, 1879, he became taxing district engineer of Memphis, and has filled this position until the present. October 25, 1855, he was united in marriage with Miss Lide P. Smith, a native of Eastern Shore, Va. They have two living daughters: Mrs. Mattie M. Betts, Huntersville, Ala., and Dr. Lucy Va Davis, New York City.

The Memphis Cider & Vinegar Works, located at 6 and 7 Howard Row, were completed by the present proprietors in August, 1886, with J. Wirlzinski, president; Sol. Morris, secretary, and H. Silverman, manager. The building occupied by this company is 48x106, three stories high and has a cellar. The boiler has a capacity of 110 horse-power, and has a copper-lined still with five departments, and capable of making 200 barrels of vinegar and ninety barrels of cider daily. This firm manufactures for the jobbing trade exclusively. Mr. Silverman, the manager of this business, is a native of Poland and came to the United States in 1870. He is the son of B. and P. Silverman. H. Silverman was engaged in business in Arkansas for thirteen years and came to Memphis in 1883. In 1880 he married Esther Harris, of this city, and two children have blessed this union.

J. S. Menken. In 1862 J. S. Menken established the foundation of the present mammoth dry goods establishment of Menken & Co., situated at 371 and 379 Main St. In 1863 Messrs. Jules A. and N. D. Menken were admitted, and in 1878 Messrs. William and J. S. Andrews, all having been previously connected with the house, filling clerkships. In 1883 the present company purchased the building at the corner of Main and Gayoso Streets and a palatial five-story building was erected, having a Main Street front of 117 feet, and extending 150 feet on Gayoso Street. The entire Main Street front is of fine, heavy plate glass. The business is divided into thirty different departments, the lower floor being devoted to dry goods, clothing, gents' furnishing goods, queens and glass wares, boots, shoes, etc.; the second floor to cloaks, shawls, millinery, carpets, oil cloths, etc. The business and private offices of the firm are also on this floor, and a ladies' parlor, handsomely fitted up for the accommodation of customers. The third and fourth floors are devoted to the wholesale dry goods and retail toy department. The fifth floor is used as a millinery and dress manufacturing department. There is also a basement or cellar under the whole structure, used as a storage and packing room. Two splendid hydraulic elevators convey patrons from floor to floor. The firm at present consists of J. S. Menken, William Horgan and J. S. Andrews, and gives employment to about 325 assistants, both male and female, being the first house in Memphis to employ salesladies. J. S.

Menken is a native of Cincinnati, Ohio, born in 1840, and at the commencement of the war was engaged in the general mercantile business with his father. He then enlisted in the Twenty-seventh Ohio Infantry, but was soon after placed on the staff of Gen. Sturges, where he remained till the date of his connection with the business interests of Memphis. He has visited Europe frequently, traveling with a different spirit from most Americans. He does not rush through as if he had an irksome task to perform; but with that cosmopolitan breadth of vision that comes from looking without onesself, he goes among the people, dances with the French, drinks beer with the Germans, sings with the Italians, and dines on plum pudding in England. In 1866 he married Miss Hart, of New York, the daughter of a wealthy merchant who had retired from business. Since, as before, he is the active spirit—ever on the move, from New York to Memphis, back again, then off to Paris, always ready, never tired. Of a cheerful, happy and impulsive disposition, gloom and melancholy vanish at his approach. He is a member of the Merchants Exchange, the F. & A. M., and the K. of H.

David A. Merrell, farmer and owner of a saw-mill, is a son of Frost and Barbara (Huffman) Merrell, both natives of North Carolina, where they grew up and were married. In the family were nine children —five sons and four daughters. In 1839 they came to Tipton County and afterward moved to Shelby where the father died. The mother still lives with her son, Alex. Our subject was born in Davidson County, N. C., in 1834, and received a very limited education. At the age of twenty-one he began working for himself, and in 1856 he married Mary J. Miller, of Tipton County, by whom he had six children, four of whom are now living. In 1862 Mr. Merrell went out in Company G, Fifty-first Confederate Tennessee Infantry. During over three years' service he was struck with six balls and once severely wounded, disabling him for life. In 1866 he engaged in the saw-mill business as one of the firm of Willey & Merrell; this partnership lasted seventeen years. Six mills and a hotel at Kerrville were the monuments of their labors. In connection with this he carries on his agricultural pursuits, owning some 250 acres. Mr. Merrell has done much to improve the stock of his county, raising fine horses, Durham cattle and Poland China hogs. He is connected with Kerrville Agricultural Association, in which he takes an active part.

Dr. J. L. Mewborn, a dentist of Memphis, was born in Madison County, Ala., in 1838 and is the second of a family of sixteen children, seven of them living. The parents were Charlton A. Mewborn, who was the son of Joshua Mewborn, who was the son of Wilson Mewborn and Mary J. (Long) Mewborn. The father was born in North Carolina in 1809, moved to Alabama when a young man and was for some time engaged in teaching; then devoted himself to farming. He died in November, 1877. The mother was born in Alabama in 1822, and now lives at the old homestead where her husband located in 1843. Dr. J. L. Mewborn received his literary education at the Macon Masonic College and at the La Grange Synodical College. In May, 1861, he enlisted in Company B, Thirteenth Tennessee Infantry, and after serving a year as private was promoted to the rank of lieutenant, and was engaged with his command in the battles of Belmont, Shiloh, Perryville, Richmond, Murfreesboro and Chickamauga. He was captured on detached service in West Tennessee in November, 1863, and held a prisoner at Johnson's Island until the close of the war. While in prison he studied dentistry and after his release, in June, 1865, he returned home, resumed his studies and then engaged in the practice of his profession. In 1870 and 1871 he attended the New York Dental College, where he graduated as valedictorian of his class. In November, 1866, he married Mary, daughter of J. B. and Mary Matthews, who was born in Fayette County in 1849. Eight children have been born to this marriage. Dr. Mewborn moved to Memphis in the fall of 1871, where he has since been most successfully engaged in the practice of dentistry, and stands high in his profession. He is a member of several dental associations and an occasional contributor to the dental journals.

Dr. J. P. McGee, surgeon and physician of Memphis, Tenn., is a native of Henry County, Tenn., born in 1835, and is one of a family of six children—three sons and three daughters. The father, Richard McGee, was born in Rockbridge County, Va., in 1775, and came to Tennessee when a young man. He was married in Kentucky about 1803 to Elizabeth Gentry, a native of that State, born about 1787, and the daughter of a prominent farmer and stock-grower of Kentucky. Richard McGee was a farmer by occupation, and located in Henry County in 1833. Previous to this he had resided for some time in Giles County and had held some prominent political offices in that county. From 1833 to 1851 he resided in Henry County, after which he removed to Gibson County, and here passed the remainder of his days. He served in the war of 1812 as captain, and died in 1865. Our subject received his literary education at Bethel College, McLemoresville, Tenn., taking the degree of B. A., and in 1881 was called upon by that institute to deliver the baccalaureate discourse. He began the study of medicine under two of the prominent physicians of Trenton in 1856, and in 1861 graduated as M. D. from the Jefferson Medical College, Philadelphia. In May, 1861, he joined Company F, Twelfth Regiment, Provisional Army of Tennessee, and when the company was organized as regular soldiers of the Confederate Army he was made assistant surgeon. From that he was promoted by degrees to the highest ranks in that department. He was once captured but remained in prison only a short time. After the war he practiced medicine at Hickman, Ky., a short time, and in April, 1867, he located at Trenton, Tenn. February 22, 1866, he married Jennie C. Elder, a native of Gibson County, and the daughter of Monroe B. and Lucy Elder. This union resulted in the birth of four children—two sons and two daughters. In September, 1883, the Doctor came to Memphis, and he is succeeding well in the practice of his profession. He is prominently connected with the Tennessee Medical Association, and as he has given his special attention to surgery, is unexcelled in that branch of the profession. He is an ardent Democrat in politics, and he and wife are members of the Presbyterian Church.

George W. McGinnis, land commissioner for the L. N. O. & T. Railroad, was born in Woodford County, Ky., in 1828, and while growing up had good advantages for an education. He is of Scotch-Irish descent. His parents, E. G. and Mary H. (Young) McGinnis, were also natives of Kentucky, and after their marriage lived in Louisville where the father engaged in the wholesale mercantile business. In their family were seven children, three of whom are now living—one son and two daughters. Both parents were members of the Presbyterian Church. Our subject came south in 1861 and five years later was united in marriage to Jane Wood, a native of Mississippi. Both Mr. and Mrs. McGinnis are consistent members of the Presbyterian Church. In 1870 Mr. McGinnis became identified with the railroad business where he has continued ever since. In 1885 he assumed the duties of his present office.

W. N. Miller, a prominent farmer of the Seventh District of Shelby County, was born in Bedford County, Va., August 7, 1817, and is a son of Simon and Martha (Rivers) Miller, who were both natives of Virginia. The father was one of the prominent men of the county, owning large tracts of land there. The grandfather, William Miller, held the rank of captain in the Revolutionary war. Our subject was raised in Bedford County, Va., and educated in that county and in West Tennessee. His father moved to Hardeman County when our subject was still young, and after completing his education he farmed with his father for several years, and in 1865 purchased a farm two miles north of Bartlett, that contained 2,000 acres. February 8, 1859, he married Miss Lucy A. Whitmore, a daughter of Charles H. Whitmore, one of the prominent citizens and commission merchants of Memphis. Six of the eight children born to them are living: William E.; Lucy A., wife of C. H. Caldwell, a merchant, of Raleigh, Tenn.; Sallie D., wife of Fred J. Warner, a merchant at Bartlett, Tenn.; Willie J.; Simon A. and Elizabeth N. Mrs. Miller is a member of the Methodist Church. Mr. Miller is a Mason and in politics a Democrat. He is a man of fine social standing and exceedingly popular in his neighborhood.

William E. Miller was born in Germantown, Shelby County, Tenn., June 5, 1860. His father, William E. Miller, was a native of Kentucky, and was brought to Shelby County by his parents when quite small, where he was raised and educated, and when of age he married Laura W. Thompson. Two sons and a daughter, our subject being the second child, were born to this marriage, two still living. The father was a farmer until he went into the drug business at Germantown and was postmaster there from 1872 to 1878. Both parents and the grandmother died with yellow fever during the scourge of 1878, the father November 16, and the mother October 12. The mother was born in Raleigh, N. C., in 1828. Our subject was raised and educated in Germantown, then took a business course in Leddin's Commercial College at Memphis, and after his father's death he continued the drug business in the old firm name. He married in Tate County, Miss., January 29, 1884, Miss Lulu Lipsey, daughter of Rev. J. W. Lipsey, formerly of Georgia, and a well known Baptist minister. She was born in Mississippi in October, 1863. Two sons—William E. and John L.—have been born to this union. Mr. Miller is a Democrat and with his wife belongs to the Missionary Baptist Church. He has been successful in business and is one of the active public-spirited citizens of his town, standing well in the community in both a social and business way.

Dr. J. L. Minor, a skillful physician of Memphis, was born in Stafford County, Va., in 1854. He is the son of Dr. John and Elizabeth (Scott) Minor, both natives of Virginia. The father, who was born in 1822, was a physician of distinction; he received his literary and professional education at the University of Virginia, and practiced medicine for many years near Fredericksburg, Va., and served four years as surgeon in the Confederate Army. He was a consistent member of the Presbyterian Church, and died in 1881. The mother was born in 1835, and now resides at Rapidan, Va. Our subject received a common-school education at the institutions of learning in his native State, and at nineteen years of age commenced the study of medicine under the direction of his father. He was graduated from the University of Virginia in 1876. After this he went to New York to pursue his studies and remained there for nearly nine years, during which time he served as house surgeon of St. Peter's Hospital, in Brooklyn, N. Y., then as house surgeon of the Brooklyn Eye and Ear Hospital; he was assistant attending surgeon to the New York Eye and Ear Infirmary for six years, and was attending surgeon to the New York City Hospital on Randall's Island, and filled the same position in St. Joseph's Industrial Home, of New York City, and for two years was pathologist to the New York Eye and Ear Infirmary. He held the position of instructor in the school of ophthalmology, otology and laryngology of the New York Eye and Ear Infirmary and was secretary and treasurer of the New York Ophthalmological Society for two years. Dr. Minor located in Memphis in October, 1885, and has met with great success in his practice, which is limited to diseases of the eye and ear. He is a member of the various medical societies of the county and State, and of the American Ophthalmological and Otological Societies. Few men of Dr. Minor's age have acquired a more enviable reputation in their professions.

Hon. William Robert Moore was born in Huntsville, Ala., March 28, 1830, and is the son of Robert Cleveland and Mary F. (Lingow) Moore, both parents being natives of the "Old Dominion," and members of two of the oldest and most highly respected families of that State. The father having died when our subject was six months old, the mother soon afterward located near Fosterville, in Rutherford County, and here William R. remained until his sixteenth year, when he went to Beech Grove; thence to Nashville and engaged in the wholesale dry goods business with Thomas and William S. Eakin, with whom he remained several years. He then for four years connected himself in the same business with S. B. Chittenden, of New York City. In 1859 he came to Memphis and established his present business under the firm name of Shepherd & Moore. His partner dying during the war, Mr. Moore has since conducted the enterprise alone, confining himself exclusively to the wholesale dry goods trade. . His establishment is, perhaps, the largest of the kind in the South, and has a flooring extent of 74,500 square feet, the building being 115x325 feet. A very large trade is enjoyed. Mr. Moore is a Republican, but has no political ambition. Being a native Southerner, his Union views during the war subjected him to much annoyance. In 1880, without solicitation on his part, he was elected to the XLVII Congress and served with honor and distinction, and in 1882 was unanimously renominated by his party, but declined to serve. In the political parlance of the State, he is what is known as a State credit man. He is enterprising, progressive, charitable, and his name is above reproach. February 14, 1878, he married Miss Lottie Heywood Blood, a native of Hamilton,

Ontario, a lady distinguished for her personal beauty and her social graces. It is the chief pride of Mr. Moore that throughout his business career of more than forty years no promise of his has ever been dishonored, and that although calamities of war, panics and pestilence have within that time caused many financial fabrics to totter and fall, his character and credit have stood impregnable and his contracts have ever been paid 100 cents to the dollar.

P. J. Moran, a member of the firm of P. J. Moran & Co., coffee roasters, dealers in teas, coffee, spices, Japanese wares and baking powder, is a native of St. Louis, Mo., and the son of Dennis and Bridget (Conway) Moran, also natives of St. Louis, Mo., where they resided during life. The father was a mechanic. In 1869, prior to his coming to Memphis, our subject was connected with the firm of Matthew Hunt & Co., and this firm in the same year established a branch house in Memphis, being the first coffee roasters and spice grinders in Tennessee. Mr. Moran conducted the business of the above firm in this city until 1872, after which he engaged in the merchant brokerage business for two years. In 1870 the old firm, Matthew Hunt & Co., became W. F. Cavanaugh & Co., and in 1874 it was purchased by our subject and became C. H. Pomroy & Co. In 1876 Mr. Moran withdrew, and the firm again became W. F. Cavanaugh & Co., and remained as such until July 1, 1885, when our subject purchased the whole interest and has since conducted the business alone. He transacts a business of about $70,000 annually, and has a man employed soliciting wholesale trade in the city. From 1876 to 1881, he served a clerkship for a wholesale grocery firm at Memphis, and was then admitted to the firm, where he remained until he established his present trade. Mr. Moran wedded Tilda J. Chandler, a native of Memphis, who died in 1882.

Judge R. J. Morgan, senior member of the law firm of Morgan & McFarland, was educated at the University of Georgia, graduating therefrom in 1848, and soon afterward began the study of law and was admitted to the bar in 1850. He practiced his profession in Georgia until 1859, when he came to this city and continued the practice until the war broke out, when he raised and was made colonel of the Thirty-Sixth Tennessee Regiment, and continued in this position until 1863, when the regiment was consolidated with other commands, and Col. Morgan was transferred to the staff of Gen. Polk, where he served until the death of the latter in 1864, near Atlanta. He was then assigned to the duty of auditing claims against the Confederate Government, and was thus engaged until the restoration of peace. He then returned to Memphis and resumed the practice of law. He was elected city attorney in 1867, re-elected in 1868, appointed chancellor in 1869, elected in 1870, and continued to hold the office until 1878, since which date he has been engaged in the practice. Judge Morgan was born March 25, 1828, in Putnam County, Ga., but was taken to LaGrange, Ga., by his parents in infancy. He is the son of John E. and Mary T. (Brown) Morgan, natives of Georgia, the father being a farmer, merchant and banker until his death in 1868. During the war he was a commissioner under the Confederate Government. The mother died in 1876. September 19, 1854, our subject married Miss Martha Fort of Milledgeville, Ga., and to them the following children have been born: Mary Louisa (Mrs. J. A. Keightley), Tomlinson F. (deceased), and John E. The mother of these children died in February, 1886. Judge Morgan is a Democrat, a Methodist and a Mason.

Dr. S. J. Morrison, of the firm of Drs. Frayser & Morrison, of Memphis, Tenn., was born in Virginia in 1834, and was one of a family of thirteen children, eight now living. The parents, Dr. E. A. and Mary (Trumbull) Morrison, were both natives of Virginia. Our subject's grandfather was a native of Ireland, born in Dublin and an eminent physician. Dr. E. A. Morrison, the father, received his medical education at the University of Pennsylvania, and was a physician of high standing for many years before his death, which occurred in 1879, at the age of seventy-five. His mother was born in 1808, and died in 1845. Dr. S. J. Morrison graduated at the University of Virginia in 1856, and soon after commenced the study of medicine, attending the New York University, afterward taking a course of lectures at Long Island Hospital Medical College, and graduated therefrom in 1860. Until 1861 he practiced medicine at his home in Virginia, when he enlisted in the Confederate Army, joining the Brunswick Guards. and was made assistant surgeon, acting in that capacity until the close of the war. In 1870 he moved to Memphis, and his extensive and lucrative practice testifies to his ability as a physician.

E. B. Moseley, proprietor of Moseley Cotton-gin, which has a capacity of twenty-five bales daily and forty bales in twenty-four hours, was born in the city of Memphis, and is a son of John B. and M. E. (Leake) Moseley. In 1882 our subject married Rosa B. Kennedy, of this city, the daughter of W. H. Kennedy. This union resulted in the birth of two children. Mr. Moseley is the proprietor and manager of the above business, which was established in the summer of 1885, and is situated at 201 and 203 Madison Street.

McKeon & Cross, real estate brokers and collecting agents, is one of the strong business partnerships of the city, and is composed of Tennie

McKeon and J. S. Cross. The firm was established in December, 1886, and has been successful since the start. J. F. McKeon is a native of Memphis, and was born September 21, 1857. He is the son of Thomas McKeon, a prominent wholesale grocer and cotton factor of this city, who died about three years after the war. Our subject grew to years of maturity in this city and was here educated. He first clerked in the grocery business and then in the real estate business five years. In 1881 he was appointed deputy sheriff for the criminal court, which position he occupied until he engaged in his present business. June 28, 1886, he was united in marriage to Miss Mollie Shea, of this city. Mr. McKeon is a Democrat and is a member of the Catholic Church and of the Catholic Knights of America. John S. Cross was born in Walker County, Tex., June 29, 1864, and is the son of John and Lucy M. (Mosley) Cross, natives of Virginia. His father died in Texas in 1864, after which his mother returned to Kentucky, taking with her our subject and his brother, and there they were reared and educated. He began business life as clerk in a mercantile establishment, working thus at Hopkinsville, Ky., and at Cincinnati, Ohio. In December, 1884, he came to Memphis and engaged with the Pullman Palace Car Company, and later entered a shoe house here; but left the same in May, 1886, and from that date until December, 1886, engaged in the real estate business for another person. In December, 1886, he began in his present business. He is unmarried, is a Democrat, a Baptist and a member of the K. of P.

Andrew J. Murray, first assistant city engineer of Memphis, is a native of Lanarkshire, Scotland, where he was born February 9, 1836, being the son of Andrew and Agnes (Jardine) Murray. Both parents were natives of Scotland, the mother being of French descent. Our subject came to the United States in 1845, and secured a fair education in the New York City schools. He then returned to his native country and remained four years, making a trip while there to the Crimea. In the spring of 1855 he returned to this country, and in 1856 went with an engineering party to Minnesota. This was the commencement of his engineering career—carrying the chain. After the financial crisis of 1857 he worked his way to St. Louis, his wild-cat money being worthless. He soon went to Chillicothe, Ohio, and in the fall of 1858 came to Memphis and worked under City Engineer E. W. Rucker until the war broke out when he enlisted in the engineer corps of the Confederate Army. In 1862 he became chief military store-keeper in the ordnance department, continuing until the winter of 1864 when he was captured at Collierville, Tenn., and was held prisoner by the Federals until the close of the war, part of the time under oath only. In 1864 while on parole he accepted an assistant professorship in Hitchcock's Commercial College of Wheeling, Va. After the war he returned to Memphis, and has since been connected with the engineer's department, having been chief assistant since 1865. In 1871 he was united in marriage with Miss Ina Saxon, a native of Alabama. They have two living sons. Mr. Murray is a Democrat, is a Master Mason, and is a member of the Episcopal Church of this city. While in the war he participated in the siege of Vicksburg.

Rev. Father Nemesius Rohde, pastor of St. Mary's Church, Memphis, was born in Rietburg, Westphalia, diocese of Baderborn. After attending the gymnasium of his native town, he went to Baderborn and completed the course at the gymnasium there, taking nine years in order to do so. For two years he reviewed the work previously gone over in the order of St. Francis, and at the same place spent two years in the study of philosophy and four years in the study of theology, being ordained March 13, 1870. For five years he was pastor in the old country, and then being expelled by Bismarck from Germany, in the time of "Cultur Kampf," he went over to Holland with all the fathers of his order, and in 1876 came to America. For eight years he was pastor of St. Peter's Church in Chicago, and in 1885 came to Memphis to administer to the spiritual wants of his present church. In all his trials and persecutions Father Nemesius has ever been found subserving the best interests of his church.

Capt. W. N. Nevill was born in Tippah County, Miss., November 1, 1840. His father, Mathew Nevill, was born in Orange County, N. C., and immigrated to Tennessee when twenty-two years of age and settled in the western part of the State. He was married before leaving North Carolina to Mahala Kirby. Two sons and six daughters were the result of this marriage, our subject being the sixth child. After remaining two years in Tennessee the father moved to Tippah County, Miss., where he lived until 1847, when he returned to Tennessee and settled in Shelby County. He was a farmer, and is now living with our subject. The mother was a native of North Carolina and died in Shelby County, Tenn., in 1848. Our subject has always made farming his business. He enlisted in the Confederate Army and belonged to the Thirty-eighth Tennessee Infantry, under Col. R. F. Looney, and participated in the battles of Shiloh, Perryville, Murfreesboro, Chickamauga, and was in the retreat from Dalton to Atlanta, and in the siege of Atlanta and at the battle of Franklin. He was slightly wounded at Chickamauga and was surrendered at Jonesboro, N. C. Mr. Nevill was married in Shelby County, Tenn., in February, 1866, to Miss Jennie Turbiville, daughter of R. W. and Ara (Harrison) Turbiville. The children born to this union are

Minnie Lou, Emma T., Charlie R. and Mary. Mrs. Nevill was born in Virginia, April 21, 1844. She is a member of the Methodist Episcopal Church South. Mr. Nevill is a Democrat. He owns 200 acres of land on the Memphis & Charleston Railroad, five miles west of Colliersville, Tenn. He is greatly esteemed by his acquaintances as a man of fine character and correct business principles.

A. W. Newsom, a member of the firm of Lawhorn & Newsom, general commission merchants and dealers in fruits and produce, 344 and 346 Front Street, is a native of this city and began business in 1866 in the grocery trade, wholesale and retail, continuing until 1868, when he engaged with Sherman & Co. in the produce trade, and in 1873 engaged in the latter business on his own responsibility, continuing until 1878, at which date the present firm was formed. The old firm of L. Lawhorn & Co. was established in 1868, and was succeeded by the present firm. They now do an annual business of from $150,000 to $200,000. In 1873 Mr. Newsom was united in marriage with Miss Emma Blair, a native of this city, who has borne five children, of whom three are living. He is a director in the Mercantile Bank and in the Merchants' Exchange, and in 1873 was elected city treasurer to fill the unexpired term of his father. The father, John, came to Memphis in 1828, and was city tax collector from 1846 to 1864. He was a native of Virginia, and died in 1873. The mother was also a native of Virginia, and is yet living in this city.

T. L. Nolley, dealer in general merchandise, is a native of Paris, Tenn., and at the age of two years went with his father to Fayette County, where he lived until he became of age, after which he went to Louisiana and engaged in planting [and merchandising. He remained there till 1878, when he came to this village and engaged in the saw-mill business. In 1880 he began merchandising in the same village and is engaged in that at the present time. His parents, Alexander and Joyce (Langley) Nolley, were both natives of Virginia. The father, by profession, was a school teacher, and at the time of his death, which occurred in 1865, was living in Oakland, Fayette County. The mother died previous to this in 1850. In 1862 our subject enlisted in the Confederate service, Third Louisiana Cavalry and remained in service until the close of the war. In 1880 he married Mrs. J. H. (Henning) Saddle, of the city of Memphis. To this union four children have been born—one son and three daughters.

D. B. Nugent was born June 12, 1850, at Cobourg, Canada West, and is the son of H. B. Nugent, a native of New York City, and Miranda (Hart) Nugent, a native of Canada West and now a resident of Wisconsin. In 1882 our subject was united in marriage to Maud R. Watson, a native of Marshall, Mo., and the daughter of B. F. and Sallie E. (Halk) Watson. To these parents was born one child, Frank H. Mr. Nugent has been engaged in the lumber business for a number of years in Wisconsin, Michigan, Missouri, Illlinois and Tennessee, and is now engaged in manufacturing lumber in northern Mississippi. He is a wide-awake, thorough-going business man and has the confidence and respect of all who know him. His prospects are bright for the future. He permanently located in Memphis in the year 1881, and is now one of the most enterprising business men of whom the city can boast.

Nutzell, Wade Wagon Company, first-class repairers of carriages, buggies, etc., established their business in August, 1884, and are situated at 60 and 62 Hernando Street, Memphis. Few companies have succeeded in business as has the above named firm, who began with experience only, and now control a trade second to none of the kind in the city. They employ in this firm fifteen skilled workmen. Mr. Nutzell, the senior member of this firm, is a native of Germany, who came to the United States in 1852 and in 1853 came to Memphis. In 1862 he enlisted in the Confederate service and remained until December, 1864, when he was taken prisoner and retained until May, 1865. He participated in many of the principal battles fought, being under the following generals: Bragg, Johnston and Hood. In 1871 he married Rosa Hammerly of this city, and to them were born five children, one of whom died during the yellow fever scourge of 1879. Mr. Nutzell's family are members of the Catholic Church. M. B. Wade, one of the members of this firm, is a native of Chicot County, Ark., and came to Memphis in 1872. He began learning his trade in 1867 and is a first-class mechanic. In 1873 he married Caroline Arnold of Memphis, and by their union has seven children, four of whom are now living. The parents of our subject are Tobias and America Wade, they having died when our subject was quite young. Thomas J. Kane, the junior member of the firm, is a native of Memphis and the son of William and Mary Kane. The parents are natives of Ireland and came to the United States in 1850 and 1848, respectively. Our subject began learning his trade in 1879, and in 1885 he became a member of this firm.

Dr. G. W. Overall, a well known physician of Memphis, was born in Rutherford County, Tenn., in December, 1849, and was one of five children that was raised. The parents were Nathaniel S. and D. H. Overall. The father was born in Rutherford County in 1812, and educated in that county, and is a farmer, now residing near Murfreesboro, Tenn. The mother was a Miss Crutchfield, born in Wilson County in 1820. Dr. Overall received his literary education at the Southwestern Baptist University at Murfreesboro, and then commenced the study of medicine under Drs. Clayton and Murfee, of that place, and afterward attended lectures at the University at Louisville and the Jefferson Medical College at Philadelphia, graduating at the latter place in the spring of 1875, then located in his native town, and practiced medicine for three years, when he moved to Memphis, and the following year was elected to fill the chair of physiology, nervous diseases and electrotherapeutics in the Memphis Medical College, and filled the position for five years, when he resigned on account of ill health. April, 1879, he married Miss Rowena, daughter of Emmet and Jane (Ewing) Eakin, the mother being a sister of the Hon. Joseph W. Ewing. Mrs. Overall is a native of Murfreesboro, Tenn. Dr. Overall has been very successful in his profession, and is regarded as a remarkably well posted physician, and his large practice is constantly increasing.

Walter L. Parker, secretary of the People's Insurance Company, is a native of this city and was born January 5, 1852. His parents were Robert A. and Lamira A. (Minter) Parker, natives respectively of North Carolina and Kentucky. In 1845 the father came to Memphis and engaged in the mercantile pursuit, continuing successfully until his death in 1864. Our subject was reared and educated in his native city, and in 1869 he left the schoolroom and entered the employ of the People's Insurance Company as clerk, and has remained with the company continuously to the present time, having by close and accurate business methods won the highest confidence of his employers. He is also agent for the following companies: Phœnix, of Hartford; Guardian, of London; American, of Philadelphia; Northwestern National, of Milwaukee; and Hibernia, of New Orleans. Mr. Parker has the enviable credit of having originated the Tennessee Society for the Prevention of Cruelty to Animals, and has been largely instrumental in securing legislation in kindred philanthropic movements. June 13, 1872, he was united in marriage with Miss Ella Burr, of this city, and to this union there are living three sons and three daughters. Mr. Parker is a Democrat, is a member of the K. of P., and in religious views is a Presbyterian.

Page M. Patterson, of the firm of P. M. Patterson & Co. (the Co. being Robt. W. Galloway), was born in Orange County, N. C., on the 8th of January, 1828. His parents moved to West Tennessee and settled near McLemoresville, Carroll County, in the year 1833, where they engaged in agricultural pursuits. In this family were ten children, six of whom are living. In 1868 his father died. His parents were Cumberland Presbyterians; of their sons two were in the Confederate service, one being killed. Our subject was of Scotch-Irish descent. He came to Memphis in August, 1850, and engaged in the stage office as agent of the different lines leading out of Memphis. In 1852 he engaged in the omnibus and transfer business, in which he has continued up to the present time. On October 11, 1854, he was married to Harriett F. Hart, near McLemoresville, by whom he had seven children, only one now living, named Nannie M. Patterson. She was married in October, 1876, to Dr. Walter Wesser, who died of yellow fever in September, 1878. They had born to them a son, August, 1877, who is living, and in December, 1885, she was married to G. W. Harris, of Louisville, Ky. Both Mr. and Mrs. Patterson are members of the Cumberland Presbyterian Church. He is a Democrat in politics. Since 1866 he has run the local ferry between Memphis and Hopefield, Ark. For thirty-six years Mr. Patterson has been intimately connected with the business of Memphis, and has ever been considered one of the most active business men of the city.

Joseph T. Penton, auditor of the L., N. O. & T. R. R., is a son of George R. Penton, a native of New York, who came when young to Louisville, Ky., where he married Emma Kendrick, by whom he had two sons, only one of whom is now living. He was a merchant by occupation, and died in 1860. Our subject was born October 21, 1859, in Louisville, Ky., where he grew up and received his education. In 1877 he began his career as a railroad man. He was clerk in the auditor's office for some time, and from that he arose, step by step, to the auditorship. In 1883 he married Florence Melone, a native of Kentucky. Upon the appointment of Mr. Penton to the auditorship of the above road in 1885, they moved to Memphis. His father was a consistent member of the Episcopal Church, and his mother, himself, and wife are members of the same.

Calvin Perkins, attorney at law, came to Memphis in 1881, and has since practiced his profession here. He is a native of Lowndes County, Miss., and was reared there and educated in the schools of that State, remaining there until he came to Memphis. His parents were Calvin and Louisa (Blakeney) Perkins and were natives of South Carolina, but were engaged in planting in Mississippi at the time of their deaths in 1863 and 1869, father and mother respectively. In 1878 our subject married Miss Susan A. Chapman, a native of Orange County, Va. She has borne her husband six children, five of whom are still living. Mr. Perkins is president of the Shorthand Type-Writer Company of this city, which company was organized in April, 1884, and incorporated with a capital stock of $100,000, James H. Anderson being secretary and treasurer. In February, 1885, they sold the patent, but retained a royalty.

George B. Peters, Jr., attorney-general of the criminal court, was born in Hardeman County, January 11, 1850, and is the son of Dr. George B. Peters, long a well known resident and physician of Hardeman County, and now a resident of Arkansas and a member of the Senate of that State. In 1870 our subject graduated at Washington Lee University, Virginia, and then entered the law school at Lebanon, Tenn., and graduated thence in 1871, and began practicing his profession in Memphis as one of the firm of Finlay & Peters. He continued thus until his election to his present official position. Mr. Peters is an unswerving Democrat, and as such was elected to the State Legislature in 1875 and again in 1877. In 1884 he declined the nomination of the Democratic convention to the State Senate. He is a member of the K. of P., K. of H., A. O. U. W. and of the Episcopal Church. June 13, 1872, he was married to Miss Katie B. Greenlaw, of this city. They have five living children—one son and four daughters.

Augustus F. Phillips, dealer in staple and fancy groceries, dry goods, etc., is a native of Shelby County, Tenn., and has been in business at Brunswick for a period of seven years. He is a son of William and Sarah W. (Purser) Phillips, natives respectively of Virginia and North Carolina. The father lived in this county for many years, and died when our subject was quite small. He was married three times, his first wife being a Miss Head. Six children were the fruits of this union. To his second marriage were born three children, two of whom are now living. In 1871 he married Mrs. Lucy A. (Thomas) Rogers, a native of Mississippi, and by her became the father of two children. After spending about nine years of his life in Arkansas, engaged in farming the principal part of the time, our subject returned to this county, about twenty-nine years ago, where he has remained up to the present time. Since locating here many improvements have been made that add greatly to the general appearance of the village, which Mr. Phillips has been quite instrumental in producing.

William E. Polk, extensive farmer and merchant, is a son of Charles G. and Mary A. (Massey) Polk, both natives of Middle Tennessee. They came to Shelby County when young; married here, and made this their permanent home. He began life with a wife, a pony and a few pounds of bacon. When he died he owned 2,500 acres of good land. Their family consisted of eight children, only one of whom is now living. One of the boys died in the Confederate service. The father died in 1876 at sixty-one years of age, but the mother is still living. Our subject was born in January, 1856, in Shelby County, and while growing up received a good English education. At the age of nineteen he began his career as a farmer, which he has made his chief business since. In 1878 he married Lena A. Wesson, of Shelby County. The fruits of this union were five children, two now living, viz.: Charley W. and Lewie R. Mr. Polk owns 960 acres of land in the best part of Shelby County, and takes an active interest in the rearing of fine stock. In 1884 he and Mrs. L. T. Anderson opened a stock of general merchandise in Millington. He is a Democrat in politics as was his father before him. Our subject's great-grandfather, Civil Charlie Polk (as he was called), helped to raise the liberty flag in Mecklenburg, N. C.

Capt. E. C. Postal was born in Jefferson City, Mo., in 1843, and is the son of William and Luna C. (Carter) Postal, natives of New York, who remained in their native State until about 1820, and then removed to Missouri; their family consisted of twelve children—six sons and six daughters. Three of the sons followed steamboating and became masters of vessels. At the age of fifteen Capt. Postal began his career on the river as clerk on a steamer. From that he went to piloting on the river in 1866, and while thus engaged gave such proof of his ability and skill, that he was made captain in 1874, which position he has since held, running almost exclusively on the White River. Through the instrumentality of himself and Capt. J. H. Rees, the steamer "Chickasaw" was built in 1883, and Capt. Postal took command of that noble vessel and has run her ever since. The Captain is a pleasant man socially, and is accounted among river men as one of the ablest masters in the service.

Poston & Poston, general legal practitioners of the Memphis bar and general attorneys for the Memphis & Charleston Railroad, is a firm consisting of D. H., W. K. and F. P. Poston, sons of W. K. Poston, Sr. The father came to Memphis in 1839, and practiced law here until his death in 1866. He was a prominent man, and was a member of the State Legislature just at the close of the war. His wife, Mary (Park) Poston, at present resides in this city. The three brothers, members of the above firm, are all natives of this city. D. H. and W. K. were admitted to the local bar in 1866, and practiced with the firm of Humes & Poston, with a few changes, until April 1, 1882, when F. P. was admitted and Mr. Humes withdrew, leaving the firm as it is at present. This firm has a large practice and the confidence of the public. The two elder brothers served throughout the war in the Confederate service and are both married. The younger brother is yet single.

George R. Powel, coroner of Shelby County, was born in Rogersville, Hawkins Co., Tenn., January 10, 1816. His parents were Benjamin and Ellen (Rutledge) Powel, natives respectively of Pennsylvania and Tennessee. In 1817 our subject was taken to Franklin, Tenn., where he was reared to manhood and given a fair education. May 4, 1843, he married

Musadora C. Jones, of Bedford County, Tenn., and to this union there are three living sons and two living daughters. John A., his eldest son, is a constable of the Fifth District, Shelby County. His son Benjamin is superintendent for a Memphis cotton storage company. His son, George R., is a traveling salesman for a Memphis company. His daughter Annie is the wife of E. E. Colby; and his daughter Sallie is yet at home. In 1844 our subject moved to DeSoto County, Miss., and in 1851 came to Memphis. He followed various pursuits until 1856 when he was appointed deputy sheriff of Shelby County, and served until 1860. He was then elected State and county tax collector, and was re-elected in 1862, but could not serve, owing to the disorder attending the civil war. In 1866-67 he again served as collector, and then for a time conducted his plantation near Memphis. In 1870 he was made deputy sheriff, and in 1871 deputy trustee. In 1872 he was again elected tax collector, and in 1876 was appointed deputy trustee and tax collector, serving thus until 1880. In 1882 he was elected magistrate, and in 1886 was elected coroner of the county, which office he yet holds. He is a notary public, and is a Jacksonian Democrat. He is one of the most useful, upright and substantial citizens of the city.

Col. Joseph D. Powell was born in Henry County, Tenn., near Paris, December 29, 1833. His father was born near Raleigh, N. C., and came with his parents to Tennessee in 1827, and settled near Paris, where he married, in 1829, Eliza Fowler, daughter of William and Morning (Cridup) Fowler. Four sons and five daughters were born to them, our subject being the second. All of them are living, but one son—John C., who died at Lauderdale Springs, Miss., from disease contracted during the Shiloh campaign. The Powells and Fowlers were among the early settlers of Tennessee; the latter family moved to the State in 1820. The father of our subject was a farmer and a carpenter, and is still living in Marshall County, Miss. The mother was born in 1812, near Raleigh, N. C., and died at Marystown, Tex., December 22, 1884, while visiting relatives. Both parents were members of the Baptist Church, having united with the church before their marriage. Our subject was raised on a farm, and has made farming his business. He enlisted in the Confederate Army May 10, 1861, and belonged to the Fourth Tennessee Infantry, under Col. R. P. Neely, and was at the battles of Shiloh, Perryville, Murfreesboro, Missionary Ridge, and the retreat from Dalton to Atlanta. Toward the close of the war he became a member of Forrest's cavalry, and was surrendered at Gainesville, Ala., in May, 1865. Col. Powell was married in Marshall County, Miss., December 28, 1870, to Miss Sarah A. McFadden, daughter of James McFadden, a tanner by trade. They have had five children, four living: James B., Joseph D., Vannoy H. M. and Edna E. The mother was born in Marshall County, Miss., March 11, 1848. Her parents were natives of South Carolina and Tennessee; her mother was born in Smith County, Tenn., in 1810, and lives near McGregor, Tex. She was a Miss Barry, and her father had been one of the first printers at Nashville. Col. Powell is an enthusiastic Democrat, and cast his first presidential vote for Buchanan; he owns 100 acres of land one and three-fourth miles northwest of Colliersville. He is sincere in his friendships, liberal in his ideas, and honest in all of his transactions.

 John H. Priddy, proprietor of the Priddy House, is a native of Virginia, born July 4, 1811. He is the son of William and Lucy (Priddy) Priddy, both native Virginians. Our subject was reared on a farm and at the age of sixteen went to Richmond, Va., where he learned the bricklayer's and plasterer's trade. In 1833 he wedded Maria A. Priddy and in 1835 he came to Shelby County with his father and located on a farm, but still worked at his trade. October 10, 1868, his wife died, leaving six children to mourn the loss of a mother. In 1869 he married Lucy A. Martin, of Memphis. She was keeping boarding-house at the time, which prospered under its new landlord until 1882, when he took a five years' lease on his present house and is running it in first-class style. Mr. Priddy is well known in Shelby County, having held responsible offices, and is well suited to the position he now so admirably occupies.

 W. P. Proudfit, manager of the DeSoto Oil Mills, is a native of Tennessee, and came to Memphis in 1853. He was for a number of years junior member of the firm of Harris, Wormley & Co., wholesale grocers and commission merchants, but severed his connection with them in 1858. He was a member of the firm of Day & Proudfit for about twenty-three years, they being commission merchants and cotton factors. At the end of that time he became stockholder and manager of the De Soto Oil Mills, this institution manufacturing crude oil, oil cake, oil meal and regin lint. The business was established in 1881, with E. Ensley, president; W. P. Proudfit, manager, and E. S. Proudfit, secretary and treasurer. Our subject is the son of William and Eliza (Walker) Proudfit, both natives of Fredericsburg, Va., and of Scotch origin. In 1852 our subject married Laura Harris, of Memphis, and the daughter of A. O. Harris. She died in 1869, leaving four children. In April, 1870, Mr. Proudfit married Fairfax Harris, half-sister to his first wife, and five children were the result of this union. He and family are members of the Episcopal Church. Mr. E. S. Proudfit, brother of our subject, was married July 1, 1874, to Virginia A. Tharpe of Macon, Ga., and the daughter of C. A. Tharpe. One child, Irene H., was born to this union. Mr. Proudfit came to this city when about ten years of age, and with the exception of eight years, has made this his home up to the present time. He and wife are worthy members of the Episcopal Church.

Benjamin K. Pullen, Jr., register of the taxing district of Memphis, was born in Richmond, Va., February 2, 1860, and is the son of Benjamin K. and Minerva A. (Smith) Pullen, natives respectively of North Carolina and Virginia. His father came to Memphis in 1860, and yet resides here engaged in the mercantile business. Our subject was reared and educated in Memphis, and first began business here as entry clerk, with Langstaff, Graham & Proudfit, but later entered the employ of the Manhattan Bank as individual bookkeeper for eighteen months. He subsequently accepted a position as traveling salesman for a New York firm, and later still became bookkeeper for the Gayoso Hotel. In September, 1886, he was appointed by the city council of Memphis, to the position of register, succeeding his father who resigned after having held the position for five years, which responsibility he has carried in a highly satisfactory and efficient manner to the present time. Mr. Pullen is a young gentleman of high character and fine promise. In politics he is Democratic, and in religion he is a member of the Central Methodist Church of this city.

Dr. Hortensius W. Purnell was born June 17, 1838, in Green County, Ala., near Greensborough, in what was known as the "canebrake and prairie" portion of the county. He grew up there and at the age of fifteen removed to Noxubee County, Miss., in December, 1853. He subsequently attended Wesleyan University at Florence, Ala., and afterward attended college at Oxford, Miss., graduating from the literary department of that institution in 1859. He also attended the Medical University of Louisiana, spending several years as resident student of medicine in the Grand Charity Hospital in New Orleans, La., and graduated in March, 1862. On the breaking out of the war, he joined the medical department of the army, on the Confederate side, and (save about two months, stationed in the hospitals at Holly Springs, Miss., until the evacuation of Corinth, after the Shiloh battle) was in the field medical service down to the close of the war. Subsequent to the surrender of the army at Greensboro, N. C., he came to Memphis, Tenn., at which place he located, and has practiced his profession, both in surgery as a specialty and the general practice of medicine since October, 1865, having practiced in the cholera epidemics of 1866 and 1873, and the other epidemics of small-pox, yellow fever, etc., he being especially well qualified to practice in these diseases, owing to his intimate acquaintance with them and on account of the favorable opportunities he had enjoyed for observation and practice in New Orleans during the days of such surgeons as Drs. Warren Stone, Samuel Choppin, Mercier James Jones, Cenas, Mandeville, Thomas Hunt, William C. Nichols, Chaille, Richardson and others. He practiced in the epidemics of yellow fever in Memphis in 1867, 1873, 1878 and 1879, reporting in 1878 as many as 685 cases of yellow fever, and with a remarkable record of successful treatment of these cases, showing a very favorable per cent of recoveries. Since that time he has resided in Memphis, and has assiduously devoted himself to the practice of surgery, both general and special, he being posted and skilled in the treatment of diseases of the eye and ear and all operative surgery. At present he is located at 279 Main Street, his residence being 393 Vance Street, in the most pleasant locality and most eligible portion of the city. Thomas Purnell, the originator of the family in America, came from England in 1664, and settled in Maryland, from which place ramify the different branches of the family. Dr. William Purnell married in Christian County, Ky., and subsequently removed to Pulaski, Tenn., thence to Green County, Ala., at which place Hortensius Purnell was born and lived, rearing a family of five children, of whom the Doctor, the subject of this article, is the second son. In 1849 his father, Hortensius P., died in Alabama. After his decease the widow, Mrs. E. W. Purnell, and three children—the Doctor, and her two daughters, Misses S. A. and M. E. Purnell (all still single)—returned to Tennessee to make their home. The other surviving son, William Purnell, resides in Issaquena County, Miss. In 1885 the widow died in the seventy-third year of her age at Nashville, Tenn. Of William's family, one son, John Hortensius, having graduated in medicine in the Memphis Hospital Medical College in 1882, was connected with the board of health at Memphis until he resigned, subsequently becoming surgeon-general of the State of Mississippi, where he now resides.

Peter J. Quigley, clerk of the county court of Shelby County, is a native of Ireland where he was born March 10, 1845. He was reared and educated in his native country, and in the spring of 1864 came to the United States, locating in Philadelphia where he followed the saddler's trade. In 1866 he came to Memphis where he continued his trade in the employ of others, but later engaged in the business for himself, continuing until 1875, when he was elected justice of the peace, and as such officer served in a faithful and efficient manner until August, 1886, when he was elected by the Democracy of the county to the office of county court clerk, and is yet discharging the duties of that office. He is a most popular officer and is highly respected. In 1873 his marriage with Miss

Martina E. Trainor was solemnized. This lady is a native of this city. She is the mother of five living children—two sons and three daughters. Mr. Quigley is a member of the K. of H., K. of I., C. K. of A., K. of L., K. and L. of H., and A. O. U. W. Himself and wife are members of the Catholic Church.

Gilbert D. Raine, general insurance agent of Memphis, was born in Lynchburg, Va., January 13, 1856, and is the son of the late Capt. Charles H. Raine by his marriage with Miss Mary Dixon, husband and wife being natives respectively of Virginia and Pennsylvania. The father entered the last war as a young lieutenant of artillery, was promoted to the captaincy, then to the command of the artillery of Johnson's division of Stonewall Jackson's aid corps, his commission as major being sent him just before his death. He was a gallant soldier, and at the time of his death was the only officer on horseback at the front. He was killed at Nine Run, succeeding the battle of Gettysburg. Our subject came to this city in 1870, finishing his education at the high schools. In 1872 he accepted a clerkship with the Hernando Insurance Company, and continued with this company six years, and then became manager of the Planters' Fire & Marine Insurance Company. In the fall of 1885 he engaged in the insurance business on his own responsibility, and to the present has met with remarkable success, doing probably the largest insurance business of any man or firm in the South. He now represents the following well known companies: New York Life, North British & Mercantile, Westchester of New York; Union of California; Equitable, of Nashville, and Knoxville, of Knoxville. He has been a member of the Memphis Board of Fire Underwriters for eight years. In 1877 he was united in marriage with Miss Julia Woodward of this city, and to this union there are two living children—a son and a daughter. Mr. Raine is a Democrat in politics and is a member of the Episcopal Church.

C. H. Raine, cashier of the Mercantile Bank, is a native of Lynchburg, Va., and was born December 11, 1857, and educated in prominent eastern institutions and in the schools of Memphis. He came to this city in the autumn of 1870, and after attending school three years clerked in a store for a short time and then did a collection business for a sewing machine company. In 1873 he became connected with the Phœnix Insurance Company, but in 1875 became collector of the Bank of Commerce, filling afterward the positions of individual bookkeeper, general-bookkeeper and teller. Upon the organization of the Mercantile Bank, April 18, 1883, he accepted the cashiership, and is thus serving at present. Mr. Raine is a Democrat, and is a member of the Episcopal Church. His father was a native of Virginia, and his mother of Pennsylvania. They were married at Lynchburg, Va., and resided there until the commencement of the war, when they moved to Appomattox C. H. The father was major of artillery November, 1863, when killed at Nine Run. (See sketch of Gilbert D. Raine.)

Richard J. Rawlings was born at Jackson, Tenn., March 17, 1845, and was a son of John Rawlings, of Alabama, who moved to Mississippi when a young man, and settled at Jackson, where he engaged in merchandising until 1837, when he moved to Jackson, Tenn., and in 1848 to Memphis. He was married at Jackson, Tenn., to Miss Sarah J. Hays, daughter of Col. Stokely Hays, who was a soldier of the war of 1812, and participated in the battle of New Orleans. She was born in Jackson, Tenn. The father continued the mercantile business for some time in Memphis, then was extensively engaged in the manufacture of bricks, and supplied nearly the entire demand during the rapid growth of Memphis before the war. He died at his home in Memphis in 1860. Our subject was but three years old when his parents moved to Memphis, where he was raised and educated, and was at La Grange College when the war broke out. He enlisted in the Confederate Army in the Second Tennessee Infantry under Col. Walker, but was transferred to the One Hundred and Fifty-fourth Senior Regiment, and participated in the battles of Belmont, Mo., and Richmond, Ky.; after the last battle he was captured and held as a prisoner at Frankfort, Ky., but was finally moved to Memphis and given the privilege of the city. When Forrest advanced he was ordered to take arms in defense of the city, but escaped and joined Forrest's cavalry. After this he was at the battle of Brice's Cross Roads, Harrisburg and various other battles, and after serving through the entire war was surrendered at Gainesville, Ala. His two brothers, Stokely and James S., were in the Confederate Army. The former died after the battle of Shiloh; the latter went through the battles of Murfreesboro, Chickamauga, Missionary Ridge, and the Georgia campaign, from Dalton to Atlanta. Mr. Rawlings was married at Memphis, June 16, 1873, to Miss Sarah F. Venable, daughter of Joseph Venable, a native of Kentucky and merchant and manufacturer of Memphis. He was born at St. Joseph, Mo., January 28, 1847. Their children were named Adelia, John H., Mary, Richard J. and George Venable. Mr. Rawlings has been in the mercantile and lumber business, and also connected with the oil-mill in Memphis, and has been very successful. He owns 900 acres of land, thirty-seven acres in the home place on Poplar Boulevard, four miles east of Memphis. He is a man of sound judgment, generous impulses and undeviating honesty.

S. P. Read, cashier of the Union & Planters' Bank, was born

in Nelson County, Ky., in 1831, and was educated at St. Joseph College, Bardstown, Ky. He came to Tennessee in 1849 and to Memphis in 1857, and engaged in the cotton and commission business, continuing until 1862, and then embarked in the dry goods trade. He remained thus engaged until he became connected with the organization of the People's Insurance Company, and of this he was made secretary. He served thus until the organization of the Union & Planters' Bank, September 1, 1869, since which date he has been its cashier. His honesty and powers of observation eminently fit him for the duties of this responsible position. He is one of three surviving children of a family of four born to the marriage of William Read and Ann Bealmear. The father was born in Kentucky and the mother in Maryland. They were married in Nelson County, Ky., and followed agricultural pursuits until the father's death in 1841. The mother afterward married William Ritchie, and is still residing in that county. In 1852 our subject married Miss Susay Hay, a native of Brownsville, Tenn., who has presented her husband with four sons and three daughters, of whom the following are still living: Myra B., Samuel P., Theodore, Pearl and Sidney. Mr. Read is a Democrat, and is a member of the orders F. & A. M. and K. of H.

James Reilly is a native of Dublin, Ireland, and was born in June, 1838. He came to the United States in 1853, and to Memphis in 1856. He was residing in Mississippi when the war broke out, and enlisted in the Fourteenth Mississippi Regiment and served three years in the Confederate service. After the war he located in Memphis, engaged in mercantile pursuits, but in 1866 accepted a position as deputy county court clerk of Shelby County, and in 1870 was elected county court clerk and served two terms of four years each. He served one year as public administrator, but resigned and organized the Brinkley Oil Company, of Arkansas, and was its president five years. In December, 1885, he became a member of his present firm. In 1859 he was united in marriage with Miss Mary Fenton, who has presented her husband with five sons and seven daughters. Mr. Reilly is a Democrat, a member of the Catholic Church, and is president of Branch 35, C. K. of A.

A. Renkert, a prominent druggist of 215 Main Street, Memphis, Tenn., is a native of Germany. He came to America in 1846, and located at Buffalo, N. Y. Three years later he moved to Ohio, and in 1852 settled in Memphis, where he has since resided. The first six years after his arrival in Memphis he filled clerkships in H. F. Farnsworth & Co.'s drug stores, and in 1860 embarked in that line of business on his own responsibility, which he has since followed at the corner of Cain and Market Streets, and without forming a partnership. He located at his present place of business in 1881. He has been quite successful, and by his close attention to affairs and courtesy to patrons has established a substantial and profitable trade. He is highly esteemed in the city, and is a director in the Arlington Insurance Company and the Manhattan Savings & Trust Company Bank. He is also an eminent member of the I. O. O. F. In 1860 he married Elizabeth Lambreth, to whom one child was born, who died in infancy. The mother passed away in 1861. In 1863 Mr. Renkert wedded Ottelia Handwerker, with whom he had a family of many children. Mrs. Renkert died December, 1883, and in 1884 he was united in marriage to Emma Heintz, of New Orleans, a daughter of Rev. Heintz. The parents of our subject, Christian and Anna M. (Bushmiller) Renkert, came to America the same year in which our subject came. The father died in Ohio. The mother is still living in Crawford County, Ohio. Our subject's eldest son, Alfred F., has lately graduated from the Memphis Medical College.

Miss Annie C. Reudelhuber. In the early part of the nineteenth century John D. and Evelyn M. (Wilhelm) Reudelhuber, who were born, reared and married in the Rhine Provinces, Germany, immigrated to the hospitable shores of America and settled in New Orleans, La. Five children were born unto them—three sons and two daughters. They then moved to Memphis, Tenn., where their children were educated in the Memphis city schools. The parents were baptized in infancy as Lutherans, but attended the First Presbyterian Church, in which their children were trained and became members. The family is noted as possessing many sterling qualities of head and heart. One of the sons, popularly known as Capt. J. S. Reudelhuber, was quite a military genius, and served in the light artillery at the age of seventeen in the late war. The daughters are the only survivors, the father having passed away in 1872 and the mother in 1881. The eldest daughter, a product of the public schools, engaged in teaching at the age of fifteen years, and step by step has been promoted, until to-day she is the principal of the largest school in Memphis, and ranks second to none in ability. Her sister, Miss Pauline, also graduated in the Memphis city schools with the first honors, and is now principal of the Merrill School. Both have distinguished themselves not only as efficient imparters of knowledge, but as able disciplinarians

William H. Robinson, attorney at law, is a native of Memphis and was born in 1858. He was educated at Washington-Lee University, Virginia, where he graduated in 1876, after which he spent three years in Europe completing and polishing his education. He returned in 1879 and studied law at Ann Arbor, Mich., and was admitted to the bar in 1881 in this city, and has risen steadily in the ranks of his profession. He is now a director of, and the attorney for, the Bluff City Stove Works. He is yet unmarried. His parents were John B. and Bettie (daughter of Burchette Douglass) Robinson, the father being a native of Kentucky and the mother of Tennessee. The father came to Memphis in 1845, and was for several years secretary of the Memphis & Little Rock Railroad, and became identified with various other enterprises of the city. He was a useful and prominent man and died October 8, 1885. He was one of the pioneer merchants of this city.

John Roper is a native of northern Ireland, and was born in August, 1843. He was reared to manhood in his native country and in 1864 came to the United States and the following year came to Memphis and engaged in the retail grocery business with his brother James, and a year or so later they merged their business into the wholesale trade and conducted it successfully until the death of James of yellow fever in 1878. Since that time Mr. Roper has been prominently connected with the success of the firm. For the last six years he has given much attention to the cotton business, and is among the heavy dealers of the city. He is a Democrat, a member of the K. of H. and the C. K. of A., and himself and family are Catholics. January 13, 1863, he married Miss Sarah McCarty, of Ireland, and by her has four sons and one daughter living.

Anthony Ross, mechanical engineer, draughtsman and paymaster of the engineer's department of the Memphis Taxing District, was born in Mayence, Germany, July 9, 1822, and was reared and educated in his native country, securing a thorough knowledge of the classics, and mastering the art of mechanical engineering. He followed this profession in his native country until 1848, when he came to the United States, and in 1851 came to the city of Memphis and accepted a situation as machinist. In 1856 he became draughtsman and store-keeper for the Memphis & Charleston Railroad, continuing until 1875, being master mechanic at Memphis for the last three years. The shops of the company were built here in 1856 under the superintendence of Mr. Ross. In 1875 he engaged in mercantile pursuits in this city, and in 1880 became time-keeper of the sewer department of this taxing district. Two years ago he was made superintendent of sewers, draughtsman and paymaster of the engineers' department, which responsible positions he yet holds to the satisfaction of the public. In 1863 he built the Brierfield (Ala.) rolling-mill, sixty-two miles north of Selma, of which he was in charge until his return to Memphis in 1865. In 1850 Mr. Ross married Mrs. Anne R. Jacobs, a native of Maryland. Mr. Ross is independent in his political views, is a member of the K. of H., and himself and wife are members of the Methodist Episcopal Church.

Maj. Frank W. Royster was born in Goochland County, near Richmond, Va., August 12, 1816, and is a son of David and Elizabeth (Sampson) Royster, both parents being natives of the same county. Frank W. grew to mature years in his native State and was there educated. In April, 1838, the father with his family, including our subject, reached Memphis and located on his plantation in this county, which was settled in 1825-26, and upon the same resided until his death, February 22, 1843. He was well advanced in years, and had served in the Revolutionary war as a soldier. Our subject early engaged in the mercantile business in this city, and continued the same until the war. During the first year of the war he served in the State ordnance department at Memphis, and later at Columbus, Miss., and Selma, Ala., continuing in the same department until the close of the war. From 1865 until the present he has been engaged in the real estate business in this city. April 23, 1849, he married Miss Helen Lake, of this vicinity, who presented her husband with eight children, four of whom are yet living, one son, William B., in partnership with his father, and three daughters, still residents of the State. He is one of the original members of the Old Folks Society of Shelby County, is a Democrat in politics, himself and family all members of the Episcopal Church.

Capt. C. B. Russell. The Memphis & Cincinnati Packet Company was organized in 1884 as successors to the Memphis & Ohio River Packet Company. They own four steamers carrying yearly over 20,000 tons from this city—the "De Soto," the "Buckeye State," the "Ohio" and the "Granite State." To represent them as passenger and freight agent at Memphis they have placed Capt. C. B. Russell, a native of West Virginia, born May 19, 1847. His parents, J. Thornton and Octavia (Wells) Russell, were both natives of Virginia. The father was owner and master of a vessel, being among the first who ran steamers. Their family consisted of four children—two sons and two daughters. Our subject was educated at a college in Wheeling, W. Va., and when twenty years of age began as second clerk on a steamer. From that he arose to first clerk and finally to master of a vessel and continued in the latter capacity about eight years. In 1884 he was appointed to his present position, which he has filled ably ever since.

George W. Rutland, merchant and farmer, was born near Raleigh, Shelby Co., Tenn., February 9, 1852, and is a son of William C. Rutland, who was born near Huntsville, Ala., and immigrated to Tennessee in 1840, settling near Germantown, Shelby County; two years later he went to Memphis and entered his father's store as clerk. He was married near Germantown to Miss Lydia A. Graham, a daughter of Joseph Graham, who was a brother of Gov. Graham of North Carolina, and one of the organizers of Shelby County, Tenn. The father followed farming from the date of his marriage until the close of the war. He was in the Confederate Army for a short time during the war. After the war he went into the mercantile business in Memphis, under the firm name of Taylor, Gay & Rutland, grocers and cotton dealers. Mr. Gay soon withdrew and the firm was Taylor & Rutland until 1873, and in 1879 Mr. Rutland went into business at Little Rock, Ark., under the firm name of W. A. Ober & Co. After the dissolution of this firm he engaged in cotton buying until his death at Little Rock in January, 1881. The mother was born near Memphis and is still living at Buntyn. Geo. W. Rutland was raised in Shelby County and received a collegiate education, having graduated at Macon Masonic College, June, 1869. He spent nine years clerking for Eckerly Bros., merchants at Memphis, but for three years has been in business for himself at Buntyn. He was married near White's Station, October 10, 1879, to Miss Euzelia M. Buntyn, daughter of Dr. G. O. Buntyn, a prominent and well known citizen. George W. and Euzelia were the children born to this marriage. The mother was born in Shelby County, August 6, 1854. Mr. Rutland is a Democrat and a member of the Methodist Episcopal Church South. He owns thirty acres of land near Buntyn Station. He is developing fine business capacity and has a genial, social disposition.

George Rutschman, retail liquor dealer, whose establishment is situated at 172 Poplar Street, is a native of Kentucky, born in the city of Louisville. He came to Memphis in 1849, and in 1861 enlisted in the Confederate Army, Seventh Tennessee Regiment, under Gen. N. B. Forrest. He displayed so much bravery and skill during many of the hard-fought battles, that in 1863 he was promoted to the rank of adjutant-general, which office he filled with honor and credit till the termination of the war. He received a wound in the right hip at the battle of Shiloh, which rendered him unfit for service for about three months. The ball was never extracted. In 1866 he returned to Memphis and engaged as clerk in a dry goods store at that place, where he remained about eight years. He then began business for himself, and although he endured many hardships during the war, and has passed through many since, he is always found at his place of business, attentive and considerate of the wants of his customers. October 2, 1877, he married Frederika Welsh, of this city. She is a native of Germany, and by marriage became the mother of three children, two now living.

Dr. D. D. Saunders, one of the leading physicians and surgeons of Memphis, Tenn., was born at Rocky Hill, near Courtland, Lawrence Co., Ala., February 26, 1835, and was one of a family of eleven children born to Col. J. E. and Mary F. Saunders. The father was born in Virginia in 1806; he was a lawyer by profession, and engaged in the practice of his profession in Alabama, where his parents had moved, for a number of years. His health becoming delicate, he quit the law, and became a commission merchant in Mobile, Ala., until the war; since then he has devoted himself to his planting interests in Lawrence County, Ala. The mother was a Miss Mary F. Watkins, daughter of R. H. Watkins, of Elbert County, Ga. She was born in 1808. Both parents are still living at the old homestead near Courtland, Ala. Dr. D. D. Saunders was educated at La Grange College, Ala., receiving his diploma from that institution in 1852. He then began the study of medicine with Dr. J. C. Nott, of Mobile, Ala., and four years later received diplomas from the medical universities of Pennsylvania and New York. He then spent some time in Europe prosecuting the study of his profession, and in 1859 located in Memphis, and was soon elected to fill the chair of surgery, and afterward that of anatomy in the old Memphis Medical College. During the war of the States Dr. Saunders served four years as surgeon, filling various positions, among the number, assistant medical director of hospitals of the Army of Tennessee, and surgeon in chief of the reserve surgical corps on the field of battle, and was required to be on the field during most of the battles fought by the Army of Tennessee. In 1861 Dr. Saunders was married to Kate S., daughter of Seth and Mary (Cook) Wheatley. She was born in Nashville in 1840; was raised at Memphis. She died at Marietta, Ga., in 1863, leaving two daughters: Mary Lou and Kate W. Dr. Saunders was elected to fill the chair of surgery in the Memphis Hospital Medical College, and, after delivering one course, resigned the chair in 1886. In February, 1867, he married Mary E. Wheatley, a sister of his first wife, and by this marriage has two children: Dudley D. and Lizzie W. Since 1860 Dr. Saunders has been a Mason, and is now Master Mason of the order, and a member of the K. of H. He is also a member of the American Medical Association, Medical Society of the State of Tennessee, of which he has been president, and the Shelby County Medical Society. In politics he is an ardent Democrat. Dr. Saunders has been a man of marked energy, and has labored earnestly and enthusiastically for all that tends to the advancement of the medical profession. He is known as an eminent physician throughout the State.

Lemuel A. Scarbrough, of the firm of L. A. Scarbrough & Co., cotton and grain merchants, is a native of North Carolina and a son of A. B. and M. L. (Morrison) Scarbrough. This firm is a continuation of what was formerly A. M. Scarbrough & Co., who established their business in 1871, the present firm beginning in 1881. For some years previous to this L. A. Scarbrough had been engaged in the same business in Savannah, Ga. Our subject came to Tennessee in 1846, and in 1859 located in Memphis. In May, 1861 he enlisted in the Confederate service, Company E, Thirteenth Tennessee Regiment, and remained during the entire war. He was wounded at the battle of Shiloh, which rendered him unfit for active duty, though he remained with the army until the surrender, except about six weeks, when he was held prisoner. In 1866 he married Ednie E. Malone, daughter of Robert C. and Elizabeth (Harper) Malone, of Tipton County. Eight children were born to this union—three daughters and five sons—one son died in 1873, and an infant son born and died February 16, 1887. Mr. Scarbrough and wife are members of the Methodist Episcopal Church South.

Daniel Schloss, clerk of Shelby County Circuit Court, was born in Yngenheim Rhine, Bavaria, Germany, September 30, 1837, and was reared and educated in his native country, learning in youth the tailor's trade, which, however, he has never followed since. He came to the United States in 1854 and spent four years in Philadelphia, with an uncle in the clothing business. In 1860 he came to Tennessee and engaged in the mercantile pursuit in Huntingdon and Union City and in 1861 came to Memphis and was a member of the local militia here during the war. He spent 1865 in Natchez, Miss. In 1868 he located in La Grange, Tenn., where he followed the mercantile business one year and then returned to Memphis and clerked until 1878, when he returned to his native country on a visit. In the spring of 1879, he engaged in the dry goods business in Memphis, which pursuit he conducted successfully until 1886, when he was elected clerk of the circuit court, and is now faithfully and efficiently discharging the duties of that office. Politically he is a strong Democrat and as such was elected to his present position. Mr. Schloss has a high reputation for integrity, and has lately served as receiver for two large business firms of the city which had failed. In 1868 he was united in marriage with Miss Johanna Besthoff, and by her had two children. In 1873 his first wife died of yellow fever and in 1875 he married her cousin, Rachel Besthoff. This lady died in the autumn of 1881 and in 1883 he married Miss Tilly Lazard. A boy eleven years old, by his first wife, was drowned in 1880. One of the three children of his second wife died in infancy. Two children by his third wife are living. Mr. Schloss belongs to the following orders: I. O. O. F.,

K. of H., K. & L. of H. and A. O. U. W., and belongs to three Jewish societies and is a member of the Jewish Church. While on his visit to the old country he brought his father, Joseph Schloss, back with him, and the old gentleman is now residing with him, and is in his eighty-fourth year.

Messrs. Schoolfield, Hanauer & Co. established their business in 1865. The firm is composed of W. W. Schoolfield, Louis Hanauer and Henry G. Miller, although at the beginning the firm contained two other members who have since died. They were Jacob Hanauer and Henry Thomas. W. W. Schoolfield is the son of John W. and Frances (Dudley) Schoolfield, and a native of Virginia. He came to Memphis in 1855 and clerked for some time in a grocery. In 1860 he married E. M. Thomas, of Virginia, the daughter of Joseph Thomas and to them was born one son, Dudley T. Mr. Schoolfield is a member of the Masonic fraternity. Louis Hanauer, one of the members of this firm, was born in Bavaria, Germany, in 1820, and is the son of Marks and Lena Hanauer, both of whom died in Cincinnati, Ohio. At the age of eighteen Louis Hanauer came to the United States, locating first in Cincinnati, and when twenty years of age went to Pocahontas, Ark., where he engaged in the mercantile business. In 1861 he enlisted in the Confederate Army, and was Gen. Hardee's staff officer. He remained but a short time and then returned home. In 1862 he came to Memphis. Previous to this, in 1845; he had married Susan Kelley, daughter of James and Sallie Kelley of Missouri. She died in 1885 in her sixty-fifth year. Henry G. Miller, the junior member of this firm, is a native of Fayette County, Tenn., and the son of Henry and Evaline Miller, natives of Pennsylvania and Virginia respectively. They came to Tennessee in 1832. In 1859 Henry G. married Lizzie S. Hart, a native of Fayette County, and the daughter of John M. and Mary M. (Armour) Hart. To Mr. Miller and wife were born three sons, one of whom died at the age of eighteen. In 1863 Mr. Miller moved to this city. He is a member of the Masonic fraternity and he and wife are members of the Methodist Episcopal Church South.

Thomas M. Scruggs, director of the Memphis Law Library and a member of the well known legal firm of Frayser & Scruggs, was born in Alabama in 1855 and came to Memphis in 1878. He became associated in the practice of law with the firm of Scruggs & Ray, continuing thus until 1882, when he entered the firm of Frayser & Scruggs. Mr. Scruggs was educated at the University of the South and at the University of Virginia, graduating from the law department of the latter institution in 1875. On the 3d of March, 1877, he was admitted to the bar at Grenada, Miss., but began the practice in this city. Mr. Scruggs is a member of the I. O. O. F. and the K. of H. He is an only child born to P. T. and Elizabeth Marshall Murphy Scruggs the father a native of Tennessee and the mother of Alabama. They were married in Alabama, and resided in that State until the father's death in 1856. The mother afterward married again, and died in Mississippi in 1878.

Miss M. L. Scudder. Among the settlers at Salem, Mass., in the latter part of the seventeenth century, was the Scudder family, of English and Scotch-Irish descent. From there they spread west and south, furnishing prominent ministers, teachers and doctors for many of the States. Among them was Samuel E. Scudder, a native of Princeton, N. J., and a graduate of the college there. When young he immigrated to Georgia and became one of the noted educators of the State. While there he married Eunice B. Safford, by whom he had seven children—two sons and five daughters. Both he and his wife were members of the Presbyterian Church. He died during the late war, but the mother still lives in Georgia. Miss M. L. Scudder was born in Greensboro, Ga., and educated at the Synodical College of that State, taking a classical course. After teaching some time elsewhere she was elected to the principalship of the Leath school in 1883. Her study of the classics has not only well fitted her for the position she now holds but furnishes a solid foundation on which to build higher.

Rev. Davis Sessums, rector of Calvary Episcopal Church, was born July 7, 1858, in Houston, Tex. While growing up he had the best educational advantages, having taken a full course in the University of the South, at Sewanee, Tenn. He graduated from the literary department of that splendid institution in 1878, from which he also received the degree of A. M. Early in 1882 he was ordained deacon, and in August of the same year was ordained priest. He then became rector of Grace Church at Galveston, Tex., and held that position until 1883, when he was called to his present position. Father Sessums is an earnest worker, and presents a commanding appearance in the pulpit.

Dr. H. J. Shaw, a physician of Memphis, Tenn., was born in Robertson County, Tenn., in 1825, and is a son of Thomas and Sarah Shaw, both natives of North Carolina. The father was born in 1798, and came with his parents to Davidson County, Tenn., in 1802, and some time afterward moved to Robertson County, Tenn. He was suveyor and colonel of the State militia of that county for a number of years. He was a farmer by occupation, and died in 1839. The mother was a Miss Binkley before her marriage, born in 1798 and died in 1881. Dr. Shaw was educated in Robertson County and studied medicine under Drs. James and R. J. Mallory, then attended lectures at the University of Louisville, Ky., and in 1854 graduated at the University of Pennsylvania, and two years later graduated in the medical department of the university at Nashville, and located near Thomasville, Tenn., where he practiced medicine until 1863, then spent two years in Philadelphia and New York, studying various branches of his profession, and in 1866 located at Memphis, Tenn., where he has since carried a most lucrative practice and is regarded as one of the best posted physicians in the State. In 1859 he married Miss Nannie W., daughter of Zachariah and Nancy Sherron. Mrs. Shaw is a native of Montgomery County. Dr. Shaw has been an earnest student in his profession and is a physician of wide experience, having always had an extensive practice. He is a Mason of long standing.

Chamberlayne Jones (deceased) was born in Virginia, and in 1827 came to Shelby County, Tenn., where he made his home and became a very extensive land owner. In 1853 he married Mrs. Ann (Smith) Lewelling, a native of Baltimore, Md., who when young came with her parents to Louisville, Ky. She here met and married Mr. Lewelling, a native of North Carolina, a farmer and a commission merchant. He died in 1851. Her second husband, Mr. C. Jones, was an elder in the Presbyterian Church. He died in 1869. In 1881 she married Mr. John Shipp, a native of North Carolina. Mr. and Mrs. Shipp are both members and active workers in the Methodist Church.

Howell Sigler, superintendent of the business of the Baltimore & Ohio Telegraph Company at Memphis, was born January 9, 1850, in Orange County, N. Y., and is the son of Peter H. and Julia A. (Howell) Sigler, both natives of Orange County, N. Y. In early life the father worked at the tailor's trade, and afterward became a commercial traveler; later still he turned his attention to agricultural pursuits. He was a member of the Presbyterian Church, and died in 1877. The mother is still living, and is a member of the Baptist Church. Their family consisted of three children—two sons and one daughter. Our subject was educated and learned telegraphy in his native county. When only fifteen years of age he took a position as a telegraphic operator, and later still operated for the Central Pacific, Kansas Pacific and Western Union until he came to Memphis in the interests of the Baltimore & Ohio Telegraph Company. In 1874 he married Lucy Berlin, a native of Virginia. By this union they had two children—one son and one daughter. Mrs. Sigler is a member of the Presbyterian Church.

Hon. David C. Slaughter, chairman of the Shelby County Court, was born in Greenville, N. C., August 25, 1831, and is the son of Abner and Mary (Cannon) Slaughter, both natives of North Carolina. In March, 1832, the parents moved to Tipton County, where they located and passed the remainder of their lives on a plantation near Covington, both dying in 1871. They were most exemplary citizens. Our subject was reared and educated on his father's plantation, and in 1858 was elected sheriff of Tipton County and served four years. In March, 1866, he was re-elected to the same office, and in 1868 was again re-elected, a merited recognition of his standing and prominence in the county. In August, 1869, he resigned and was elected State senator. He served until 1871 and then followed agricultural pursuits in Tipton County until February, 1877, when he removed to Shelby County and located on a small plantation where he yet resides. In 1878 he was elected magistrate and became cashier for George B. Fleece, county trustee. He served as cashier two years and as magistrate ever since. From 1882 to 1885 he served as adjuster of claims against the Chesapeake & Ohio Railroad, and in January, 1886, he was elected chairman of the county court, in which position he is yet serving, to the acceptance of the people. In 1850 he married Susan A. Overall, of Tipton County. They have three sons and three daughters living. He is a Royal Arch Mason, a member of the K. of H., K. & L. of H. and the A. O. U. W., and himself and wife are members of the Methodist Episcopal Church.

John D. Slaughter was born in Tipton County, Tenn., in 1850, and is a son of Dr. Wyatt and Mary Ann (Fleming) Slaughter. The father was a native of North Carolina and the mother of Tennessee. Dr. Slaughter was a practicing physician in Tipton and Shelby Counties for twenty-five years, then moved to Fort Smith, Ark., where he now carries an extensive practice. John D. Slaughter was educated in Tipton County. He spent some time clerking after finishing his education. He married Miss Mary M. Stewart, a daughter of J. D. Stewart, a well known farmer of Shelby County. Eight children have been born to this union, only five of them living. Mrs. Slaughter is an earnest member of the Cumberland Presbyterian Church. In 1885 Mr. Slaughter established himself as a merchant at Stewartsville, in Shelby County, and has conducted his business in an enterprising, liberal manner, and has a large patronage. He is independent in politics and a man of generous disposition, and broad views.

Charles M. Small, a farmer of Shelby County, was born in Giles County, Tenn., November 7, 1836. His father, George Small, was born in Mecklenburg County, Va., and immigrated to Giles County, Tenn., in early life, where he was an overseer for different planters in that part of the country for a few years, and married Mary J. Jones, a native of King and Queen County, Va., and daughter of James Jones and a sister of G. W. Jones, who represented the Lincoln County (Tenn.) District in

Congress for sixteen consecutive years, besides filling many other prominent positions in public life. The father moved to Shelby County, Tenn., in 1846, and settled at the place where our subject now lives, and engaged in farming until he died in August, 1880. The mother died in 1873. Charles M. Small was raised on a farm and received a common-school education, and has made farming his occupation. He enlisted in the Confederate Army and belonged to Owens' Arkansas battery, serving until the war closed; he was at the bombardment of Fort Pillow, and the evacuation of Corinth, and was surrendered at Meridian, Miss. Mr. Small has never married; he makes his home with his sisters, Mary J. Small and Mrs. L. J. Bilderback. He is a Democrat and a K. of H. and cast his first presidential vote for S. A. Douglass. He owns a half section of land five miles south of Germantown, and is one of the progressive farmers of the county.

Gen. William J. Smith was born in Birmingham, England, September 24, 1823, and came to America when a child, and served four and a half years at the painter's trade, in Goshen, Orange Co., N. Y. In 1846 he removed South and joined James Wheat's mounted rangers for the Mexican war. He participated in all the battles from Vera Cruz to Mexico City, and on that memorable campaign was one of Gen. Scott's body guard. In July, 1848, he was mustered out at the city of Memphis. He then worked at his trade of painting in this city for ten years, and in 1858 purchased a plantation at Grand Junction, Hardeman County, which he conducted successfully until the breaking out of the last war. He opposed secession from the start. His opinions becoming known, he was arrested four times by the Confederate authorities for disloyalty to the South, but was released, as the arrests were found unjustifiable. Soon afterward he joined the First West Tennessee Cavalry, afterward known as the Sixth Union Tennessee Cavalry, and after two months was made regimental quartermaster, six months later major, and a little later lieutenant-colonel. In 1864 he was made colonel of the united Sixth and Thirteenth Union Cavalry Regiments. Soon after this he was promoted to brevet brigadier-general. In 1865 he was a delegate to the State Constitutional Convention to reinstate Tennessee in the Union, and later was elected to the Legislature from Hardeman County, and two years later was elected to the State Senate from Shelby County, and in November, 1868, was elected to Congress. In 1871 he was appointed surveyor of the port of Memphis by President Grant and served three terms. In 1878 he was very active in relieving the victims of the yellow fever at Grenada and was taken down with the scourge, but recovered, having been sent home. He was married in New York City, by Rev. Dr. William Berryan, to Miss Mary A. R. Slack, a native of New Brunswick. They have had eleven children, three now living—one son and two daughters—Victor R., Irene and Lillian. He is United States commissioner and notary public, and has been engaged in the real estate, lumber and abstract businesses in company with L. B. Eaton, of Memphis, for several years. Two years ago he was elected to the State Senate from Shelby County.

James H. Smith, cashier of the Memphis National Bank, of Memphis, was born in Shelbyville, Ky., July 6, 1835, and is the son of Abraham and Margaret (Campbell) Smith, both parents being natives of Kentucky. Our subject passed his youth and received his education in his native county, and in early manhood served as deputy circuit court clerk six years. In 1858 he came to Memphis and served as deputy sheriff of Shelby County four years. During the first years of the war he served as first assistant provost-marshal of the Confederate Government in West Tennessee. From the close of the war until 1882 he was engaged in the grocery and cotton businesses at Memphis. During the yellow fever epidemic of 1878 he was secretary of the Howard Association, of Memphis. In 1882 he went to Birmingham, Ala., and was made secretary of the Pratt Coal & Iron Company, the largest institution of the kind in the South, and he still serves as secretary and director of the same. In 1882 he was appointed postmaster of Memphis by President Arthur, and held the position until August 1, 1885. From 1879 to 1882 he represented Shelby County in the State Legislature. He was elected secretary of the Planters' Fire & Marine Insurance Company, of Memphis, in August, 1885, and resigned this position February 1, 1887, to accept his present position as cashier of the Memphis National Bank, of Memphis, one of the most solid institutions of the city, having a capital of $500,000. In politics he is a stanch Republican. He is married and has living three sons and two daughters. He is a deacon in the Linden Street Christian Church, of Memphis.

W. A. Smith, proprietor of the Avery Gin Company—business located at 391 and 393 Front Street, and established in 1879—was born in Alabama in 1845. He spent his youthful days clerking, and afterward engaged in the grocery business. In 1855 he immigrated to Arkansas with his parents, William H. and Minerva (Leverque) Smith, and in 1866 came to the city of Memphis. In 1862 he enlisted in the Confederate Army and remained in service until the close of the war. In 1866 he was united in marriage to Miss Georgia Sheffield, of Memphis, and by this union became the father of seven children, five of whom are now living. Mr. Smith is a member of the K. of H. and A. O. U. W., and his wife is a member of the First Baptist Church.

Albert H. Smith, proprietor of the Memphis Cotton Beam Manufactory & Scale Repair Works, established his business, which is located at 83 East Court Street, January 1, 1884. Mr. Smith is a native of Buffalo, N. Y., and served his apprenticeship in the Buffalo Scale Works; was also with the Howe Scale Works for some time. In 1874 he was married in the State of New York, and in December, 1883, he came to the city of Memphis. He is a skilled workman and makes a specialty of erecting and repairing scales.

W. M. Sneed, of the law firm of Myers & Sneed, was educated at Chapel Hill College, N. C., and afterward began the study of law and was admitted to practice at the bar of Oxford, N. C., in 1874. Soon after that date he came to Memphis and was associated with the firm of McRae, Myers & Sneed, which firm existed until 1877, when the present firm of Myers & Sneed was formed. In 1885 Mr. Sneed was elected president of the Woodruff Lumber Company, one of the leading lumber firms of this city. He has also been one of the directors of and attorney for the State National Bank of Memphis since its organization. Our subject was born August 7, 1848, and is one of a family of six children, all of whom are still living. Mr. Sneed is recognized as one of the rising young attorneys of the Memphis bar. His parents are W. M. and Louisa (Bethell) Sneed, and are natives of North Carolina, and were married in Granville County, where they followed agricultural pursuits. The mother died in 1863, and the father married Mrs. Sarah A. Bullock, who is also deceased.

John K. Speed, senior member of the firm of J. K. Speed & Co., grain and commission merchants, and member of the firm of J. M. Phillips & Co., grain dealers in West Memphis, is a native of Kentucky, and in 1835 was taken by his parents to Chicago, and in 1866 came to this city with his mother and engaged in the retail grocery trade. A few months later he established the grain and commission business to which he has since devoted his attention. He was the pioneer grain merchant of Memphis and loaded and unloaded the first barges of grain at this port. In 1874 in connection with the grain trade he began the milling business, and the Memphis City Mills are now among the best in the city. In West Memphis the company has a large elevator and a wharfboat, said to be the largest in the United States. Mr. Speed was the first president of the Board of Trade and of the Board of Exchange. He is interested in the extensive grain elevator at this city and is vice-president of the Home Insurance Company and is a director in the State National Bank. In 1871 he married a Miss Clark, of Peoria, Ill. His father died in Chicago.

Prof. Andrew J. Steele, principal of Le Moyne Normal Institute, was born July 2, 1848, in Wisconsin, and secured his education at Milton College, in that State, graduating from the State Normal School of Wisconsin in 1870. He then came South and took charge of the normal department of Tongaloo University, near Jackson, Miss., where he remained till 1873, after which he came to his present position. His parents, Samuel and Olive (Pierce) Steele, were natives, respectively, of Vermont and New York. The father, when young, moved to New York where he met and married Miss Pierce. In 1842 they moved to Wisconsin. In the family were eight children—five sons and three daughters. Three of the sons served in the Federal Army. Our subject when only seventeen years of age left home without the consent of his parents and entered Company L, Eighth Illinois Cavalry, and served nearly two years of the latter part of the war. In 1871 he married Amelia Crandall, a native of Wisconsin and a graduate of Milton College, by whom he had two children: Jessie (deceased) and Howard. Both Mr. and Mrs. Steele are members of the Congregational Church.

J. D. Stewart, a farmer, residing in the First District of Shelby County, was born in Gibson County, Tenn., in 1824, and is a son of James T. and Mary A. (Craig) Stewart. The father was a resident of Gibson County and engaged in farming. He was a moral and industrious man, highly esteemed in his neighborhood. Our subject was educated in the common schools in Gibson County, the advantages offered by the primitive schools in the country at that time being meager. He enlisted in the Confederate Army under Col. Aaron Burrows, in 1862, but remained only a short time as his eyes were seriously affected, and when he returned home the citizens of his neighborhood petitioned for his release, that he might manage a mill, that was at that time much needed. In 1848 he married Miss Mary Epperson, daughter of Joseph Epperson, a farmer of Wilson County, Tenn. Ten children have been the issue of this union, seven of them now living. Mr. and Mrs. Stewart are members of the Cumberland Presbyterian Church. He is a Mason, but does not adhere to any political party. He is a well-informed man, and a genial companion.

Dr. Cyrus M. Stewart, a leading physician in the First Civil District of Shelby County, Tenn., was born in Gibson County in 1832. He is a son of James T. Stewart, who was born in Sumner County, Tenn., in 1802, and moved from that county to Gibson County, where he lived for twenty years, then moved to Shelby County and engaged in farming until he died, January 31, 1880. He was a member and an elder in the Cumberland Presbyterian Church. He married Miss Mary A. Craig, a native of

Tennessee, born in 1821, and a daughter of Maj. Craig, who was a prominent officer in the Indian war during the early settlement of West Tennessee. Our subject was but thirteen years of age when his father moved to Shelby County, Tenn. He was educated in the county, attending New Salem Academy. He has been practicing medicine since 1859. In March, 1860, he graduated in medicine at Cincinnati, and afterward graduated from the Memphis Medical College. Dr. Stewart was married February 16, 1860, to Miss Virginia A. Walker, a daughter of Rev. J. R. Walker, of Shelby County. They had two children, but both died, and Mrs. Stewart died August 18, 1864. She was a devout Christian and a member of the Methodist Church. Dr. Stewart was married the second time to Miss Kate J. Douglass, daughter of G. L. Douglass, a prominent farmer of the First District. Four children have been the issue of this marriage, only two of them living. Dr. and Mrs. Stewart are active members of the Cumberland Presbyterian Church. He is a Mason and a K. of H. He ranks high in his profession, and has met with marked success in his extensive practice. He is a Democrat and an influential citizen of Shelby County.

Prof. W. B. Stewart is a native of New Orleans, La., was born in 1843 and immigrated to Memphis with his parents, E. P. and Mary (Battle) Stewart, in 1846. The father was an extensive building contractor, also handled cotton on the factorage system. He was the second president elected for the Elmwood Cemetery, and held the office at the time of his death, which occurred in 1859; the mother followed in death in 1865. In 1861 our subject left his desk in the school room and enlisted in the One Hundred and Fifty-fourth Senior Tennessee Regiment Infantry, Confederate Army, and was discharged the same year at Columbus, Ky., on account of being afflicted with inflammatory rheumatism. In 1863 he re-enlisted, joining the Twelfth Tennessee Regiment Cavalry and remained in service until the close of the war. He then began teaching school and has continued in that business up to the present time. In 1871 he located in the village of Arlington, and has since made it his home. He is a member of the Masonic fraternity and a good citizen.

A. A. Strange is one of the wholesale and retail coal dealers of Memphis, with yards at the corner of Clinton and Beale Streets, and at the corner of Market and Front Streets, where he handles Kentucky coal. Mr. Strange is a native of Memphis, born in 1858, but when a mere boy was taken to New York City where he received his education. At the age of fifteen he engaged in the mercantile business and in 1876 he came to Memphis. He was engaged in different occupations till 1883 when he opened a coal yard. He began at first by hiring teams, but by industry and close attention to business has attained a position among the leading coal dealers. His father, W. R. Strange, was one of the first book dealers in Memphis. He died in 1861. The mother, Maria (Merrill) Strange, is a daughter of Dr. A. P. Merrill. She is still living. Our subject is an experienced coal dealer, having worked formerly for C. B. Bryan & Co., and having been, also, traveling salesman for a mining company.

Dr. A. S. Stratton, of the firm of Stratton & Humphreys, was born in Athol, Mass., July 5, 1820. He is a son of David Stratton, who was a native of Athol, Mass., where he was raised and educated and married to Sarah Wadsworth, who was of an English family. Three sons and three daughters were born to this marriage, our subject being the fifth child. The father was a farmer and by trade a shoemaker. He died in his native State in 1854. He was of Scotch descent. The mother was born in Grafton, Mass., and died in Athol, Mass., in 1825. Our subject was raised, and educated in the common schools of Grafton, and his time has been given to the practice of medicine and to merchandising all of his life. In 1845 he immigrated to Mississippi and settled near Como, where he read medicine under Dr. D. W. Harris, and afterward graduated at the Memphis Medical College in 1848, and commenced practicing at Colliersville, Tenn., where he became a member of the firm of Moore & Stratton, dealers in general merchandise. Afterward Dr. Stratton sold goods at Centerhill, Miss., for a year and a half; then returned to Colliersville, Tenn., where he again went into business, with E. J. Kindred, but in May, 1868, their store was destroyed by fire, and he formed a partnership with J. T. Biggs and Co., which lasted sixteen years. In 1884 Dr. Stratton opened his present dry goods store under the firm name of Stratton & Humphreys. July 10, 1849, he married, in Shelby County, Miss Mary E. Chamberlain, a daughter of Jacob Chamberlain, who was a native of Connecticut. Mary Eudora, now the wife of T. H. Humphreys, junior member of the firm of Stratton & Humphreys, was the only child born to this marriage. Mrs. Stratton was born in Sharon, Conn., in November, 1821, and is a sister of the distinguished Rev. Dr. Jacob Chamberlain, who is a resident missionary at Manda Palla, India; also of W. J. Chamberlain, formerly secretary of the State board of agriculture of Ohio, and is now president of the Iowa State Agricultural College. Dr. Stratton has been successful as a business man, and popular as a physician. He owns a pleasant home in Colliersville, and in politics is an influential Democrat. Dr. Stratton and wife are prominent members of the Presbyterian Church.

John H. Sullivan, superintendent of the Kansas City Railroad, and of the Memphis, Birmingham & Atlantic Railroad, was born in 1850, and is a native Tennessean in which State he was reared and educated. His parents were natives of Ireland, and came to America settling in Missouri, where the father followed agricultural pursuits. Our subject has been prominently connected with several railroads. He was with the Hannibal & St. Joseph Railroad in various capacities in Missouri; was with the Northern Pacific Railroad as superintendent from 1872 to 1876, and with the M. K. & T. Railroad as superintendent from 1876 to 1878. He then returned to the Northern Pacific and was superintendent of that during its building through the Yellowstone Valley in Montana. In 1880 he married S. P. Orrick of Kirkwood, St. Louis Co., Mo., and to this union were born two children. In 1882 Mr. Sullivan was called to his present position. He has been an able and diligent official, as may be seen from his successive promotions.

Jeremiah Sullivan, secretary of the Memphis Board of Fire Underwriters, is a native of Memphis, Tenn., and was born December 7, 1862, being the son of Jeremiah and Mary (Powers) Sullivan, both parents being natives of the Emerald Isle. Our subject grew to manhood and received his education in the Memphis City public schools. In 1883 he became connected with the fire department and served in various positions—pipeman, driver, captain and secretary, to Chief Clary—receiving steady promotion for meritorious conduct. In September, 1886, he was elected to his present position, and is now faithfully and efficiently discharging the duties assigned him. He is yet unmarried, is a Democrat, and a member of the Catholic Church. He is chairman of the finance committee of the Memphis Fire & Relief Association, and is also secretary of the K. of I.

Julius A. Taylor, a member of the law firm of Taylor & Carroll, began reading law while acting as deputy clerk and master, at the age of seventeen years, and when the war broke out was reading in an office. He stopped his studies and enlisted in the Twenty-first Tennessee Confederate Infantry, with which command he served a year as lieutenant and was then transferred and held the same rank under Gens. Chalmers and Forrest until the cessation of hostilities. He then returned to Memphis and resumed the reading of law, and in 1866 was admitted to the bar. Except a few months he practiced alone until 1878 when the present firm of which he is a member was formed. From January, 1876, to January, 1882, he was attorney for the county of Shelby. He is one of a family of ten sons and four daughters, of whom four sons and two daughters survive. In 1866 he was married to Miss Margaret Ruffin, a native of Mississippi, who bore the following children, all living; James R., Fanny H., Rosa R. and Julius A. His wife died in 1879, and in 1881 he married Miss Louise Crawford, who has presented her husband with two children, both living: Margaret and West C. Mr. Taylor is a member of the following orders: F. & A. M., K. of P., K. of H. and A. O. U. W. His father was Dr. William V. Taylor, who was born in Yorktown, Va., in 1790. His mother was Fanny H., daughter of Chief Justice Henderson, of North Carolina, and was born in 1796. Dr. Taylor was assistant surgeon in the United States Navy during the war of of 1812. He practiced medicine for sixty years and died in 1872. After his marriage he lived in North Carolina, until 1836, then at LaGrange, Tenn., until 1840, then in Holly Springs, Miss., till 1848, then in Memphis until his death.

George W. Thomas, an enterprising merchant at Germantown, Tenn., was born in Mississippi, May 23, 1837. His father, L. W. Thomas, was a native of North Carolina, and immigrated to Mississippi in 1837, settling at Pontotoc, where he was a merchant and a farmer, doing business with his brother, Dr. Thomas. He was married in North Carolina to Miss Nancy McClintock. Eight children were born to them, George W. being the fourth child. Both parents died in Mississippi, the mother in April, 1847, and the father August 25, 1851. Our subject was raised on a farm, and through his own efforts secured a good education. He served in the late war; although opposed to the manner of settling the trouble between the North and the South, he entered the army and discharged his duty in a faithful, courageous manner. He was married in Fayette County, Tenn., October 3, 1865, to Miss M. F. Scott, daughter of M. Scott, a farmer, and a native of Virginia. They have had five sons and four daughters. The mother was born in Fayette County, where she was raised and educated. The Thomas family is an old one in this country, and is of English and Scotch descent. Mr. and Mrs. Thomas are active members of the Missionary Baptist Church; he is a Democrat, a Mason, and a K. of H. He owns 1,000 acres of land, 150 acres of it being in the home place at Germantown, Tenn., where he has a beautiful residence. Mr. Thomas has a frank, sincere disposition, and is known as a man of probity and kind heart, and has many friends.

The Memphis Carriage Works, located at 81 to 83 Madison Street, was established in December, 1886. Mr. G. W. Tomlin, the manager of this great enterprise, was reared in Jackson, Tenn., and came to Memphis in 1865. He has since that time been identified with the carriage business, having acted as manager for Woodruff & Oliver for fifteen years. At the time of the failure of said firm, he and William Benges purchased their stock and manufacturing department, and engaged in business under the firm name of Tomlin & Benges. Mr. Tomlin withdrew from the firm in November, 1886. He is the son of James S. and M. L. (Hawkins) Tomlin. In 1867 our subject married Martha Tanner, of this city, and a daughter of John A. Tanner. To this union were born eight children, two of whom died during the yellow fever epidemic of 1878. In May, 1861, Mr. Tomlin enlisted in the Confederate Army, Sixth Tennessee, as orderly sergeant, and near the close of the war was promoted to first lieutenant. He is a member of the I. O. O. F., the K. of H. and the K. of P.

William A. Tucker, one of the leading citizens of Kerrville, is a son of William B. and Elizabeth (Murphy) Tucker, both natives of North Carolina, where they were reared and married. They came to Tipton County in 1833, and here passed the residue of their days. Their family consisted of nine children—two sons and seven daughters. Our subject was born in Tipton County, Tenn., in 1834, and followed farming and merchandising until 1872, when he went to Memphis and was here engaged in mercantile pursuits till 1881. He then moved to Kerrville, and is still engaged in his last named occupation. In connection with this he carries on his farming interest, being the owner of about 600 acres of land. In 1861 he volunteered in a company of Arkansas cavalry, but ill health prevented his remaining long in service. In the fall of the same year, having sufficiently recovered, he enlisted in Company I, Fifty-first Tennessee Infantry, and during three and a half years of service was never taken prisoner. At the battle of Murfreesboro he received a wound from a bursting shell. At the conclusion of the war he returned home and engaged in mercantile pursuits until he removed to Memphis. Previous to the war, in 1857, he married Helen Montague, of Fayette County, who bore him four children—one son and three daughters. Mr. and Mrs. Tucker are both members of the Cumberland Presbyterian Church. Mr. Tucker has been in business for about fourteen years, and has added much to the business progress of the county.

T. B. Turley, a member of the law firm of Turley & Wright, attended the University of Virginia one year in the literary department, and one year in the law department, from 1865 to 1867, and began the practice of law at Memphis in 1870, continuing alone one year, and then as a member of the firm of McKissick & Turley, until 1875; then with Harris, McKissick & Turley until 1880; then with Harris & Turley, and subsequently the firm of Turley & Wright was formed. They have a good practice, which is steadily increasing. Thomas J. Turley, the father of our subject, was a native of Virginia, and the mother, whose maiden name was Flora Battle, was a native of North Carolina, but was reared mainly in Shelby County. The father came to West Tennessee in his youth, and located in this county previous to 1840, and here married our subject's mother. He practiced law in Memphis until his death in 1854. The mother is still living. Our subject was an only child, and was born in April, 1845, and has always resided in this county. When the war broke out he enlisted in the One Hundred and Fifty-fourth Senior Tennessee Confederate Regiment as a private, and participated in the battles of Shiloh, Perryville (Ky.), and numerous ones on the Georgia campaign, serving with honor and distinction until peace was declared. In 1869 he was joined in matrimony to Miss Irene Rayner, daughter of Eli Rayner, of this county, and by her has the following children: Rayner, Flora, Thomas and Mary. Mr. Turley is a Democrat, a member of the K. of H., and is one of the leading citizens of the city and county.

Gen. Alfred J. Vaughan, clerk of the criminal court of Shelby County, was born in Dinwiddie County, Va., May 10, 1830. In 1851 he graduated from the Virginia Military Institute, and then adopted the profession of civil engineering. Locating at St. Joseph, Mo., he surveyed the Hannibal & St. Joseph Railroad, and was afterward appointed deputy United States surveyor of California. November 6, 1856, he was united in marriage with Miss Martha J. Hardaway, of Mississippi, and to this union there are five living children—three sons and two daughters. After his marriage he settled in Mississippi, where he resided until the late war broke out. He at first opposed a dissolution of the Union, but finally went with his adopted State, Mississippi. He raised a company in Marshall County, of that State, but they could not be received, owing to lack of military equipments. He then joined a company at Moscow, Tenn., and was elected captain. He followed the fortunes of the grand army of Tennessee, fighting gallantly at Belmont, Shiloh, Richmond, (Ky.), Murfreesboro and Chickamauga, and rising steadily in rank and in the confidence of his superiors. At the bloody battle of Chickamauga he was made brigadier-general by President Davis, on the field, for conspicuous gallantry. In the fight near Marietta, Ga., on the 4th of July, 1864, he unfortunately lost his leg. After the war he engaged in farming in Mississippi. In 1872–73 he was connected with the Grange movement, and was located at Memphis. In 1878 he was elected, on an independent Democratic ticket, clerk of the criminal court. In 1882 he was unanimously nominated for the same office by the Democratic convention, and was, at the election following, again elected. He was not a candidate in 1886. In this election his majority over his opponent was 5,701, one of the greatest ever given for any candidate in the county. He is a very popular officer, and is the soul of honor, and accordingly no citizen stands higher in the estimation of the public. He is a Royal Arch Mason, and a member of the K. of H. and the R. A., and himself and wife are members of the First Methodist Episcopal Church of Memphis.

Rev. Father John Veale was born October 2, 1846, in County Waterford, Ireland. He received instruction at the national schools, the Christian Brothers' school and then began his classical studies under the famous Mr. Dwyer of Dungawan, who had educated over 400 priests. He then attended Mt. Mellary Seminary and graduated from this institution in 1865. After this he entered the Foreign Missionary College of All Hallows, Dublin, being ordained priest in 1870. The same year he came to America and located at Nashville. After acting assistant of the late Very Reverend M. Riordan for a time he was sent to Jackson, Tenn., where he remained three years as pastor. In 1876 he was recalled to the cathedral at Nashville where he served in various capacities till 1881 when he came to Memphis and assumed the duties of pastor of Patrick's Church at that place.

A. J. Vincent is manager for C. W. and S. G. Boyd, dealers in pine and hardwood lumber, making a specialty of walnut, ash and poplar lumber. Their offices are at No. 1 Madison Street, Memphis, and No. 91 Water Street, Cincinnati, Ohio. Our subject, the manager of this branch of their business, is a native of Michigan and a son of W. H. and Rachel (Shimmel) Vincent, both natives of Watertown, N. Y. Mr. Vincent has devoted many years of his life to the lumber business, trading in Indiana, Illinois, Kentucky, Arkansas and Mississippi and is not only one of the most energetic and thorough-going business men of this section of the country but has the respect and esteem of all who know him. In 1879 he married Jennie Snodgrass of Metropolis, Ill., the daughter of David and Annie Snodgrass. To this marriage were born two children: Harry S. and Gertrude. In October, 1885, our subject permanently located in this city and engaged with C. W. and S. G. Boyd, one of the largest hardwood lumber firms in the United States. Later—since the above was first put in type the lumber firm has failed in business and is succeeded by Charles C. Boyd & Co., who occupy the same offices here and at Cincinnati and transact the same business. Mr. Vincent remains with the new company.

Joseph K. Waddy was born in Roane County, Tenn., May 11, 1820 His father, Samuel Waddy, was a native of Virginia, and in early life immigrated to Huntsville, Ala. Before leaving Virginia he married Martha H. Kimbrough, and of ten children born to them five sons and three daughters lived to be grown, our subject being the seventh child born.

The father moved to Roane County, Tenn., in 1818, and remained till 1825, when he moved to Davis, Tenn. He was engaged in farming until 1830, then went into the hotel business at Paris, where he died in 1840. The mother was born in Virginia, and died in 1845 while on a visit to friends in East Tennessee. Joseph K. Waddy was raised in Paris, Tenn., and received a good English education, and has been a merchant since leaving college. In 1849 Mr. Waddy moved to Colliersville, Shelby County, and was married in that county, September 24, 1851, to Miss Virginia H. Vaden, a daughter of William Vaden, a farmer and native of Virginia. The children born to this marriage were William S., born October 31, 1853, and died December 18, 1864; Vaden S., born February 18, 1856, and died February 14, 1857; Mollie Holmes, born July 29, 1859, and died December 30, 1884. She graduated from Bellevue College in 1877, and April 25, 1878, she married Mr. T. H. Canon. They had four children: Emma Holmes, Joe Waddy, Thomas Hope and Alfred Orville. Mrs. Waddy, the wife of our subject, was born in Virginia in 1833. In 1849 Mr. Waddy went into the mercantile business in Colliersville and still continues that business. He was an old line Whig, but is now a Democrat. He is one of the leading business men of the place and a man of fine character and correct business principles, and is the president of the board of directors of Bellevue College, and also of the board of directors of Magnolia Cemetery. Mr. and Mrs. Waddy are active members of the Christian Church. They have six acres of land in the center of the town, with a handsome residence upon an elevated and beautiful site, and they contribute a great deal to the pleasure of the social circle of their town. Mr. Waddy is justly recognized as a leading citizen.

Rev. William Walsh, rector of St. Brigid's Church, Memphis, was born in Callan, County Kilkenny, Ireland, May 4, 1850. He was educated at Prof. Walter Hawe's Intermediate School and at the Augustinian College, Callan, and later at St. Jarlath's College at Tuan. From 1869 to 1874 he attended and graduated from All Hallow's College, Dublin, and was ordained priest at this institution June 24, 1874. He came to the United States in September of the same year, and was attached to St. Peter and Paul's Church, Chattanooga, and to several missions in Tennessee east of Nashville. In October, 1876, he was sent by Bishop Feehan to Memphis to serve as an assistant to Rev. Martin Walsh, pastor of St. Brigid's Church, continuing thus until the death of the latter, August 29, 1878, since which time he has been in charge of the church. He is a very able pastor, a courteous gentleman and is greatly respected by his congregation.

Hiram Campbell Warinner, a member of the law firm of Eastes & Warinner, graduated at Bethany College, Virginia, in 1857, and at the commencement of the war enlisted as a private in Clark's Second Missouri Battery, Confederate States Army, and after seven months was promoted to first lieutenant. He participated in the battles of Oak Hills, Mo.; Lexington, Mo.; Elkhorn Ridge, Corinth, Iuka, Van Dorn, Atlanta and elsewhere, serving the last few months of the war in Forrest's command. In December, 1865, he came to Memphis and resumed the study of law, and was admitted to the Memphis bar in August, 1866. He was first with Chalmers, Lee & Warinner, then with Lee & Warinner, then with Warinner & Lee, and in January, 1884, formed the present partnership with Mr. Eastes. Willis W. Warinner, the father of our subject, was born in Lincoln County, Ky., in 1810, and was married there to Miss Clemence Mason, who bore him five children. The mother died in about 1847, and the father then married Margaret Scales, who bore him eight children. These parents live at Richmond, Mo. The father followed merchandising and banking at that place, and at Kansas City, but is now retired. Our subject was born in February, 1841, and was married in 1867 to Miss Sally T. Ardinger, a native of Missouri, who has presented her husband with the following children: Annie Bodieu, Carrie Belle, Hugh Lee, Gussie and Ardinger. Mr. Warinner is a Democrat, but has no political aspirations.

Fred J. Warner, merchant and resident of Bartlett, Tenn., is a son of F. L. and Matilda (Young) Warner, and was the second of six children born to this marriage. The father was captain in the Confederate Army, in Gen. Sneed's command, and was the founder of the German National Bank, of Memphis, and was considered one of the prominent and influential citizens of that city. The mother was a native of Germany, and came to this county when quite young. Fred J. Warner was educated at Memphis, and after completing his education engaged in farming, on a farm belonging to his mother in the Seventh District. In 1883 he established his present business at Bartlett, and has succeeded well with it. He married Miss Sallie Miller, daughter of W. N. Miller, a prominent farmer in the Seventh District of Shelby County, and has one child by this marriage. Mrs. Warner is a member of the Methodist Church; he is a member of the K. & L. of H., and is a true Democrat. He possesses many excellent qualities that have won for him a host of friends.

Cæsar Weatherford, collector of delinquent revenue, was born in North Carolina, May 29, 1843, son of William and Frances G. (Hooper) Weatherford, natives of Virginia. At the breaking out of the war,

Cæsar Weatherford was at college in Cheatham County. He responded to the call to arms, left college and enlisted in the Fourteenth Tennessee Regiment, Company H, of the Confederate States Army. He served during the entire war and so conducted himself as a soldier that he enjoyed the confidence of both officers and men, and especially of his immediate commander. He was promoted for gallantry at the battles of Sharpsburg and Shepherdstown, and was complimented by his commander for individual gallantry at the battle of the Wilderness. While in the trenches in front of Petersburg his name was forwarded for promotion for meritorious conduct during the campaign. It was through the lines of the brigade to which he belonged that the enemy made their entrance into Petersburg, the men being stationed behind the works eight feet apart. After the line was broken and the brigade surrounded and retreat almost cut off, he was directed by Gen. McComb, commanding, to take such men as were available and skirmish with the head of the Federal column in order to aid the retreat and save as much of the brigade as possible. This he did, until finally he was surrounded and captured, near the banks of Hatchie River, while making an effort to swim across. He was carried to Fort Delaware prison, where he remained until the breaking up of the war. He returned home and went to college at Russellville and to the law school at Lebanon. He located in Memphis in 1870 and practiced law in the firm of Weatherford & Weatherford, and afterward of Heiskell, Weatherford & Heiskell. December 19, 1870, he married Eliza Heiskell, of East Tennessee, and they have five living children. Mr. Weatherford is a Democrat in politics, a Knight of Honor and a Methodist Episcopalian in religious belief.

Dr. A. M. West, a talented physician of Memphis and professor of chemistry and hygiene in the Memphis Hospital Medical College, was born in Memphis March 5, 1849, and is one of a family of nine children, six of whom are still living. The parents are A. M. and C. O. (Glover) West. The father was born in Alabama in 1818, and for many successive terms, before the war, served in the State Senate of Mississippi. In the early part of the late war he served as brigadier-general in the Confederate Army, and was afterward candidate for governor. He was defeated by Gen. Charles Clark, who had returned home permanently disabled by wounds received in the service and was therefore invincible before the people of his State. Gen. West afterward served as quartermaster-general of his State until the termination of the war, when he was elected president of the Mississippi Central Railroad Company (now the Illinois Central Railroad), and was elected to Congress. He was one of the Tilden electors for the State at large in 1876, and was afterward a candidate for Vice-president of the United States on the Greenback ticket with B. F. Butler. Although not a partisan Democrat he has uniformly acted with that party and voted its ticket, save when he had the opportunity to support a worthy Greenbacker. He is now a resident of Holly Springs, Miss., and one of the prominent men of the State. The mother, who has been an invalid for many years, is generally known and recognized as possessed of rare intellect. Our subject graduated from the University of Mississippi in 1869 with high honor, receiving the degree of B. A., and served as assistant professor of mathematics in the same institution after graduating. He also graduated with honor at the University of Pennsylvania, and was unanimously elected by a class of over 300 students to deliver an address to the faculty and board of trustees. He read law a short time, but preferring the medical profession began the study of medicine and spent eighteen months in the medical department of the University of Virginia and while here served as editor of the college magazine. In August, 1876, he located at Holly Springs, Miss., where he practiced his profession successfully and was for a number of years health officer of the county. December 5, 1877, he married Eva W., daughter of Judge J. W. and E. D. Clapp, of Memphis, and to them have been born three children: Evlyn L., Alston Madden and Jere. Dr. West has built up a large practice since moving to Memphis and is recognized as an excellent citizen and a most skillful physician.

William A. Wheatley, United States commissioner and real estate broker, is a native of this city and was born January 4, 1843. His father was Seth Wheatley, a distinguished lawyer of this city in *ante bellum* days. Our subject was educated at Macon College, Randolph, Va., and upon the breaking out of the war enlisted with the Culpeper riflemen, Thirteenth Virginia Confederate Regiment, under Capt. Stockton Heath, and in this command served one year, and then came to Memphis and enlisted in Saunder's cavalry, and served as a non-commissioned officer until the surrender at Shreveport, La., in 1865. He returned to Memphis in 1867 and engaged in the real estate business, at which occupation he has since been continuously engaged. He now has one of the largest businesses of the kind in the city. He is a Democrat in politics and is one of the solid men of the city. October 1, 1867, he was joined in marriage with Miss Bettie Bowen, of Winchester, Va., and by her has three living children—one son and two daughters.

Col. F. M. White. Among the emigrants who came to America from Leicester, England, as early as 1720, was one by the name of John White, then aged twenty years, who settled in Orange County, Va. One of his grandsons was Thomas White, a native of Orange County, Va., whose father, when quite young, removed to Elbert County, Ga., where he grew to man's estate. Among the fair daughters of Virginia he sought a wife in Elizabeth G. Clarke, with whom he returned to Georgia to make that their permanent home. Their family consisted of twelve children, only two of whom are now living. In early life the father followed merchandising and later became a planter. Politically he was a Whig, and for a number of years was a member of the Georgia Legislature. Having lived an active and useful life they passed away and are now sleeping in the soil of their adopted State. Col. F. M. White, son of the above and president of the Mississippi & Tennessee Railroad, was born December 16, 1810, in Jones County, Ga. He was reared on a farm and received an academic education. In 1834 he married Lucinda S. McGehee, who was born 1815, and this union resulted in the birth of four children—three sons and one daughter. In 1847 his first wife died and later in the following year he wedded Frances Hamilton, who bore him one son, Francis H. Soon after his second wife died, and in 1858 he married Catherine Gardner, of Augusta, Ga. He and his present wife are members of the Episcopal Church; his other wives were also professors of religion. In 1840 the Colonel moved to Miss. to engage in farming and has since been thus interested. In 1852 he was appointed by the State Legislature as commissioner to assist in organizing the Mississippi & Tennessee Railroad Company. The following year he was elected president of the same, holding that position continuously since. He is also interested in the great Gayoso Hotel. He was a Whig till that party went down, and since then has been a Democrat. He has always been just in dealing and pre-eminently successful in business.

Dr. Elbert A. White, an old resident and physician of Memphis, was born in Alabama in 1825, and was one of a family of six children, four of them living. The parents were John D. and Sabra White; the father was born in Georgia in 1794, and moved to Shelby County, Tenn., in 1830, and at one time owned much of the land where the city of Memphis now stands. He was a farmer, and died in 1849. The mother's maiden name was Sabra McNees; she was born in 1792, and died in 1860. Dr. White was educated at Cumberland College at Princeton, Ky., and read medicine under Dr. Brown, of Memphis; then attended the Memphis Medical College and graduated in 1850, and has met with marked success as a physician, and has rendered valuable service during the visitations of yellow fever, doing a great deal as a physician and a citizen to alleviate the suffering. In 1849 he married Miss Almeda Waldran, who died in 1862. Three of the four children born to this marriage are living. In 1865 Dr. White married Miss Susan, daughter of James Felts. Mrs. White is a native of Shelby County. They are members of the Methodist Episcopal Church, and Dr. White is a Mason, a K. of H. and an ardent Democrat.

A. J. Whitney, master of trains on the Little Rock Railroad, was born in Jersey City, N. J., and is one of the three sons born to the union of C. O. and Adelia (Swartz) Whitney, natives of New Jersey. For a calling in life the father followed railroading. He filled the position of superintendent of the Alabama & Chattanooga Railroad for some time. He died in 1872. The mother is still living. The subject of this sketch was educated principally at Elmira, N. Y., but completed his scholastic training at Lookout Mountain Educational Institute. For three years Mr. Whitney was operator at Chattanooga and was subsequently train dispatcher, which position he held for nine years. In 1885 he assumed the duties and responsibilities of master of trains on the Memphis & Little Rock Railroad. He is an obliging young man, and one whose business qualifications are highly spoken of by his company.

Dr. E. Miles Willett, Sr., well known as one of the leading physicians in Memphis, Tenn., is a native of Kentucky; he was graduated in the classical department of St. Joseph's College, Bardstown, Ky., in 1851, and two years later received the degree of Master of Arts in the same institution. Having decided to adopt the profession of medicine he repaired to Philadelphia, where he remained more than four years, attending the lectures of the eminent professors of that day, in the colleges and hospitals of that city, then the most famous seat of medical instruction in this country. He graduated in Jefferson Medical College in the class of 1855, and then had the good fortune to be elected one of the resident physicians of Philadelphia Hospital, where he served a term of one year. This hospital, better known as Blockley Almshouse, had a population of 2,300 and 280 children, besides 1,000 beds for the indigent sick, who were afflicted with all the ills that human flesh is heir to. As resident physician he was not a mere looker on, but it was his duty to treat disease in all its countless manifestations, the medical department being under the management of one chief resident and eight resident physicians. In the deadhouse opportunities were offered every day to study the ravages of disease. His term of office having expired, he decided in the spring of 1857 to make Memphis, Tenn., his future home, not on account of personal friendships, for he did not know any one in that city, but simply on account of what he supposed to be the advantages of the location. As he was quite youthful in appearance, he did not jump at once into practice; his success was gradual but permanent. Since 1860 he has enjoyed a large and lucrative practice. During the four terrible epidemics of yellow fever, which visited this ill-fated city, he might have always been seen in the front ranks of that noble band of physicians, who by day and through the lonely hours of the night, regardless of personal danger, were in constant attendance on the victims of this dreadful scourge. To his praise be it said, he was equally prompt and conscientious in the discharge of his professional duty to the poor as to the rich. He has always manifested great devotion to his profession, and with the exception of an extensive tour of Europe, and an occasional visit to the northern cities, he has rarely taken a trip for pleasure, but is always engaged in the active duties of his calling, visiting the sick, or he may be found in his library reading up in connection with his cases, or it may be, studying kindred branches of science as an ornamental part of education. He was one of the original members of the faculty of the Memphis Hospital Medical College, and as such lectured on the diseases of women and clinical medicine for five years. At present he is professor of clinical medicine, physical diagnosis and diseases of the chest. He has always been regarded with great favor by the various classes of medical students as a fluent and pleasant lecturer and impressive teacher. He has always been held in high esteem by his professional brethren because of his uniform courtesy and great sincerity. He was one of the medical directors of the Southern Life Insurance Company for ten years, the term of its existence, and he had the honor to be elected the first supreme medical examiner of the C. K. of A., which place he has held for six years. These offices were not simply positions of empty honor but there was attached to the one as there was to the other a great deal of work and a substantial salary. The organization of Catholic Knights of America is a mutual benevolent society composed of between 400 and 500 branches and 20,000 members, scattered through the States and Territories of this country. When you are told that all of the medical examinations, made for this order throughout the United States, must be superintended by the supreme medical examiner, the nature of the office will be understood, and when it is stated that since the office was created Dr. Willett, the present incumbent has rejected nearly 1,000 applicants, the importance and responsibility of the office will be appreciated, especially when you remember that each accepted application represents a liability of $2,000.

John W. Willey is a son of Willis and Mary (Perkins) Willey, natives of Halifax County, N. C. The father was born in 1790 and moved to Tennessee in 1803. The mother was born in 1800, and when young came to Tennessee. Their marriage occurred in Dickson County, where both passed the remainder of their days engaged in agricultural pursuits. The father was a soldier in the war of 1812 under Jackson. Their family consisted of ten children, our subject being the fourth. He was born in Dickson County, May 28, 1825, and when twenty-three years of age came to Tipton County. In 1849 he began running mills, and from that time till the breaking out of the war he continued in that business. In 1862 he enlisted in Company G, Fifty-first Tennessee Infantry, Confederate Army, and was one of the brave defenders of Fort Donelson, where he was captured. For seven months he was imprisoned at Camp Butler, Ill., and such was his health when released that he did very little more in the service. After the war he engaged in the firm of Willey & Merrell. Mr. Willey is largely interested in landed property, owning about 900 acres. In 1856 he married Nancy E. Miller, of Tipton County, by whom he has one child—Mary, now the wife of H. N. Smith. Mr. Willey is also interested in the Kerrville Agricultural Association. He is a Democrat in politics, and he and wife are members of the Presbyterian Church.

W. N. Wilkerson, vice-president of the Security Bank of Memphis, and a member of the wholesale drug firm of W. N. Wilkerson & Co., 334 Main Street, was born in 1831 in Montgomery County, Tenn. His parents were Samuel M. and Mary A. (Wyatt) Wilkerson, natives of Virginia. The father had been school director in Haywood County for about forty years next prior to his death in 1884. The mother, in her seventy-eighth year, is still living. Upon reaching manhood our subject studied medicine and practiced the same a short time before the war. He served three years in the Confederate service, and in 1864 came to Memphis and established his present drug business in 1865. He is a member of the firm of D. B. Blair & Co., Australia, Miss., where they own a large plantation and a general merchandise store. He wrote the charter of the Memphis City & General Insurance Company, of which he is vice-president, and with which he has been connected since its organization. His wholesale drug trade varies from $250,000 to $300,000 annually. In April, 1878, he was joined in marriage to a daughter of Judge L. V. Dixon, and has by her four living children and two deceased.

George Winchester was born in Baltimore, Md., July 14, 1818, and is the son of William and Henrietta (Cromwell) Winchester. The father was a son of William Winchester, who was a brother of Gen. James Winchester, two of the original proprietors of the Chickasaw Bluffs. The father, who was a first cousin to Marcus B. Winchester, came to Tennessee in 1800 and located in Sumner County, but returned East after a three-years' residence. In 1831 our subject came to Tennessee, locating first in Jackson, but three years later moved to Brownsville, where he married and resided eleven years. In 1845 he came to Memphis and carried on the mercantile business two years, and then engaged in the cotton business, and has thus been engaged, with a short intermission, from that day to this, being one of three *ante bellum* cotton buyers of this city. Mr. Winchester is a Democrat, but takes no active interest in politics. In 1859 he was one of the organizers of the De Soto Insurance Company, and was its secretary until the war stopped business. In 1839 he married Miss Jane, daughter of Col. Richard Nixon, of Hayward County, and by her has had twelve children, of whom only four are now living.

Woods & Swoope, dealers in wagons, buggies, carriages, all kinds of agricultural implements, harness, saddlery, engines, and mowers, are the sole agents in this city for the Studebaker wagon. This firm is unequaled for variety of stock in the South. The members are Frank F. Woods and W. C. Swoope, who established their business in September, 1885, and are located at 332 Second Street, Memphis. Mr. Woods was born in Nashville and came to Memphis in 1873. He is a son of Joseph L. and Fannie (Foster) Woods, and grandson of Robert Woods, a distinguished member of the old firm of Woods & Yateman of the Tennessee Iron Manufacturing Company. Mr. Woods engaged with Orgill Bros. of this city in the hardware business and from them obtained his knowledge of his present business. He is the principal manager of the business. December 16, 1880, he married Annie H. Hancock, of Florence, Ala., and the daughter of James Hancock, the well known member of the firm of Hancock, Jones & Co. Mr. Woods is a member of the K. of H. Woods & Swoope were lately succeeded by Woods & Woods, composed of F. F. and R. J. Woods.

Hon. Archibald Wright (deceased) was for over thirty years the recognized leader of the Memphis bar. He was born in Maury County, Tenn., November 29, 1809, but was reared in Giles County and studied law at Pulaski under Judge Bromlett. He was admitted to the bar at that place in 1832. He secured his education partly at Mt. Pleasant Academy, near Columbia, and partly at Giles College, Pulaski. His parents, John and Nancy (McIntyre) Wright, were both natives of North Carolina and both of Scottish parentage. Our subject practiced at the Pulaski bar until October 1, 1861, and then moved to this city where, at different times, he was associated with Judges Eldridge, Turley and Curran. In August, 1858, he received an appointment from Gov. I. G. Harris, to the supreme bench of the State to fill an unexpired term. In November of the same year he was elected to the same position, which he filled with credit until the breaking out of the war. He was not a regular soldier during this unpleasantness, but helped the soldiers fight, followed them in their battles, bivouacked with them and shared their dangers and privations. He had two sons in the service; one was killed at Stone's River; the other, Gen. Luke Wright, is a resident of this city. Our subject's name was mentioned in connection with the supreme bench long before he was placed there, but he was never a strong aspirant for office, preferring rather to prepare for, than to seek office. He served in the Florida war, and soon after his return married Elizabeth Eldridge, May 29, 1837. He was a member of the Methodist Church and led a true devoted Christian life. At the bar he was not demonstrative in language or polished in oratory, but his arguments were always clear, comprehensive and convincing. He was noted for simplicity of character and by his death, which occurred September 4, 1884, Tennessee lost one of her noblest men, the bar one of her greatest leaders and Memphis one of her most prominent and beloved citizens.

Hon. Thomas B. Yancey, United States marshal for the Western District of Tennessee, was born in Fayette County, Tenn., October 10, 1843, and is the son of Alexander L. and Elizabeth (Bragg) Yancey, both natives of North Carolina. Thomas B. passed his youth in his native county without noteworthy event, and having graduated in medicine and dentistry at Baltimore College he entered upon the practice of his chosen profession in Somerville, Fayette County. He at once secured an encouraging practice which steadily increased until he left to accept the position he now holds (September, 1886). During the war Dr. Yancey served two years in the Confederate service as a private and two years on the staff of Gens. Preston Smith and Vaughan, ranking as first lieutenant and afterward as captain. In November, 1884, he was elected to the State Legislature and served in the session of 1885-86, securing his election from the Democracy, of the principles of which party he is a strong supporter. He is a member of the Odd Fellows' fraternity and of the Episcopal Church. In April, 1871, he was united in marriage with Miss Narcissa J. Warren, and by her has a family of three sons and three daughters.

James Yonge, a member of the firm of Mullins & Yonge, cotton factors and commission merchants, and a director of the Home Insurance Company, is a native of England and came to America in youth. He returned to England to educate himself, and then again came to the United States, locating in Georgia, where he connected himself with the lumber and manufacturing business until 1870, when he came to Memphis and became superintendent of the Memphis & Tennessee Railroad.

Two years later he became a member of the firm of F. M. White & Co., wholesale grocers and cotton factors, which firm existed about one year, when Col. White withdrew and the firm of J. W. Caldwell was formed and continued to exist until February, 1885. In August of that year the present firm was formed. It is now doing a handsome and profitable business. In 1866 our subject was married to Miss Wilson, of Augusta, who has borne four children, all living. The parents of our subject were natives of England. The family remained in that country, while the father followed boating along the American coast, where he finally died off of Georgia.

James W. Young was born in Memphis, Tenn., July 17, 1852, and is a son of Dr. James Young, an eminent physician, who was born in Chambersburg, Penn., September 13, 1800. He was raised and educated at that place, and graduated in medicine from the University of Pennsylvania; then moved to Tennessee, bringing with him letters of introduction to some of the leading citizens of Nashville, and by their advice established himself in Jackson, Tenn., and was soon recognized as a successful practitioner. In 1832 he married Miss Rebecca R. Hogg, daughter of Dr. Hogg, a well known physician of Nashville. Soon after his marriage Dr. Young moved to Nashville and formed a partnership with Dr. Hogg in the practice of medicine, and from Nashville moved to Natchez, Miss., where he continued to practice until 1840; then moved to Memphis, Tenn. His wife died without children in 1847, and he afterward married Mrs. Mary N. Coffee, a daughter of John Brahan, who was a native of Farquier County, Va. Two sons and two daughters were born to this union, three now living: our subject, William B. and Rebecca L. The mother was born in Huntsville, Ala., May 10, 1817, and is still living in Shelby County. She had one son by her first marriage: John D. Coffee, who died at Devall's Bluff, Ark., in 1874. Our subject was raised on the farm, and well educated under Prof. Tutwiler, of Alabama. He was married in Shelby County, Tenn., December 14, 1876, to Miss Kittie McConnell, daughter of James McConnell. One daughter, Mary, was born to this union. Mrs. Young died July 13, 1881, and June 18, 1884, Dr. Young married Miss Louisa Johnson, daughter of the Rev. W. C. Johnson, D. D., of the Memphis Conference of the Methodist Episcopal Church. She was born in Holly Springs, Miss., February 24, 1859. Dr. Young is a prominent Democrat, and is at present a member of the executive committee of the county, and with his wife belongs to the Methodist Episcopal Church South; his mother and sister are members of the Presbyterian Church. He owns 160 acres of land four miles northeast of Memphis, on the Raleigh Road, which is devoted entirely to garden planting. Dr. Young is well known in social, business and political circles, and is a man of influence and integrity.

Zellner & Co., one of the leading wholesale and retail boot and shoe firms of Memphis, was established in the year 1872, by David Zellner and Emil L. Goldbaum, both of whom were born in Germany. Mr. Zellner came to America when quite young, being the only one of his family who crossed the waters. After clerking a number of years he saved sufficient means to open a shoe store in St. Louis, under the firm name of Green & Zellner. Some time later he dissolved this partnership and came to Memphis, which city he recognized at once as most promising for future development and concluded to make this his permanent home. There he met his present partner, Mr. E. L. Goldbaum, with whom he again engaged in the boot and shoe business. The firm took high rank at the start, and from a modest beginning became the leading shoe house in the Southwest, and is noted for its liberality, enterprise, push and energy. Their reputation for highest class foot wear is not confined to Memphis alone, but extends into many adjoining States, from which they derive a large share of their business through orders by mail. In 1874 Mr. Zellner married Miss Annie Sonfield, of Memphis, by whom he has two sons and two daughters. Mr. Goldbaum came to the States in 1864, coming direct to Memphis, where he has resided ever since. After being a traveling salesman for Schwab & Co. for eight years he gave up his position and joined Mr. Zellner in establishing the now famous firm of Zellner & Co. In 1885 he wedded Miss Louise Andrews, a daughter of Mr. J. I. Andrews, one of the pioneers, and who built the first three-story brick house, now known as the Commercial Hotel, of Memphis. Both of the firm are thoroughly identified with the commercial and financial interests of the city, Mr. Zellner being a director of the Merchants' Protective Association, and trustee of the Security Savings Bank & Trust Company. Mr. Goldbaum is a director in the Memphis Building & Loan Association, and also a trustee of the Manhattan Savings & Trust Company.

INDEX

SHELBY COUNTY, TENN.

Prepared by
Frances Maynard
Fort Worth, Texas

Abban...847
Abbington, H. H. 832
  J. B. 914
Abernathy, J. R. 903
Acock, Samuel 819
Adams...1001
  David 920
  J. D. 815,824
  Nathan 891
Agelasto, A. M. 898
Ainsley, John A. 890
Ainslie...905
  John 904
Albrecht, John 833
Albright, C. H. 917
  John G. 917
  Jonathan 917
  Mary 917
  Sallie E. 917
  William A. 917
Alemany, James S. 854
Alexander...931
  Amma 981
  James P. 918
  John D. 918
  John McKnitt 799
  Lucy P. 959
  Mary A. 931
  Robert 852
  W. B. 959
Allen...919
  D. J. 852,853
  Docia 978
  Elizabeth 978
  Geo. 818
  J. W. 819
  R. C. 817
  Sallie 1003
  S. M. 910
  Thomas 812,916
  Thomas H. 892,898
  W. B. 978
Allison, Robt. 826
Alphonso, Mother 881
Alrich, W. P. 848
Alston, Augustus 815
  Philip 863
  William 799
Amandus...858
Amonett, E. 916
Ander...926
Anderson...824
  Agnes Brooks 919
  Bailey 820
  Charles 936
  C. L. 814
  D. R. (colored) 862
  E. M. 825
  Florence Modena 919
  J. A. 833
  James 918
  James H. 1021
  Janie Sanford 919
  J. C. 825
  J. D. 918,919
  Louisa A. 949
  L. T. 1023
  Maggie E. 191
  Mary Rolly 919
  M. J. 918
  Mathan 881
  Nathaniel 869,902
  R. M. 825
  R. T. 915,916
  S. M. 898

Anderson, Sophia 956
  S. R. 826
  W. L. 814
Andrews, David O. 919
  J. I. 863,1063
  J. S. 1008
  Louisa 1063
  Lula 919
  William 1008
Apperson, E. M. 823,919
  John 920
  Susan 920
  Susan B. 920
  Thomas 832
  T. M. 890
Arbuckle, J. A. 914
Ardinger, Sally T. 1053
  Drucilla 920
Armistead, John 891,895
  T. B. 920
  T. R. 920
Armour, Arthur 920
  E. B. 842
  Mary M. 1037
  Sarah Frances 920
  Spencer F. 920
  Susan 920
Armstrong...829,977
  A. J. 876
  Martha 994
Arnold, Caroline 1019
  George 891,895
  John 813
  S. C. 877
Arrington, Emma C. 921
  James H. 921
  Mary W. 921
  W. T. 921
  William T. 921
Arthur...1042
Asbury 853
Ashe, Annie A. 922
  Cora H. 922
  Haywood 922
  John B. 922
  Maggie L. 922
  Martha 922
  Samuel 922
  Samuel P. 922
  Shepherd M. 922
Ashford, B. 816
  J. A. 829
Asinius...877
Atkins, Evelina P. 975
Athey, P. R. 814
Athy...936
  P. R. 889
Atwood, N. B. 881
An-fat-char (Indian) 817
Austin, Azalia 923
  J. A. 922,923
  Lillie 923
  Margaret B. 923
  Robert S. 923
Avent, V. W. 876
Avery...1042
  Estelle 997

Babb, Benj. 898
  Benjamin 923
  Elizabeth 923
  John 923
  Mary 923
Bailey, A. F. 877
  S. 813

Bailey, S. 813
  Sylvester 814,880
Bain, J. 832
Baird, Drucilla 920
Baker...917
  Annie 935
  Ann W. 957
  William C. 957
Balch, J. K. 814
  John K. 881
Baldwin, A. E. 860
  Sarah 930
Ballentine, J. G. 833
Bamberger, M. 863
Bankhead, S. P. 834
Banks, David 882
  Enoch 882,883,884
  Richard G. 993
  Sarah A. 993
Barbee, W. J. 861
Barbiere, Joe 835
Barbour, Elizabeth S. 992
Bard, O. P. 907
Barn, Sarah 1002
Barnes, Esther A. 847
  J. 818
Barnett...841
Barr, Benjamin 891
Barret, A. R. 923
  J. H. 923
  Rebecca 923
Barrett, Dover J. 924
  Edmund 926
  Hosmer J. 924
  Maria J. 924
  M. Ford 926
  Thomas 926
  R. Frost 924
Barrow, John 817
Barry, Henry 824
  Jennie J. 954
  V. D. 814,819
  V. T. 911
Bartholomew, O. D. 876
Bartlett, G. M. 914,915
Barton 940
Bassett, Cornelius 924
  Elizabeth 924
  G. T. 924
  Lucretia 925
  S. P. 833
Bate...940
  H. C. 833
  H. R. 908
  William B. 806
Bateham, Sarah C. 847
Bates, W. H. 861
Bath, Victor 887
  William 898
Battier, Alice 925
  George J. 925
  Mary 925
  R. 925
  R. C. 925
Battle, Cornelia 944
  Flora 1045
  Fred 832
  Mary 1045
  William, 818,944
  Wm. 911,913
Baugh, R. D. 855
Baxter...924,997
  Katie V. 959
Bayless, Abram 817,818, 910

Bayless, B. 898
  Paul 815
Bayliss, B. 903
Bealmear, Ann 1030
Beamish, John 903
Bean, Jacob 816
  Joab 818
  Mary C. 818
  Russell 816,818
Beard...939
  Amelia 925
  Jacob 818
  J. H. 830
  Lee 925,926
  Peggy 818
  R. H. 925,926
  W. D. 925
Beasley, James E. 894
Beatty, J. D. 825
Beauregard...825
Bedford, B. W. 926,927
  Benjamin 927
  Ellen 926
  Hugh L. 927
  Hugh R. 927
  Julian 926
  Louisa 927
  M. A. 927
  Martha A. 926
  Rosa 926
  Virginia 926
  William H. 927
  Willie H. 926
Beecher...823
  P. D. 876
Belcher...823
  Edward 946
  E. J. 946
  Eliza 946
  Evelin 943
  Laura 973
Bell...841
  John 805,905
Benges, William 1048,1049
Bently, David 819
Bensen, Thomas 864
Benton, Jesse 955
  Jessee 810,817
  Samuel 963
  Thomas H. 817
Berlin, Ike 913
  Lucy 1039
Bernardine, Sister 877
Berry...1025
  Henry 911
  Mary J. 985
  V. T. 824
Berryan, William 1041
Berryhill, S. L. 915
Berryman, William 819
Besthoff, Johanna 1036
  Rachel 1036
Bethel, B. 891
Behtell, H. E. 928
  Louisa 1043
  Pinckney C. 928
  W. D. 892,893,894,897,900
  William D. 928
Bethnell, Bessie P. 928
  Cynthia S. 928
  Jennie W. 928
  J. Pillow 928
  William D. 928
Bettes, Drury 817
  John 816
  L. 816
  Tilman 814,818,864,869
  William 815
Betts, Lula 919
  Mattie M. 1008
Beyer, Paul 864
Bickford, Elizabeth 929

Bickford, Henry H. 929
  Louise 929
  Lydia 928
  Moses 928
  W. A. 870,872
  William A. 928,929
Bicknell, B. J. 929,930
Bierce, Lucy C. 996
Biffle...928
Bigelow, J. B. 806
Bigger, E. E. 850
Biggs, J. T. 1046
Bigley...957
Bignon...845
Bilderback, L. J. 1041
Bingham, J. B. 905
  Julia 943
Binkley, Sarah 1038
Biscoe, J. H. 892
Black...842
  Fannie M. 930
  J. E. 889
  Jane 930
  Janie 930
  Joseph S. 930
  R. J. 891,892,895,930
  William 930
Blackley, T. C. 814
Blackwell, Joe 819
  Joseph 915
  L. V. 931
  M. H. 852
  Nicholas 930
  Sarah 930
  Willie 931
Blaine, James G. 806
Blair, D. B. 1059
  Emma 1018
  W. C. 848
Blakeney, Louisa 1021
Blalack, M. F. 908
Bleckley, E. M. 914
  T. C. 903
  Thomas 914
Bledsoe, John 818
Bliss, T. E. 860
Blood, Caroline 931
  Charlotte 931
  Emma A. 931
  George H. 931
  Henrietta 931
  Joshua 931
  Lottie Heywood 1013
  Margaret 931
Bloom, M. 863
Bloomer, R. M. 857
Blount, John Gray 799
  Thomas 799
  William 921
Boddie, Elijah 945
  Ella D. 945
Boekel, J. A. 856,857,877
Boggs, W. E. 849
Bohlen, P. R. 973
Bollinger, Emma E. 986
Bolten, Henrietta 937
  Leonidas 937
Bolton, A. Wade 822
  Isaac 822
  Josephine 822
  Lavinia Ann 822
  Lucassa 822
  Marcua D. 820
  Mary L. 822
  Sarah W. 822
  Seth W. 822
  Wade H. 822,823
  Washington 822
Bond...916
  John 915
  Lewis 1006
  Samuel 915
  T. W. 876

Bond, Washington 915
Bone, Andrew M. 931
  George A. 932
  J. P. 931
  Mary A. 931
  Nettie 931
Boneparte, Napoleon 971
Booker, Grace 945
Booth, Anne 947
Borland, Solon 805,904
Borner, George C. 932
  Herman G. 932
  Mary E. 932
  Mary W. 932
Bostick, L. 814
Boucher, Joshua 851
Boulton, Charles 818
Bourland, A. B. 839
Bowdoin, Emily 842
Bowen, Bettie 1055
Bowles, Nannie V. 958
Bowman, F. H. 848
Boyd...842
  Alston 895
  C. W. 1051
  Charles C. 1051
  L. C. 849
  S. G. 1051
Boyle, Patrick 908
  Thomas 892
Bradford, Alex. B. 814, 817
  R. M. 898
  Wat. 1001
Bradley, Edward 810
Brady, Catherine H. 933
  Edward 932
  Elizabeth 932
  Thomas Van 932,933
Bragg...830,835,1019
  Elizabeth 1061
Brahan, John 1062
  Mary N. 1062
Bramlett, L. M. 815,819
Bransford...971
Breckenridge, John C. 805
Brett, James 805
Briggs, J. T. 913
Briney, J. B. 861
Brinkley...1030
  Robert C. 862
  W. A. 908
Brock, Moses 853
Brogan...806
Bromlett...1060
Brooks...832,890,898
  B. F. C. 886
  Joseph H. 853
  S. H. 893
  T. J. 835
Broome, Frances C. 1000
Brower, D. A. 905
Brown...890,898,911,991, 1056
  A. V. 825
  Aaron V. 804
  Annie 933
  B. C. 900
  E. L. 1005
  Eliza 979,980
  Eugene L. 933
  J. W. 824
  James 801
  John 814,817,832,853, 880
  John C. 806
  Mary T. 1015
  Neill S. 804
  Pauline 964
  S. R. 814
  Sam (Indian) 817
  Sam'l R. 809
  Samuel R. 814,815

Brown, T. W. 822,1006
  Thomas J. 895
  W. H. 830,991
  W. N. 889,895
  W. T. 824
  William 820
Brownlow, W. G. 805
Bruce, Alice 935
  Joseph 891,892
  Sallie L. 945
  W. S. 886,891,893,895,
    900,902,935
Bruse, James 1000
  W. S. 1000
Bryan, A. M. 851
  C. B. 891,900,1046
Bucey, Sarah M. 988
Buchanan, E. C. 896
  James 804
Buchholz...858
Buckingham, Anne Gifford
  933
  Cornelia Beckwith 933
  Eliza 934
  Henry G. 933,934
  M. S. 891,933
  Miles Gifford 933
  Theophilus Nash 933
Buford, S. B. 913
Bulkley, H. D. 905
Bullington, Caroline 934
  D. E. 934
  R. E. 934
  S. A. 934
Bullock, Sarah A. 1043
Bunch, B. 819
  Elijah 818
Buntyn, Euzelia M. 1034
  G. O. 1034
Burcham, R. 876
Burford, J. W. 832
Burke, Annie 935
  Catherine 934
  M. 888,889,901
  Michael 934
Burns, Caroline R. 972
  D. E. 854
  Daniel 818
  Jermiah 972
  W. F. 832
Burr, Ella 1020
Burroughs, Frances 988
Burrow, Reuben 851
Burrows, Aaron 1044
Burton, Andrew 925
  Mary 925
Busby...898
  J. J. 891
  Powel 802
Bushmiller, Anna M. 1031
Butler, B. F. 1055
  J. J. 886
  Matilda 978
Buttinghaus, F. W. 886
Bybee, Joseph N. 849
Byler, W. L. 800
Bynum, H. L. 825
Byars 981
Byrd, Alice 935
  C. L. 935
  Charles 935
  Mary 935

Cabell 836
Caldwell, A. S. 849
  Alexander S. 849
  C. H. 1012
  E. W. 861
  J. W. 1062
  Lucy A. 1012
  Martha 849
  Samuel A. 850
Callahan, John 935

Callahan, Mary 935
  P. 935
Callis, C. M. 915
Cameron, J. F.
  W. L. 900
Campbell...907
  Margaret 1042
  Polly 818
  William B. 804
Canada, Annie 936
  C. J. 936
  John B. 936,937
  Willis C. 936
Canale, D. 895
Cannon...823
  Charles Devereaux
    Dunlap 949
  Elizabeth Love 949
  Henry E. 948
  Henry Hugh 949
  Henry J. 935,948
  Mary 1039
  Mary Dunlap 949
  M. Florence 936
  Robert Dudley 949
  Sarah 935
  Sarah P. 948
  Sarah Virginia 949
  Susie Dunlap 949
  Susie Virginia
    Devereaux 949
  W. D. 807,814
  William D. 935,936
Canon, Alfred Orville 1052
  Emma Holmes 1052
  Joe Waddy 1052
  Mollie Holmes 1052
  T. H. 1052
  Thomas Hope 1052
Capers, Alice J. 937
  Benjamin H. 937
  Rebecca J. 937
  Richard S. 937
  Richard T. 937
Carbery, B. H. 895
Carey, B. V. 857
Carmon, Simon 820
Carnes...835
  S. T. 900
Carr...926
  A. B. 801,818
  Anderson B. 815,864,
    868,869
  Gideon 815,816
  Mary 818
  O. W. 818
  T. D. 801,809,815,816,
    817
  Thomas 816
  Thomas D. 800,808,816,
    817,864
Carrington, E. J. 971
Carrol, W. H. 892
Carroll...805,841,1047
  C. M. 832
  O. 832
  W. H. 829,830,831
  Thomas B. 885
  William 800,896
  William H. 896
  Wm. H. 829,830,831
Carter, J. C. 832
  Luna C. 1023
Caruthers...801,953
  J. P. 814,815,824
  R. L. 832
Carver, S. B. 898
Cary...954
Cash, Benj. 977
  Mildred Spotswood 977
Caskey, T. W. 861
Cass, Lewis 804
Cassady, Nancy A. 940

Cassarly, Margaret 950,
  951
Castleman, Cynthia 926
Catherine...848
Cavanaugh, W. F. 1014
Cayce, M. C. 903
Cenas...1027
Chaille 1027
Chalmers...945,1047,1053
  J. R. 930
Chamberlain, Jacob 1046
  Mary E. 1046
  W. J. 1046
Chambers...998
  A. T. 937,938
  Henrietta 937
  J. P. 937
  Rebecca 937
Chandler, James 819
  John 818
  Rachel 819
  Sarah 818
  Tilda J. 1014
Chapman, James L. 852
  Susan A. 1021
Charlotte (Negro) 817
Chase, W. J. 891,896,897
Cheatham...830
  Anderson 938
  Charlotte W. 938
  Edward 938
  Elizabeth 938
  John A. 938
  Leonard P. 938
  Richard 938
Cheney, Martha 945
Cherry, George 913
Chester, John 969
Chevis, L. A. 876
Chew, R. E. 861
Chilton, Thomas H. 894
Chisholm, W. S. 812
Crittenden, S. B. 1013
Choppin, Samuel 1027
Christian...883
  Frederick 808,818
  J. R. 820
  Wyatt 870
Christman, Elizabeth 999
Church, C. B. 891
Cirode...898
Claiborn, Thomas 833
  William C. 820
Clanton, Catherine 948
Clapp...928
  Aubrey B. 939
  E. D. 1055
  Eva W. 1055
  J. W. 925,1055
  Jerl 939
  Lamira 939
  Lucas 939
  Parker 939
  Robert 939
  W. L. 925,939
Clark...935,1043
  Charles 1054
  E. 916
  F. H. 860
  W. L. 971
Clarke, E. E. 898
  Elizabeth G. 1056
  G. B. 875
  S. R. 876
Clarkson, J. H. 856
Clary...1047
  Ellen 939
  J. W. 932
  James E. 939
  Nettie 932
  Patrick 939
Clay...898,962
  C. C. 833

Clay, Henry 804
Clayton...1020
Cleary, E. M. 832
  J. E. 889
  J. R. 856
Cleaves...974
Cleveland, Grover 806
Clinton, Charles 824
Cloth...982
  H. 891
Cobb, J. W. 979
Cochraham, Sarah 818
Cochran...841,898,1004
  Anna E. 940
  C. A. 941
  Conley 940
  D. 965
  Henry L. 940
  Ida 940
  Ida C. 940
  J. W. 924,940
  John F. 914
  John Knox 940
  John W. 890,892
  M. A. 941
  M. E. 924,940
  Mable 940
  Maggie 940
  Mamie 940
  Marcus E. 940
  Nancy A. 940
  R. L. 892,940
  Richard L. 940
  Sophy 941
  William T. 940
Cody, Elsie 941
  Harriett A. 941
  J. C. 814
  Jane 941
  Joseph L. 941
  Maude 941
  Miles F. 941
  Minerva 941
  Ola 941
  Thomas 941
Coe...911
  Joseph 808
  L. M. 824
Coen, M. 901
Coffee, E. 868
  Elijah 851
  John D. 1062
  Mary N. 1062
  Sallie R. 966
Coffin...898
  H. E. 891
  R. L. 891,893
Coghill, Lucy 916
Cohn, A. 892
Colby, Annie 1024
  E. E. 1024
Colden, Cadwallader D. 802, 804
Cole...924,970
  A. E. 941,952
  E. A. 815,828
  E. M. 915
  E. W. 812
  Frances 959
  Frances A. 941
  J. C. 829,830
  Mattie 941,952
  Sallie F. 993
  Susan 959
  Wesley 916
  William I. 894
  Winfield 941
  Winfred 916
  Wingfield 959
Coleman...911
  Amelia 942
  B. F. 814
  Daniel 942

Coleman, David 910
  George B. 942
  J. M. 911,912
  James 812
  James M. 942
  Milton 819
  Robt. 830
  Sol. 892
  Susan 942
Collier, Charles H. 942,943
  C. Miles 942
  Elizabeth 945
  Evelin 943
  H. W. 832
  Julia 943
  Sarah 942
Collins, J. F. C. 852,853
Collis, Joseph 616
Colyar, A. S. 812
  Chas. H. 843
Connell, H. D. 843
Conner...898
Conway, Bridget 1014
  Clara 845,846,997
Cook...841
  J. B. 806,809
  J. G. 832
  M. B. 825
  Mary 1035
  R. A. 861
Cooke, A. M. 943,944
Coons, George W. 848
Cooper 945
  Cornelia 944
  Frances 980
  Henry 944
  L. P. 943,944
  M. 896
  M. T. 943
  N. 897
  Pauline H. 944
  R. T. 891
  Sallie A. 944
  T. C. 852
Coopwood, W. C. 914
Corbett, Ellen 937
Cornelius...916
Cosgrove, John 824
Cothron, Alex 913
Coulter, H. W. 832
Countee, R. N. 908
Covington, W. C. 820
Cowles, Sarah 942
Cox. A. A. 830
Craft...943
  Alfred D. 945
  Charles K. 945
  Elizabeth R. 945
  Ella D. 945
  Henry 944,945
  Hugh 945
  Martha 945
  Mary E. 945
  Mary F. 945
  Paul 945
Craig...1045
  Mary A. 1044
  R. G. 854,902
  Richard G. 945
  Sallie L. 945
Cranberry, G. W. 909
Crandall 836
  Amelia 1044
Crawford, Anna 1004
  Bettie 994
  Louise 1048
  W. J. 895,899,1004
Creighton...841
  J. C. 824
  John C. 887
Crenshaw...915
  Grace 945
  Ida E. 979

Crenshaw, L. H. 979
  Thomas B. 945,946
  William A. 979
Cridup, Morning 1024
Crigley, J. D. 920
Crockett, Davy 931
  E. J. 946
  Elise B. 946
  William H. 946
Cromwell, Henrietta 1059
Cross, David C. 946
  J. S. 1015
  John 1016
  John S. 1016
  Lucy M. 1016
  Loula 947
  Mary 979
  Richard 799
  W. R. 914
  William R. 946,947
Cruse, David 824
Crutchfield, D. H. 1019
Cubbins...1001
  John 900
Cubero, Francis 856
Cullen, Anne 947
  H. B. 814
  Hugh B. 947
  Hugh M. 947
  Lizzie 947
Cullom, Alvin 972
  Shelby M. 972
  Verlinder 972
Cummings, Emily S. 975
Cummins, Bettie 947
  Holmes 969
  John 947
  William 947
Cunningham, Fannie 948
  Mary 948
  P. 947,948
Curran...1060
Curry, A. P. 806,814
  David M. 805
Curtis, C. T. 898
Cushing, Caleb 924
  Elizabeth 924

Dale, Catherine 948
  D. M. 948
  Elizabeth A. 948
  Hugh 948
  J. C. 948
  W. H. 948
Daley, J. R. 857
Daniel, Eugene 849
  Lizzie 984
  R. C. 891,898,899
  William 984
Darby, Willie 875
Dare, W. B. 818
Darnall, William 850
D'Artaguette...798
d'Arusmont, Frances 821
  Frances Sylva 821
  Phiquepal 821
Dav, Wilhelm H. Th. 864
Davidson, T. P. 851,852
Davis...836,841,939,944, 1050
  A. C. 851
  A. W. G. 819
  C. H. 835,836
  F. A. 890
  F. S. 899
  G. H. 914
  George W. 880
  J. M. 914
  J. W. 824
  James D. 886
  John 818
  Jospeh L. 881,882
  Lewis W. 949

Davis, Lucy Va 1008
  Margaret C. 949
  Nancy H. 950
  W. B. 825
  W. C. 889
  William 819
  William A. 802,815
  William C. 949,950
  Wm. O. 809,817
Davison, Thomas 916
Dawson, John W. 829
  S. R. 876
Day...898,1025
  Isaiah 819
  J. S. 895
Dayton, A. C. 909
Deadrick, Anna May 950
  Elese Garland 950
  Eliza G. 950
  J. G. 950
  Jennie Barron 950
  Mattie S. 950
  Rachael J. 950
  Sam Hays 950
  William P. 950
Dean, J. H. 831
  William 815,818
Deason, E. 810
Degman, James 950,951
  Margaret 950,951
  Philip 950
DeGraffenried...829
DeGroat, S. B. 889
Delacy 836
Deloach, Mary 967
Denie, John A. 892,895
Dennis, C. J. 936
  J. S. 936
  Samuel 851
DeRoach, Josiah 896
Desota 797,798
Dewese, Henrietta 982
Dewitt...883
Dewoody, W. L. 814
D'Iverville, M. 798
Dickason, J. S. 827
Dickens...851
  Thomas 822
  Tom 822,823
  Samuel 801,823
Dickerson, J. S. 808
  P. M. 876
Dickinson, C. C. 908
  Mary L. 983
Dill, W. F. 904
Dillahunty, Edmund 1001
Dillard...898
Dixon, L. V. 1059
  George 885
  Mary 1028
  Thomas 883
d'Lagerty, Eugene 821
Doak, H. M. 905
Dobyns, Carrie Deslonde 845
  Flora R. 1007
Dollar, James 820
Donelson...1005
  Alexander 912,913
Donnell, Alice 925
  Robert 851
Donnelly, John 912
Doty, J. C. 819
Dougherty, John R. 881
Douglas, Andrew J. 951
  C. L. 952
  Carrie T. 951
  G. L. 941
  J. 941
  J. P. 952
  Laura 951
  Mattie 941
  Oscar P. 952

Douglas, S. A. 951
  Stephen A. 805
Douglass, A. C. 952
  A. H. 815,825,828,885
  Adda H. 953
  Alice 952
  Anna 952
  Ann Eliza 954
  Bettie 952,1032
  Bettie S. 970
  Burchett 953
  Burchette 1032
  E. W. 831
  Edward 953
  Eliza A. 953
  Eliza B. 953
  Elizabeth 953
  Elmore 953
  Emma 952
  Eugene B. 953
  G. L. 913,952,970,1045
  G. R. 952
  H. L. 832
  Ida May 953
  Ila 953
  J. B. 952
  J. W. 952
  Joanna 952
  John 952
  John 952
  Kate 952
  Kate J. 1045
  Margaret 953
  Martha 953
  Martha A. 953
  Mattie 952,953
  Mollie 952
  Richard R. 953
  S. A. 1041
  Samuel 882
  William H. 953
Dow, Elizabeth 967
Doyle, Edward 859
  Margaret 841
  W. J. P. 814
Dozier...943
Drane, T. J. 854
Dresser, R. 825
DuBose, A. B. D. 954
  Camilla F. 954
  J. J. 815,906
  Julius J. 954
  Mary M. 954
Dubose...806
  J. J. 807
Duckworth, Alex. 833
  W. L. 833
Dudley, Frances 1037
  R. 891
Duffin, T. F. 895,901
Duffy, Bridget 955
  Ella M. 955
  James 954
  Jennie J. 954
  John 955
  John J. 954
  Maggie 955
  P. H. 955
Duke, B. 916
  Jane 941
Dunavant, W. P. 891,894,895
Duncan...911
  Albert B. 956
  Annie 956
  Benjamin 910,955
  Edith V. 956
  Elizabeth 956
  G. K. 810
  George K. 955
  Julia 986
  Nancy 955

Duncan, Sophia 956
Dunlap...805
  Devereaux 949
  Hugh 974
  Hugh W. 949
  Martha 974
  Susie Virginia Devereaux 949
  S. Virginia 949
  W. C. 815,817,820,824,949
  William C. 804
Dunn, Camilla F. 954
  Daniel 818,911
  David 818,869,950
  Dudley 851
  Eliza G. 950
  Emma 956
  Hattie 956
  Oliver M. 956
  Paulina 851
  Seely 956
  William B. 956
Dunscomb, Ann W. 957
  J. S. 892
  Marietta C. 957
  S. H. 892,899,900,902,903
  Samuel D. 957
  Samuel H. 956,957
Durfee, Philip R. 898
Durward, Sarah 907
Duval, Albert L. 957,958
  George W. 957
  Margaret 957
  Nannie V. 958
Dwyer...1051
  John 912
  Owen 814,947
Dye, R. J. 825

Eager...854
Eakin, Emmet 1020
  Jane 1020
  Rowena 1020
  Thomas 1013
  William S. 1013
Earnshaw, W. B. 837
Easley, E. T. 876
Eason, E. J. 824
Eastes...1053
Eaton, Clara 958
  Lohn 958
  L. B. 958,1006,1042
  Lucian B. 958
  Valentine W. 958
Ebbert...842,843
Echols, W. S. 825
Eckerly...1034
Eckles...933
Ecklin, Joshua 916
  Robert 916
Eddins, B. H. 959
  John 959
  John W. 959
  Joseph H. 959
  Lucy P. 959
  Nancy 959
  Samuel C. 959
  Susan 959
Edgington, Katie V. 959
  T. B. 959
Edmonson, Alexander 973
  Fannie 973
  J. H. 828
Edwards, J. B. 819
  J. S. 814
  James W. 959,960
  Jennie 960
  Lizzie 960
  M. E. 960
  Martha J. 959
  Mordecai 959

Edwards, R. M. 806
  T. E. 960
  W. A. 960
  W. O. 914
Elder, James 843
  Jennie C. 1011
  Lucy 1011
  Maretta C. 957
  Monroe B. 1011
Eldridge...807,1060
  Elizabeth 1061
  Thomas D. 815
Ellett...836
  Charles 835
  Chas. R. 836
  H. T. 815
  Henry T. 807
Elliott, John T. 960
  Sarah 961
Ellis, B. R. 961
  Emmit 961
  Ida E. 979
  J. T. 978,979
  L. D. 961
  Mary 979
  R. A. 961
  R. E. 961
  Robert E. 961
  Robert L. 979
  Rosa Lee 961
  W. E. 986
Ely...898
English...905,990
Ensley, E. 891,1025
  Enoch 893
Epperson, Joseph 1044
  Mary 1044
Erb, Adolphus L. 961
  Edna 961
  Esther 961
  Fannie 961
  L. 896
  Louis 893
  Newman 961,962
Erben, Henry 856
Erasmus...858
Erwin...841
  R. W. 854
Erskine, John H. 876
Estes...898,1006
  B. M. 850
  L. H. 807,815,902
  Z. N. 891
Etheridge, Emerson 805
Eustis, W. Tracy 898
Evans...806,915
  J. H. 853,854
  W. 916
  Wm. 916
Everett, Edward 905
Ewing, Jane 1020
  Joseph 1020
Extein...824
Exum, Mary 980
  Wm. 913

Fagan...1001
Fall, Jonnie Winston 845
Falls, G. 898
  J. W. 891,894
Fannehill, W. F. 883
Farabee, J. R. 835
Fargason...898
Farggson, J. T. 962
  Mary 962
  Sarah A. 962
  Thomas H. 962
Farley, J. Boyce 963
  Nancy M. 963
Farnsworth...854
  H. F. 1030
Farrington...804
  W. M. 886

Farrington, William M. 891,893
Farro, Rebecca 937
Fearn, Robert 818,882
Feehan...858,1052
  Patrick 860
  Patrick A. 847
Fellon, Zulu E. 847
Felts, J. E. 814
  James 1057
  Mattie 996
  Susan 1057
Fenton, Mary 1030
Fentress, James 808,910
Ferguson, Alexander 814,815
  J. T. 990
  William D. 902
Fewkes, William 802
Fick, W. 863
Field, Penelope P. 963
Fields...806,807
Fife, Mary 986
Fillmore...804,805
Finlay...1022
  John 854
  L. W. 833
  Luke W. 805,966
Finnie...890
Fisher...898
  Clemmie 975
  George W. 804,842
  H. C. 813,962
Fitch...836
  H. S. 924
Fitzgerald...829
  E. 828
  John 830
Fizer...898
Flannery, D. T. 895
Fleece, George 839
  George B. 1040
Fleming, A. B. 963
  Eliza 963
  Fannie A. 963
  James 962
  John M. 962,963
  Margaret 994
  Mary Ann 1040
  Nancy 962
  Nancy M. 963
  Samuel C. 962
  Samuel T. 963
Flegcher, J. 818
  J. M. 872
  Joshua 810,816,864
Flint, Austin 980
Flippen, J. R. 815,902
  John R. 887
Flowery, George 802,804
Floyd, Polly 818
  Thomas W. 818
Fly...982
Foley, T. 806
Folkes, W. C. 843
Folz, T. 863
Fontaine...890,898
  N. 892
  Noland 894
Foote, G. P. 837
Fooy, Benjamin 868
Forbes, J. G. 876
  Samuel H. 820
Force, F. H. 876
Ford...898
  J. N. 963
  Miles H. 917
  Newton 903
  R. P. 825
  S. H. 854,855,856
  Sallie E. 917
Fordan, Charlotte 868
Forrest...937,950,952,975,
  988,993,1024,1029,1047,
  1053

Forrest, Jane 824
  Jeff 968
  N. B. 834,930,1034
  Shin 824
Fort, Martha 1015
  R. B. 876
Foster, Bessie P. 928
  E. H. 804
  Fannie 1060
  J. P. 886
  J. S. 825
Foute, W. H. 843
Fowler, Azalia 923
  Eliza 1024
  J. W. 901
  John W. 814
  Morning 1024
  William 1024
Fowlkes...841
  J. M. 899
  Jepha M. 896
  Sterling 828
Fox, George S. 902
  John 948
Foy, Benjamin 798,816,868
  Frances 848
Frank, J. F. 898
  J. T. 894
Fraser, E. 819
Frayser...1015,1037
  C. L. 981
  C. W. 830
  Florence 964
  J. R. 981
  John R. 964
  Mary 964
  Pauline 964
  R. W. 964
  R. Dudley 892,963
Frazier...883
Freck, Nick 832
Frederick (slave) 803
Freeman...898
  A. A. 806
  J. J. 891
  James 808,830,910
  Margaret C. 949
Freemont, S. L. 993
Friend, Phillip H. 809
Fritz, Louis G. 906
Frohman, Alfred 806
Frost, J. T. 891
  Maria J. 924
Fry, Calvin 964
  Emily 964
  J. A. 964
  Lucy 964
Fuller, John W. 814
Fulmer, J. W. 899,965
Fulton, Martha J. 959
Furstemheim...898
Fussell, Joseph H. 806

Gage...898
  W. A. 894
Gaines, O. P. 904
Gaither...1002
Galbreath, W. B. 891,898,
  899
Gale, Tom 861,903,999
Galleger, Mary 935
Galloway, C. B. 965
  Charles B. 965
  Emma 965
  J. S. 807,815
  Jacob S. 806,965,966
  Lotta 965
  M. C. 896,905
  Mary 966
  Mary E. 966
  R. 889
  Rebecca 965
  Robert W. 966,1020

Galloway, Sallie R. 966
  Samuel 965
  W. D. 1003
Galvin, James 821
Gant, John 916
Gantt, George 966,967
Gardner, Catherine 1056
Garfield, James A. 806
Garner, Elizabeth 967
  Frank R. 967
  Matilda A. 967
  Mattie C. 967
  Robert 967
  Samuel C. 967
  Willie A. 967
Garnett, B. G. 887
  H. Y. 967
  John W. 967
  K. 967,968
  Kenneth 967
  Louisa C. 968
  William 968
Garrard, D. W. 853
Garth, Eliza G. 992
Gaston, Annie 969
  Jean 969
  John 968,969
  John Patrick 969
  Julia 969
  Peter 969
Gates, Annie E. 940
  S. M. 898,986
  Sam M. 899
Gavin, M. 891,892,894,898
Gay...1034
  W. W. 888
Gayle...841
  Fannie 842
  P. S. 854
Gayoso, Don 798
Gebhardt, C. E. 908
Genet, J. 828
Gentry, Elizabeth 1010
  Meredith P. 804
Gertrude, Sister 817
Gibbs, Lizzie 947
Gibson, Henry 816
  Pininah Lucinda 998
  Robert 898
  Sam 817
Gilbert, Annie E. 987
Gilchrist, M. M. 969
Gill, C. 825
Gillam, J. M. 819
Gilliland...971,972
  F. M. 914
Gillium, John 802
Gilmore, W. D. 814
Gist, Robert C. 896
Glass, Sarah 987
Glenn, John 825
Gloreing, Mary 935
Glover, C. O. 1054
Godwin...941
  Bettie 952
  Bettie S. 970
  D. G. 952,969,970
  J. R. 891,892,893,898,
    899,900
  Seth 969
Goff, James D. 849
Goldbaum, E. L. 1063
  Emil L. 1063
  Louise 1063
Goldsby, Martin S. 820
Goldsmith, Belle 970
  Celestia S. 847
  Dora 970
  Edward 890,891,892,970,
    971
  Elias 970
  Emanuel 971
  I. 970

Goldsmith, Isaac 970
  J. 970
  Regina 971
Goodbar, A. P. 971
  J. H. 972
  J. M. 889,891,893,972
  James B. 971
  James M. 971
  Jane 971
  Jennie E. 971
  Luan 972
  Mammie o. 971
  Mary 971
  Verlinder 972
  William M. 971
  William P. 971
Goode, Fannie A. 963
Goodlet, J. H. 808
Goodlett...898
  J. E. 903
Goodloe, Robert 799
Goodlow...965
Goodman, W. A. 843
Gorman, Caroline R. 972
  E. W. 915,916
  Edward W. 972,973
  Fannie T. 973
  P. A. 973
  Patrick 972,973
Gorrell, J. O. G. 876
Gorth, Horace E. 890
Gotsch, G. M. 864
Gotten, M. 914
Gould, John H. 837
Goyer, C. W. 889,891,903
Grace, John 816,817,864
  Peggy 816,818
  T. L. 847
  Thomas L. 856,857
Graham...903,1026
  C. C. 892,900
  Daniel 800
  George F. 881
  J. D. 819,882
  Joseph 808,810,814,819,
    910,1034
  Lydia A. 1034
  Q. J. 889
Grandison (slave) 802
Grant...833,904,1041
  G. R. 843
  George M. 990
  Juliet M. 990
  U. S. 805
  Ulysses S. 806
Glasgow, J. 800
Graves...824
  Amanda 973
  J. R. 909
  Laura 973
  R. C. 824,891,973
  W. M. 973
Gray, J. 913
  John H. 849,850
  M. V. 833
  W. C. 830
Greaves, Rebecca J. 937
Greeley, G. M. 814
  Horace 806
Green...1063
  Annie 933
  Colton 891,894
  Rebecca M. 847
Greenlaw, A. 820
  Katie B. 1022
  L. D. 830
  W. B. 834,891
Greenlee, E. E. 913
Greer, David S. 974
  Hugh D. 974
  J. M. 815
  John R. 973
  Martha 974

Gregory, John 819
Grible, H. W. 814
Grierson...833
Griffin, Ann E. 991
  George W. 991
  Luella 991
  Martha 985
  Nancy 990
Griffith, Oliver 819
Griswold, W. C. 861
Gronauer, Herman 983,984
Groom, John 819
Grubbs...922
Grundy, R. C. 849
Guion, H. L. 842,903
  Henry L. 974
  Lucy D. 974
  Margaret 974
Gunn...1001
  John 889
Gunter, Temperance 941
Guthridge, J. W. 819
Guy...898
Gwathmey, Hannah T. 978
Gwynn, A. B. 891

Hadden, D. P. 891
  David P. 888,889,892,
    894,899
Halk, Sallie 1019
Hall, B. F. 861
  Mary 966
  Sidney G. 996
Haller, Anna 975
  Benjamin F. 975
  Clemmie 975
  George W. 975
Hamilton...838
  E. E. 853
  Ella A. 847
  Frances 1056
  H. A. 900
  J. W. 832
  James 828
Hamlin...861
Hammerly, Rosa 1019
Hampton, Henrietta 842
  Henry 830
  Wade 917
Hanauer...897,940,990
  Jacob 1037
  L. 892,893
  Lena 1037
  Louis 890
  Marks 1037
  Susan 1037
Hancock, Annie H. 1060
  James 1060
  W. S. 806
Handwerker, J. G. 892
  Otellia 1031
Hanson, H. P. 908
  J. P. 908
  T. E. 908
Harbin, G. C. 990
  George C. 990
  John N. 893
  Juliet M. 990
Harcott, Nathan 852
Harcourt, T. J. 907
  Thomas 907
Hardaway, L. P. 814
  Martha J. 1050
Hardee...1037
Hardin. G. M. 814
  W. F. 903
Hardy, William A. 882
Hargan, C. J. 903
Harlan, L. B. 876
Harke...958
Harklerood, Mary C. 818
Harper, Elizabeth 1036
Harrell, J. E. 914

Harrington, G. 894
Harris ..804,805,826,827,
   828,831,898,1004,1025,
   1049
  A. O. 1025
  Andrew J. 807,975
  D. W. 1046
  Elizabeth 953
  Emily S. 975
  Esther 1008
  Evelina P. 975
  Fairfax 1025
  G. W. 1021
  George C. 862
  I. G. 1060
  Isham G. 805
  J. L. 814
  James M. 806
  John 953
  Laura 1025
  Nannie M. 1021
  Polly 988
  Samuel 799
  Thomas H. 886
  W. R. 815,824
  W. T. 852,854
  William 818,819
  William R. 815,975
Harrison...931
  Ara 1017
  Fannie E. 976
  Henry 976
  Jerusha 976
  N. F. 807,814,916
  Needham F. 976
  William Henry 804,904
Hart...1009
  B. N. 824
  Harriett F. 1021
  John M. 1037
  Lizzie S. 1037
  Mary M. 1037
  Miranda 1018
Hartmus...898
Harvey...898
Haskell...819
  Joshua 815,818
Hastings, David 977
  Janet 978
  Margaret 978
Hatch, Emma 956
Hatcher...915
Hatchett, Americus 978
  Hannah T. 978
  William 978
Hawe, Walter 1052
Hawkins...955,973
  Alvin 806
  Benjamin 910
  M. L. 1049
Hay, Patrick 820
  Susan 1030
Hayes, A. J. 903
  Benjamin A. 853
  R. B. 806
Haynes...806,807
  Docia 978
  Henry G. 978
  Matilda 978
  T. B. 898,978
Hays,...825
  O. B. 800
  Rachel J. 950
  Samuel J. 950
  Sam'l. J. 912,913
  Sarah J. 1029
  Stokeley 1029
Head...1022
  Jas. M. 812
Heady...876
Heakes, Frederick 931
  Margaret 931
Heard, Isaac 852

Heard, J. A. 854
Jeath, Stockton 1055
Heintz, Emma 1031
Hein, C. C. 962
Heiskell, C. W. 815,899,979
  Eliza 979,980,1054
  F. H. 979
  Frederick S. 979, 980
  Gussie L. 979
  J. B. 979
  Sarah A. 979
Henderson, Amelia 925
  Fannie H. 1048
  Irene M. 980
  John F. 980
  John L. 980
  L. 848,916
  Letitia e. 980
  Margaret J. 981
  S. J. 852,853
  W. L. 839,980
Hendrickson, C. R. 854
Hennepin...798
Henning, Ann B. 981
  B. G. 981
  C. L. 981
  D. M. 981
  J. H. 1018
Henry (slave) 802
  J. F. 830
Hensband, Richard 802
Herbers, Christina 982
  Clara 982
  George H. 982
  Lizzie 982
Herring, Joel 913
  Lewis 913
Herron...898
  F. B. 982
Hess...838
Hester...878
Hetherington...941
Hickey, Emily 964
Hickman...883
  E. 883,884
  Edwin 883
Hicks, John B. 876
Higbee, H. H. 843
  Jennie M. 845
Hughtower, R. 800
Hill...890,930
  A. Bruce 982
  C. H. 833
  E. W. Thomas 982
  H. M. 822
  Hattie E. 983
  Henrietta 982
  I. M. 886,895
  Isabelle R. 983
  James M. 982
  John S. 982
  J. Sloan 982
  Mary 818
  Napoleon 891,892,894,
   899
  Rebecca 923
Hillhouse, Adelaide 983
  Catherine M. 983
  J. F. B. 983
  John 983
  Mary L. 983
Hillsman...898
Hindman...832,946
Hines, Richard 843,862
Hirsch, Samuel 983,984
Hitchler, John 905
Hitzfeld, August 906,907
Hobart, E. 898
Hobson...982
Hodge, Samuel 848
Hodges, J. B. 814
  W. R. 876
Hoffman, John P. 891

Hogan, J. S. C. 904
Hogg, Rebecca R. 1062
Holeman, James 984
  Lizzie 984
  Mary 984
  Thomas 814
  Tom 984,985
Holiman, Charles 816
Holland, C. H. 831
Holman, Charles 810
  Thomas 813
Holmes, John B. 808,818
Holter, Henry 899
Hood...829,830,831,834,
   1019
Hooke, John 881
Hooker, Nancy 959
Hooks, J. C. 853
Hooper, Frances G. 1053
  Nimrod 819
Hopson, H. R. 876
Horgan, William 1008
Horne, J. B. 985
  Martha 985
  Mary J. 985
  Rosa L. 985
  W. D. 985
Horrigan, L. B. 815,825
Horton...969
  W. H. 839,840,985
Hotter, Emma E. 986
  Henry 986
Hough, Frances 999
Houston, Eliza 849
  John W. 914
  W. 880
Howard...1042
  Annie E. 987
  Emmett 986,987
  John 986
  Julia 986
  M. H. 801
Howell, Julia A. 1039
  R. B. C. 909
Howland, Louise 929
Howze...933
Hoxie, H. M. 989
Huehlefeld, J. B. 906
Hudson, John 968
Huffman, Barbara 1009
Hughes...941,970
  Bernard 986
  Edward 986
  Edward 986
  Emma Grace 942
  F. M. 941
  Luna May 942
  M. E. 942
  Mary 986
  Robt. 817
Hulbert, H. T. 886
Humes...1023
  W. T. C. 834
Humphrey...805
  Augustus L. 882
Humphreys, J. C. 815,824,
   1046
  J. H. 900
  H. W. 818
  Mary Eudora 1046
  P. W. 819
  Parry E. 815
  T. H. 914,1046
  W. H. 817
Hunt. C. P. 899
  F. R. 814
  J. M. 819
  Matthew 1014
  Thomas 1027
Hunter, Jacob 818
  James 820
  James F. 806
  Wm. 818

Huntington, C. P. 812
Hurt, C. S. 832
Huse...973
Huskey, B. 819
Hutton, William 904
Hyler, T. B. 825

Imes, Benjamin A. 847
Ingalls...876
Inman...823
Irby, Harriseon 987
  M. J. 987
  Sarah 987
  William H. 987
Irvine, Chas. 825
  Mary 818
  William 809,810,814,815,
  816,817,818,864
Irving, Washington 925
Irwin, Nancy 1007
Isaac (slave) 820
Isaacs, Mattie L. 875

Jackman...925
Jackson...835,933,938,1005,
  1006
  Andrew 802,815,816,817,
  820,865,866,867,868
  C. E. 988
  Emma 988
  Frances 988
  James D. 988
  M. Florence 936
  Stonewall 1028
  T. J. 823
  W. H. 833,930,948
Jacob (slave) 803
Jacobs, Anne R. 1033
James...903,1038
  H. M. 894
  Henry 818
  Joseph 816,818
  W. M. 813
Jansen, Ambrosius 858
Jardine, Agnes 1016
Jarnagin, Milton P. 964
Jefferson, J. W. 898
Jenkins, Amanda 824,841
Jennings, Robert 802,804
Jenny, J. J. 891
Jeter, Benjamin W. 988
  Eliott 988
  Frances 988
  Hariet D. 988
  Polly 988
  Sarah M. 988
Jetton, Robert 808,910
Jobe...842
Juliet, M. 798
Johnson...898,1028
  Andrew 804
  Anna 975
  B. M. 853
  Bertha 989
  C. O. 989
  G. D. 886
  J. C. 850
  John 887,895,903
  Lucile 967
  Louisa 1062
  Mary V. 989
  Samuel 800
  Samuel C. 897
  Thomas 817
  W. C. 1062
  W. R. 845
  William 850
  William P. 989
Johnston...970,1019
  A. S. 1001
  Albert Sidney 828
  C. W. 814
Jones...890,898,1060

Jones, Andrew 802
  Ann 991,1039
  C. 1039
  C. S. 991
  Calvin 815,821
  Carrie 990
  Chamberlayne 1039
  D. C. 861
  Eliza G. 992
  Elizabeth S. 992
  Ella 990
  F. G. 971
  G. W. 989,990,1040
  Guilford 853
  H. A. 851
  H. S. 832
  Heber 992
  Henry T. 916
  J. E. 851
  J. L. 914
  J. N. 861
  James 1040
  James C. 804,872
  John T. 992
  Luella 991
  M. 914
  Mary J. 1040
  Mercier James 1027
  Musadora C. 1024
  N. M. 890,991
  Nancy 990
  P. S. 898
  Phil B. 894
  Philip B. 992
  R. L. 990
  Rebecca 990
  Roger 875
  S. E. 991,992
  Stephen 990
  Valeria 992
  W. A. 920
  Wharton Stewart 991
  William S. 992
  William W. 886
Jordan, Alfred B. 993
  Bettie 994
  Elvin 994
  George S. 993
  Laura B. 994
  Louise C. 994
  R. D. 843
  Rix 993
  Sallie F. 993
  Sarah A. 993
Josepha, Sister 877
Jost, Marie 845
Joy, Luan 972

Kahn, Julius 907
Kalleher, Margaret 994
  P. 889
  Patrick 994
Kane, Mary 1019
  Thomas J. 1019
  William 1019
Katzenberger...898
  J. 892
  M. H. 892
  William 892
Kay, S. 848
Kearnes, J. W. 879
Keating...905
  J. M. 905
  M. T. 876
Keck, Elias 996
  Jennie 996
  Mattie 996
Keeling, E. A. 896,897
  Edward A. 994
  Martha 994
  Mary 995
Keightley, J. A. 1015
  Mary Louisa 1015

Keiser, J. P. 880
Kellar, A. J. 831
  J. R. 905
  Joseph 832
Kelley, D. C. 834
  J. E. 913
  James 1037
  Sallie 1037
  Susan 1037
Kelly, M. J. 995
  Morgan 806
  Morgan J. 995
Kelso, G. W. 832
Kendrick, Emma 1021
Kenkert, A. 892,894
Kenneday, W. H. 894,895
Kennedy...935
  James 880
  Mary 923
  Rosa B. 1015
  W. H. 1015
  Walker 907
Kenney, Edward 926
  Lucy 926
  Virginia 926
Kent, John R. 808,818,868
Kerr, Andrew H. 951
  Carrie T. 951
  John L. 900
Ketchum, A. C. 832
  A. R. 900
Kettman, H. 982
  Louis 982
Kilpatrick...841
Kimbrough 915
  A. G. 916
  Jas. 916
  John 810
  Martha H. 1051
  Nat. 810
Kindred, A. J. 1046
King...915
  E. W. 814
  E. W. M. 815,824
  Ephriam W. M. 820
  H. C. 833
  J. R. 814,910
  J. W. 814
  W. M. 913
Kinney, Minerva A. 847
Kirby, Mahala 1017
Kirkendal, Jacob 913
Kirkland, I. B. 891
  J. B. 842
Kitty (slave) 803
Klein, William 862
Klinck, J. C. 904
Knapp, A. J. 996
  A. G. 996
  Burke R. 996
  Edmonds S. 996
  Elizabeth 996
  Julia C. 996
  Lucy C. 996
  Mamie R. 996
Knott, J. W. 852
Knowlton, L. S. 896
Kortrecht...945,1006
  Charles 815,885
  Chas. 843
  F. D. 825
Kuey, Charles 889,891

Lafayette...802,804,821
Lake, Helen 1033
  Jenry 814
Lamar, A. W. 856
  Gussie L. 979
  L. Q. C. 979
Lamaster, Jas. S. 818
Lamb, Estelle 997
  Isaac N. 996
  Lawrence 824

Lamb, Sidney, G. 996
   Spence H. 996
Lambreth, Elizabeth 1031
Lamphier, Annie 956
   John 956
Lancaster, William 815
Landis, Janet 978
   W. H. 978
Landrum, Sylvanus 856
Lane, Aurelia 845
   Catherine 934
   Fletcher 964
   Mary 964
   R. C. 861
Langley, Joyce 1018
Langstaff...1026
Lanier, John C. 815
Lapsley, R. A. 850
   Samuel H. 955
La Salle..798
Latham, Edmund P. 997
   F. S. 895
   T. J. 846,861,900,997
   Thomas J. 891
Latimer, J. F. 849,850
Lausburg, Leon 845
Lavalette...871
   Margaret 957
Law, S. C. 827
Lawhon, L. 895
Lawhorn...1018
Lawler, J. B. 833
   J. T. 833
Lawrence, A. A. 889
   James H. 869
   Robert 814,882
   William 800,802,808,814,
     816,864,868,869
Laxton, A. G. 998
   Amanda 998
   John 998
Lazard, Tilly 1036
Leach, C. D. 920
Leake, M. E. 1015
   Sophy 941
   Virginius 987
Leath...901,902
   Carrie 990
   H. W. 990
   J. T. 843,844
Leatherman, D. M. 814,824,
   901
Lee...1053
   Adelia N. 999
   Elizabeth 999
   James 888,889,896,973,
     998
   James C. 999
   Peninah Lucinda 998
   Rowena 998
   T. L. 999
Leftwich, John T. 805,806
   John W. 887
Leigh, W. H. 853
Leith, David 853
LeMaster, James S. 963
   Margaret 974
   Nathaniel F. 963
   Olivia 963
   Penelope P. 963
Lemaster, J. S. 911
Lemmon, H. T. 891,893
   Henry T. 999
Le Moyne, F. Julius 846
Lenow, Frances 999
   Frances C. 1000
   Henry 999
   Henry J. 1000
   Jessie L. 1000
   Joseph 999
   Lizzie A. 1000
Leonard, Thomas 814
Leverque, Minerva 1042

Levett, J. S. 849
Levy, Archibald 921
   Christiana 621
   D. 863
   Emma C. 921
   L. 892
Lewelling, Ann 1039
Lewis...806
Lieck, H. 864
Lilly...903
   Kate 1000
   M. D. 857,1000
   Owen 1000
Lincoln...933
Lingow, Mary F. 1013
Linn, W. H. 825
Lipsey, J. W. 1012
   Lulu 1012
Livermore, A. S. 1001
Locke, G. B. 840,841,874
   Gardner B. 883
   Joseph 915
Lockhart...827
Lockwood, Lucretia 925
Loeb, A. 983
Lofland, W. O. 886,887
Lofton, G. A. 854
Logue, John 886,887,894
Logwood...930
   T. H. 824,825,833
   Thomas H. 815
Long, Mary 1010
   N. M. 850,860,861
Loomis...973
Looney, R. F. 1017
   Robert F. 1001
   Robt. L. 832
   W. H. 820
Loop, C. L. 812,1001,1002
Loring...833
Love...971
   Elizabeth 949
   Matthew 949
Lovel...835
Lovejoy, A. B. 832
Lovin, J. J. 861
Lowe...967
Lowenstein, B. 891
   Bobeth 1002
   E. 1002
   Leopold 1002
   Samuel B. 907
   Sarah 1002
Lowery, M. P. 919
   Maggie E. 919
Lowry, W. R. 876
Loyd, Thomas 819
Lucas...937
Lucker...915
Ludwig, H. M. 895
Luehrmann, H. 893
Luiselli, Antonio 860
Lundy, W. L. 813
Lurry, A. B. 914,1002
   Mary L. 1003
   Sallie 1003
   Thomas 1003
Lyles, O. P. 900
Lynch, A. J. 1003
   G. B. 1003
   J. 914
   John 1003
   Joseph F. 1003
   Lillie E. 1003
   Mary Irene 1004
   Polly 1003
Lynn, Henry J. 894

McAdam, Hugh 814
McAlur, Michael 856
McAllister, Robt. 816
McAlpin, Benjamin 910
McBride, E. J. 907

McBride, Edward J. 907
   William 820
McBrooks, John 914
McCadden, P. 908
McCallum...814
   S. M. 900
McCampbell, Andrew 815
McCarty, Sarah 1032
McClanahan, John R. 904
McClellan...898
McClintock, Nancy 962,1048
McCloy, W. A. 889,905
McClure, W. C. 890
   William 802,804
McComb...1054
McConnell, James 1062
   Kittie 1062
   Neil (negro) 817
McCrae, G. W. 900
McCrere...818
McCullock, Alexander 800
McCullough, Fannie E. 847
McDavitt, E. 892,903
   Flora R. 1007
   George 1006
   J. C. 834
   J. H. 892
   James Clare 1006,1007
   Linnie 1006
   Mattie 1007
McDonald, James H. 891
   Rosa 926
McDowell, Bessie 823,1007
   John D. 1007
   Lizzie A. 1000
   Nancy 1007
   S. I. 815,892
   Samuel Irwin 1007
   W. W. 815,1000
McElroy, W. 895
McEven, S. E. 992
McFadden, B. J. 814
   James 1024
   M. 889
   Sarah A. 1024
McFarland...853,1014
   Felix 953,954
   R. 806
McGarney, J. R. 877
McGarvey, S. R. 857
McGaveney...829
   Michael 828
McGee, Elizabeth 1010
   J. P. 1010
   Jennie C. 1011
   Martha 953
   Richard 1010
McGeehee, Lucinda S. 1056
McGeveney...840,841
McGill, M. J. 918
McGinnis, E. G. 1011
   George W. 1011
   Jane 1011
   Mary H. 1011
McGlathery, Polly 1003
McGowan...963
   Bessie 1007
   E. L. 815,893
McGregor, T. H. 876
McGuire, Ann 861
McHenry, E. B. 901
McIntosh, Eliza 934
   Mary 861
McIntyre, Nancy 1060
   P. 893
McKay...898,965
McKever, John 824
McKeon, J. F. 1016
   Mollie 1016
   Tennie 1015,1016
   Thomas 1016
McKim, J. W. 876
McKinley, J. S. 806

McKinney, Jane 971
  Sarah A. 979
McKinzie, James 818
McKissick...1049
McLean, Charles D. 820
  Chas. D. 902,903,916
  Louisa 927
  Robert D. 927
McLemore...801
  J. C. 810
  John C. 866,869
McMahon...843
  Dan 887
  J. H. 904,905
McMillan...823
McMullen...852
McNeal, J. 819
McNees, Sabra 1056
McPherson...830
McRae...1043

Mabry...883
Maddox...823
  J. W. 842
  S. C. 985
Magdalen...848
Magee, Patrick 816
Magen, Samuel F. 885
Mageveny, Michael 903
Magevney, Eugene 902,903
Magruder...917
Mahaffy, J. S. 909
Mahan, T. M. 900
Mahon, R. H. 852,854
Malatesta, N. 891
Mallman, Maternus 858
Mallory T. Geo. 898
  G. J. 889
  R. J. 1038
  W. B. 892,1004
Malone, Ednie E. 1036
  Elizabeth 1036
  Robert C. 1036
Mandeville...1027
Mangum, S. D. 914
Mann, A. P. 852
Manning, John 851
Mansfield, Mary B. 1005
  S. 894
  Samuel 1004,1005
Maria (slave) 820
Marquette...798
Markham, J. H. 819
Marks, A. S. 806
Marley...877
Marr, Mary 917
Mars...965
Marsh, Sarah A. 962
Marshall, Cyrus 825
  G. W. 837
Martin...898
  A. J. 1005,1006
  Elizabeth 996
  H. B. 969
  J. D. 818,828,829
  J. E. 910
  J. H. 897
  J. H. T. 969
  J. L. 850
  John 885
  John D. 817,1005
  Lillie 923
  Lucy A. 1025
  Mary 1005
  Robert 853
  Rosa A. 1005,1006
  Rosadelle 1005
  R. R. 895
  Shelton W. 1005
  William 808,910
Mary Dolora "Sister" 877
Mary Veronica "Sister" 877
Mason...861

Mason, C. 902
  Carrington 850
  Clemence 1053
Massey...914,916
  E. D. 1006
  Frances 959
  Frances A. 941
  Mary A. 1022
  Rueben 1006
  Sallie 1006
Master, F. W. 816
Mathes, Benjamin Cash 977
  J. H. 806
  J. Harvey 906
  James Harvey 976,977
  Lee Dandridge 977
  Mildred Overton 977
  Mildred Spotswood 977
  Talbot Spotswood 977
Matternus...877
Matthews, Ella 990
  James A. 990
  J. B. 1010
  Mary 1010
  Sandy 824
  W. 813
Meacham...969
  M. L. 891
Mead, W. C. 876
Meagher, M. 877
  Michael 850
  Patrick 816,817,818,
    864,868,869
Means...989
Meau...989
Meier, Julia S. 969
Mellersh...957
Melone, Florence 1021
Mendal...971
Menees, T. W. 876
Menken, J. S. 1008,1009
  Jules A. 1008
  N. D. 1008
Menton, William 819
Menus, H. H. 880
Mercer, I. B. 914
  J. L. 942
  Luna May 942
  Mary Grace 942
Meriweather, Minor 997
Meriwether, J. T. 853
  Miles 889
Merrell, Alex. 1009
  Barbara 1009
  David A. 1009
  Frost 1009
  Mary J. 1009
Merrill...1059
  A. P. 842,843,901,1046
  Maria 1046
Merriman, James E. 935
  J. E. 880,886
Merriwether, Garrett M.
  1007
  Lide P. 1008
  Lucy Va 1008
  Mary 1007
  Mattie M. 1008
  Miles 1007
  Minor 824
Messick, J. 819
  Jefferson 910
Mette, Christina 892
Mewborn, Charlton A. 1009
  J. L. 1009
  Joshua 1009
  Mary 1010
  Mary J. 1010
  Wilson 1009
Meyer, Bertha 989
Mhoon, J. C. 889
Muckleberry, Robert 810
Milburn, T. H. 846

Milburn, Thomas H. 890
Miles...856
  J. R. 898
Mill, W. M. 820
Millard, W. D. 860
Miller, A. B. 854
  A. J. 886
  Elizabeth N. 1012
  Evaline 1037
  Henry 1037
  Jenry G. 1037
  John L. 1012
  Laura W. 1012
  Lizzie S. 1037
  Lucy A. 1011
  Lulu 1012
  Martha 1011
  Mary J. 1009
  Nancy E. 1059
  Sallie 1053
  Sallie D. 1012
  Simon 1011
  Simon A. 1012
  W. C. 965
  W. E. 915
  Wilie B. 901
  William 1011
  William E. 1012
  Wrilie J. 1012
  W. N. 1011,1053
Milliken, L. H. 854
Mills, Adelia N. 999
  J. C. 893
  J. W. 999
Milton, E. O. 903
Miner, Mary 1007
Minor, Elizabeth 1012
  J. L. 1012,1013
  John 1012
Minter, Lamira A. 1020
Mitchell, George (colored)
  875
  Rosa Lee 961
  R. W. 843
  W. P. 903
  W. Z. 843
Molitor, Francis, M. 967
  Matilda A. 967
Momack, R. B. 854
Monsarat, G. H. 828
Montague, Helen 1049
Montedonico, J. D. 806
Montgomery, A. H. 808
  Ed. 835
  H. A. 889
  R. B. 876
Moody...877
  Samuel 821
  S. S. 852
Moore...890,924,1046
  Caroline R. 972
  Charlotte 931
  James C. 987
  Jane 818
  John 914
  John B. 864
  Lottie Heywood 1013
  Mary F. 1013
  M. J. 987
  Robert Cleveland 1013
  S. W. 854
  T. M. 972
  Warner 853
  W. H. 894
  William R. 931
  William Robert 1013,
    1014
  W. R. 886
Moran, Bridget 1014
  Dennis 1014
  J. P. 857
  P. J. 1014
  Tilda J. 1014

Morecock, Susan 920
  Susan B. 920
Moreland...828
Moegan...823,916,992
  J. B. 971
  J. H. 831
  John E. 1015
  John H. 882,883
  Martha 1015
  Mary 971
  Mary Louisa 1015
  Mary T. 1015
  R. J. 964,1014
  S. T. 843,886
  Tomlinson F. 1015
  W. H. 886
Morrow, Angello 824
  Wm. 812
Morris, Lotta 965
  Moses S. 851
  R. E. 965
  Sol 1008
Morrison, E. A. 1015
  Mary 1015
  M. L. 1036
  S. J. 1015
Moseley, E. B. 1015
  Eliza 963
  H. W. 817,818
  J. B. 814,902
  John B. 902,1015
  M. E. 1015
  Rosa B. 1015
Moses (slave) 820
Mosley, Lucy M. 1016
Moss...807
  J. T. 916
  R. F. C. 914
Mulbraden...878
Mullins...1061
  Emmit 961
  L. D. 853,961
  Martha A. 961
Mumford, Robinson 799
Murfie...1020
Murphy, Elizabeth 1049
  Elizabeth Marshall 1038
  J. J. 895
Murray, Agnes 1016
  Andrew 1016
  Andrew J. 1016,1017
  Ina 1017
  Joseph 978
Myers...1043
  A. S. 892
  D. B. 894

Nabers, B. D. 995
  Mary 995
Nancy (servant) 823
Nash, Annie Gifford 933
Nathan, James 892
Neal, F. M. 895
Neighbors, Katie 875
Neely...890,898,993,
  E. A. 909
  Fannie E. 976
  H. M. 895
  J. C. 812,894
  R. P. 830,1024
  William D. 881
Nellie (slave) 803
Nelson...876,998
  F. M. 891,892
  J. B. 825
  T. N. 891
Netherland, Eliza 980
  John 805,979
Nettleton, George H. 812
  G. H. 812
Nuuhardt...914
Nevill, Charlie R. 1018
  Emma T. 1018

Nevill, Jennie 1017
  Mahala 1017
  Mary 1018
  Mathew 1017
  Minnie Low 1018
  W. M. 1017
Newell...1004
Newson, A. W. 891,1018
  Emma 1018
  John 1018
Nickerson, I. B. 819
  W. N. 895
Nicholson...953
Nichols, S. S. 905
  William C. 1027
Nightingale, T. 908
Nixon, Jane 1060
  Richard 1060
Nolley, Alexander 1018
  J. H. 1018
  Joyce 1018
  T. L. 1018
Nooe, John A. 843
Norris, A. A. 819
  C. P. 889
Norton...824
Nott, J. C. 1035
Nowlin, Linnie 1006
Nugent, D. B. 1018
  Frank H. 1019
  H. B. 1018
  Maude R. 1018
  Miranda 1018
  P. G. 876
Nunn, David A. 805,806
Nutzell, Rosa 1019

O'Banner...965
Ober, W. A. 1034
O'Brien, Anthony 856
  D. A. 857
  M. J. 812
O'Conner, Kate 1000
O'Haver, Benj. 825
Oldham, G. S. 820
  John W. 817
  J. W. 818
Oliver...890,903,1048
  C. B. 895
Omberg, J. A. 892
Only, John 910
Orengo, Aloysises 856
Orgill...1060
Orrick, Mary V. 989
  S. P. 1047
Osborn, Jessee 913
Osborne, Thomas 820
Osterhout, Lotta 965
Otey, James H. 862,863
  Paul H. 876
Ottenheim, Dora 970
  L. 970
Overall, D. H. 1019
  G. W. 1019
  Nathaniel S. 1019
  Rowena 1020
  Susan A. 1040
Overton, John 800,801,817,
  864,865,868,868,869,888,
  892,893,894
Owen, F. A. 813
  Francis A. 851,852
  J. G. 886
  Robert 802,804
  Robert Dale 802,804

Padam, J. W. 816
Page...863
Painter, Jacob B. 819
Palmer, Thomas 817
Park, David 950
  John 836,885,887
  Mary 1023

Park, Mattie S. 950
Parker, Ella 1020
  Lamira A. 1020
  O. B. 898
  R. A. 892,903,962
  Robert A. 1020
  Walter L. 1020
  W. L. 893
Parkerson, J. T. 892
Parr, S. S. 854
  W. G. 820
Parson, R. J. 830
Parsons...877
Partee, Hiram A. 1000
  Jessie L. 1000
Passmore, Mary E. 932
Pattilo, M. A. 849
  M. C. 849
  M. L. 849
  P. C. 849
  R. H. 849
Patton, A. A. 898
Patrick, J. M. 968
  Louisa C. 968
  M. 828
  Marsh 829
Patterson, E. C. 822
  Harriet F. 1021
  Josiah 966,967
Peabody, Ida 902
Pearce...898
  M. C. 897
Pearle, J. F. 842,843
Pearson, Emily 985
  D. 813
  James L. 985
  Rosa L. 985
  Thomas J. 840
Pearsons, G. W. 900
Peck, Esther 961
  Jacob 913
Peden, Jerusha 976
Peebles, Sarah P. 948
  Sarah S. 935
Peete, Ann E. 934
  John S. 934
  S. A. 934
Pell, James 833
Pendleton, J. M. 909
Penn, J. L. 825
Pennington, J. 819
Penton, Emma 1021
  Florence 1021
  George R. 1021
  Joseph T. 1021
Pepper, John R. 891,896
  J. R. 892
Peres, J. J. 843
Perez, Hardwig 892,893
Perkins, Calvin 1021
  James P. 814
  J. P. 813
  Louisa 1021
  Mary 1058
  Paulina 851
  Thomas 819
Person, Benj. E. 818
  John B. 820
  Loula 947
  T. F. 816
  Thomas C. 817
Persons, T. H. 802
  Thomas H. 810,817,818
Peters...991
  George B. 807,1021,1022
  Geo. P. 814
  Katie B. 1022
Pettit...898
  Florida 842
  J. T. 891,899
  J. W. A. 808,814,840,
  841,842
Petway, F. S. 853

Peyton, Craven 873
Phelan, Isaac 1001
Picard, N. 907
Pickett, A. 843
  A. B. 905
  Ed. 829
  Ed. S. 832
Pidgeon, Phil 1001
Pierce, Franklin 804
  George F. 853
  Hiram M. 876
  James O. 815
  Olive 1044
Pike...799
  Albert 904,966
Pillow...828,928
  Cynthia S. 928
  F. G. 835
  Gideon 800
  Gideon J. 826,827
  Jerome B. 928
Pirtle, Emma 918
Pittman, C. L. 952
  Henry 912
  M. T. 952
Pitts, Mary E. 945
Pharr, Elias 910
Phillips, Augustus F. 1022
  Charles J. 900
  J. M. 893,1043
  Lucy A. 1022
  P. E. 845
  Sarah W. 1022
  W. 852
  William 1022
Phoebus, Thomas 904
Plant, H. B. 812
Plantz, T. G. 864
Polk...801,938,1006,1014
  Charles G. 1022
  Charley W. 1023
  Civil Charlie 1023
  George W. 954
  Henrietta 937
  James K. 804
  Lena A. 1023
  Lewie R. 1023
  Mary A. 1022
  Mary M. 954
  William E. 1022
Pollock, Ann 991
Pomroy, C. H. 1014
Poore, John 913
Pope...804,827
  Elizabeth 923
  John 814
  Leroy 842,843
  Lizzie 914
  W. S. 833
Porter...801,841,898
  D. H. 912
  D. T. 888,891,893,902
  Edward 849
  E. H. 910
  Herschell S. 851
  James D. 806
  J. B. 819
  Joe 819
  W. A. 825
  W. N. 825,826
Postal, E. E. 1023
  Luna C. 1023
  William 1023
Poston...824
  D. H. 1023
  F. P. 1023
  Mary 1023
  W. K. 1023
Powel, Annie 1024
  Benjamin 1023, 1024
  Ellen 1023
  George R. 1023,1024
  John A. 1024

Powell, Musadora C. 1024
  Sallie 1024
Powell, Edna E. 1025
  Eliza 1024
  James B. 1025
  John C. 1024
  Joseph D. 1024,1025
  Sarah A. 1024
  Vannoy H. M. 1025
  William 819
Power, Thomas L. 847
Powers, J. J. 809
  Mary 1047
Pratt...1042
Preston, T. W. 843
Price...835
  B. F. 893
Priddy...905
  John H. 1025
  Lucy 1025
  Lucy A. 1025
  Maria A. 1025
  William 1025
Pritchett, A. L. 854
  M. J. 849
  T. 849
Proudfit...824
  Eliza 1025
  E. S. 1025,1026
  Irene H. 1026
  Laura 1025
  Virginia A. 1025
  William 1025
  W. P. 1025
Proudfitt...898
Pruden...914,915
Puers, Eugenius 858
Pullen, Benjamin K. 1026
  B. K. 889
  C. L. 907
  Minerva A. 1026
Pulliam, E. 916
Pulliams...915
Purnell, E. W. 1027
  Hortensius W. 1026,1027
  Hortentius P. 1027
  John Hortentius 1027
  M. E. 1027
  S. A. 1027
  Thomas 1027
  William 1027
Purser, Sarah W. 1022
Putman...938

Quigley, Peter J. 1027,1028
  P. J. 814,946
  Martina e. 1028
Quimby...864
  Robert 818
Quinby...827
Quinche, Helen Marion 845
Quinn...859,860
Quintan, Bettie 947
Quintard, C. T. 862,863

Radford...898
Ragland, Edward D. 949
  Elizabeth 949
  Louisa A. 949
  M. E. 949
  Nathaniel 949
  S. Virginia 949
Ragsel, A. 881
Raine, C. H. 891,1028
  Charles H. 1028
  Gilbert D. 1028,1029
  Julia 1028
  Mary 1028
Ralston, John 800,810,818, 869
Rambeau, G. B. 920
Rambert, M. E. 949
Rambout, G. V. 843

Ramsay...806
Ramsey, A. J. 1003
  John 799,800
  R. W. 914,1003
Randall, John E. 900
Randle, J. E. 889
  John E. 929
Randoll, G. W. 916
Randolph...806
  Eliza B. 953
Ranger, Louis 898
Ransom, L. C. 851
Rawlings...910
  "Ike" 867
  Isaac 814,818,819,865, 866,881,882
  James S. 1029
  J. J. 891,898,911
  John 1029
  Olivia 962
  Ricahrd J. 1029
  Sarah F. 1029
  Sarah J. 1029
  Stokeley 1029
Ray...878,1037
  J. E. R. 815,825
  Veronica 848
Rayburn, Ann W. 957
Rayliss, Rowena 998
Raymond, D. F. 1002
Rayner, Eli 1050
  Irene 1050
Read, Ann 1030
  John 814,815
  Myra P. 1030
  Pearl 1030
  Samuel P. 1030
  Sidney 1030
  S. P. 891,892,899,1029, 1030
  Theodore 1030
  William 1030
Reaves, W. P. 814
Rees, J. H. 1023
Reese, William 960
Reeves, George W. 814,815
  John 810
  John Jones 984
  William 815
  W. P. 910
Reid...944
  Frank T. 806
Reiley, James 814
Reilly, James 894,947,995, 1030
  Mary 1030
Reinach...863
Reinjurst...910
Reinke, Chrysostom 858
Rembert, Andrew 820
  James 818,911
Renkert, A. 1030,1031
  Alfred F. 1031
  Andrew 886
  Anna M. 2031
  Christian 1031
  Elizabeth 1031
  Emma 1031
  Ottelia 1031
Renner, J. G. 876
Repis, W. J. 857
Reudelhuber, Annie C. 1031
  Evelyn M. 1031
  John D. 1031
  J. S. 1031
  Pauline 1031
Revell...988
Reville, Dalmatius 857
Reynolds, Benjamin 808,910
  Frances 980
  Letitia E. 980
  Mary 980
  R. 818

Reynolds, William 980
　Rhodes, Joseph H. 1002
Rice, Elisha 864
　Frank 832
　John 799,800,864,865,881
　John H. 849
Richards, Channing 886
　L. R. 886
　Lydia 928
Richardson...898,1027
　C. A. 842
　E. M. 849
　James 802,804
　J. W. 894,895
　W. B. 809
Ricketts, H. P. 907
Riddle, J. M. 818
　John M. 816
Riley, M. J. 900
Ring...841
Rinklage, Lee 858
Riordan, M. 877,1051
　Martin 858,859,860
Risk, E. F. 903
Ritchie, Ann 1030
　William 1030
Rivers, Bill 824
　E. C. 988
　Martha 1011
　Minerva 985
　T. M. 988
Roach, A. J. 898
Robb, W. C. 853
Roberts, William 817
Robertson, A. C. N. 953
　Elizabeth 938
　James 799,938
　Martha A. 953
　Mary B. 1005
Robins, Benj. 808,819
　B. J. 819
　Mary L. 1003
　W. H. 876
Robinson...827
　Bettie 1032
　John B. 1032
　J. S. 891,892
　M. F. 914
　Pleasant B. 851
　R. A. 933
　William H. 1031,1032
Rochell...943
Rockett, F. Y. 906
Rode, S. W. 895
Rodgers, B. B. 1000
　H. R. 832
Rogers, James A. 891
　J. M. 876
　John C. 876
　Julia C. 996
　Lucy A. 1022
　Martha 922
Rohde, Nemesius 858,1017
Rolon, G. L. 825
Root...841
　Amanda 973
Roper, Bridget 955
　James 995,1032
　John 995,1032
　Sarah 1032
Rose...924
　J. M. 849
　Sister 877
Roseborough, Jennie 960
　W. D. 960
Rosebrough, S. 868
Ross, Anne R. 1032
　Anthony 1032
　Chas. E. 832
　Nancy 955
　Stephen 820
　Stephen 820
　W. B. 829

Rosser, Thomas H. 835
Rowan, Thomas J. 856
Royster, David 1033
　Elizabeth 1033
　Frank W. 903,1033
　Helen 1033
　J. 913
　William B. 1033
Rozell, Ashley B. 851
Rucker, E. W. 930,1016
Rudisill, J. A. 814
Ruffin, Lucy 926
　Margaret 1947
　William 901
Rumsey...807
Russell, C. B. 1033
　Frank 824
　J. B. 833
　J. Thornton 1033
　Octavia 1033
　S. H. 914
Tuth, E. F. 825,874
Rutland...898
　Euzelia 1034
　George W. 1033
　Geo. W. 1034
　ydia a. 1034
　William C. 1033
Rutledge, Ellen 1023
Rutschman, Frederika 1034
　George 1034
Ryan, C. R. 919
　Frank T. 919
　Michael 860

Saddle, J. H. 1018
Safford...798
　Eunice B. 1038
Samfield, M. 863
Sampler, William A. 848
Sampson, Elizabeth 1033
Sandac, Julius 863
Sander, Enno 911
Sanderford, Joanna 952
　J. W. 952
Sanderlin, Wilson 808,910
Sanders...932
　William 910
Sappington...841,833
　M. B. 870
Saunders...1055
　D. D. 1035
　Dudley D. 1035
　J. E. 1035
　Kate S. 1035
　Lizzie W. 1035
　Mary E. 1035
　Mary F. 1035
　Mary Lou 1035
Savage, William 819
Sawrie...991
　W. D. F. 852
Sawyer, Jacob 820
Saxon, Ina 1017
Say, M. S. 914
Scales...945
　Lemuel A. 1035
　Margaret 1053
　M. L. 1036
　Pauline H. 944
　Robert 944
Scarbrough, A. B. 1036
　A. M. 898,1036
　Ednie E. 1036
Schafer, C. A. 834
Schieley...915
Schloss, D. 814
　Daniel 1036,1037
　Johanna 1036
　Joseph 1037
　Rachel 1036
　Tilly 1036
Schlosser, Kilian 857

Schneider, L. 857
Schoefield, J. 824
Schoolfield, Dudley T.
　1037
　E. M. 1037
　Frances 1037
　John W. 1037
　W. W. 896,899,902,1037
Schorr, J. M. 892
Schulte, C. W. 890,931
　Emma A. 931
Schuyler...877
Schwab...1063
Schwill, Otto 895
Scipio, (slave) 848
Scott...826,1041
　Elizabeth 1012
　M. 1048
　M. F. 1048
　Winfield 804
　W. L. 815,834
Scruggs...911,963
　A. T. 852
　Elizabeth Marshall 1038
　Minerva 985
　P. T. 815,825,853,877,
　　985,1038
　Thomas M. 1037
Scudder, A. M. 960
　Eunice B. 1038
　Lizzie 960
　M. L. 1038
　Rebecca 965
　Samuel E. 1038
Searcy, G. D. 825
Seawell, James 883
　J. P. 877
　P. J. 857
Seely, Hattoe 956
Semmers, R. E. 894
　B. J. 957
Sessums, David 863
　Davis 1038
Seymore, Horatio 805
Shane...898
Shank, Lewis 817
Shanks...883
　L. 842
Shaw...806
　A. B. 880
　H. J. 1038
　Nannie W. 1039
　Sarah 1038
　Thomas 1038
Shea, Mollie 1016
Sheehy, J. D. 857
Sheffield, Albert H. 1043
　Georgia 1042
Shelby...925,957
　Isaac 807
Shelton, Irene M. 980
Shepherd...915,1013
　James G. 819
　John H. 846
Sheridan, P. H. 924
Sherman...833,1018
Sherron, Nancy 1039
　Nannie W. 1039
　Zachariah 1039
Sherry, Patrick 886
Shimmel, Rachel 1051
Shipp, Ann 1039
　John 1039
Shoemaker, Jane 818
　Lindsey 818
Shortt, Laura 845
Shotwell, A. 850
Shouse, Mary 845
Shryock, E. A. 832
Sigler, Howell 1039
　Julia A. 1039
　Lucy 1039
　Peter H. 1039

Signaigo, A. J. 812
Silverman, B. 1008
  Esther 1008
  H. 1008
  P. 1008
Silvers...807
Sim...909
  T. B. 891,894,895
Simons, Moses 863
Simpson...898
  Lawrence J. 900
Slater, E. C. 852,854.877
Slaughter, Abner 1039
  David C. 1039,1040
  D. C. 814
  G. J. 825
  H. C. 843
  John D. 1040
  Mary 1039
  Mary Anne 1040
  Mary M. 1040
  Susan A. 1040
  Wyatt 1040
Sledge...898,965
Small...911,914
  Charles M. 1040,1041
  George 1040
  H. D. 813
  Henry 824
  L. J. 1041
  Mary J. 1040
Smith...806,807,829,833, 876,935
  A. 819
  Abraham 1042
  Ann 1039
  C. C. 833
  C. E. 814,947
  C. F. 898
  Curtis J. 861
  Dennis 923
  Frank 839
  Georgia 1042
  H. E. 928
  Henry G. 827,886
  H. G. 886
  H. N. 1059
  Irene 1042
  J. A. 830,831
  James H. 896,1042
  J. H. 861,893
  J. M. 891,894
  John E. 887
  J. W. 812,814
  Laura 951
  Lidde P. 1008
  Lillian 1042
  Margaret 1042
  Mary 923,1059
  Mary A. R. 1042
  Minerva 1042
  Minerva A. 1026
  Morgan L. 886
  O. H. 832
  Preston 828,829,1061
  Samuel 818
  T. B. 910
  Thomas 851
  Thos. R. 843
  Victor R. 1042
  W. A. 1042
  William H. 1042
  William J. 1041,1042
  William M. 815
  W. J. 805,806,903
Sneed...1053
  J. L. T. 814,825,829,831
  J. W. 833
  Louisa 1043
  R. C. 825
  Sarah A. 1043
  W. M. 891,1043
Snodgrass, Annie 1051

Snodgrass, David 1051
  Jennie 1051
  Maria 1051
Snowden, I. N. 902
  Isaac N. 891
  R. B. 892,893
Snyder, Jacob 852
Somerdell, Fannie M. 930
Somerville...830
  J. W. 833
Sonneshein, H. 863
Sonfield, Annie 1063
Spain, T. J. 835
Speed, John K. 846,891,893, 895,896,1043
  R. A. 901
Speer, Charles 821
  Nelson 821
Spence, J. M. 853
Spiers, Abram 820
Spinkernagle, William 874, 883
Spira, Polly 817
Spruill, Benjamin 921
  Mary W. 921
Stainback, G. W. 851
Stanislaus, Sister 877
Stanley, Mary 962
Stanton, F. P. 804,820
Starks, S. G. 852
Starr, C. A. 913
Stedman, James O. 848,850, 918
Steel, John 981
  Margaret J. 981
  S. A. 852
Steele, Amelia 1044
  Andrew J. 847,1044
  Howard 1044
  Jessie 1044
  Olive 1044
  Samuel 1044
Stein, Belle 970
  C. H. 839
  L. 970
Stephens...821
Sterling (slave) 820
Stern, Regina 971
Stevens, C. M. 847
Stevenson, J. S. 876
Stewart, A. B. 925
  A. P. 991
  C. M. 952
  C. S. 991
  Cyrus M. 1044,1045
  E. P. 901,1045
  Hugh 891
  J. A. 952
  James 895
  James T. 942,1044
  J. D. 1044
  J. J. 1040
  Kate 952
  Kate J. 1045
  Margaret A. C. 847
  Mary 942,1044,1045
  Mary M. 1040,1044
  M. D. L. 814,815,898
  M. E. 942
  Mollie 952
  Robt. M. C. 817
  Virginia A. 1045
  W. B. 1045
Stinson, Ruth E. 847
Stock, J. C. 833
  J. G. 833
Stoddert, William 817
Stokes, Thomas 830
Stoltz...864
Stone, Warren 1027
  W. T. 895
Storm, Ad 898
Stovall, W. H. 828
Stover...821
Strahl, O. F. 830,831

Strange, A. A. 1045
  Maria 1046
  W. R. 1046
Stratton, A. S. 914,1046, 898,913
  B. M. 978
  David 1046
  John T. 903
  Mary Eudora 1046
Strauss, Joseph 863
Streight...834
Strickland...932
Stubblefield, Caroline 934
Sturges...1009
Sturgis...834
Sturm...983
Stutts, Amelia 942
Suggs...898
  A. B. 963
  L. B. 895,899
  George 998
  John S. 908
  John H. 1047
  Jeremiah 1047
  Mary 1047
  Nancy H. 950
  S. P. 1047
Surratt, S. B. 852,854
Swarford, Jacob T. 817
  Thomas 816
Swartz, Adelia 1057
Sweeney, G. W. 861
  Mary 935
Swoope, W. C. 1060

Taft, Frank 814
Tagg, Joseph 886
Tah, Jung Yung 875
Talbot, Joe H. 821
  Joseph H. 815
Talley, W. F. 814
Talmadge...907
Tanner, John A. 1049
  Martha 1049
Tapp...910,011
Tapscott, Alice J. 937
Tarbox...842,843
Tate, Jease M. 910
  R. H. 876
  Samuel 811
Tatum, H. A. 1001
Taylor...826,898,969,1034
  A. B. 814,880,885,910
  Alfred 800
  Alfred A. 807
  Fannie H. 1048
  H. R. 832
  James R. 1048
  Julius A. 1047,1048
  Louise 1048
  Mamie 940
  Margaret 1047,1048
  Robert L. 807,942
  Rosa R. 1048
  Thomas 814,815,910
  Thomas D. 816,817
  West C. 1048
  W. F. 833,892,903
  William V. 1048
  Zachary 804
  Zack 806
Teahue, John 814
Teas, Jane 930
Temple, W. C. 852
Templeton, Amelia 838
Teslard, O. 825
Thacher, W. W. 898
Thacker, N. H. 890
Tharpe, C. A. 1026
  Virginia A. 1025
Thoma, Corneluis 857
Thomas...877
  A. H. 852,853

Thomas, A. S. 814
  E. M. 1037
  George W. 1048
  G. W. 915
  Henry 1037
  Jane 941
  J. E. 826
  J. M. 913
  Joseph 1037
  Lucy A. 1022
  L. W. 1048
  M. F. 1048
  Nancy 1048
  Squire 813
Thompkins, William C. 934
Thompson...842,930
  Anna 1004
  Anna D. H. 896
  George 932
  Hattie E. 983
  J. A. 915
  Jeff 835
  Laura W. 1012
  Margaret 931
  M. Jeff 835
  Nettie 932
  R. A. 905
  Rebecca 990
  William 816
Thornton, G. B. 889
  J. J. 965
  Robt. G. 817
Thrasher, J. C. 832
Thumel, N. 828
Theveat...852
  Jennie 996
  J. O. 996
Tichnor, I. T. 854
Tighe, Sam 887
Tilden...1054
  Samuel 806
Tilghman...833
Tilley, Geo. H. 812
Tillman, H. 829
Tipton, Jacob 800,801,807,
  809,815,817,818
Titus, Ed 824
  F. 827
Tobey, S. H. 842,843
Tobin...878
  A. F. 892
Tomlin, G. W. 1048,1049
  James S. 1049
  Martha 1049
  M. L. 0149
Tonti...798
Toof, Jno. S. 898
  John S. 896,899,900,903,
  986
  S. C. 861
Topp...805
  R. 824
  Robertson 842
Toppin, Sarah 961
Torrance, Hugh 898
Torrey, Robt. 825
Tours, Judah 863
Tradeau, Martha 845
Tradewell, D. C. 810
Trainor, Martina E. 1028
  Wm. T. 824
Trask, W. L. 906
Treadwell, A. B. 896
  A. C. 898
Trent, John 833
Trester...874
Trezevant, B. R. 841
  John T. 880,903
  J. P. 814
Trible, J. M. 861
Trousdale, Leon 904
  William 804
  Wm. 825

Trumbull, Mary 1015
Tucker...943
  Elizabeth 1049
  Helen 1049
  Mary E. 966
  Sallie R. 966
  William A. 1049
  William B. 1049
Tuerk, P. 876
Tuggle...915
  E. C. 988
  Philip 853
Turbivelle, Ara 1017
  Jennie 1017
  R. W. 1017
Turley...1060
  Flora 1050
  Irene 1050
  Rayner 1050
  T. B. 1049
  Thomas 1050
  Thomas B. 893
  T. J. 814
  W. B. 824
  William B. 814,819
Turnage, Amanda 998
  Isaac 998
Turner, G. P. M. 807,814
  824,907
  J. T. 908
  William T. 819
Turnley, P. T. 924
Tuska, S. 863
Tuther, A. G. 898
Tutwiler...1062
Twyford, Wm. 916
Tyler...839
  R. C. 832
Tyner, T. J. 878

Uhl, Joseph 814
Ulander, N. J. 916
Urguhart, Henrietta 931
  E. 931

Vaccaro, A. 891,892,893,
  903
Vaden, Virginia H. 1052
  William 1052
Valentine...998
  R. 819
Van, Bryant 932
  Elizabeth 932
Van Buren, Martin 804
Bance, R. H. 891
  Lucy D. 974
  C. F. 903,974
Van Dorn...833,835
Fan Fleet...990
Van Hook, Mary 984
Van Pelt, Henry 904
Vanse, Isabelle R. 983
Vantroostemburg...877
Vaughan...1061
  Alfred J. 1050,1051
  Martha J. 1050
Vaulx, James 800,801
Van Vranken, Catherine M.
  983
Veale, J. 859
  John 1051
Venable, Joseph 1029
  R. A. 854
  Sarah F. 1029
Vernon...806,807
Villepique...835
Vincent...848
  A. J. 1051
  Gertrude 1051
  Harry S. 1051
  Henry 944
  Jennie 1051
  Rachel 1051

Vincent, Sallie A. 944
  Sister 877
  W. H. 1051
Vincentia...848
Virgin, F. J. 812

Wade, America 1019
  Caroline 1019
  E. D. 820
  M. B. 1019
  Tobias 1019
Waddell, J. N. 849
  John A. 850
Waddy...988
  J. K. 913
  Joseph K. 1051,1052
  J. R. 914
  Martha H. 1051
  Mollie Holmes 1052
  Samuel 1051
  Vaden S. 1052
  Virginia H. 1052
  William S. 1052
Wadsworth, Sarah 1046
Waldran, Almeda 1056
Walk, David 861
Walker...926,990,1029
  Eliza 1025
  Harriet D. 988
  James 801,819,829
  J. Knox 829
  John 863
  Joseph 914
  J. R. 1045
  Sam'l P. 897
  S. P. 806,815,889
  Virginia 1045
Wall...832
Wallace...837
  Symmes 889
Walsh, John 908
  John J. 860
  Margaret 951
  Martin 858,859,860,877,
  1052
  Robert 951
  William 860,908,1052
Ward...914,989
  Jane 902
  J. C. 903
  Joseph 915
  J. P. 931
  L. V. 931
Ware, G. P. 886
Warinner...998
  Annie Bodieu 1053
  Ardinger 1053
  Carrie Belle 1053
  Clemence 1053
  Gussie 1053
  Hiram Campbell 1053
  Hugh Lee 1053
  Margaret 1053
  Sallie T. 1053
  Willis W. 1053
Warner, F. J. 914
  F. L. 886,1053
  Fred J. 1012,1053
  Matilda 1053
  Sallie 1053
  Sallie D. 1012
Warren, Narcissa J. 1061
  Wesley 852
Washburn, C. C. 886
Washington, George A. 938
  Joseph E. 938
Waters, W. H. 1002
Watkins, H. W. 833
  Lucy 964
  Mary F. 1035
  R. H. 1035
Watson, B. F. 1019
  Joab 852

Watson, J. W. C. 944
  Maud R. 1018
  P. K. 876
  Sallie E. 1019
  Samuel 852
Weatherford, Caesar 1053,
  Eliza 1054
  Frances G. 1053
  William 1053
Weaver, James 814
Webber, E. B. 898
Weidt, Charles 906
Weir, J. S. 916
Welch, Mary 948
Weller, Jacob 891
Wellford...898
  Thomas 895
Wells, Octavia 1033
Welsh, Fredericka 1034
Wesley, John 853
Wesser, August 1021
  Nannie M. 1021
  Walter 1021
Wesson, Lena A. 1023
West, Alston Madden 1055
  A. M. 1054,1055
  C. O. 1054
  Eva W. 1055
  Evlyn L. 1055
  Jere 1055
  John 953
  Margaret 953
Wetherill, J. B. 886
Wetter, H. 893
Wheat, C. R. 825
  James 1041
Wheatley, Bettie 1055
  J. L. 825
  Kate S. 1035
  Mary 1035
  Mary E. 1035
  Seth 817,824,871,882,
    1035,1055
  W. A. 969
  William A. 1055
Whelan, James 857
Whitley, Richardson 802,
  804
White, A. J. 891,989
  Albert T. 1005
  Almeda 1056
  Alphonsus C. 1005
  Catherine 1056
  C. C. 1005
  Elbert A. 1056
  Elizabeth G. 1056
  Emily E. 1006
  Eppy 810,819,916
  F. M. 892,898,1055,1062
  Frances 1056
  Francis H. 1056
  George 863
  Jennie 875
  J. D. 916
  Joe 833
  John 1055
  John D. 1056
  Lucinda S. 1056
  Martha A. 926
  Mary E. 1005
  R. A. 856
  Rosa A. 1005
  Sabra 1056
  Shelton, W. 1006
  Susan 1057
  Thomas 1056
Whitford, A. S. 918
  Emma 918
Whitmore, Charles H. 1011
  E. 906
  Lucy A. 1011
  W. 906
  William 906

Whitney, Adelia 1057
  A. H. 1057
  C. O. 1057
Whitsett, S. H. 825
Whyte, M. A. 927
  Robert 927
Wick, M. J. 833
Wickersham...804
  James 885
Wiener, Aloysius 858
Wight, A. J. 916
Wilbar, J. L. 825
Wilcox, R. E. 849
Wilford, John 819
Wilhelm, Evelyn M. 1031
Wilhelmina, Sister 877
Wilkerson, Mary A. 1059
  M. M. 892
  Samuel M. 1059
  W. N. 891,894,1059
Wilkes, Annie 936
Wilkins, James S. 903
  J. S. 903
Willet, B. 916
Willett, E. Miles 1057
Willey...1009
  John W. 1058,1059
  Mary 1058,1059
  Nancy E. 1059
  Willis 1058
Wilkinson...799
Williams...916
  Humphrey 816,818
  J. A. 830
  J. D. 903
  James M. 821
  Jessie 916
  J. T. 914
  Lewis 808
  R. B. 876
Williamson, James M. 815
  J. M. 811,901
  J. N. 901
  S. M. 848
  William A. 891,892
Williford, J. B. 913
  S. 914
Willins, J. T. 892
Willis (slave) 803
Willis, A. W. 837
  Benj. 815,816
Wills, P. B. 905
Wilson...823,834,904,925,
  973,1062
  B. F. 812
  Catherine H. 933
  James 910
  John 819
  LeGrand W. 933
  Robert 803,824
  R. T. 811
Winchester, Elizabeth 929
  George 869,929,1059,
    1060
  Henrietta 1059
  James 817,865,867,868,
    869,1059
  Jane 1060
  Marcus B. 809,815,816,
    866,868,1059
  M. B. 804,810,814,817,
    818,864,867,869,881,882,
    895
  N. B. 817
  William 865,867,868,869,
    929,1059
Winkelman, Sister 877
Winters, Clara 958
  P. M. 814,886
  Valentine 958
Wirlzinski, J. 1008
Wise, J. M. 863
  Julius 909

Wisener, W. H. 806
Witherington...923
Withers, Mary E. 1005
  Sterling 1005
Witherspoon, T. D. 849,
  850
Wood...842
  Jane 1011
  J. M. 1005
Woodruff...903,925,926,
  930,1043,1048
  George W. 900
Woods, Annie H. 1060
  Fannie 1060
  F. F. 1060
  Frank F. 1060
  Joseph L. 1060
  Mary E. 842
  R. J. 1060
  Robert 1060
  Walker 814
Woodson, E. L. 962
  S. T. 825
Wooldridge...997
  Egbert 861
Wooten, John W. 992
  Mary 992
  Valenia 992
Wormeley, Ralph 898
Wormley...1025
Worsham, J. J. 903
Wren...910
  Sallie 1006
Wright...1049
  Archibald 825,1060
  Camilla 802
  Elizabeth 1061
  E. M. 806
  Frances 801,802,803,
    821,916,988
  J. 840
  John 1060
  John V. 806,973,984
  Luke 1061
  Marcus J. 805
  M. J. 814,828,829
  Nancy 1060
  W. B. 832
Wyatt, E. J. 825
  Mary A. 1059
Wykoff...850
Wynn, Peter D. 820
  Thomas S. 820
Wynne, Ann Eliza 954
  W. D. 954

Yancy...916
  Alexander L. 1061
  Elizabeth 1061
  Narcissa J. 1061
  Thomas B. 1061
Yateman...1060
Yerger...911
  Ed 824
  E. M. 815
  Orville 825
Yonge, James 893,1061
Young...1005
  H. Casey 806
  H. Y. 967,968
  J. 819
  James 1062
  James W. 1062,1063
  Kittie 1062
  Louisa 1062
  Mary 1062
  Mary H. 1011
  Mary N. 1062
  Matilda 1053
  Rebecca L. 1062
  Rebecca R. 1062
  William B. 1062

Zack...875
Zeller, David 1063
    Annie 1063
Zimmerman...906

www.ingramcontent.com/pod-product-compliance
Lightning Source LLC
Chambersburg PA
CBHW020643300426
44112CB00007B/225